Teaching Middle Level Social Studies: A Practical Guide for 4th–8th Grade (3rd Edition)

Teaching Middle Level Social Studies: A Practical Guide for 4th–8th Grade (3rd Edition)

Scott L. Roberts
Benjamin R. Wellenreiter
Jessica Ferreras-Stone
Stephanie L. Strachan
Karrie L. Palmer

INFORMATION AGE PUBLISHING, INC.
Charlotte, NC • www.infoagepub.com

Library of Congress Cataloging-In-Publication Data

The CIP data for this book can be found on the Library of Congress website (loc.gov).

Paperback: 978-1-64802-698-0
Hardcover: 978-1-64802-699-7
E-Book: 978-1-64802-700-0

Copyright © 2022 Information Age Publishing Inc.

All rights reserved. No part of this publication may be reproduced, stored in a retrieval system, or transmitted, in any form or by any means, electronic, mechanical, photocopying, microfilming, recording or otherwise, without written permission from the publisher.

Printed in the United States of America

CONTENTS

    Acknowledgements vii

    Preface 3rd Edition ix

1. Middle Level Students: Who Are They? How Are They Different? 1
2. Social Studies in the Middle Grades 17
3. Teaching Middle Level Social Studies: The Basics 53
4. Teaching Middle Level Social Studies: Advanced Strategies and Methods 77
5. Planning Middle Level Social Studies Lessons and Units 121
6. Assessment: Formal and Informal 141
7. Best Practices for Teaching State History 167
8. Best Practices for Teaching United States History 191
9. Best Practices for Teaching Geography 217
10. Incorporating Economics and Government in Middle Level Social Studies 233
11. Building Literacy in Middle Level Social Studies 255
12. Integrating the "Core" Subjects in Middle Level Social Studies 279

13. Using your Social Studies Resources Effectively 295
14. The Recent Past and New Directions in Social Studies 319
15. Becoming a Social Studies Professional 347
16. Concluding Remarks 363

APPENDICES
TEACHING MIDDLE LEVEL SOCIAL STUDIES: A PRACTICAL GUIDE FOR 4TH–8TH GRADES

A. Lesson Plan Template 371
B. Hollywood or History Lesson Plan/Graphic Organizer 375
C. 25 Resources for Teaching History 383
D. 25 Resources for Teaching Geography 389
E. 25 Resources for Teaching Economics 395
F. 25 Resources for Teaching Civics/Government 401
    About the Authors 407

ACKNOWLEDGEMENTS

While writing a textbook is both a challenging and exhilarating task, updating a prior book offers both unique tests and successes. Ben and Scott believe the first two editions of this book were good, however, asking Jessica, Karrie, and Steph to join us as authors to provide their ideas and expertise made the book even better. Ben and Scott can't thank them enough for their hard work and dedication to this process, especially during the COVID-19 pandemic.

We would like to thank our families and friends who have supported us during our educational journeys. They were there for us from the time we decided we wanted to become teachers, to going to graduate school, to telling them we were writing a book. We could not have done it without their love and support.

There are also many others who played key roles in the development of at least one edition of the book that we would like to show our appreciation. Most notably, we would like to thank Dr. John Hoge, Professor Emeritus: University of Georgia. Dr. Hoge was Scott's major professor and the founder of Digital Textbooks, the publisher of the first two editions of the book. Dr. Hoge's long hours editing, commenting, and revising the first two editions are still evident in this one. We can't thank him enough for his commitment to helping us write the best middle level textbook that we possibly could.

There were also several people who offered their feedback and suggestions on the books over the past several years. They include Kenneth Blum (Fayette Coun-

---

Teaching Middle Level Social Studies: A Practical Guide for 4th–8th Grade (3rd Edition),
pages vii–viii.
Copyright © 2022 by Information Age Publishing
www.infoagepub.com
All rights of reproduction in any form reserved.

ty Schools), Dr. Brandon Butler (Old Dominion University); Dr. Hilary Conklin (Du Paul University); Dr. Debbie Daniell (Gwinnett County Public Schools); Dr. Charles Elfer (Clayton State University) and Dr. Kimberly Logan (The University of Georgia). Thank you all for all of your assistance!

Finally, we would like to acknowledge the students who contributed work samples to the book. We are certain their work will help the readers better visualize some of the strategies in practice. Thanks to Chance Barr, Jakeb Barr, Calista Chimbos, Eva Chimbos, Kimberly Palmer and Ella Thomson for your hard work on these projects. We wish you the best as you continue your own educational journeys!

PREFACE 3ʳᴰ EDITION

Social studies courses have long been described as boring and as being inapplicable outside the classroom (Heafner, 2004; Key et al., 2010; Schug et al., 1982). Popular media portrays social studies classes as having teachers who dump unending facts into uninterested, and sometimes unconscious, students. Classroom activities in these portrayals are generally limited to one-way transmissions of information through lectures and slideshow presentations. An occasional discussion or debate may be sprinkled into the schedule, the storyline goes, but the thinking usually ends with the merciful ringing of the dismissal bell. Social studies assessments characterized in popular media portrayals are often excruciating exercises in the regurgitation of decontextualized trivia with no application in the world beyond 2ⁿᵈ Period United States History. If popular media is to be believed, students feel as if the nature of the subject itself is pointless and would rather be anywhere else. Essentially, history is dead, geography is rote, civics is work, economics is dense, and sociology is fluff.

Professional educational climates at the national, state, and local levels generally treat the social studies only marginally better. While the methods employed in many schools *may* be better than seen in popular media, the place of social studies within their curriculums is tenuous, at best. Even forward-looking elementary schools often relegate social studies to the last few minutes of the day when the students and teachers are often physically and mentally spent. Many schools have

---

Teaching Middle Level Social Studies: A Practical Guide for 4th–8th Grade (3rd Edition),
pages ix–xxi.
Copyright © 2022 by Information Age Publishing
www.infoagepub.com
All rights of reproduction in any form reserved.

no scheduled time for formal social studies curriculum at all. Though many current curriculum standards, specifically within the English Language Arts (ELA), purport to encourage more focus on subjects such as social studies and science, the practice of integrating deeply meaningful social studies experiences into classrooms is woefully sparse (Anderson, 2014; Sunal & Sunal, 2007). Because many states do not test students in social studies skills, knowledge, or concepts, it takes place when everything else is done. States, school districts, individual schools, and many teachers concentrate their time, energy, and budgets on the subjects that are tested. For social studies, there is little in the way of school supported opportunities for professional development, there is infrequent discussion at faculty meetings, and often there is only passing mental effort given toward social studies curriculum.

Popular understanding of adolescents fares no better than popular perceptions of social studies. Grumpy, disrespectful, gawky, disengaged, and just plain delinquent are frequent adjectives used to describe the 10–15-year-old age group. Glued to the walls during school dances, these "not children and not adults" are seen as having no real roots in either the world of children or the world of adults. When in the realm of school, they are often described as uneducable. A former teacher described a common view of this age group when he stated on the radio program *This American Life*; "I basically came away thinking you're sort of wasting your time trying to teach middle school students anything." (This American Life, 2011)

Bullying, academic disengagement, apathy, and sassiness are generally seen as the norms in middle schools. Preservice teachers most frequently want to either work with elementary school children because they enjoy the age group or with high school students because they enjoy the subject. Being a middle school teacher is often seen as a last-chance, "fall back" profession. Who in their right mind would want to spend any length of time with 30 adolescents who have, according to popular belief, few redeeming qualities?

There is a perception problem with social studies; There is a perception problem with adolescents. These perceptions should not exist. These perceptions must not continue to exist. We believe that popular media have presented a false perception of social studies and adolescents. These false perceptions are not only fundamentally wrong, they are damaging to the youth of our nation and the welfare of our society. We ask that you keep reading to understand why these false perceptions are incorrect. We will detail can be done to help promote a more accurate view of the rich, engaging, and essential learning that social studies should provide and the deeply rewarding and impactful interactions that are possible with young adolescents. While negative perceptions of social studies are deeply entrenched, it is certainly possible to challenge and move away from them through the provision of middle level social studies instruction that is immediately applicable, vitally important, and deeply meaningful.

Though the focus of this text is social studies, we approach the subject with adolescents in mind. Developmentally, adolescents are experimenting with their understanding of who they are and what their world is. The topics that naturally exist within the social studies are wonderful fits for the adolescents who struggle with them whether they realize it or not.

Engagement in the concepts, topics, people, and places within the social studies are inevitable as we proceed through life. From the time we are born to the time we die, we are students of the social processes that inform, surround, affect, and are affected by us. We deeply consider our histories and their impacts on our present and future lives as we struggle with our own individual identities. We struggle with and marvel at geographic truths and the processes that created them when we walk to school in the snow or realize we are not the only inhabitants of the planet. We feel infuriated, disillusioned, or justified with civic processes, locally, nationally, and globally. We focus much of our daily activity on economic endeavors as we work, spend, and save. We continually work to refine our understanding of complex social processes in our middle school cafeterias, in our romantic relationships, and in our increasingly diverse communities. Either we as individuals and as a society can embrace the social studies as a way of working to better understand ourselves or disregard the area of study as an isolated subject of trivial importance. We believe adolescence is a perfect age for these, and countless other, considerations. The adolescents in our middle schools are entering a developmental stage where deep consideration of these concepts is beginning to take hold. Different from children who struggle with abstract concepts, the adolescents in our middle schools practice with the abstract and with the global. It is the job of the middle level social studies teacher to stimulate this struggle.

When you become a middle level social studies teacher, you will have immense influence on how your students view the human experience and the subject areas within the social studies. Their engagement in politics, their wonderment of psychological and sociological processes, their appreciation for cultures, and their curiosity about themselves are, in part, informed by the experiences you provide them inside your classroom. Through the experiences you plan and execute, students can be encouraged to ask questions they had as three-year-olds but forgot as their curiosity was stunted. Through the discussions you stimulate, your students can learn of other cultures and practice civil disagreement in a safe environment. By demonstrating genuine interest in historic events, students can become compelled to learn more on their own. As an engaging, student-centered social studies teacher, you have the power to deeply influence how students view life in general. What a joy and what a responsibility this is.

If you have a teaching assignment not labeled as a social studies teacher, you will still teach concepts found within the social studies discipline. We believe every teacher is a social studies teacher. The math teacher provides students with experiences in which students can better analyze—and perhaps work to correct— economic injustice. The Language Arts teacher helps students develop argumentation and logic skills that can be employed in the civic arena. Science teachers who insist upon systematic processing of observable data help refine social interaction and interpretation skills. The music teacher exposes connections between philosophical and historical trends and the creative spirit. The examples are nearly endless.

Even if you do not formally teach a middle level social studies curriculum, you and your future classroom will still model concepts found within the social studies. Do your classroom rules demonstrate compassionate citizenship? Have you considered the histories and cultures of your students while planning for parent conferences? What type(s) of patriotism are encouraged within your classroom procedures and school policies? The nuances of your classroom practice, no matter what course you teach, are all informed by concepts found in history, geography, economics, sociology, and civics, among other subjects within the social studies. It is our hope that regardless of whether you become a teacher who has a middle school social studies class, you will embrace the beauties, the angers, the accomplishments, and the struggles that come with working with this age group and this subject.

With this said, the third edition of *Teaching Middle Level Social Studies: A Practical Guide for 4th–8th Grade* will help you learn about and process these important ideas with your classmates. We are happy that this formerly digital textbook is now part of Information Age Publishing's catalog. In addition, for anyone who read or used the one of the older editions we are excited that Drs. Steph Strachan and Jessica Ferreras-Stone, and classroom teacher Karrie Palmer, Ed.S, have joined Scott and Ben as co-authors of this edition. The important insights they provided and additions they made to the book has made it, in our humble opinion, one of the best resources for strategies and ideas to teach middle level social studies. We hope you find this new edition to be a useful guide to high quality middle school social studies instruction.

MAKING SOCIAL STUDIES MEANINGFUL

As Scott passed by an 8th grade social studies class at Obama Middle School he noticed that several students were crying. Intrigued, he paused outside the door and listened. Several had tissues and many were wiping away tears. Other's faces showed distressed. Poking his head into the room he could see images were being shown of Emmett Till, a 14-year-old African American child, who was killed for whistling at a white woman in rural Mississippi in 1955. Along with the photographs the teacher was playing the Death of Emmett Till by Bob Dylan, to tell the story of what happened. This lesson brought a personal connection to a young man who had been brutally murdered over 50 years before. How did the teacher gain such emotion from his students? What were his objectives? What consequences might come from this lesson?

No matter what your answers are to these questions, there is no doubt that the teacher had established an emotional connection to this story. Social studies courses are often the only courses that can bring such reactions in students. Social studies helps students understand the past, present, and future of our society and their role in it. Though social studies can be powerful, it can also be boring. It is a subject that is often viewed as the memorization of trivia, endless lecture, and mind-numbing note taking. It is our hope that this book will help you avoid these potential pitfalls.

Unfortunately, since the advent of No Child Left Behind (NCLB) and standardized testing, social studies is also becoming the most overlooked and underfunded core subject in America's public schools (Jacob, 2005; Pace, 2011; Willis, 2007; Willis & Sandholtz, 2009). Research has shown that the average elementary school teacher spends anywhere between 90 to 230 minutes a week on the subject in comparison to 699 minutes per week on reading and mathematics (Bailey et al., 2006; Center on Educational Policy, 2008; VanFossen, 2005; VanFossen & McGrew, 2008). While the social studies disciplines are core subjects (e.g., History, Geography, Economics, and Government) at both the middle and secondary levels, it is a subject that usually does not count toward NCLB's Adequate Yearly Progress (AYP) for elementary and middle schools. It is often only a three-year requirement at the high school level, thus receiving less attention than other subject in these schools as well (Bailey et al., 2006; Pace, 2011; van Hover et al., 2010; Willis, 2007; Willis & Sandholtz, 2009).

Due to the lack of emphasis on social studies at the elementary and middle level, teachers are often told to focus more on reading and writing and less on the standards that are still required for state mandated tests (Jacob, 2005; Pace, 2011; Willis, 2007; Willis & Sandholtz, 2009). Regrettably, teachers often find themselves believing the myth that the only way to "cover the standards" in a timely manner is to rely heavily on lecture and the use of textbooks and worksheets to quickly go through the material (Pace, 2011; Treadaway, 2009). In turn, social studies teachers are often disappointed, and even angry, with their students' low test scores, even though they "know they covered the content" (Pace, 2011). This cycle often starts anew the next school year.

After reading the last few paragraphs about the place of social studies in the elementary and secondary schools, we hope that we have not sent you running to your advisor to change your major to avoid this fate. Though the introduction was based on research and our many conversations with K–12 social studies teachers over the years, in many school districts and classrooms, social studies is neither viewed nor taught in this manner. In fact, in our experience, social studies is a discipline that is supported in many ways, taught by teachers who are passionate about the subject, and believe in its importance in their students' everyday lives—just as the Emmett Till lesson illustrated. As Scott's former supervisor Dr. Debbie Daniel often says, social studies is most certainly thought of in many school districts as the "subject that we do for the rest of our lives." There are many social studies curriculum advocates and instruction resources to help both beginning and experienced social studies teachers improve their content knowledge and teaching methods.

With that said, Scott wrote the first edition of this book with a special audience in mind: the middle level social studies teacher. In our opinion, the educational needs of those who aspire to teach in the middle grades are not met in most social studies methods' textbooks. The authors of these books far too often lump middle level teacher preparation with early childhood (grades K–5) or secondary social studies education (grades 6–12). As experienced middle level teachers, middle grades methods instructors, and supported by the research of Conklin (2010), we believe these texts fail to prepare their readers for the special needs of the middle level student (grades 4–8). We hope that this book will help you learn the best strategies for teaching middle level social studies students.

THE PHILOSOPHIC FOUNDATION OF THIS BOOK

In the simplest of terms your personal philosophy is the foundation for all your actions and beliefs. In education there are several established philosophies that teachers use to make decisions about their instruction. Most teachers and administrators find themselves identifying with elements of several different philosophic foundations at different times in their career. A social studies teacher for instance, may hold a progressive philosophy and create many lesson plans that incorporate its elements, such as giving students a choice of "hands-on" projects. In other lessons the teacher may take an essentialist approach and spend an hour lecturing to their students about the impact of World War II on the modern world because they do not feel that students would learn this material while working in a collaborative group setting.

Personally, we have always considered ourselves to be progressive educators and tried to incorporate this philosophy in my classroom management and lesson planning. Progressivism is rooted in the works of John Dewey (e.g., 1902, 1933, 1938), and is based on the primary belief that students learn by "doing" especially when it comes to incorporating real life scenarios in the classroom such as debating the merits of an important historical decision or analyzing primary sources like a historian. Contrary to the critiques of some of the detractors of this philosophy (e.g., Chall, 2000; Hirsch, 1996; Ravitch, 2000; Ravitch & Finn, 1987; Schug & Western, 2002), our own experiences have demonstrated to us that middle level learners thrive in social studies classes that implement a progressive philosophy. We have seen this in both students' interest of social studies and their achievement on their standardized test scores. Therefore, this book is primarily based on the progressive philosophy and there are many methods and strategies that will be introduced based on these ideals. In sum, just a few of the actions of a progressive social studies educator include:

- Taking a role in helping students understand who they are (Kincheloe, 2001).
- Offering students opportunity to form a "critical consciousness" about their society (Kincheloe, 2001).

- Using curriculum and content standards as a guide in the interpretation, understanding, celebration, and critique of the topics and themes of social studies (Liss, 2003).
- Offering students a variety of choices in their own learning (Liss, 2003).
- Using multiple strategies and differentiation in an effort to stimulate each student's passion for learning (Liss, 2003, p. 247).
- Helping students develop an awareness of community problems and the tools with which to address them (Liss, 2003, p. 247).
- Serving more as a facilitator, not the keeper or provider, of knowledge.
- Allowing students to make connections and draw their own conclusions about social studies topics.

Despite the obvious appeal of such methods, it should be understood that in today's classrooms progressivism is often viewed as the antithesis of the essentialist, test orientated, and standards-based curriculum that has stemmed from several federally mandates over the past 20 years. With this in mind, we have found that the key to any successful classroom experience is, quite simply, balance. As a classroom teacher you will need to do what is best for both your students and for you as an educator.

However, for better or worse, as a social studies educator, one of the primary ways that you will be evaluated as an effective educator is based on your students' test scores. While we contend that progressive methods and strategies do lead to higher student performance on standardized tests, the primary goal of the readers of this book should be to learn how to incorporate several educational philosophies in the development of the methods and strategies that they use in their social studies classes for their middle grade students.

WHAT MAKES THIS BOOK DIFFERENT?

The primary purpose of this book is to provide methods and strategies to education majors who are earning an undergraduate or master's degree in middle grades education. In addition, this book should be useful to those secondary social studies teachers who find themselves teaching at the middle school level. In our experiences working with middle grades education students, and supported by the research of Conklin (2010, 2012a, 2012b) and Tanner (2008), many preservice teachers do not have the same social studies content knowledge or overall interest in the subject as possessed by their peers who major in secondary social studies education. In turn, secondary social studies majors usually do not receive adequate preparation for working with middle level students. In fact, most of the secondary social studies student teachers that we have mentored were terrified about being assigned to teach the middle grades despite being certified to teach grades K–5 or 6–12.

This book offers in-depth guidance for teaching middle grades social studies. Readers will learn many progressive and traditional teaching methods and strategies that have been studied by social studies researchers and proven effective in the middle school classroom. The content of the book consists of both conventional chapters found in most texts offering information about topics such as "What is Social Studies?" and "Unit and Curriculum Planning," as well as unique chapters such as "The Middle Level Learner" and "Best Practices for Teaching State History." A brief summary of each chapter is provided below:

- Chapter 1 offers information about what makes middle level learners different from students at the elementary and secondary level. The chapter offers a summary of the traditional views about the challenges of teaching students at this level but, more importantly, offers information and about the capabilities that middle level students have to learn at high levels. An overview of the more effective strategies to teach middle level students is provided as well.
- Chapter 2 summarizes the purposes of teaching social studies and how to incorporate the NCSS 10 themes and C3 Framework for teaching social studies. We also discuss the NCSS' four motifs for the development of high-quality middle grades instruction.
- Chapters 3 and 4 offer several basic and advance strategies for teaching middle grades social studies. You'll learn about the appropriate use of textbooks and lectures as well as more advanced teaching strategies such as conducting inquiry lessons and using simulations.
- Chapter 5 offers information about how to plan lessons and units using the basic and advanced strategies provided in Chapters 3 and 4. The chapter also provides ideas for incorporating state and local standards into your lessons as well as ways to create differentiated lessons that meet the learning styles of all students.
- Chapter 6 provides information about the different types of assessments, how to prepare students to take state mandated tests, and ideas for how to create formal and informal assessments.
- Chapter 7 offers a unique view of the best practices for teaching state history, a subject that is required for middle level students in most states but ignored in most methods textbooks. The chapter presents examples of lessons that incorporate the 10 NCSS themes and C3 Framework into state history courses.
- Chapters 8–10 offer "best practice" suggestions for teaching U.S. history, World Geography, Government/Civics, and Economics.
- Chapters 11 offers specific suggestions for using social studies to help build literacy.
- Chapter 12 offers ideas about how to integrate social studies with other "core" disciplines such as English/Language Arts and science.
- Chapter 13 offers ideas for using social studies resources effectively such as textbooks and audio/visual tools.

- Chapter 14 provides an eclectic examination of the recent past and new directions for social studies. Topics include the C3 Standards being adopted or adapted by many states, how the NCLB act and state standards have affected middle level social studies, the effects of federal mandates on middle grades social studies, and recent controversies that have brought national attention to social studies curriculum. The bulk of the chapter focuses on how technology impacts social studies courses and specific programs that can immediately be used in social studies courses.
- Chapter 15 offers suggestions on how to transition from being a novice social studies teacher into a social studies professional.
- Chapter 16 concludes the book by offering a summary of ideas and strategies that you should take away from reading the book.

Additionally, the appendices offer exemplary lesson plans specifically geared to meet the needs and interests of 10/14-year-old students. These lesson plans correspond to the chapters concerning historical inquiry, state history, U.S. history, world geography, and incorporating economics and government in the social studies classroom. Readers will note many references to teaching in Georgia and Illinois. All authors, working to remain true to their classroom-experience roots, reference lessons they have explored with students. As you read about these lessons, it is our hope you use them as springboards to consider how lessons, cultural references, and state histories might be employed in your own contexts. We hope that these lesson plans will be useful when you enter the classroom, are given a textbook and teacher guide, and are told to "get started."

FEATURES OF THE BOOK

In addition to the unique chapters and lesson plans many additional features of the book will be useful when you begin your student teaching experience as well as when you become an experienced teacher. These features include:

- A list of "website resources" that will take you to thousands of lesson plans, state and national standards, and other multimedia tools that can be used in your classroom. You may note that we often duplicate these resources across chapters. Because college instructors are known for selecting specific chapters or for assigning chapters out of order, we include multiple references to ensure you are aware of these fantastic resources.
- Individual, collaborative, and whole class activities that will help you develop a better understanding of the topics, lessons, and strategies discussed.
- High quality lesson ideas and classroom tested teaching strategies embedded throughout the book.
- Images of student work samples that will help you visualize the finished product that is being discussed.

- An examination of state and national standards that will help guide you in your lesson planning

USEFUL PUBLICATIONS FOR SOCIAL STUDIES TEACHERS

In addition to textbooks and websites, there are several great publications that can be useful in learning more about social studies and helpful in creating lessons plans. These include:

- **Middle Level Learning** (http://www.socialstudies.org/publications/mll) is a "special publication featuring lessons and activities for middle school teachers. MLL is published online only, three times a year. The current issue and MLL back issues are available to NCSS members only at the Archive of Publications."
- **Middle School Journal** (https://www.tandfonline.com/toc/umsj20/current) is the official journal of the Association for Middle Level Education. A blend of research and practice-based articles, this journal is of interest to those working with young adolescents.
- **Social Education** (https://www.socialstudies.org/publications-resources) is an NCSS publication that is offered to members once every two months. The publication features articles, lessons, and activities for social studies practitioners at varying grade levels.
- **Social Studies and the Young Learner** (https://www.socialstudies.org/publications-resources) is an NCSS publication that is offered to members. The publication features articles, lessons, and activities for social studies practitioners who teach grades K–6.
- **The History Teacher** (http://www.thehistoryteacher.org) is the "most widely recognized journal in the United States devoted to the teaching of history" at all grade levels. The journal has articles of interest to both K–12 teachers and history professors.
- **The Social Studies** (https://www.tandfonline.com/toc/vtss20/current) "is a peer-reviewed journal that publishes articles of interest to educators at all levels." Topics found in the journal include "those concerned with the social studies, the social sciences, history, and interdisciplinary studies."
- **Theory and Research in Social Education** (https://www.socialstudies.org/publications-resources) is a journal "designed to stimulate and communicate systematic research and thinking in social education." Though geared toward researchers K–12 teachers may be able to gain better insight about the field and even some practical ideas from reading the journal.

WEBSITE RESOURCES

- **The Association for Middle Level Education** (http://www.amle.org/) is the only national education association dedicated exclusively to those in

the middle grades, though not specifically about social studies. Their website offers resources, information about their advocacy programs, opportunities for professional development, research, and publications for those interested in teaching at the middle level.
- **The Council for Economic Education** (http://www.councilforeconed.org/) offers resources, materials and standards to K–12 social studies teachers. The website also includes information about their annual conference, on-line teacher training, a free on-line personal finance video game, and offers teachers the opportunity to purchase the Virtual Economics CD that contains 1200 K–12 lesson plans and 51 videos.
- **The National Council for Geographic Education** (https://ncge.org/) offers geography-based resources, materials, and standards to K–12 social studies teachers. The website includes information about their annual conference, publications, and collaborations with other organizations.
- **The National Council for History Education** (http://www.nche.net/) "builds bridges between K–12 teachers, college and university faculty and museums/libraries/historical societies who all share a common passion for teaching history." The website includes information about their annual conference, professional learning opportunities, lesson ideas, and their advocacy for history in schools.
- **The National Council for the Social Studies** (http://www.socialstudies.org/) provides "leadership, service, and support for all social studies educators. Founded in 1921, National Council for the Social Studies has grown to be the largest association in the country devoted solely to social studies education. NCSS engages and supports educators in strengthening and advocating social studies." The NCSS website offers teachers access to the 10 NCSS themes for teaching social studies, information about their annual conference, lesson plans and resources, position statements, and a list of notable trade books.

REFERENCES

Anderson, D. (2014). Outliers: Elementary teachers who actually teach social studies. *Social Studies, 105*(2), 91–100.

Bailey, G., Shaw Jr., E. L., & Hollifield, D. (2006). The devaluation of social studies in the elementary grades. *Journal of Social Studies Research, 30*(2), 18–29.

Chall, J. S. (2000). *The achievement challenge: What really worked in the classroom?* Guilford Press.

Conklin, H. G. (2010). Preparing for the educational black hole? Teachers' learning into two pathways into middle school social studies teaching. *Theory and Research in Social Education, 38*(1), 48–79.

Conklin, H. G. (2012a). Company men: Tracing learning from divergent teacher education pathways into practice in middle grades classrooms. *Journal of Teacher Education, 63*(3), 171–184.

Conklin, H. G. (2012b). Toolboxes for teaching in the middle grades: Opportunities to learn in two preparation pathways. *Theory and Research in Social Education, 40*(2), 161–191.

Dewey, J. (1902). *The child and the curriculum.* University of Chicago Press.

Dewey, J. (1933). *How we think* (rev. ed.). D.C. Heath.

Dewey, J. (1938). *Experience in education.* Touchstone.

Heafner, T. (2004). Using technology to motivate students to learn social studies. *Contemporary Issues in Technology and Teacher Education, 4*(1), 42–53.

Hirsch, E. D. (1996). *The schools we need.* Doubleday

Jacob, B. A. (2005). Accountability, incentives, and behavior: The impact of high stakes testing in the Chicago public schools. *The Journal of Public Economics, 89*(5–6), 761–796.

Key, L., Bradley, J. A., & Bradley, K. S. (2010). Stimulating instruction in social studies. *Social Studies, 101*(3), 117–120.

Kincheloe, J. L. (2001). *Getting beyond the facts: Teaching social studies/social sciences in the Twenty-first century.* Peter Lang.

Liss, N. J. (2003). What we talk about when we talk about social studies: A reply to Schug and Western's article on the homeless social studies teacher. *The Social Studies, 94*(6), 245–250.

Pace, J. L. (2011). The complex and unequal impact of high stakes accountability on untested social studies. *Theory and Research in Social Education, 39*(1), 32–60.

Ravitch, D. (2000). *Left back: A century of failed school reforms.* Simon & Schuster.

Ravitch, D., & Finn, C. (1987). *What do our 17-year-olds know?* Harper & Row.

Schug, M. C., Todd, R. J., & Beery, R. (1982). *Why kids don't like social studies.* Paper presented at the Annual Meeting of the National Council for the Social Studies. Boston, MA, November 1982.

Schug, M. C., & Western, R. D. (2002). The homeless social studies teacher: How muzak progressivism has harmed social studies education. *The Social Studies, 93*(6), 251–256.

Sunal, C. S., & Sunal, D. W. (2007). Reports from the field: Elementary teacher candidates describe the teaching of social studies. *International Journal of Social Education, 22*(2), 29–48.

Tanner, L. (2008). *No Child Left Behind* is just the tip of the iceberg. *The Social Studies, 99*(1), 41–45.

This American Life. (2011). *Middle school.* http://www.thisamericanlife.org/radio-archives/episode/449/middle-school

Treadaway, T. S. (2009). How social studies teachers teach: State standards and their impact on teachers' pedagogical strategies. In L. P. McCoy (Ed.), *Studies in teaching: 2009 research digest* (pp. 157–163). Wake Forest University

van Hover, S., Hicks, D., Stoddard, J., & Lisanti, M. (2010). From a roar to a murmur: Virginia's history and social science standards, 1995–2009. *Theory and Research in Social Education, 38*(1), 80–113.

VanFossen, P. J. (2005). "Reading and math take so much of the time...": An overview of social studies instruction in elementary classrooms in Indiana. *Theory and Research in Social Education, 33*(3), 376–403.

VanFossen, P. J., & McGrew, C. (2008). Is the sky really falling? An update on the status of social studies in the K–5 curriculum in Indiana. *International Journal of Social Education, 23*(1), 139–179.

Willis, J. S. (2007). Putting the squeeze on social studies: Managing teaching dilemmas in subject areas excelled from state testing. *Teachers College Record, 109*(8), 1980–2046.

Willis, J. S., & Sandholtz, J. H. (2009). Constrained professionalism: Dilemmas of teaching in the face of test-based accountability. *Teachers College Record, 111*(4), 1065–1114.

CHAPTER 1

MIDDLE LEVEL STUDENTS

Who Are They? How Are They Different?

A teacher who knows he is sensitive to students questioning his authority can anticipate that middle grades students will, in fact, question his authority.
—*Mary Ellen Beaty-O'Ferrall, Alan Green, and Fred Hanna (2010)*

As a result of working in middle school, I am much more self-reflective. It is the kids that show us what they need and where we need to go next
—*Juli Kendall, Teacher*

Activity List
- Reflecting on Your Middle Grades Experience
- Reflecting on Piaget's Cognitive Stages
- The Challenges of Teaching at the Middle Level
- The Benefits of Teaching at the Middle Level
- Suggestions for Teaching Middle Level Students
- Reflecting on the Chapter

COLLABORATIVE ACTIVITY: REFLECTING ON YOUR MIDDLE GRADES EXPERIENCE

Think back to your time in upper elementary and middle school. Review these questions and discuss them with a classmate:

- What were you like as a middle school student?
- What were your interests?
- What were your greatest challenges?
- Did you like school?
- What were your experiences like in the hallways, cafeterias, and locker rooms of your school?
- What were your favorite subjects?
- What did you wish your teacher knew about you as a young adolescent?
- What type of learning opportunities do you wish your teacher had created?
- Would you like to teach students that were just like you were at that age? Why or why not?
- What types of teaching strategies would you use if you were to teach a room full of students who were just like you were?

INTRODUCTION

Middle level students, who range in age from approximately 10–15 years, are unique in comparison to students in the lower elementary and high school levels. Generally seen as a stage that is more mature than children and less mature than adults, adolescence is defined in large part by its transitory nature. Middle level students undergo more rapid physical, intellectual, and emotional changes than at any other point in their lives (e.g., Alexander, 1988; Allen, 1988; Association of Middle Level Educators (AMLE) formerly National Middle School Association (NMSA), 1982, 1995, 2003, 2012; Carnegie Council on Adolescent Development, 1989; Cohen Kadosh et al., 2013; Jackson & Davis, 2000; National Council for the Social Studies, 1991; Toepfer, 1988). While research has shown that young adolescents possess great potential and desire for learning (AMLE, 2012; Conklin, 2018), middle grades students have traditionally been considered to be the most at risk to become engaged in negative behaviors such as alcohol and drug abuse, sexual activity, violence, suicide, and dropping out of school (Alexander, 1988; Carnegie Council on Adolescent Development, 1989; Jackson & Davis, 2000; NCSS, 1991; Toepfer, 1988).

Furthermore, once students enter middle school, they find a different environment than the elementary school they left. Gone are the self-contained classrooms where elementary students spend the majority of their days. Many students feel lost in the shuffle. The change in environment may present significant challenges to students when they transition to middle school (Holas & Huston, 2012). Middle school is often a place where students fall behind in one or more subjects and where a lack of knowledge and skills finally catches up with those who were just getting by in earlier grades. Additionally, middle school is where students often first encounter teachers who are content focused and grade more targeted than elementary school teachers. Finally, the middle school level is sometimes when parents admit that they have lost control of their children and give up any hope for their academic success. The changes taking place with adolescents themselves, layered with changing relationships with their parents, blended with changes in their school environments, combine with other elements to create a time of transition for 10–15-year-olds that can be both exciting and downright scary at the same time.

Both the popular press and academic research offer some very disturbing images about the social and academic lives of middle level students. Different from previous generations, the current, and potentially future, generations of middle school students are networked with influences and pressures not seen before. Social media and the ubiquity of communication has fundamentally changed how adolescents experience their adolescence. For example, the PBS television show, Frontline, reported adolescents, as they strive for "likes," are influencing and being influenced by markets that are potentially at the global scale (Koughan & Rushkoff, 2014; Libresco, 2019).

A *Time Magazine* article points out that the levels of "emotional and physical problems are higher among U.S. middle school students than their peers in 11 other countries" (Wallis, 2005, para. 8). The article also argues that there is almost a 30% increase in the number of incidents requiring a police report from the elementary to the middle school and "more than half of eighth-graders fail to achieve levels of proficiency in reading, math, and science on national test scores" (Wallis, 2005, para. 10–11). In the area of social studies, students also perform poorly. For example, in 2018, 26% of 8th graders taking the National Assessment of Educational Progress (NAEP) scored below the basic level of understanding and only 2% scored at the "advanced" level in their knowledge of civics (U.S. Department of Education, 2018).

Articles in academic journals and books report similar concerns. For instance, the works that have been credited for paving the way for middle grades education and the middle school movement, *This we Believe* (1982), *Turning Points* (1989), and *Turning Points* 2000 (2000), offer claims that middle level students are often impulsive, rebellious, easily pressured by their peers, and prone to see moral situations in shades of gray. Eccles and Wigfield (1997), in turn, report that adolescents, as a group, have the highest levels of arrest rates in comparison to any other age group in the United States (p. 15). More recently, Curry and Choate (2010) found that, due to societal influences, middle level girls are more susceptible to experience negative physiological outcomes such as anxiety, poor self-esteem, and eating disorders than any other age group (p. 8).

Recently, the Centers for Disease Control reports that; 29% of high school students report drinking alcohol in the past 30 days; 38% of high school students report having had sexual intercourse; and that suicide is the second leading cause of death for people 10–34 years of age (Centers for Disease Control, 2020). Many of these concerning statistics find their roots in the middle school years. Over the long term, these trends change, but remain concerning. In the 1990s, researchers found both increases and decreases in risky behaviors of middle grades students as compared to this age group in the 1970s and 80s. For instance, there was a 9% increase in the use of illicit drugs from 1991–1998, as well as a report that 52% of middle school students drank alcohol (Jackson & Davis, 2000, p. 7). Nonetheless, there were also some positive trends being shown by adolescents during this time period. For example, middle level students reported being less sexually active and more educated about contraception and the risk of HIV. From 1990–1998 the number of pregnancies and abortions went down among middle grades students; however, these statistics were still higher than the rates of all other developed countries (Jackson & Davis, 2000). This trend appears to have continued through the early 2010s (Sedgh et al., 2015). Nevertheless, it should be pointed out that even though today's adolescents mature faster and are exposed to more violent and sexually explicit images, songs, movies and TV shows, most of the respondents have a good relationship with their parents, and 60% say that they should wait until marriage before having a sex (Curry & Choate, 2010; Gibbs, 2005). Broadly, these behaviors have been—and continue to be—of deep concern to middle school teachers as they work to assist young adolescents in their overall development.

In addition to all of the societal pressures that middle level students face, there are also many physical differences found in this age group. The middle school years bring about rapid physical growth and the onset of puberty—the point at which an individual reaches sexual maturity and becomes capable of reproduction. Rapid growth can challenge coordination, making middle school students notoriously clumsy at times. Puberty brings about a rise in hormone levels that influence body odor, voice changes, hair growth, and problems such as acne. These physical changes are major factors that affect the lives of middle grades students and are significant influences on their behavior at both home and school (AMLE, 1982; Brown & Knowles, 2014; Repetto et al., 2006).

These physical changes also affect the middle level student emotionally. Adolescents can show mood swings, egocentrism, a search for self-identity, and have self-esteem issues (Brown & Knowles, 2014; Jackson & Davis, 2000; Repetto et al., 2006). Though many of these issues are often considered normal for this age group, a middle grades teacher should be aware that "50% of all serious adult psychiatric issues—such as depression, anxiety, and substance abuse— begin at 14 years old…" and should be ready to help these students as much as they can (Kessler et al. as cited in Mulhall, 2007, p. 6). The best, and lawful, approach is to always report any sign of an emotional or physical issue to the school counselor or an administrator immediately (Akos, 2007; Rischel, 2007).

Physically, though the 10–15-year old's brain is usually the same size as an adult's, internally it is still developing cognitively (Brown & Knowles, 2014; Cas-

1. Sensorimotor (birth to about age 2):
   Infants "think" by acting on the world with their eyes, ears, hands, and mouth. As a result, they invent ways of solving sensorimotor problems, such as pulling a lever to hear the sound of a music box, finding hidden toys, and putting objects into and taking them out of containers.
2. Preoperational (age 2 to age 7):
   Preschool children use symbols to represent their earlier sensorimotor discoveries. Development of language and make-believe play takes place. However, thinking lacks the logic of the two remaining stages.
3. Concrete Operational (7–11 years):
   Children's reasoning becomes logical. School-age children understand that a certain amount of lemonade or play dough remains the same even after its appearance changes. They also organize objects into hierarchies of classes and subclasses. However, children think in a logical, organized fashion only when dealing with concrete information they can perceive directly.
4. Formal Operations (11 years on):
   The capacity for abstract, systematic thinking enables adolescents, when faced with a problem, to start with a hypothesis, deduce testable inferences, and isolate and combine variables to see which inferences are confirmed. Adolescents can also evaluate the logic of verbal statements without referring to real-world circumstances.

FIGURE 1.1. Piaget's Cognitive Stages. Source: Berk, L. E. (2017)

key & Ruben, 2007; Eccles & Wigfield, 1997; Repetto et al., 2006). This is why middle level students often fail to understand a concept that appears simple and obvious to adults. Many of these students are still in what psychologist Jean Piaget identified as the Concrete Operational stage (see Figure 1.1), a time in adolescent development when they have difficulty understanding abstract concepts (Brown & Knowles, 2014). However, adolescents who display characteristics of concrete operational thought should be provided with activities that involve Formal Operations as these are needed to further develop their thinking. Middle grades students simply require a bit more assistance, for example scaffolding, to benefit from such activities. At this higher stage students are able to do more advanced problems (Brown & Knowles, 2014).

COLLABORATIVE ACTIVITY: REFLECTING ON PIAGET'S COGNITIVE STAGES

Think about the middle level students that you will be teaching and the likelihood that they will be using concrete operational thought. Answer the following questions in your reflective journal and discuss them with a classmate:

> 1. Create a collaborative learning environment.
> 2. Ensure that social interactions with peers and adults are positive.
> 3. Establishing structure and clear limits.
> 4. Make connections to real life scenarios.
> 5. Make participation meaningful.
> 6. Offer praise for achievement.
> 7. Plan for physical activity and active learning.
> 8. Provide interactive "hands-on" activities.
> 9. Use diverse learning and teaching approaches.

FIGURE 1.2. Best Practices for Teaching Middle Level Students

- Think of a common social studies topic that may be taught at the middle level (i.e., the Civil War, the geography of the United States, Harriet Tubman).
- What types of social studies activities could you use in teaching this subject to concrete operational thinking students?

Some researchers believe that because their brains are still developing, adolescents are extremely curious by nature and not afraid to take risks (Brown & Knowles, 2014). The fact that adolescents often display these two characteristics can be both intimidating and frightening to middle grades teachers. However, channeled correctly, the characteristics of curiosity and risk taking afford teachers the opportunity to provide thought provoking and worthwhile lessons (Brown & Knowles, 2014). These cognitive differences have a major impact on the type of learning environment that middle level students need to thrive (AMLE, 1982; Gallagher-Polite et al., 1996; Jackson & Davis, 2000).

Due to physical needs, most middle level students will not thrive in a classroom setting that is geared solely to sitting and taking notes (Brown & Knowles, 2014). A large amount of research has been conducted on the physical needs of middle grades students and this body of research supports a list of best practices (see Figure 1.2) that teachers need to keep in mind (AMLE, 1982, 2010, 2012; Anfara et al., 2007; Brown & Knowles, 2014; Jackson & Davis, 2000; North Carolina Area Health Education Centers Program, 1996; Repetto et al., 2006; Silvis, 2017).

Using all of these best practices may seem somewhat daunting. No teacher can create lessons incorporating all these suggestions, all the time. However, with careful planning many of these best practices can be built into lessons. Eventually, they will become a natural part of your instructional style.

THE CHALLENGES AND JOYS OF TEACHING MIDDLE LEVEL STUDENTS

As educators who have taught at the elementary, middle, high, and postsecondary levels, we argue that middle level students can be the most difficult group to teach. Working with individuals in this group can also present the deepest rewards. Some students walk into the building not caring about school, about being in your class, or learning the subject you teach (Carnegie Council on Adolescent Development, 1995). While many students may not show such negativity, the fact is that some will, and the middle level teacher will have to contend with these negative attitudes on a daily basis (Anderman & Midgley, 1997). These negative attributes are balanced with students who have unbridled enthusiasm for school, deep interest in the activities that take place in your classroom, and perhaps even more subject knowledge in certain topics than the teacher. Looking beyond academics, a teacher entering the middle level classroom should also keep in mind that the main focus of many middle level students is the development of relationships with their peers (Brown & Knowles, 2014). Any educator about to embark on a middle level teaching career should understand that, more often than not, when asked what they like best about school students will reply "hanging out with my friends" or simply "lunch" (Brown & Knowles, 2014). Rather than view young adolescents as volatile and negative, we like to look at this age group as dynamic and energetic. The changes through which your students are going can be embraced to develop a classroom climate and subsequent learning experiences that can be life changing. Rather than fighting the negative aspects that are so often the focus when approaching this age group, we have found success when embracing them and integrating them into the learning environment. Ben, for example, employs adolescents' developing sense of critique and voice when encouraging students to provide opinions on tax collection and spending. Rather than remaining distant and abstract, the taxation discussion focuses on sales tax that is applied to the gas station sodas students buy before and after school. Getting students "riled up" about where their money goes is a great way to embrace what is often erroneously viewed as purely negative complaining.

Middle school students are easily distracted and impulsive (release a cockroach in the middle of an 8th grade classroom and watch the mayhem ensue). Many educators believe that in order to prevent chaos and maintain student attention you have to be either extremely authoritarian (which will make everyone's life worse) or extremely funny and silly (which may backfire for those times when you need to be serious) (Beaty-O'Ferrall et al., 2010; Bennett, 1997). We must admit that we have used both approaches, especially early in our careers, with varying levels of success. Scott is not ashamed to admit that sometimes he had to dress up like a Teletubby or Care Bear, and even take a pie in the face to motivate his students to perform to their full potential on standardized tests. Likewise, it is not uncommon for Ben to use a large stuffed animal to represent mammoths crossing Beringia. Rather than shy away from the balance between childhood and adulthood, we blend together the advantages of both to create educational and interesting learning environments. Essentially, the distractedness and impulsivity demonstrated by many adolescents can be used to the class's advantage. While Scott's social studies students were not required to pass an end-of-course standardized test for promotion to the next grade, such tests were used as an indicator of his success as a teacher. For instance, one month after earning his Ph.D., Scott dressed like a clown as a reward for his students because they met their goal for the overall score on the state standardized test. It should be noted that Scott's students chose the clown costume because two of their other teachers were supposedly afraid of clowns. Indeed, students actually received two rewards as they watched these teachers run away from him in mock horror.

We have found that in order to keep our classrooms from reaching the point of anarchy, we have had to work extremely hard at planning and being very creative every day. Ben often says that an engaging lesson plan can serve as its own classroom management system. Nonetheless, many middle level students find everything to be "boring." In many cases all you can hope for is that the lesson you spend hours developing is considered to be "okay." This means that each day must be different yet have enough routine to keep students within the behavioral expectations and boundaries required for them to learn and not hurt themselves or others (Beaty-O'Ferrall et al., 2010; Bennett, 1997).

As a middle level educator, you will have to be willing to accept that students are going to ask you "Why?" when it comes to almost everything, and they will not accept "I don't know" or "because I said so" as answers (Beaty-O'Ferrall et al., 2010; Bennett, 1997). Rather than see them as negative, it is helpful and productive to use these inquiries as opportunities to provide rationales for the class activities and to build class cohesiveness. It also helps to possess an extensive knowledge of the content you teach because middle school students will often ask you specific and sometimes nonsensical questions about a historical figure or event, and if you do not know the answer, the students will say in frustration, "You're a teacher and you don't know the answer!" This will inevitably lead to a verbal free-for-all between students who support you and those who do not. One of Ben's techniques when put in this situation by students is to ask the student to explain the importance of the question. Students often enter his class positioned as adversaries to the learning environment and it often takes months to develop the trust necessary to get past trivial questions that are posed to challenge the teacher, rather than advance the learning. While you will not be able to answer every question, you will need to review their course's content thoroughly, and not simply stay one chapter ahead of the class. Furthermore, if students are asking high quality questions for which they can provide rationales, it is a sign that you have students engaged beyond the basics of simply acquiring knowledge.

Middle grades teachers will find themselves being a student's "favorite" teacher one day and the "meanest" teacher the next (Brown & Knowles, 2014). One should be aware that students will argue (and sometimes fight) over things adults find silly such as chairs, computers, pencils, cookies, the last chocolate milk, girlfriends, boyfriends, and for more disturbing and "adult important" reasons such as drugs or being in rival gangs (Repetto et al., 2006). You may have students "get in your face" while screaming at you and telling you to "get out of my face" (Beaty-

O'Ferreal et al., 2010). You will have students lie to you and steal from you. You will have students who "don't get it" and students who "don't care" (Jackson & Davis, 2000). You will have students who interpret your words and actions in very different ways than you do (Wellenreiter, 2018). You will bring your work home with you every night and work many more than the contractual 40 hours a week year after year. So…are you sure you are ready to teach this age group? Whether the answer is "yes" or "no" we ask you to keep reading. We deeply believe the rewards of working with this age group far outweigh the perceived costs.

COLLABORATIVE ACTIVITY: CHALLENGES OF TEACHING AT THE MIDDLE LEVEL

Teaching middle school is a challenging job. Answer the questions below in your reflective journal and discuss your answers with a partner.

- Why did you decide to teach at the middle level?
- What do you think will be your biggest challenge in teaching this age group?
- What do you think are the best ways to overcome these challenges?

THE BENEFITS OF TEACHING MIDDLE LEVEL STUDENTS

The task of teaching middle level students can appear daunting. Raging hormones, mood swings, and general negativity are all challenges that can send a pre-service teacher running for the hills, or at least dreading to teach at this level. Still, the unique physical, social, and cognitive characteristics of middle level students are also the best reasons to teach them. If you are willing to put the time and effort into working with 4th–8th graders, they will reward you every day with their enthusiasm, their willingness to take risks, their eagerness to speak their mind, and the unconditional respect they have for their "favorite" teachers (Beaty-O'Ferreal et al., 2010; Gallagher-Polite et al., 1996). Middle grades students will entertain you every day with the hilarious things that only a 10–15-year-old can say and do, and, for that matter, get away with. Middle school classrooms are places where many teachers do not dare tread, but they richly reward those who are drawn to truly adventurous learning environments.

As a middle-grades teacher you will always need to be creative (Brown & Knowles, 2014). For the most part your students are not going to thrive in the "sit and get" environment of the high school (Brown & Knowles, 2014; Jackson & Davis, 2000, NMSE, 1982). They will tell you frankly if an assignment is perceived as too childish for them, and you will need to develop strategies and activities that keep them interested but are not so difficult that students decide to quit and give up. This constant need to stay creative is challenging but will transform you into a great teacher. After developing countless lessons that have kept 10–15-year-olds actively engage the majority of the time, teaching college classes or making presentations to educators at any level is a breeze.

Teaching middle grades students never gets boring or dull. There will always be problems or issues you will have to solve while managing 30 students. Once you put out one fire another ignites, but you will never complain of having nothing to do. As a middle-grades teacher you will play several roles. Counselor, surrogate parent, police officer, psychologist, and referee are all hats that you will wear in any given school year (Brown & Knowles, 2014).

No matter what roles you take on, you may be the final chance that a student in trouble has to turn his or her life around. Or you may be the teacher that helps a student understand the real-life relevance of the subject you teach or inspires a student's future academic achievement. At the very least, you can be the person who shows students that your subject can be fun. As your students cross the bridge between childhood and adulthood, this may be the last chance to reinforce to them the deep, intrinsic joy of learning that they often had in earlier grades. The positive effect you can have on your students' lives and helping them reach their full potential is the largest benefit of being a middle grades teacher.

COLLABORATIVE ACTIVITY: BENEFITS OF TEACHING AT THE MIDDLE LEVEL

Think back to when you were a middle school student. In your reflective journal answer the following questions and share your answers with a partner:

- Who were some of your favorite teachers?
- What did they do to make them your favorite? What types of strategies and lessons did they use?
- Using them as an example what can you take away from the experience and bring into your own classroom?

THE IMPORTANCE OF TEACHING MIDDLE LEVEL STUDENTS

Why is it important to teach the middle level student? Quite simply, after reading about all of their physical, social, and cognitive changes and development it should be obvious these students need caring, motivated, and knowledgeable teachers. It has been recommended that in order to have a middle level classroom that ensures student success, schools need to be staffed with teachers specifically trained for the middle grades (Jackson & Davis, 2000). Nonetheless, especially in subjects such as social studies, many teachers who teach at the middle grade level are from secondary education programs that usually focus on high school teaching. Though most states offer secondary social studies teacher certification in grades 6–12, many have not received the educational opportunities necessary for teaching middle level learners (Conklin, 2012; Tanner, 2008).

We have witnessed how this lack of teacher understanding can be detrimental to the development of middle level learners. Due to the fact that they are still particularly impressionable, we have seen how "bad" teachers can cause students to dislike a subject for the rest of their academic career. More importantly, a teacher who lacks the understanding to work with this age group may be the cause of a student to withdraw from all elements of school entirely, thus adding to the possibility of this student becoming one of the negative statistics discussed previously. Simply put, many middle level teachers do not understand the long-lasting impact that they can have on the lives of the students they teach (Beaty-O'Ferrall et al., 2010; Jackson & Davis, 2000; Repetto et al., 2006).

SUGGESTIONS FOR TEACHING MIDDLE LEVEL LEARNERS

There are many ways middle level educators can structure a classroom conducive to the needs of middle level learners. To target the potential challenges middle level students bring to the classroom, a teacher should listen to and acknowledge their viewpoints, provide opportunities for inquiry and research in areas of choice, and help students explore both the concrete and abstract aspects of ideas (Brown & Knowles, 2014; Repetto et al., 2006). To work with their tendencies of self-interest, a middle level teacher should use activities that allow students the opportunity to share their opinions, beliefs, and thoughts (Conklin, 2011). To acknowledge the physical changes and needs of adolescents, activities should invoke movement and spatial skills whenever possible. In creating safe environments, teachers should make sure that students feel that their privacy is respected and set clear boundaries to help students remain secure (Beaty-O'Ferrall et al., 2010; Repeto et al., 2006).

To support the need for students to build positive relationships with one another, teachers should build positive relationships with their students. Talking about appropriate elements of your personal life such as your favorite sports team, your family, pets, and your own childhood will certainly help the students view you as a person with whom they can talk. Middle level teachers should also carefully use humor. They should recognize individual students for effort, perseverance and success. Finally, middle level educators should allow time in their classes for students to work with one another, even allowing them to occasionally choose their own partners. (Beaty-O'Ferreal et al., 2010; Brown & Knowles, 2014; Repeto et al., 2006).

As middle level educators, we have found that our students needed equal amounts of freedom and structure in the classroom to be successful. This delicate balance encourages safe risk-taking while maintaining clear focus on goals. Teachers need to consciously adjust to this balance in order to keep students engaged. As far as classroom management is concerned, middle level students do not need their teacher to be their friend, but someone who will be an empathetic mentor (Beaty-O'Ferreal et al., 2010). We believe that this position can be developed and maintained when the teacher is flexible with students, transparent in decision-making, empathetic, and includes student voices in the classroom. Middle level educators should be educational mentors who students view as trustworthy, flexible, and worthy of respect.

1. A belief in the process of collaborating with both students and co-workers (AMLE, 2012; Brown & Knowles, 2014; Jackson & Davis, 2000).
2. A belief in all students' ability to succeed (AMLE, 2012; Brown & Knowles, 2014; Jackson & Davis, 2000).
3. A rationale concerning why one wants to teach middle level learners (Hole & McEntree, 1999; Repetto, 2006).
4. A passion for learning (Brown & Knowles, 2014; Jackson & Davis, 2000; Repetto et al., 2006).
5. A philosophy and action plan that places students at the center of the learning processes (Beane, 2005; Brown & Knowles, 2014; Vagle, 2007).
6. A sense of humor (Brown & Knowles, 2014).
7. A wealth of knowledge about young adolescent development (AMLE, 2012; Brown & Knowles, 2014; Jackson & Davis, 2000).
8. An awareness of adolescent health issues, the willingness to discuss these issues with students, and an understanding of how these issues can affect student success (Brown & Knowles, 2014; Jackson & Davis, 2000; Mulhall, 2007).
9. Instructional and curricular flexibility (AMLE, 2012; Brown & Knowles, 2014; Repetto et al., 2006).
10. The ability to actively listen to your students (Brown & Knowles, 2014; Gallagher-Polite et al., 1996; Repetto et al., 2006)
11. The ability to show unconditional caring for your students (Brown & Knowles, 2014; Noddings, 1992; Gallagher-Polite, 1996)

FIGURE 1.3. Characteristics of an Effective Middle Level Educator

So, in conclusion, what makes a good 4th–8th grade teacher? The qualities and characteristics of an effective middle level educator have been suggested in prior works and are summarized in Figure 1.3.

The good news is, even if you do not possess all of the qualities now, if you care about your students and their success, you will learn to adapt. Starting your teaching career understanding about why it is important to teach middle level students and how to teach them will put you ahead of many teachers who arrived at their middle level classroom unprepared. We hope this book will provide that knowledge. For the remainder of the book, the focal point will be the concepts discussed in this chapter and how to incorporate them into your middle level social studies classroom.

Individual Activity: Suggestions for Teaching Middle Level Students

In your reflective journal:

- Using Figure 1.3, rank from most to least important, the needed characteristics for teaching middle level students.
- Write a few sentences explaining why you made your selections.

SUMMARY

In this chapter, we examined important information about middle level students and how to teach them. You should now have a better idea of the challenges that middle school students face and the characteristics that their teachers need in order to effectively teach them. The most important understanding you should take from this chapter is that middle school students are not only capable of learning in a progressive and interactive fashion, research has proven that they need this type of instruction to perform at their highest potential. The next chapter will examine the discipline of social studies and how to teach the subject to middle level learners.

COLLABORATIVE ACTIVITY: REFLECTING ON THE CHAPTER

In your reflective journal:

- List the teaching strategies you think will be the most and least effective for teaching middle level students.
- Based on what you learned in this chapter describe what should be taking place in a "perfect" middle level classroom.
- Draw a map of what your middle level classroom will look like and explain your drawing to a classmate using what you learned in this chapter as your rationale.

REFERENCES

Akos, P. (2007). The unique nature of middle school counseling. In S. B. Mertens, V. A. Anfara, Jr., & M. M. Caskey (Eds.), *The young adolescent and the middle school* (pp. 183–200). Information Age Publishing.

Alexander, W. A. (1988). Schools in the middle: Rhetoric and reality. *Social Education, 52*(2), 107–109.

Allen, M. G. (1988). Middle grades social studies: A modest proposal. *Social Education, 52*(2), 113–115.

Anderman, L. H., & Midgley, C. (1997). Motivation and middle school students. In J. L. Irvin (Ed.), *What current research says to the middle level practitioner* (pp. 41–48). National Middle School Association.

Anfara, V. A., Mertens, S. B., & Caskey, M. M. (2007). Introduction. In S. B. Mertens, V. A. Anfara, Jr., & M. M. Caskey (Eds.), *The young adolescent and the middle school* (pp. ix–xxxiii). Information Age Publishing.

Association of Middle Level Education (formerly National Middle School Association). (1982). *This we believe.* Author.

Association of Middle Level Education (formerly National Middle School Association). (1995). *This we believe: Developmentally responsive middle level schools.* Author.

Association of Middle Level Education (formerly National Middle School Association). (2003). *This we believe: Successful schools for young adolescents: A position paper of the National Middle School Association.* Author.

Association for Middle Level Education. (2010). *This we believe: Keys to educating young adolescents*. AMLE.
Association of Middle Level Education (formerly National Middle School Association). (2012). *This we believe in action: Implementing successful middle level schools*. Author.
Beane, J. A. (2005). *A reason to teach: Creating classrooms of dignity and hope: The power of the democratic way*. Heinemann.
Beaty-O'Ferrall, M. E., Green, A., & Hanna, F. (2010). Management strategies for difficult students: Promoting change through relationships. *The Middle School Journal, 41*(4), 4–11.
Bennett, B. J. (1997). Middle level discipline and young adolescents: Making the connection. In J. L. Irvin (Ed.), *What current research says to the middle level practitioner* (pp. 73–85). National Middle School Association.
Berk, L. E. (2017). *Development through the lifespan: Seventh edition*. Allyn & Bacon.
Brown, D. F., & Knowles, T. (2014). *What every middle school teacher should know: Third edition*. Heinemann.
Carnegie Council on Adolescent Development. (1989). *Turning points: Preparing American youth for the 21st Century*. Carnegie Council on Adolescent Development.
Carnegie Council on Adolescent Development. (1995). *Great transitions: Preparing adolescents for a new century*. Carnegie Corporation.
Caskey, M. M., & Ruben, B. (2007). Under construction: The young adolescent brain. In S. B. Mertens, V. A. Anfara, Jr., & M. M. Caskey (Eds.), *The young adolescent and the middle school* (pp. 47–72). Information Age Publishing.
Centers for Disease Control. (2020). *Information for parents with teens*. https://www.cdc.gov/parents/teens/index.html
Cohen Kadosh, K., Linden, D. E. J., & Lau, J. Y. F. (2013). Plasticity during childhood and adolescence: Innovative approaches to investigating neurocognitive development. *Developmental Science, 16*(4), 574–583.
Conklin, H. G. (2011). Teaching intellectually challenging social studies in the middle school: Problems and possibilities. *Social Education, 75*(4), 220–225.
Conklin, H. G. (2012). Toolboxes for teaching the middle grades: Opportunities to learn in two preparation pathways. *Theory and Research in Social Education, 40*(2), 164–191.
Conklin, H. G. (2018). Caring and critical thinking in the teaching of young adolescents. *Theory into Practice, 57,* 289–297:
Curry, J. R., & Choate, L. H. (2010). The oversexualization of young adolescent girls: Implications for middle grades educators. *Middle School Journal*, 6–15.
Eccles, J. S., & Wigfield, A. (1997). Young adolescent development. In J. L. Irvin (Ed.), *What current research says to the middle level practitioner* (pp. 15–30). National Middle School Association.
Gallagher-Polite, M. M., DeToye, L., Fritsche, J., Grandone, N., Keefe, C., Kuffel, J., & Parker-Hughey, J. (1996). *Turing points in middle schools: Strategic transitions for educators*. Corwin Press.
Gibbs, N. (2005). What does it mean to be 13. *Time Magazine*. http://content.time.com/time/magazine/article/0,9171,1088701,00.html
Holas, I., & Huston, A. C. (2012). Are middle schools harmful? The role of transition timing, classroom quality, and school characteristics. *Journal of Youth and Adolescence, 41*(3), 333–345.

Hole, S., & McEntree, G. H. (1999). Reflection is at the heart of practice. *Educational Leadership, 56*(8), 34–37.

Jackson, A. W., & Davis, G. A. (2000) *Turning points 2000: Educating adolescents in the 21st century.* Teachers College Press.

Koughan, F., & Rushkoff, D. (Writers). (2014). Generation like [Television series episode]. In F. Koughan & D. Rushkoff (Producers), *Frontline*. WGBH. http://video.pbs.org/video/2365181302/

Libresco, A. S. (2019). Surviving eighth grade. *Middle Level Learning, 64*, 17–18.

Mulhall, P. F. (2007). Health promoting, high performing middle level schools: The interrelationships and integration of health and education for young adolescent success and well-being. In S. B. Mertens, V. A. Anfara, Jr., & M. M. Caskey (Eds.), *The young adolescent and the middle school* (pp. 1–26). Information Age Publishing.

National Council for the Social Studies. (1991). *Social studies in the middle school: A report of the Taskforce on Social Studies in the Middle School.* National Council for the Social Studies. http://www.socialstudies.org/positions/middleschool/

Noddings, N. (1992). The challenge to care in schools: An alternative approach to education. In *Advances in contemporary educational thought* (vol. 8). Teachers College Press.

North Carolina Area Health Centers Program: Health Careers and Minority Work Force Development Council. (1996). *Guide for working with Adolescents: Preceptor/mentor handbook.* NCAHCP.

Repetto, J. B., Webb, K. W., Neubert, D. A., & Curran, C. (2006). *The middle school experience: Successful teaching and transition planning for diverse learners.* Pro-Ed.

Rishel, T. J. (2007). Suicide, schools, and the young adolescent. In S. B. Mertens, V. A. Anfara, Jr., & M. M. Caskey (Eds.), *The young adolescent and the middle school* (pp. 297–322). Information Age Publishing.

Sedgh, G., Finer, L. B., Bankole, A., Eilers, M. A., & Singh, S. (2015). Adolescent pregnancy, birth, and abortion rates across countries: Levels and recent trends. *Journal of Adolescent Health, 56*(2), 223–230.

Silvis, R. (2017). Giving up control: Action research in the middle school. *Middle Level Learning, 58,* 15–17.

Tanner, L. (2008). No Child Left Behind is just the tip of the iceberg. *The Social Studies, 99*(1), 41–45.

Toepfer, C. F. (1988). What to know about young adolescents. *Social Education, 52*(2), 110–112.

U.S. Department of Education. (2018). *The Nation's Report Card: Civics grade 8 national results.* https://www.nationsreportcard.gov/civics/results/scores/

Vagle, M. D. (2007). Middle school teacher qualities: Looking for signs of dignity and democracy. In S. B. Mertens, V. A. Anfara, Jr., & M. M. Caskey (Eds.), *The young adolescent and the middle school* (pp. 323–342). Information Age Publishing.

Wallis, C. (2005, August 1). Is middle school bad for kids? *Time Magazine.* http://content.time.com/time/magazine/article/0,9171,1088694,00.html

Wellenreiter, B. R. (2018). Hallways paved with good intentions: Analyzing rules and procedures in non-classroom middle school spaces. *Middle School Journal, 49*(2), 10–15.

CHAPTER 2

SOCIAL STUDIES IN THE MIDDLE GRADES

History without politics descends to mere Literature
—*Sir John Robert Seely*

The causes of events are ever more interesting than the events themselves
—*Cicero*

Activity List
- Reflecting on Your Middle Level Social Studies Experiences.
- Reflecting on the Common Terms and Phrases in Social Studies.
- Where Do You Stand on the Texas Curriculum Controversy?
- State and NCSS Standards.
- Reflecting on the Four Motifs of Teaching Middle Level Social Studies.
- Multicultural Education in Middle Level Social Studies.
- Reflecting on the Chapter.

Teaching Middle Level Social Studies: A Practical Guide for 4th–8th Grade (3rd Edition),
pages 17–51.
Copyright © 2022 by Information Age Publishing
www.infoagepub.com
All rights of reproduction in any form reserved.

COLLABORATIVE ACTIVITY: REFLECTING ON YOUR MIDDLE LEVEL SOCIAL STUDIES EXPERIENCES

Think back to your time in upper elementary and middle school social studies classes.

- Review these questions and discuss them with a classmate:
- What was your favorite subject?
- How did you feel about the subject of social studies?
- Do you remember the focus and topics of your social studies classes from grades 4–8? What were they?
- How were they different from your early elementary and high school social studies classes?
- Have your thoughts about social studies changed since you have been in college?
- Based on what you remember about your social studies classes, what do you think the rationale for the program was; that is, what were your middle level social studies teachers trying to accomplish and teach you in their classes?

INTRODUCTION

When hearing the word "social studies" many people think of only one element of the discipline: history. However, social studies is much more than just the study of the past. The National Council for the Social Studies (NCSS), the largest social studies organization in the world, defines social studies as:

> ...the integrated study of the social sciences and humanities to promote civic competence. Within the school program, social studies provides coordinated, systematic study, drawing upon such disciplines as anthropology, archaeology, economics, geography, history, law, philosophy, political science, psychology, religion, and sociology, as well as appropriate content from the humanities, mathematics, and natural sciences (NCSS, 2010, p. 7).

Based on this definition, this chapter offers an in-depth examination of the purposes of teaching social studies and of the NCSS' national curriculum standards called the 10 Themes of Social Studies. Next, the chapter provides information about the more recently released NCSS C3 frameworks (2013) and the Religious Studies Companion document (NCSS, 2014). The chapter then moves on to inspect the purposes of teaching social studies in the middle grades and to explain why good social studies instruction is important at the middle level. The chapter also offers information about the NCSS' Task Force on Social Studies in the Middle Schools' four motifs of middle grades social studies instruction (NCSS, 1991) and how these motifs correlate to the 10 NCSS themes. Finally, this chapter concludes with information about teaching diverse learners and celebrating diversity in the middle level social studies classroom

PURPOSES OF TEACHING SOCIAL STUDIES

The NCSS (2010) contends that the primary purpose of teaching social studies in America's schools is to "help young people develop the ability to make informed and reasoned decisions for the public good as citizens of a diverse, democratic society in an interdependent world" (p. 9). The organization's primary aim is for the promotion of civic competence, which it defines as "the knowledge, intellectual processes, and democratic dispositions required of students to be active and engaged participants in public life" (NCSS, 2010, p. 7). The NCSS (2010) argues that a focus on civic competence allows social studies students to learn and use important skills such as data collection and analysis, collaboration, decision-making, and problem solving as they seek knowledge, learn to improve our democratic way of life, and participate as members of our global community (p. 7).

In addition, it can be argued that there are several other core purposes and goals for the study of social studies, along with important skills that students should learn from its study. These themes recur in the social studies literature and in the individual disciplines that make up the social studies. In summary, these basic beliefs include promoting critical thinking and making educated value judgments about issues, instilling knowledge about our own society, gaining knowledge of other cultures around the world, acquiring basic understanding of the social sciences and humanities, building decision making/ problem solving skills, and developing self-awareness (e.g., Barton & Levstik, 2004; Ravitch & Finn,

- Active and Engaged Citizens
- Civic Competency
- Collaboration
- Critical Thinking
- Cultural Responsiveness
- Decision Making/Decision Makers
- Democratic Principals/Values
- Data Collection/Analysis Skills/Information Analysis
- Environmental Awareness and Action
- Financial Awareness and Skill
- Global Citizenship
- Instilling Knowledge
- Self, Social, Cultural Awareness
- Social Justice

FIGURE 2.1. Common Terms and Phrases used in the Rationales for Teaching Social Studies and other Social Science Disciplines (In Alphabetical Order)

1987; Saxe, 1991; Wineburg, 2001). Indeed, US and world events such as global COVID-19 pandemic and events surrounding the 2020 Presidential election and electoral college process demonstrate ongoing need for citizens deeply informed in civic processes, economic concepts, and data analysis. Figure 2.1 lists common terms and phrases used in rationales for teaching social studies and other social science disciplines. The breadth of these terms and concepts reflects the multifaceted goals of deep, meaningful social studies education.

CLASS ACTIVITY: REFLECTING ON THE COMMON TERMS AND PHRASES IN SOCIAL STUDIES

Examine the terms listed above. Answer the following questions in your reflective journal and share your answers with your classmates:

- Which terms and phrases are similar and which are different?
- Do you agree that all of these terms explain the purposes for teaching social studies?
- Which term or phase do you think is the most/least important for teaching social studies? Why?
- How would a historian view the phrase you chose as the most important for their discipline? How about an economist or political scientist?
- What strategies would you use to teach the term or phrase you chose as the most important in your middle grades social studies classes?
- What are terms you would add to this list?

The "Social Studies Wars"

Though we support the NCSS definition and purpose for teaching social studies what social studies should *be* and *do* is an ongoing topic of debate (Evans, 2004; Hawley & Crowe, 2016). In America's public schools, the "social studies wars" have been raging since at least the late 19th century, and they continue to this day (Evans, 2004; Evans & Passee, 2007). For example, one of the major sources of friction between social science educators, history educators, and historians concerns history's place within social studies education. Various camps argue whether history should be the core social studies subject from which all other disciplines branch, or if history should be but one area of a larger interdisciplinary study (Brophy & VanSledright, 1997; Evans, 2004, 2007; Saxe, 1991). Nevertheless, it should be noted that no matter their political biases or differing views about the methods that should be used for history instruction, the vast preponderance of authors, researchers, theorists, historians, and educators believe that teaching the subject of history in some form is not only worthwhile but absolutely essential in America's schools (e.g., NCHE, 2011; NCSS, 2010; Saxe, 1991; Stearns et al., 2000).

Another source of friction is the differing beliefs about "what" or "whose" history should be taught (Brophy & VanSledright, 1997). The *1619 Project,* which; "...aims to reframe the country's history by placing the consequences of slavery and the contributions of black Americans at the very center of the [United States'] national narrative." (1619 Project, 2019) presents challenges to a historical narrative learned in schools by generations of Americans (Riley, 2020; Wright, 2020). Working to counter the 1619 project, President Trump proposed the *1776 Commission* to create a "...restoration of American education grounded in the principles of our founding that is accurate, honest, unifying, inspiring, and enabling..." (Exec. Order No. 13958, 2020, p. 2). A perfect example of the on-going debate regarding what "should" be taught in schools is found in the 2010 Texas social studies curriculum controversy (see Figure 2.2). Due to the influence that the large textbook adoption state of Texas has on the content found in the textbooks written for school systems throughout the United States, the controversy received nationwide attention. In sum, the Texas Board of Education, dominated by conservatives, made several changes to the state's K–12 social studies curriculum. Some of these changes included removing Thomas Jefferson from a list of writers who inspired 18th century revolutions (due to his advocacy for the separation of church and state), supporting the efforts of Senator Joseph McCarthy's communist "witch hunts" of the 1950s, and voting down proposals by Hispanic board members to include more historical figures of Latino descent in the standards (McKinley, 2010). The inclusion and exclusion of individuals, events, or concepts is one of the most hotly debated topics in social studies curriculum.

More recently, the College Board (2020) released a new AP US history framework the board claimed would meet the needs of AP teachers who had complained that the existing courses covered too much content and did not allow their students to delve deeply into the material. However, opponents of the changes claimed the framework did not include important content in American history such as Benjamin Franklin and Martin Luther King Jr. Another complaint was that the new

---

- The New York Times: Texas Conservatives Win Curriculum Change
    - http://www.nytimes.com/2010/03/13/education/13texas.html
- The Daily Beast: In Texas Textbooks, Moses is a Founding Father
    - http://www.thedailybeast.com/articles/2014/09/22/in-texas-textbooks-moses-is-a-founding-father.html
- The Magazine of the American Historical Association: Texas Revises History Education, Again.
    - https://www.historians.org/publications-and-directories/perspectives-on-history/january-2019/texas-revises-history-education-again-how-a-good-faith-process-became-political

FIGURE 2.2. Articles Describing the Texas Curriculum Controversy

AP US history framework focused too much on the darker aspects of American history. Even prior to this most recent change, the AP US History Framework has been a focal point of controversy. In 2014, the content from the framework prompted students in one Colorado school district to protest a school board proposal that required teachers to emphasize that patriotism be taught in their US history classes (Strauss, 2014).

Class Activity: Where do you stand on the Texas curriculum controversy?

Read two of the articles listed in Figure 2.2. With your classmates answer the questions below:

- Summarize why the Texas curriculum controversy was so controversial.
- With which side do you agree? Why?
- As a class, develop a list of the 10 most important historical figures that should be in the U.S. history curriculum for any state. Make sure that there is a rationale behind why these figures should be included.
- Read the top 10 list, who are some of the most important historical figures who you had to leave out?
- Is there anyone that your classmates listed that you would remove in favor of the person who was left out?
- How would each side of the Texas curriculum controversy feel about the historical figures on your list?
- Based on your reading and class activity, why do you think that it is so difficult to develop social studies curriculum and standards?

The common belief about the importance of history is not true of social studies education in general. Some still disregard social studies as a discipline and believe that all the disciplines should be separated and individually studied at all grade levels (e.g., Brophy & VanSledright, 1997; Cheney, 1987; Evans, 2004; Gagnon, 1989; Ravitch & Finn, 1987; Saxe, 1991). Though, it should be noted, that no matter the philosophical camp to which they belong, many educators, researchers, and theorists continue to identify at least one of the same purposes when writing about why their chosen discipline should be taught and studied either in a multidisciplinary social studies approach or as a separate subject in schools. While critics spend a great deal of time pointing out the politics behind the rationale supported by each camp, they do not take note of the similarities found in the rationales of each group (Brophy & VanSledright, 1997; Evans, 2004, 2007).

No matter with whom you side in the debate on the nature of social studies, in the middle grades you will likely use an interdisciplinary approach for teaching social studies. The 2013 NCSS publication of the College, Career, & Civic Life C3 Framework for Social Studies Standards points toward an interdisciplinary approach emphasizing questioning/inquiry, investigative, and communication skills across the traditional social studies disciplines while maintaining some elements of subject specificity. In short, you will not teach "just history" or "only geography," but will teach "historical thinking," "geographic thinking," "civic thinking" and "economic thinking." Indeed, Chapter 12 is wholly dedicated to connecting the social studies with other subject areas. As a starting point, we recommend that middle grades social studies teachers consciously plan lessons around the 10 NCSS themes.

THE 10 NCSS THEMES FOR TEACHING SOCIAL STUDIES

Though there is much conflict about the place of social studies in the schools, an overarching set of goals for teaching social studies has been adopted by the National Council for the Social Studies. First published in 1994, these themes can be adapted to traditional history, civics, economics, and geographic instruction, or any interdisciplinary social studies course, depending on the needs found at the local level (NCSS, 2010). The ten strands are: 1) Culture; 2) Time, Continuity, and Change; 3) People, Places, and Environments; 4) Individual Development and Identity; 5) Individuals, Groups, and Institutions; 6) Power, Authority, and Governance; 7) Production, Distribution, and Consumption; 8) Science, Technology, and Society; 9) Global Connections; and 10) Civic Ideals and Practices. For the complete NCSS explanation of the strands, we encourage you to visit their website, as written in the references section. Additionally, in the most recent version of the NCSS standards the organization offers "Learning Expectations for Middle Grades" (NCSS, 2010, pp. 94–124).

We will spend the next few pages describing the themes and offering examples of their application in lessons.

Theme 1: Culture

The first NCSS theme is culture. The NCSS (2010) explains that "social studies programs should include experiences that provide for the study of culture and cultural diversity" (p. 14). The NCSS states this theme can be found in courses and units that deal with anthropology, geography, history, and sociology. However, this theme can be incorporated in the social studies courses that are taught in grades 4–8 such as state history, U.S. history, and world geography/cultures. Discussions in history courses about immigration and migration, for example, may explore the creation, adaptation, and evolution of culture as people from different backgrounds interact. In a unit on immigration to the United States in the latter half of the 19th century, for example, your class may investigate elements that make up culture and how they change given various circumstances. Languages, traditional family unit structures, religious beliefs, holidays, foods, and histories of immigrants coming to the United States are all elements that influence and are influenced by changes in an individual's or family's setting. The concept of the United States as being the great melting pot is challenged as students read primary sources and find examples of adjustment and assimilation of various ethnicities that also maintain aspects of their uniqueness. The charge of the NCSS Theme regarding the study of culture and cultural diversity is seen when students discuss and debate whether or not immigrant groups of the past and present are fully homogenized into the "American culture" and, more fundamentally, whether there actually is an American culture. Culture may be explored in a contemporary way as well. Dramatic changes in economic conditions, such as were seen in 2020 during COVID-19 shutdowns, certainly impacted short-term and long-term cultures of students. Sports culture, family celebration culture, and civic culture such as Independence Day celebrations were forced to adapt to new circumstances. As we will see, the 10 themes are deeply rooted in interdisciplinary and multidisciplinary thinking. For more on how to incorporate this theme in social studies courses see Chapters 7–10.

Theme 2: Time, Continuity, and Change

The second NCSS theme is Time, Continuity, and Change. Of the 10 themes, this is the most history focused. In explaining this theme, the NCSS (2010) states; "social studies programs should include experiences that provide for the study of the past and its legacy" (p. 15). For the middle level learner, the formal study of history allows students to "continue to expand their understanding of the past" (para. 9). In addition, the NCSS (2010) recommends that middle level students begin working with historical inquiry in their social studies classes. Putting this very broad theme into practice in Ben's US History class for example, students analyzed the strengths and weaknesses of primary and secondary sources, refine inquiry skills by asking history-oriented questions, find examples of historic accounts that disagree with one another, and continue to hone the same research skills used by historians. In a more contemporary setting, students may explore similarities and differences between the Black Lives Matter movement and the broader Civil Rights movement of decades past. We will focus on historical inquiry in more detail in Chapters 4 and 8. It should be noted, however, that inquiry-based lessons are also important in the middle level studies of economics, geography and government.

Theme 3: People, Places, and Environments

This theme states that social studies programs "should include experiences that provide for the study of people, places, and environments" and is often the basis of world cultures and geography courses (NCSS, 2010, p. 16). While this theme has a geography focus, it is easily incorporated across the social studies disciplines. For instance, teachers can create cross-disciplinary lessons based on this theme that incorporate historical, economic, political, and geographic issues. An 8th grade class in Scott's former school district won the statewide *We the People* competition with their study on the "Water Wars" in the Southeastern United States. This case involved the states of Alabama and Florida suing Georgia concerning each state's water rights to the Chattahoochee River and was based on this theme. Whether it is an economics class studying a nation's resources and access to capital, a sociology class investigating causes of poverty, a geography class looking at connections between population patterns and access to navigable water, or a history class that is looking to see how mountain ranges affect borders and cultures, the interactions of people, places, and environments is fundamental in all human activity. We believe the common statement, "without geography, you are nowhere" and without this theme as a basis, investigations in the disciplines of the social sciences are incomplete. Using this theme for creating middle grades world geography lessons will be discussed in more detail in Chapters 4 and 9.

Theme 4: Individual Development and Identity

The fourth NCSS theme focuses on the disciplines of psychology, sociology, and anthropology and states that social studies programs should help students understand that "personal identity is shaped by an individual's cultures, by groups, by institutional influences, and by lived experience shared with people inside and outside the individual's own culture" (NCSS, 2010, p. 17). Questions related to identity and development are central to the understanding of who we are and studying this theme will help students become aware of the factors that have shaped their personal identity.

This theme is critically important to middle school students who are grappling with finding out their role in our pluralistic society (e.g., identifying their talents, preferences, etc.). The NCSS suggests that incorporating this theme into middle school social studies offers students opportunity to gain a broader context for understanding their personal identity issues. Incorporating this theme into social studies courses also allows students to collaborate with peers who may come from different socio-cultural backgrounds.

Theme 4 also encourages connections between the curriculum and the student. As discussed in the preface, it is, sadly, a common belief that social studies classes and experiences are disconnected from the lives of students to the point of irrelevancy. One of the challenges and one of the joys of teaching middle level social studies is putting this theme into practice. Not only through curricular objectives involving topics such as culture, immigration, civic controversies, and civil liberties, the way your class participants interact with one another can work toward achieving the goals of Theme 4. A class that is studying factors that influence voting choices, for example, can do so in heterogeneous groups to encourage diverse perspectives and lively discussions. Theme 4 will be discussed in more detail in Chapters 5 and 10.

Theme 5: Individuals, Groups, and Institutions

The fifth NCSS theme focuses on helping students understand the social, economic, and political functions of institutions and their influence on all aspects of society. The NCSS maintains that this theme should appear in anthropology, history, political science, psychology, and sociology courses, though it can be argued that this theme fits within the study of economics as well. There are many topics middle level teachers can explore with their students with this theme in mind, including the impact that their own school or school district has on the community. For example, Scott's students were always amazed that their school district was one of the largest employers in the State of Georgia. Due to their interest, Scott provided opportunities for them to debate the merits and issues of a school system being so large. In Ben's class, this theme was addressed in discussions about taxes and the investigation of various levels of government. Students enjoyed wandering around the school searching for examples of taxpayer expenditures, then evaluating whether these expenditures were in the interest of the public good. Broadening beyond governmental institutions, this theme encourages students to describe different groups of which they are a part or are aware of and describe what role(s) these groups have in individual identity formation and community cohesiveness. This theme will be discussed in more detail in Chapters 5, 7, 8, 9, and 10.

Theme 6: Power, Authority, and Governance

The sixth theme has a political science focus and the NCSS (2010) asserts that social studies programs should "include experiences that provide for the study of how people create, interact with, and change structures of power, authority, and governance" (p. 19). In the state history courses Scott taught, his students examined this theme in a lesson about Nancy Hart, the only woman in Georgia with a county named in her honor. While the Georgia standards only required that students learn this simple fact, Scott developed a lesson where students were given the opportunity to examine why only one county out of 159 was named to honor a woman. The lesson provided students with the opportunity to determine which women in Georgia's history should have received this honor and which counties should consider changing their name based on this evidence. After making their name change decisions, students were urged to write that county's state representative or senator explaining why the county should change its name. With less than 70 of America's 3,141 counties being named in honor of women, such as Bremer County, Iowa and Florence County, Wisconsin, this lesson can be adapted for any state or U.S. history course (Roberts, 2013). When studying the Bill of

Rights in Ben's US history course, students had multiple opportunities to discuss and debate the balance the government's responsibility to protect individual liberties while ensuring domestic tranquility. Activities involving discussions about schools requiring students to submit urine samples for drug tests, religious observances at school, and student free speech issues all work toward Theme 6. This theme will be discussed in greater detail in Chapters 5, 7, 8, 9 and 10.

Theme 7: Production, Distribution, and Consumption

The seventh NCSS (2010) theme has an economic focus and suggests that social studies programs should "include experiences that provide for the study of how people organize for the production, distribution, and consumption of goods and services" (p. 20). This theme offers the skills-based goal that students will be able to collect and analyze data and use critical thinking in discussing economic concepts. A great way to analyze this theme is have students study a locally based business such as Burger King® (Florida); Ford® (Michigan); Amazon® (Washington); Caterpillar® (Illinois); and Nike® (Oregon). Students can identify companies headquartered in their own state and explore local, national, and global impacts of those companies.

For example, students in Georgia might study the Coca-Cola® Company and the hamburger sandwich alternative company, Chick-Fil-A®. Using these companies as a guide, they can examine many of the components of this theme including the concepts of limited resources (e.g., why Coca-Cola® uses corn syrup and not real sugar), decision making in production, distribution, and consumption (e.g., why Chick-Fil-A® is closed on Sunday and how some of their controversial polices and beliefs impact sales), and how to best deal with market failures (e.g., how Coke® managed to survive the Great Depression).

In a history context, the study of the dramatic increase in cotton production in the first half of the 19th century serves as an example of how increased supply can have profound economic and social effects. Blending discussions of the cotton gin and railroad advancements with increase in demand and production of cotton, students are challenged to see the dynamic interaction production, distribution, and consumption of goods and services with ethical and moral values as well as legal circumstances. This theme will be discussed in more detail in Chapters 5, 7, and 10.

Theme 8: Science, Technology, and Society

The eighth theme argues that social studies programs should "include experiences that provide for the study of relationships among science, technology, and society" (NCSS, 2010, p. 21). The NCSS recommends middle school students use this theme to explore, for example, how scientific discoveries can change human values and whether new technology is always better. Scott wrote a lesson based on this theme for the Georgia Council on Economic Education. This lesson, called "All Progress is Precarious: The Growth of Georgia 1790–1840," was a favorite among his students as they were given the opportunity to analyze and discuss two differing paintings concerning both the positive and negative impacts of the railroad on Georgia and all of America in the 1830s and 1840s (Roberts, 2009). Throughout his US History class, Ben's students continually return to the question; "How does technology influence our daily lives?" From studying battle tactics as a result of smoothbore vs. rifled firearm barrels to the impact the steam engine had on transportation and industry, students were frequently challenged to explain how technology works to shape their lives. To exemplify this, Ben enthusiastically encouraged students to "go home and hug your refrigerator!" because; "your life without it would not be the same!" On occasion, a student will return to class with photographic proof of the appreciation of this technological marvel. The science, technology, and society theme will be discussed in more detail in Chapters 5 and 8.

Theme 9: Global Connections

The NCSS (2010) advocates that social studies programs should "include experiences that provide for the study of global connections and interdependence" (p. 22). This theme should be present in all social studies disciplines, even state and local history courses. For example, many cities have a connection to the rest of the world through the development of the "sister cities" program. Sister Cities International is a nonprofit organization that hopes to build global understanding, cooperation, and economic development through partnering cities throughout the United States with cities in other nations around the world. With this theme in mind teachers can create lessons that allow students to research their city's "sister," learn more about the partner cities, and determine what commonalties exist between them. See the Sister Cities website in the website resources near the end of this chapter for more information about this program. Put into practice, Theme 9 can also be seen in studies of the Silk Road, the Columbian Exchange, and increasing globalization. Blending history, geography, sociology and economics, Ben challenged his students to go to the local superstore to find products from all seven continents. (They have yet to find a product that originated in Antarctica). The strength in this activity lies in the everyday nature of the concept of global interdependence. So commonplace is our use of products from across the globe we rarely give the concept a second thought. By having students list only products they knew to be made in Illinois (construction equipment, corn, pumpkins, and pork), Ben reinforced the ideas of global connections and interdependence.

Theme 10: Civic Ideals and Practices

The 10th theme of the NCSS standards is civic ideals and practices. This theme has a civics/political science base and the NCSS (2010) suggests that social studies programs should "include experiences that provide for the study of the ideals, principles, and practices of citizenship in a democratic republic" (p. 23). As with all others, we argue this theme should be found in all social studies courses.

In the middle grades, creating lessons that incorporate this theme often come from students' questions or "teachable moments." For example, one of the questions Scott found himself constantly answering when he was in the classroom was "why do we take so many tests?" After hearing this question asked for what seemed like the millionth time, Scott developed a lesson called "'Why Do We Take So Many Tests?' How the Federal, State, and Local Governments Fund Your School" (Roberts, 2009). This lesson provided students with an opportunity to explore the intricacies of how the cost of their schooling was funded and allowed them to critically analyze the ongoing educational climate of testing and how it balances with local, state, and classroom desires and needs. This lesson sprang from a civics-based "teachable moment" and describes the influence that the varied levels of government have on students' everyday lives by examining the one thing many of our adolescent students were interested in: themselves.

In addition to taking a curricular approach to this theme, Ben enjoyed working Civic Ideals and Practices into his classroom management philosophy. Similar in concept to Scott's "teachable moment," Ben's students find times when they; "... expand their knowledge of democratic ideals and practices, along with their ability to analyze and evaluate the relationships between these ideals and practices." (NCSS, 2010). When issues were brought to Ben's attention, he often decided they would make good fodder for discussion for the class. A few years ago, to the horror of the students, the school's cafeteria stopped serving French fries in the a la carte line. Ben's students wanted to stage a protest to demonstrate their dissatisfaction with the decision. Ben overheard students discussing an anonymous letter that they wanted to have the principal sign. Ben stepped in and suggested a well-written, professional petition instead. The students followed the suggestion and wrote a letter requesting the French fries be reinstated. Though they were not successful in their petition, the students had the genuine opportunity to practice active citizenship. More information about this theme will be offered in Chapters 5, 7, 8, 9, and 10.

Individual Activities: State and NCSS Standards

Choose a grade level (4–8) and use Table 2.1 to locate the standards for your state. Use the state and NCSS standards to answer the following questions:

- How are the state and NCSS standards similar and different?
- Do you see more similarities or differences between the two sets of standards?
- Choose one of the NCSS themes and your state standards and write some ideas about how you would combine the two in a social studies lesson plan.

TABLE 2.1. Social Studies Standards by State

State	Standard Website
AL	https://alex.state.al.us/browseSS.php
AK	https://education.alaska.gov/standards
AZ	https://www.azed.gov/standards-practices/K–12standards/standards-social-studies
AR	http://dese.ade.arkansas.gov/divisions/learning-services/curriculum-support/humanities/social-studies/social-studies-standards-and-courses
CA	https://www.cde.ca.gov/ci/hs/
CO	http://www.cde.state.co.us/cosocialstudies/statestandards
CT	http://www.ctsocialstudies.org/wp-content/uploads/2014/05/ctsocialstudiesframeworks2015.pdf
DE	https://www.doe.k12.de.us/domain/392
DC	https://osse.dc.gov/publication/social-studies-standards
FL	https://www.fldoe.org/academics/standards/subject-areas/social-studies/
GA	https://www.georgiastandards.org/Georgia-Standards/Pages/Social-Studies-6-8.aspx
HI	http://www.hawaiipublicschools.org/TeachingAndLearning/StudentLearning/Pages/standards.aspx
ID	https://www.sde.idaho.gov/academic/shared/social-studies/ICS-Social-Studies.pdf
IL	https://www.isbe.net/Pages/Social-Science.aspx
IN	https://www.doe.in.gov/standards/social-studies
IA	https://iowacore.gov/sites/default/files/K–12_socialstudies_508.pdf
KS	https://www.ksde.org/Agency/Division-of-Learning-Services/Career-Standards-and-Assessment-Services/Content-Area-F-L/History-Government-and-Social-Studies
KY	https://education.ky.gov/curriculum/standards/kyacadstand/Documents/Kentucky_Academic_Standards_for_Social_Studies_2019.pdf
LA	https://www.doa.la.gov/osr/lac/28V121/28v121.pdf
ME	https://www.maine.gov/doe/learning/content/social
MD	http://marylandpublicschools.org/about/Pages/DCAA/Social-Studies/MSSS.aspx
MA	https://www.doe.mass.edu/frameworks/hss/2018-12.pdf
MI	https://www.michigan.gov/documents/mde/Final_Social_Studies_Standards_Document_655968_7.pdf
MN	https://education.mn.gov/MDE/dse/stds/soc/
MS	https://www.mdek12.org/sites/default/files/Page_Docs/final_2018_mississippi_ccr_social_studies_standards.pdf
MO	https://dese.mo.gov/sites/default/files/gle-social-studies.pdf
MT	http://opi.mt.gov/Educators/Teaching-Learning/K–12-Content-Standards-Revision/Social-Studies-Standards
NE	https://cdn.education.ne.gov/wp-content/uploads/2019/11/Nebraska-Social-Studies-Standards-Final-11-2019.pdf

TABLE 2.1. Continued

State	Standard Website
NV	http://www.doe.nv.gov/uploadedFiles/nde.doe.nv.gov/content/Standards_Instructional_Support/Nevada_Academic_Standards/Social_Studies/NVACSforSocialStudies.pdf
NH	https://www.education.nh.gov/sites/g/files/ehbemt326/files/inline-documents/standards-socialstudies-framework.pdf?2
NJ	https://www.nj.gov/education/aps/cccs/ss/
NM	https://webnew.ped.state.nm.us/wp-content/uploads/2018/01/SocialStudiesStandards_5-8.pdf
NY	http://www.nysed.gov/curriculum-instruction/social-studies
NC	https://sites.google.com/dpi.nc.gov/social-studies/standards/standards
ND	https://www.nd.gov/dpi/sites/www/files/documents/Academic%20Support/Final%20Social_Studies_Content%20Standards_Rev5_6.3.2020.pdf
OH	http://education.ohio.gov/Topics/Learning-in-Ohio/Social-Studies
OK	https://sde.ok.gov/sites/default/files/documents/files/Oklahoma%20Academic%20Standards%20for%20Social%20Studies%208.26.19.pdf
OR	https://www.oregon.gov/ode/educator-resources/standards/socialsciences/Pages/Standards.aspx
PA	https://www.education.pa.gov/Teachers%20-%20Administrators/Curriculum/SocialStudies/Pages/default.aspx
RI	https://www.ride.ri.gov/InstructionAssessment/CivicsSocialStudies.aspx
SC	https://ed.sc.gov/instruction/standards-learning/social-studies/
SD	https://doe.sd.gov/contentstandards/
TN	https://www.tn.gov/education/instruction/academic-standards/social-studies-standards.html
TX	http://ritter.tea.state.tx.us/rules/tac/chapter113/index.html
UT	https://www.uen.org/core/socialstudies/
VT	https://education.vermont.gov/student-learning/content-areas
VA	https://www.doe.virginia.gov/testing/sol/standards_docs/history_socialscience/index.shtml
WA	https://www.k12.wa.us/student-success/resources-subject-area/social-studies
WV	https://wvde.us/tree/middlesecondary-learning/social-studies/
WI	https://dpi.wi.gov/social-studies/standards
WY	https://edu.wyoming.gov/educators/standards/social-studies/

THE NCSS C3 (COLLEGE, CAREER, AND CIVIC LIFE) FRAMEWORK

In 2013, the National Council for the Social Studies released the C3 framework for state social studies standards. This framework took many of the skill-based concepts found in the Common Core standards and developed an inquiry-based approach to teaching the four primary disciplines of social studies education. This "inquiry arc" of the framework includes four dimensions. Though the dimensions are relatively complex they can be broken down into simple concepts. In a nutshell, the first dimension asks social studies teachers to develop questions and plan inquiries. The second dimension asks students and their teachers to apply disciplinary concepts and tools to their study. Dimension 3 states that students

Dimension 1: Developing Questions and Planning Inquiries	Dimension 2: Applying Disciplinary Tools and Concepts	Dimension 3: Evaluating Sources and using Evidence	Dimension 4: Communicating Conclusions and Taking Informed Action
Developing Questions and Planning Inquiries	Civics	Gathering and Evaluating Sources	Communicating and Critiquing Conclusions
	Economics		
	Geography	Developing and Using Claims	Taking Informed Action
	History		

FIGURE 2.3. The Inquiry Arc of the C3 Framework (NCSS, 2013)

should evaluate their sources using evidence. The final dimension asks students to communicate their conclusions and take informed action (The National Council for the Social Studies, 2013).

Many states have adopted this framework in its entirety or adapted the concept to best fit their unique needs. As you explore the standards listed in Table 2.1, you will see various interpretations and applications of the C3 Standards in state standards. If your state does not align their standards to this framework, keep in mind that social studies lessons that are inquiry-based, hands-on, and involve higher order thinking skills are ideal for middle level learners. Throughout the book, we offer many examples of lessons that meet all four of these dimensions and correlate well with both the new C3 framework as well as the Common Core standards. Figure 2.3 shows the Inquiry Arc of the C3 Framework, (NCSS, 2013) and Figure 2.4 provides an example of the application of the framework in a geography class.

Dimension 1: Developing Questions and Planning Inquiries	Dimension 2: Applying Disciplinary Tools and Concepts	Dimension 3: Evaluating Sources and using Evidence	Dimension 4: Communicating Conclusions and Taking Informed Action
In what ways is global warming caused by human activity?	Comparison of maps or other sources of information showing various human activities that produce Carbon Dioxide	Questioning the relationship between the sources of information	Presenting a proposal to the school board to decrease local carbon footprint

FIGURE 2.4. Example of the Inquiry Arc in Practice in a Geography Classroom

Dimension 1: Developing Questions and Planning Inquiries

Dimension 1 of the Inquiry Arc requires students to develop questions and plan social studies-oriented inquiries. The standards within this first dimension work to assist students in going beyond rote questions with answers that may have little impact on their lives outside the classroom. In working to formulate impactful and compelling questions, the standards require students to evaluate how the question represents key ideas in the field and determine the kinds of sources that would be helpful in answering a question. Standard D1.3.6-8, for example, connects questions to current discourse in social science disciplines; "Explain points of agreement experts have about interpretations and applications of disciplinary concepts and ideas associated with a supporting question" (p. 25).

Put into practice, this dimension is similar in approach to the inquiry-based lesson plans discussed in Chapter 4. Students spend time in class and outside of class developing questions important to the field they are studying. Students are encouraged to go beyond the question and investigate current understandings of the question being asked. They may provide rationales for the importance of these questions, research how experts agree or disagree on the question, and begin researching potential responses to the question. If addressing the question; "In what ways is global warming caused by human activity?" in a geography class, for example, students would investigate expert opinions on the matter and then discuss how the expert opinions agree or disagree with one another.

Dimension 2: Applying Disciplinary Tools and Concepts

The second element in the Inquiry Arc is the integration of the four "core" disciplines of Civics, Economics, History, and Geography. The C3 document states Dimension 2 of the framework; "…is intended to serve as a frame for organizing curricular content, rather than [serve as a] prescription for the specific content to be taught" (p. 29). In this way, Dimension 2 places focuses on skills important to each of the core areas, rather than on specific content to be covered. Each core discipline has concepts and skills that are emphasized in its area. In Civics for example, students would "examine the origins, purposes, and impact of constitutions, laws, treaties, and international agreements" (p. 32). Remaining broad in their concepts, the standards in Dimension 2 of the C3 framework are intended to be applicable given many different specific content standards states may already have in place. Content, according to the C3 document, is specifically left up to more local units such as states; "The C3 Framework…[describes] concepts and skills rather than curricular content because there are significant differences among states in terms of what is taught and when. If and when the Irish potato famine might be taught, for example, is a decision best left to state and local decision makers" (p. 29).

In our example of a geography class studying humans' influence on global warming, students learn geography "content" such as climate patterns, biomes, map skills, and human environment interaction through their interaction with maps, charts, and other modes of data used by climatologists. In this way, coverage of the content is not the end, but rather a natural product of the process of investigating the question.

Dimension 3: Evaluating Sources and Using Evidence

Building upon Dimensions 1 and 2 which seek to develop questions and skills from content perspectives, the focus of Dimension 3 is on using evidence to develop and support claims. Subsections of this dimension encourage students to gather pertinent information from a variety of reliable sources, develop evidence-based claims, and prepare for argumentation. Standard D.3.4.6-8, for example, requires students to; "Develop claims and counterclaims while pointing out the strengths and weaknesses of both" (p. 55). If applied well, the standards within Dimension 3 will strengthen you students' ability to discuss and debate content-based arguments. Rather than stopping at the gathering of information, Dimension 3 works to have students take the next step and evaluate, process, and synthesize information collected into coherent arguments.

Put into practice, these standards will require students research a discipline-based question, using skills a professional within the discipline might use, and then prepare and defend a stance on the question. The potential for deeply meaningful civic dialogue is great if the standards within the C3 are employed as intended. In our climate change example, students would be challenged with varying viewpoints as to the causes of global warming. Climatic data tracing millions of years of climate change may be used to bolster or erode arguments that recent human activity has had influence. With standards in Dimension 3, students are challenged to evaluate the data they are looking at and are required to summarize their findings.

Dimension 4: Communicating Conclusions and Taking Informed Action

The final dimension of the C3 standards, Dimension 4 focuses on action upon the first three dimensions. Rather than leaving questions, data, and conclusions in the classroom, Dimension 4 encourages students to communicate their findings to a larger audience and take informed action. We find this dimension to be the most exciting because it is a cumulative action based upon the first three dimensions and it encourages students to be engaged citizens beyond the classroom. Working to make irrelevant the question; "Why are we learning this?" Dimension 4 puts into action the skills and concepts learned and refined in the social studies classroom. In Dimension 4, students are charged with critiquing the credibility of arguments, assessing how a problem manifests itself at local, state, national ,and international levels, and applying; "…deliberative and democratic procedures to make decisions and take action in their classrooms and schools, and in out of school civic contexts" (p. 62). In our examples, students might create a presentation regarding the impact of carbon emissions on global temperature then design a presentation to their school board on how they might reduce their carbon footprint. From investing in new energy-efficient windows to lowering winter classroom temperatures, students might encourage their school to take action based upon their classroom activities. Ben has a colleague whose environmental studies class convinced the school to move from Styrofoam lunch trays to biodegradable trays in a similar process. The end results were empowered students and a smaller environmental impact.

Most social studies educators believe that an overarching goal of social studies education is to foster the engagement of informed, articulate, and engaged citizens. Dimension 4 charges social studies educators with applying systematic approaches to social issues with their students. Rather than the stereotypically isolated and inapplicable content-based approaches, Dimension 4 takes a final step by looking beyond the classroom. This Dimension is exciting because for too long has social studies been described by students, parents, and the general public as irrelevant and useless beyond the semester-end test. With work, effective application of Dimension 4 will bring your social studies classes to the forefront of your school and greater community.

Impact on Social Studies Instruction

The C3 Standards Framework represents a fundamental change in how the social studies are perceived, taught, and learned in the 21st Century. It remains too early to tell the long-term impact the C3 Standards will have on the learning and teaching of social studies in the United States. Many states have already worked the C3 standards approach into their state standards in an effort to maintain relevance given the ubiquity of information via the Internet. Indeed, recent societal dialogue regarding fake news and social media has demonstrated the deep importance of this framework, particularly Dimensions 3 and 4. Gone, hopefully, are the days of the teacher pouring isolated facts into their students through hour-long lectures. Needed are the days of student-centered, deeply meaningful approaches that connect students to the curriculum inside and outside the classroom. We do warn, though, if history teaches us anything about social studies curriculum movements, it is that the C3 will be vigorously debated by those inside and outside the social studies profession and will ultimately itself be revised.

LOOKING TOWARD SOCIAL STUDIES IN THE MIDDLE LEVEL CLASSROOM

As we have seen, various frameworks, themes, and standards assist teachers in conceptualizing what, how, and why to teach and learn social studies. Focusing in on middle school students specifically, this section explores how social studies class activities can be merged with the unique needs and strengths of young adolescence.

Social studies is taught in middle and junior high schools throughout the country. While the study of history makes up the bulk of this subject, other disciplines, such as geography and economics, are often included in state standards (Allen, 1988; Bradley Commission, 1989; National Association of State Textbook Administrators, 2007; Stern & Stern, 2011). In addition to U.S. history being one of the core subjects of middle school social studies, many states also require that their own history be taught during the middle school years, often in the fourth or eighth grade (Menton, 1993; Moore, 1969; Percy, 2003).

Interestingly, the literature points out that, until the 1970s and 1980s, middle level social studies was largely ignored by social studies professionals (e.g., Alexander, 1988; Levy, 1988; Lounsbury, 1988; NCSS, 1991). Once researchers began to study middle level social studies, they began to suggest that the methods and purposes of teaching the subject should be altered to meet the unique needs of middle grades students (e.g., Allen, 1988; Levy, 1988; Toepfer, 1988). Based on the recommendations of the middle school research and the resulting proposals in the 1970s and 1980s, the NCSS developed a committee to study and make further recommendations about teaching social studies to middle level students. The NCSS Task Force on Social Studies in the Middle School (1991) offered suggestions about how to improve instruction of the subject.

The NCSS Task Force on Social Studies in the Middle School

The National Council for the Social Studies Task Force on Social Studies in the Middle School (1991) made several suggestions about the purpose and importance of properly teaching social studies at the middle level that are still relevant today. This report echoed the suggestions of the middle school literature during the time period and discussed the risks faced by adolescents. The report identified "three areas of developmentally appropriate needs" of middle school students (i.e. physical, social-emotional, and intellectual) and designed a social studies curriculum that would meet these needs.

The report suggests incorporating four "unifying motifs" that are needed for a focused social studies curriculum in the middle schools. It supports a curriculum that uses more of an "integrated" social studies approach (NCSS, 1991). The Task Force believed that instruction with a focus on the four motifs could "function throughout the program to personalize academic instruction and increase its relevance to the students and connection to societal imperatives" (NCSS, 1991, para. 28). The report explains the rationale behind each motif, how the subject of social studies is useful in meeting the challenges faced by middle level students, and strategies that teachers can use in their classes to meet the stated goals of the motifs. The Task Force developed "anticipated student outcomes," that they believed middle school students would develop if they were exposed to these motifs and subsequent strategies.

The four motifs are: "Concerns with Self: Development of Self-Esteem and a Strong Sense of Identify;" "Concern for Right and Wrong: Development of Ethics;" "Concern for Others: Development of Group and Other-Centeredness;" and "Concern for the World: Development of Global Perspective" (NCSS, 1991). Though written over 20 years ago, we believe these motifs have grown in relevance and importance and, paired with the 10 NCSS themes discussed earlier, should still be used as guiding rationales for teaching middle level learners in a progressive manner. The motifs are discussed in more detail below. We encourage you to keep them at the forefront of your mind as you begin developing your own middle level lessons.

Motif 1: Concern with Development of Self-esteem and a Strong Sense of Identity

One of the major concerns of middle level learners is low self-esteem. Combined with growth in social media use, this lack of confidence and self-worth can lead middle level students to make poor or risky decisions that may affect the rest of their lives. Fortunately, the study of history, culture, and humanities provide many opportunities that can allow students to address self-esteem issues and develop a strong sense of identity. With this motif in mind, middle grades social studies teachers should include strategies such as interest inventories, journals, independent research, student diaries biographies, presentations, and portfolios (NCSS, 1991, para. 28).

The five anticipated outcomes associated with the first motif are the "acquisition of appropriate skills and outcomes to be a lifelong learner;" the "ability to communicate effectively;" a "competence in conducting activities necessary for research, critical thinking, and problem solving;" the "ability to recognize and capitalize upon the relationships between school subjects, as well as integrate experiences with academic knowledge;" and the "awareness of primary sources" (NCSS, 1991, para. 29).

Motif 2: Concern for Right and Wrong: The Development of Ethics

Middle level students need assistance with developing a sense of right and wrong and making positive decisions. Helping middle school students develop a strong sense of morality is a more difficult task than one might expect. Social studies courses should offer adolescents the opportunity to develop their own beliefs, standards, and values that will "guide their decisions and actions for life, and thus influence our society" (NCSS, 1991, para. 31). As the task force stated, "the middle school is the last best place to provide a strong sense of right and wrong" and social studies courses with their focus on problem solving and decision making are the best subjects for students to practice these skills (NCSS, 1991, para. 31).

According to the NCSS Task Force (1991), the best classroom strategies that support this motif include the use of role playing, simulations, interviews, discussion of controversial issues, and prejudice reduction activities (para. 31). Using these activities can lead to anticipated student outcomes such as a commitment to democratic values and ethical standards as well as the ability to think critically and analyze one's own thoughts and actions (NCSS, 1991, para. 31). Though some teachers have reservations about teaching controversial issues, discussing controversial issues is important in the social development of middle level learners. Indeed, if we expect students to be citizens who can effectively engage in productive dialogue as adults, they need practice as adolescents. Our social studies classrooms can provide them with this practice.

Motif 3: Concern for Others: The Development of Group and Other-centeredness

Middle grade social studies instruction should help students learn how to become responsible citizens through positive interactions with others. One of the most effective ways for students to learn this skill is by participating in service activities for their school and community. According to the NCSS Task Force (1991) students who learn social studies content through such experiences are able to interact with people of diverse background and they also gain a broad understanding of society (para. 32).

In order to meet the goals of this motif, social studies teachers can incorporate several strategies in their classrooms. Some of these include participating in school or community service, peer tutoring, cooperative learning, small group discussions, and conducting oral histories (NCSS, 1991, para. 33). This motif blends well with Dimension 4 of the Inquiry Arc as both encourage active citizenship. A middle grades social studies teacher using these strategies can anticipate that their students will gain the insight on how to become an active participant in the community and contribute in a positive fashion. Since middle school students tend to have a concern for the oppressed and less fortunate, this motif most certainly should be featured in middle level social studies courses (NCSS, 1991, para. 34).

Motif 4: Concern for the World: The Development of a Global Perspective

The final motif asks middle level social studies teachers to use strategies that offer their students the opportunity to gain an "awareness of the pluralistic, interdependent, and changing nature of the world community" (NCSS, 1991, para. 35). In today's technologically linked world this goal makes even more sense than it did in 1991. The NCSS Task Force (1991) argues that middle level students should be developing a broad world view, and that schools, and more importantly social studies classes, must "engage them in examining the content and context of persisting global issues, the elements of human values and cultures, global systems, and global history" (para. 35).

There are several strategies that teachers can use to meet the goals of this motif. Some of these include inviting "guest speakers representing other lands," collaborating with foreign language classes to create cultural programs, and attending international festivals (NCSS, 1991, para. 35). Today a teacher can add international Skype or Facebook friends to the list of opportunities for helping students develop a global perspective.

The NCSS Task Force (1991) contends that the anticipated student outcomes associated with these activities include "respect for cultural diversity, knowledge of diverse cultures, and intercultural competencies;" "understanding of and appreciation for the delicate relationship between humans and the natural world;" and "knowledge of temporal and spatial relationships and of the world as a dynamic system" (para. 36). Though some may believe that this motif corresponds best with courses in world geography and cultures, it should be pointed out that this motif should be incorporated into state and U.S. history courses as well. With the large number of immigrants that come to the United States every year, along with our historical and contemporary cultural, economic, and political interdependence with the rest of the world, this motif has a place in all social studies disciplines.

COLLABORATIVE ACTIVITY: REFLECTING ON THE FOUR MOTIFS OF TEACHING MIDDLE LEVEL SOCIAL STUDIES

With the same state standards you used in the last activity, list ways that you can incorporate the motifs in the study of your state standards. Discuss your answers with a partner.

THE IMPORTANCE OF HIGH-QUALITY MIDDLE GRADES SOCIAL STUDIES INSTRUCTION

The first two chapters of this book focused on the challenges facing students in our nation's middle grades and why it is important for them to have caring, understanding teachers. As Jackson and Davis (2000) contend, middle level students should be taught by those who have the proper knowledge and training to teach at this level. A teacher who comes into the classroom using the traditional methods of rote memorization, worksheets, and constant lecture will be doing themselves and, most importantly, their students a great disservice. Generally, these strategies will bring little success for everyone involved and have potential to dissuade students away from further study in the academic area to which we dedicate our professional lives.

Additionally, this chapter offered several rationales on the purposes of teaching social studies. These rationales were drawn from the works of many experts in the field of social studies education, the 10 themes of the NCSS, the C3 Framework, and the recommendations of other subject-specific organizations. To review, some commonly listed rationales for teaching social studies include:

- Promoting critical thinking skills;
- Promoting democratic citizenship;
- Developing knowledge of society (collective memory) and knowledge of other cultures and the world (cultural/global awareness);
- Developing knowledge about other subjects both within the fields of the social sciences as well as in other disciplines (interdisciplinary knowledge);
- Promoting decision making and problem-solving skills; and
- Understanding ourselves through the various disciplines of social studies instruction (self-awareness).

As a reader of this book, your goal is to one day teach middle school social studies. As a middle level social studies educator, you will need to have a combination of social studies content knowledge, understanding of the unique characteristics that often define adolescents, and the most appropriate pedagogy to effectively teach all your students (Association for Middle Level Education, 2012). In our opinion, along with the 10 NCSS themes and C3 framework for teaching social studies, the best explanation about why it is important to teach social studies to middle level students is found in the four motifs of the NCSS Task Force.

Starting in the next chapter, we will offer you specific strategies and methods to help you in your preparation as a middle school social studies teacher. All the strategies we discuss can be linked back to the NCSS themes and the four NCSS Task Force motifs and most are based on the progressive philosophy described in the Preface. Keeping these themes and motifs in mind as you begin the preparation for your teaching career will help secure success for you and your students.

Next, it is important to examine major considerations that beginning teachers must keep in mind about diversity as they embark on their careers. As mentioned in the NCSS four motifs for teaching at the middle level social studies, teachers should be prepared to teach their students about diversity. Events such as the murders of unarmed Black citizens, subsequent social justice protests, and ongoing societal dialogue regarding diversity, inclusion, and privilege reinforce the need for experiences in this discourse. Additionally, all teachers should be mindful of the challenges faced by diverse learners. The following section will examine these topics in more detail and offer suggestions for maintaining a classroom that recognizes and honors diversity.

Diversity and the Social Studies Classroom

America's population is ever changing. Today the United States' population is much more diverse than it was 50, 20, or even 10 years ago. America's public schools reflect these changes. There is little doubt that you will teach students who vary widely in their cultural background, first language, religious beliefs, socioeconomic status, gender identities, and family structures. However, even if you find yourself teaching at a school where all the students seem similar, it is still vital for your students to have educational experiences exploring diversity in

America. The NCSS recognized the importance of this task by making culture the first of its 10 themes and by including diverse perspectives in the nine additional themes. At the middle school level, the NCSS' third and fourth motifs also stress the need for teaching students about diversity.

Socioeconomic Status and Academic Skills

From 2007–2009, America faced its worst economic crises since the Great Depression. The housing market collapsed, unemployment hovered around 9%, gas prices were at an all-time high, and the United States government bailed out the American banking and auto industries. Even the federal government was close to a financial default that would have led to its inability to borrow money from the U.S. treasury and hurt the nation's credit rating. This economic crisis affected almost everyone in the country including the middle class. More recently, the lockdowns and broad economic catastrophe of COVID-19 has fundamentally changed the economic circumstances of billions of people around the globe. Even in the best economic times, you will still have students who struggle with poverty, homelessness, hunger, and other forms of economic injustice.

Simply put, a student's socioeconomic status is based on measures such as their family's income, their parent's education level, occupation, and standing in the community (American Psychological Association, 2011). These collective measures offer an economic, cross-sectional view of the U.S. population. While culture, ethnicity, race, and gender are important factors in understanding and predicting a person's opportunity for success in the United States, one of the most potent is their socioeconomic status. In America's public schools, socioeconomic status is closely related to student achievement with students living in poverty gaining less from school than more affluent students.

In 2019, the number of Americans living in poverty was about 34 million people, or about 10.5% of the population (U.S. Census Bureau, 2020). Black and Latinx populations are overrepresented in this demographic. Living below the poverty line impacts a student's ability to perform in school. Children living in poverty suffer from malnutrition and hunger throughout their school career. They often have more health problems but receive less medical attention. They often live in substandard housing and suffer more abuse and/or neglect than students from higher socioeconomic levels (Borich, 2006; Bowe, 2005; Johnson, 2010; Park et al., 2002; Salend, 2004). In addition to facing these challenges, students who live in lower socioeconomic areas often have limited access to books, computers, and other learning tools (Borich, 2006). Certainly, students in poverty face more internet connectivity challenges than peers from higher income levels. Additionally, their higher income peers constantly out-perform them on tests for all subjects and grade levels (Johnson, 2010; Park et al., 2002; Salend, 2004; Woolfolk, 2006). Due to this lack of success in school, students from lower socioeconomic levels are much more likely to drop out of high school than their age peers from higher socioeconomic levels (Bowe, 2005; Johnson, 2010; Salend, 2004).

Ethnicity and Culture

Ethnicity and culture are words that are often used interchangeably but are not entirely synonymous. Ethnicity refers to "a shared sense of identity or a pattern of characteristics" (Johnson, 2010). One's ethnicity often includes characteristics such as language, nationality, race, or religion—which are considered elements of culture (Woolfolk, 2006). Thus, ethnicity is unavoidably intertwined with culture. However, the term culture is also used to refer to a larger collection of attitudes, beliefs, behaviors, and values that may be shared by people of many different ethnicities (e.g., "American" culture; "Hip Hop" culture or LGBTQ+ culture). While ethnicity is firmly rooted in inherited characteristics, culture can be independent of physical characteristics. Finally, ethnicity is a more fixed classification while cultures typically vary their essential characteristics over time.

In schools, students' ethnicity and culture, because of their close relationships to socioeconomic status, have correlations to their performance in the classroom and collectively influence the reputation of the school that the students attended. Typically, students from lower socioeconomic groups have not performed as well in the traditional classroom setting and on standardized tests. Unfortunately, many members of the global majority have a disproportionate number of their members at lower socioeconomic levels, which then correlates to their standardized test scores.

Beyond test scores, it is the ethical, moral, and democratic responsibility of all educators to meet the needs of all their students. The backgrounds from which our students come—and the contexts in which they currently live—inform their views of history, economics, and social processes. As middle level social studies teachers, it is one of our foremost responsibilities to embrace our students' perspectives, then work to grow those perspectives with others in respectful, responsive, and socially just ways.

Sexual Orientation and Gender

In 2015, with the landmark case *Obergefell v. Hodges,* the United States Supreme Court affirmed that the U.S. Constitution guarantees the fundamental right of same-sex couples to marry. No matter what your own personal beliefs are on this topic, it is important to understand that one of the core values of social studies is social justice. This includes the truth that everyone must be treated with respect and are entitled to live their lives free of discrimination, harassment, and violence. This is especially true in public schools. The Centers for Disease Control and Prevention finds that:

> Sexual minority students—those who identify as gay, lesbian, or bisexual, those who are not sure about their sexual identity, and those who have had sexual contact with the same sex—experience higher prevalence of health-risk behaviors like substance use, sexual risk, and suicide risk, and experience greater risk of violence victimization than sexual majority students (Centers for Disease Control and Prevention, 2019, p. 7).

It is clear that to provide safe and effective classrooms in which all our students grow, we must acknowledge and work toward improving upon this unacceptable truth. As a middle-grades teacher you will teach students who are struggling with their own sexual identities. As a social studies teacher it is up to you to not only teach tolerance in your classes but also to help protect and offer a safe environment to these students. Simply put, no one has the right to infringe on the rights of others. Name calling, physical intimation, and violence, whether it concerns class, culture, race, religion, or sexual orientation should never be tolerated in your classroom. As mentioned previously, one of your most important responsibilities as social studies educator is to promote social justice so derogatory or marginalizing terms should not be tolerated in your classroom. In addition to letting your students know as firmly as possible that you will not accept the use of derogatory language in your classes, you should also introduce the principles of respect and tolerance, integrate age-appropriate discussion about LGBTQ+ issues into curricula, and most importantly, communicate your commitment to creating a safe, nurturing environment for all of your students (Johnson, 2010, pp. 35–36).

When discussing gender, it is easy for both teachers and students to find themselves inadvertently participating in the promotion of gender stereotypes. It is important to be aware of the use of these stereotypes in the materials you create or use in your classes. There are several strategies you can use in developing a gender-neutral classroom. These include using instructional materials that are gender balanced, attempting to model and use gender-neutral language at all times, encourage the use of self-identified pronouns such as they/them instead of she/he, introducing/including female perspectives, and most importantly, establishing a zero-tolerance policy on sexual harassment (Johnson, 2010, pp. 33–34).

Religion

Another important factor of which you need to be aware is your students' religious or non-religious beliefs. Unless you work at a private religious school, you will teach students from varied religious or non-religious backgrounds and should be sensitive to the fact that many of your students' beliefs may differ from your own. Religion can and should be discussed in social studies classes. Indeed, in its 2014 position statement on study of religions, the National Council for the Social studies states: "Religious literacy dispels stereotypes, promotes cross-cultural understanding, and encourages respect for the rights of others to religious liberty." (NCSS, 2014). Reflecting the importance of—and need for—deeper understanding of religion and religious diversity, many of history's greatest conflicts, debates, and wars stem from religious differences. As a social studies teacher, your job will be to take an academic approach to the study of religious thoughts, beliefs, and practices. This should be done in an impartial manner and should include the goal of helping students understand the First Amendment and the influence that freedom of religion has played in our pluralistic and democratic society.

Content Integration	In applying content integration to a classroom and school, teachers must "use examples from a variety of cultures and groups to illustrate concepts from across the current curriculum" (Johnson, 2010, p. 30). For example, when discussing the Declaration of Independence or the Pledge of Allegiance, discuss the phrases "…all men are created equal" and "…and justice for all." Bring in examples of how members of different socioeconomic levels, races, and gender had to struggle to turn these powerful ideals into a reality.
Equity Pedagogy	This dimension involves adapting your teaching style to your students' various learning styles. This practice is often called differentiation. There has been much research about student learning styles based on socioeconomic and cultural factors (e.g., Anderson, 1988; Melton, 1990, Stanley et al., 1999; Wilson-Jones & Caston, 2004) and, in order to achieve classroom success, teachers should keep these in mind. While it is impossible to meet all learning styles all the time, teachers should vary their instructional methods frequently. For example, introducing a topic such as the Bill of Rights through lecture is perfectly fine, but it should be followed by collaborative, hands-on, or kinesthetic learning activities (For a kinesthetic learning activity to help students learn the first 10 amendments see the Youtube video, "The Bill of Rights Hand Game" www.youtube.com/watch?v=LYG_f-y8-VY).
Empowerment of School, Cultural, and Social Structure	This dimension suggests that schools and classroom teachers "create a school culture that values and empowers all cultures" (Johnson, 2010, p. 31). School personnel should make sure that there is an equitable balance of all students participating in clubs, sports, and events in the school. In classrooms teachers should make sure that all students feel safe and empowered. For example, teachers should avoid always calling on or asking for aid from the same students.
Prejudice Reduction	This is the simple action of finding out your students' perceptions, attitudes, and biases about race, religion, gender, and sexual orientation either formally or informally. Once you have an idea of your students' prejudices you should try to alter and reduce their stereotypes and misinformed ideas, though teaching, class discussion, and/or group work.
Understanding of the Construction of Knowledge	It is important for teachers to realize that much of our social knowledge has been constructed with a particular bias. Ben often states that there is no such thing as an unbiased view, either by students or by the teacher. In the United States the dominate bias found in most social studies courses, and in most other disciplines for that matter, comes from a white, male, Judeo-Christian perspective. While there is nothing inherently wrong with this perspective, with the large number of students in the nation's schools who do not come from this background, it is important to balance social studies courses with other perspectives. Even with students who have this background, introducing multiple perspectives is vital to do if we are to promote understanding in our classrooms. In his experience teaching in "minority-majority" schools Scott was told by several of his students that they did not like social studies because it was about "a bunch of rich white dead guys." Scott promised them he would make sure to include in their class activities information about a diversity of races, religions, and social classes. Students appreciated his honesty and enjoyed their class discussions, and the resources he brought in about people, topics, and events from all perspectives.

FIGURE 2.5. Applications of Banks' Five Dimensions of Multicultural Education

When discussing and teaching religion, make sure to structure lessons in an academic fashion and not a devotional one (Johnson, 2010). Discuss all religions required by your state or district standards, and not just the religion that you know the most about or are a member of. Most certainly never disparage a religion or a member of a certain religion in your classes. Open conversations with your students about how religion is approached in schools before your specific discussions can assist students in framing the topic. One resource that can help with this is *Teaching about religion in the social studies classroom* by Haynes (2019). Having a culture in which students and teachers freely talk about this topic can help prevent misunderstandings as to the role of the teacher and the purposes of the discussion. As always, we recommend discussing specific issues with your administrator or mentor teacher. Resources can be found in the "Website Resources" section below. Additionally, the National Council for the Social Studies released a position statement regarding the study about religions in the social studies curriculum (NCSS, 2014).

Multicultural Educational Approaches

Many authors and educational researchers have written about multicultural education and culturally relevant pedagogy in order to help you gain a better understanding of these education approaches (e.g., Banks, 1996, 1997; Gay, 2000; Grant, 2003; Ladson-Billings, 2001). For instance, Dr. James Banks (1997), who is credited as one of the leaders in the development of multicultural education, describes multicultural education as a process that consists of five dimensions. These dimensions include content integration, equity pedagogy, an empowering of school culture and social structure, prejudice reduction, and a knowledge construction process. We work to describe and apply these dimensions in Figure 2.5. All five of these dimensions should be used in schools to combat the negative impact of overt prejudice or ignorance concerning all genders, races, cultures, religions, and sexual orientations.

COLLABORATIVE ACTIVITY: MULTICULTURAL EDUCATION IN MIDDLE LEVEL SOCIAL STUDIES

What are some ways you can incorporate Banks' dimensions in your middle level social studies classes? Discuss these with a partner.

Keeping these five multicultural dimensions in the forefront of your mind, begin thinking about how you want to structure your classroom and plan lessons to sustain a multicultural classroom. In addition, there are other ideas you can incorporate to meet this goal. For example, always use multiple sources from different perspectives and include them in historical discussion and inquiry. We will discuss the use of historical inquiry in more detail in Chapters 4 and 8.

TABLE 2.2. ELL, Gifted, and Special Education Organizations

TESOL (formerly Teachers of English to Speakers of Other Languages)	https://www.tesol.org/
National Association for Gifted Children	http://www.nagc.org/
National Association of Special Education Teachers	http://www.naset.org/

English Language Learners, Gifted and Talented Students and Special Education Students

English language learners (ELL) are students for whom English is not their primary language. These students sometimes have difficulties in school based on their limited ability to read and speak English. Gifted and talented students are those students who demonstrate the ability to solve problems or perform at exceptionally high academic levels. Special education students are those students who may have a learning disability, emotional or behavioral disorders, or attention deficit hyperactivity disorder (ADHD). In your career you will certainly teach students that fall into all three categories.

Because there are several organizations, courses, and texts directed to teaching students in these categories, we will not discuss them in detail (see Table 2.2), As a social studies teacher you should be aware that at some point in your career you will teach students who fall into these different specialized categories. This is because even though there are separate classes and certified teachers for these students, quite often in the middle level there is limited ability level "tracking." There are also federal mandates to place special education and ELL students in the least restrictive environments as possible. Many school systems offer certification and staff development courses with a focus on ELL, special education, and gifted education and, even if you do not plan to teach these students exclusively, these classes are worth taking. More broadly, we believe that meaningful inclusion of all students enriches the tapestry of classrooms and encourages students of all perspectives to interact more deeply.

SUMMARY

In this chapter we examined several important topics for teaching middle level social studies including the social studies wars, the 10 NCSS themes, the NCSS C3 Framework and the four NCSS motifs for teaching middle level social studies. Links to the standards for all states were provided as well. Additionally, we looked at the importance of teaching diversity in middle level social studies classrooms and analyzed James Banks' dimensions of multicultural education. Finally, we provided several strategies and lesson ideas for the 10 NCSS themes, the four motifs, and Banks' dimensions. In the next chapter, we will provide you with basic strategies for teaching middle level social studies.

Individual Activity: Reflecting on the Chapter

Answer the following questions in your reflective journal:

- How do you think social studies should be taught at the middle level: though the study of separate disciplines or as an interdisciplinary course? Explain your answer.
- What are some of the challenges you will face as a social studies teacher? Did the examination of the NCSS standards and motifs help in your understanding of meeting the challenges? Why or Why not?
- What do you need to do to prepare for teaching social studies to a diverse group of students?

Website Resources

- **Facing History and Ourselves** (http://www.facing.org/) is an organization that "combats racism, anti-Semitism, and prejudice and nurtures democracy though education programs worldwide. Their website offers teachers lessons, teaching strategies, podcasts, and information about seminars and workshops.
- **iCivics** (https://www.icivics.org/) provides a wealth of free resources and lesson plans regarding government processes, politics, and civic engagement. A widely respected resource, iCivics is recognized by students and their teachers for a multitude of interactive games, scenarios, and activities that promote understanding of civic processes and engagement in civic activities.
- **National Association of Gifted Children** (http://www.nagc.org/) is an organization whose primary purpose is to support the educational needs of gifted and talented students. Their website includes information and resources for teachers, administrators, and parents. The site also includes sections regarding the organization's publications, conferences, and advocacy and on behalf of gifted programs.
- **National Association of Special Education Teachers** (http://www.naset.org/) is the "only national membership organization dedicated solely to meeting the needs of special education teachers and those preparing for the field of special education teaching." Their website offers special education teachers access to resources, publications, information about board field certification, and professional development opportunities.
- **National Council for the Social Studies** (http://www.socialstudies.org/) provides "leadership, service, and support for all social studies educators. Founded in 1921, National Council for the Social Studies has grown to be the largest association in the country devoted solely to social studies education. NCSS engages and supports educators in strengthening and advocating social studies." The NCSS website offers teachers access to the

10 NCSS themes for teaching social studies, information about their annual conference, standards for teaching about religion, lesson plans and resources, position statements, and a list of notable trade books.
- **Religious Freedom Center** (https://www.religiousfreedomcenter.org/) This organization: "…is a nonpartisan national initiative focused on educating the public about the religious liberty principles of the First Amendment." The website provides professional development opportunities for social studies teachers.
- **Rethinking Schools** (http://www.rethinkingschools.org/index.shtml) is an organization founded in 1986 by Milwaukee, WI teachers who wanted to improve their schools. The organization is a non-profit, independent publisher of education materials that advocates "the reform of elementary and secondary education with a strong emphasis on issues of equality and social justice."
- **Sister Cities International** (http://www.sister-cities.org/) "is a nonprofit citizen diplomacy network that creates and strengthens partnerships between U.S. and international communities." The organization strives to "build global cooperation at the municipal level, promote cultural understanding and stimulate economic development." The website offers a page for educators that discusses programs, projects, and resources offered by the organization for K–12 teachers.
- **Teachers of English to Speakers of other Languages** (http://www.tesol.org/) is an organization that seeks to "advance professional expertise in English language teaching and learning for speakers of other languages worldwide." Their website offers ELL/ESOL teacher resources, a directory of degree and certificate programs, ELP standards, and publications.
- **Teaching Tolerance** (http://www.tolerance.org) is an organization founded in 1991, by the Southern Poverty Law Center and dedicated to "reducing prejudice, improving intergroup relations, and supporting equitable experiences for our nation's children." The site provides free, award-winning education materials to teachers.

REFERENCES

The 1619 Project. (2019). *The 1619 Project.* https://www.nytimes.com/interactive/2019/08/14/magazine/1619-america-slavery.html

Alexander, W. A. (1988). Schools in the middle: Rhetoric and reality. *Social Education, 52*(2), 107–109.

Allen, M. G. (1988). Middle grades social studies: A modest proposal. *Social Education, 52*(2), 113–115.

American Psychological Association. (2011). *Socioeconomic status.* http://www.apa.org/topics/socioeconomic-status/index.aspx

Anderson, J. A. (1988). Cognitive styles and multicultural populations. *Journal of Teacher Education, 39*(1), 2–9.

Association for Middle Level Education (Formerly National Middle School Association). (2012). *This we believe in action: Implementing successful middle level schools.* Author.

Banks, J. A. (1996). *Multicultural education, transformative knowledge and action.* Teachers College Press.

Banks, J. A. (1997). *Educating citizens in a multicultural society.* Teachers College Press.

Barton, K. C., & Levstik, L. S. (2004). *Teaching history for the common good* (2nd ed.). Lawrence Erlbaum Associates.

Borich, G. D. (2006). *Effective teaching methods* (6th ed.). Pearson.

Bowe. F. (2005). *Making inclusion work.* Pearson.

The Bradley Commission. (1989). Building a history curriculum: Guidelines for teaching in schools. In P. Gagnon & The Bradley Commission on History in Schools, (Eds.), *Historical literacy: The case for history in American education* (pp. 16–47). Macmillan Publishing Company.

Brophy, J., & VanSledright, B. (1997). *Teaching and learning history in elementary schools.* Teachers College Press.

Centers for Disease Control and Prevention. (2019). *School health profiles 2018: Characteristics of health programs among secondary schools.* Author.

Cheney, L. (1987). *American memory: A report on the humanities in the nation's public schools.* National Endowment for the Humanities.

College Board. (2020). *AP© U.S. History: Course and Exam Description.* Author. https://apcentral.collegeboard.org/pdf/ap-us-history-course-and-exam-description.pdf?course=ap-united-states-history

Evans, R. W. (2004). *The social studies wars: What should we teach the children?* Teachers College Press.

Evans, R. W. (2007). *This happened in America: Harold Rugg and the censure of social studies.* Teachers College Press.

Evans, R. W., & Passee, J. (2007). Dare we make peace: A dialogue on the social studies wars. *Social Studies, 98*(6), 251–256. DOI: 10.3200/TSSS.98.6.251-256

Exec. Order No. 13958, 85 FR 70951, (November 2, 2020).

Gagnon, P. (Ed.) (1989). *Building a history curriculum: Guidelines for teaching history in schools.* Educational Excellence Network.

Gay, G. (2000). *Culturally responsive teaching: Theory, research, and practice.* Teachers College Press.

Grant, C. A. (2003). *Turning on learning: Five approaches for multicultural teaching plans for race, class, gender, and disability* (3rd ed.). Wiley.

Hawley, T. S., & Crowe, A. R. (2016). Making their own path: Preservice teachers' development of purpose in social studies teacher education. *Theory & Research in Social Education, 44*(3), 416–447.

Haynes, C. C. (Ed.) (2019). *Teaching about religion in the social studies classroom.* National Council for the Social Studies.

Jackson, A. W., & Davis, G. A. (2000) *Turning points 2000: Educating adolescents in the 21st century.* Teachers College Press.

Johnson, A. P. (2010). *Making connection in elementary and middle school social studies.* Sage.

Ladson-Billings, G. (2001). *Crossing over to Canaan: The journey of new teachers in diverse classrooms.* Jossey-Bass.

Levy, T. (1988). Making a difference in the middle. *Social Education, 52*(2), 104–106.

Lounsbury, J. H. (1988). Middle level social studies: Points to ponder. *Social Education, 52*(2), 116–118.

McKinley, J. C. (2010, March 12). Texas conservatives win curriculum change. *The New York Times.* http://www.nytimes.com/2010/03/13/education/13texas.html

Melton, C. D. (1990). Bridging the cultural gap: A study of Chinese students learning style preferences. *RELC Journal, 21*(1), 29–47.

Menton, L. K. (1993). Researching and writing state history: Theory and practice. *The History Teacher, 26*(1), 221–231.

Moore, J. R. (1969). State history textbooks: Essays in ethnocentrism. *Social Education, 33*(1), 267–278.

National Association of State Textbook Administrators. (2007). *Instructional materials websites.* http://www.nasta.org/instm.htm

National Council for History Education. (2011). *Core purpose: Leading the teaching and learning of history.* http://www.nche.net/what_we_do/

National Council for the Social Studies. (1991). *Social studies in the middle school: A report of the Taskforce on Social Studies in the Middle School.* http://www.socialstudies.org/positions/middleschool/

National Council for the Social Studies. (2010). *National curriculum standards for social studies.* Author. https://www.socialstudies.org/national-curriculum-standards-social-studies-chapter-2-themes-social-studies

National Council for the Social Studies. (2013). *Social studies for the next generation: Purposes, practices, and implications of the College, Career, and Civic Life (C3) Framework for social studies state standards.* Silver Author.

National Council for the Social Studies. (2014). *Study about religions in the social studies curriculum.* Author. https://www.socialstudies.org/position-statements/study-about-religions-social-studies-curriculum

Park, J., Turnbull, A. P., & Turnbull, H. R. (2002). Impacts of poverty on quality of life in families of children with disabilities. *Exceptional Children, 68*(2), 151–170.

Percy, W. A. (2003). *Georgia history textbooks.* http://www.georgiaencyclopedia.org/nge/Article.jsp?id=h-859&hl=y

Ravitch, D., & Finn, C. (1987). *What do our 17-year-olds know?* Harper & Row.

Riley, N. S. (2020). "The 1619 Project" enters American classrooms: Adding new sizzle to education about slavery—But at a significant cost. *Educations Next: A Journal of Opinion and Research, 20(4),* 1.

Roberts, S. L. (2009). *Georgia economic history: Lessons for implementing the GPS at grade 8.* Georgia Council on Economic Education.

Roberts, S. L. (2013). Women of action and county names: Mary Musgrove County-Why not? *Middle Level Learning, 48,* M12–M16.

Salend, S. (2004). *Creating inclusive classrooms* (5th ed.). Pearson.

Saxe, D. W. (1991). *Social studies in school: A history of the early years.* State University of New York Press.

Stanley, C. A., Rhodieck, S., & Tang, L. (1999). An exploration study of the teaching concerns of Asian American students. *Journal of Excellence in College Teaching, 10*(1), 107–127.

Stearns, P. N., Seixas, P., & Wineburg, S. (Eds.) (2000). *Knowing, teaching, & learning history: National and international perspectives.* New York University Press.

Stern, S. M., & Stern, J. A. (2011). *The state of state U.S. history standards: 2011.* The Fordham Institute.

Strauss, V. (2014, October 1). College board says it 'revised' controversial AP U.S. History framework. *The Washington Post.* http://www.washingtonpost.com/blogs/answer-sheet/wp/2014/10/01/college-board-says-it-revised-controversial-ap-u-s-history-framework/

Toepfer, C. F. (1988). What to know about young adolescents. *Social Education, 52*(2), 110–112.

U.S. Census Bureau. (2020). *Income, expense, poverty, and health insurance coverage in the United States: 2019.* Author. https://www.census.gov/newsroom/press-releases/2020/income-poverty.html

Wilson-Jones, L., & Caston, M. C. (2004). Cooperative learning on academic achievement in elementary African American males. *Journal of Instructional Psychology, 31*(4), 280–283.

Wineburg, S. (2001). *Historical thinking and other unnatural acts: Charting the future of teaching the past.* Temple University Press.

Woolfolk, A. (2006). *Educational psychology* (10th ed.). Allyn & Bacon.

Wright, M. M. (2020). 1619: The danger of a single origin story. *American Literary History, 32(4)*, e1–e12.

CHAPTER 3

TEACHING MIDDLE LEVEL SOCIAL STUDIES

The Basics

Learning is something students do, NOT something done to students.
—*Alfie Kohn (AZ Quotes, n.d.)*

Too often, we give children answers to remember rather than problems to solve.
—*Roger Lewin (Goodreads, 2021)*

Activity List
- Student Centered Strategies
- Strengths and Weaknesses of Textbooks
- Good and Bad Worksheets
- Improving Lecture
- Great Social Studies Movies
- Incorporating Basic Teaching Strategies

COLLABORATIVE ACTIVITY: STUDENT CENTERED STRATEGIES

In your reflective journal:

- Make a list of student-centered strategies that you have learned about in your education courses, or that you remember from middle school, that will be easy to bring in to your social studies classes.

With a partner:

- Discuss what you think are the strengths and weaknesses of each strategy.

INTRODUCTION

Life is a series of "firsts." At some point most of us take our first steps, lose our first tooth, and buy our first car. One day it will be your first day as a middle-grades teacher. What are you going to do? How are you going to teach? What do you hope to accomplish? All of these questions will be rushing through your mind as you look out at the group of 10–15-year-olds staring back at you. They too will be waiting to see what happens next. As the school year progresses, you will become more comfortable with what you are going to do and how you will teach on a daily basis. Nevertheless, as a new teacher you should also have an idea of what you hope to accomplish for the class period, the week, and the entire year.

While many first-year teachers begin their careers asking these questions and slowly find their role in the classroom, early on, most educators tend to teach the same way they were taught. Unfortunately, teachers often revert back to the solely curriculum-centered use of textbook, lectures, and worksheets. Though there is nothing wrong with the thoughtful, balanced and critique-based use of these tools, methods, and strategies, research has shown that most teachers display an over-reliance on them (Loewen, 2010; Shaver et al., 1979). "What will I teach?" is a common question that informs the activities in the classroom. It is our hope that you will progress through this early stage and settle in on the more important question; "What will the students experience?" This shift from focus on the teacher to focus on the student can have a fundamental impact on what takes place in your classroom.

This chapter has been written with the first-year teacher in mind. At the beginning of the chapter, we offer an explanation of how to use some of the traditional classroom tools and strategies more effectively, including textbooks, worksheets, lectures, and movies. This section is based on the suggestions made by educational researchers as well as ideas we developed as teachers and teacher educators. The second part offers specific research-based teaching strategies that are simple to plan and can be easily incorporated into any middle level social studies course. Many of these strategies have been proven to increase student engagement and achievement. The goal is to provide the beginning teacher with an array of ideas for employing effective strategies in the classroom.

BEST PRACTICES FOR USING TEXTBOOKS

The standard social studies textbook is by far the most critiqued educational tool used in American's public schools. Critics often argue that these books are overused by teachers, are full of inaccurate, biased, and politically motivated information, are too difficult for students to read, or are intentionally designed to be visually appealing with the actual text offering little substance (Loewen, 1995). By the very nature of their topics, social studies and history textbooks are arguably the most lambasted of any subject and have been since the 1930s (Alridge, 2006). Consider how current topics of social discourse might be approached in future social studies textbooks; marriage equality, police/community relations, health care law, and immigration law, to name a few. If the social studies textbook is the main source from which students learn about their past, their present, and their world then it is clear that much attention will be paid to its contents.

Though it has been argued that social studies is not a highly regarded subject in the age of the Common Core standards, it is amazing how much attention and debate history textbooks and standards receive during certain states' adoption cycles. An example of this is the 2010 Texas curriculum controversy, which made national headlines based on the influence the large and populous state has on the content found in U.S. history textbooks used throughout the nation (Birnbaum, 2010; Marshall, 1991; McKinley, 2010; Moyer, 1985).

As soon as they are hired, many first-year teachers are handed the textbook or digital resources/platforms that they are expected to use in their classes and are strongly advised to go home and read it. Due to this initial professional experience, combined with the common experience new teachers had as students in middle and high school, the textbook or digital textbook is typically used as the center of lesson planning. Teachers often require that their students read the books (either silently or aloud), answer questions at the end of the chapter or section, and then fill out a worksheet or take a multiple choice or "true/false" quiz to document understanding of what they read (Berkeley et al., 2016). While this approach is traditional, it is most certainly not the best way to gain students interest in the subject matter, or reading in general (Berkeley et al., 2016; Dean et al., 2012; Dole et al., 1991; Johnson, 2010; Ogle et al., 2007).

Though often used ineffectively, there are many reasons that a textbook *should* be used in social studies classes (Berkeley et al., 2016; Ogle et al., 2007; Roberts, 2011, 2014). The textbook offers the most straightforward means of providing students with information about the course of study. In turn, with the focus on standards and standards-based testing, many textbooks, especially for younger students, are designed to meet a state's standards. When using the textbook as a guide in your lesson planning, it will often guarantee that your lessons meet the standards required by the state. Along with providing a condensed narrative concerning the topic of study, today's social studies textbooks contain a variety of maps, photos, charts, and graphs that can be useful in teaching students some of the skills encouraged by the NCSS and other social studies advocates. These skills include problem solving and synthesizing information. Textbook publishers are also providing a wealth of information online as supplementary material to the textbook, or even in place of the book. For schools with adequate technology access, these online resources can complement and add depth to what students experience in the pages of a hard copy book.

The textbook should not, however, be used as the sole source of information (Loewen, 2010; Ogle et al., 2007; Roberts, 2011, 2014). A text is most useful when students compare the information in it to other sources (Loewen, 2010; Ogle et al., 2007). As the classroom teacher you may have to find these sources on your own, or it may be possible to have more advanced students find other sources about the topic of study. The textbook can be seen as a starting point for social studies, but it should not be seen as the only source of information in an increasingly information-saturated world.

Textbooks should also not be used every day. Diversifying your lessons and differentiating your instructional methods should naturally pull you away from the exclusive use of the textbook by offering students activities that are more hands-on and collaborative (though textbooks can be used as tools in these types of activities as well). At the very least, your students will appreciate a break from lugging their heavy textbook around all day. A good approach is to introduce a concept or topic through the textbook, then elaborate and deepen students' understanding of the concept or topic with other materials or activities. Another alternative is to present a concept using your own sources first, then have students review the textbook. When Ben does this after discussing the basic tenets of the concept or event, his students then discuss discrepancies or differing perspectives between the two sources. Taking this approach can assist students with background knowledge and terminology that may be challenging.

Finally, the least useful assignment a middle level teacher can request of their students is one that ends with a statement similar to "read pages 35–42 and answer the questions 1–5 on page 42." This approach does little to help the student improve their reading comprehension skills or learn the material they need for any standardized assessment (Dole et al., 1991; Johnson, 2010; Loewen, 2010; Ogle et al., 2007). According to literacy experts Stevenson and Mussalow (2019), students should be active in their reading. When students are simply scanning the text to find the correct answers to the questions in their book, they are not actively processing the information that they are being asked to learn. Ben once saw a student copying definition out of the back of a science textbook during a study hall. As he watched, Ben realized the student was not going to comprehend the material:

"Whatcha doing?" Ben asks.
"Copying definitions like we were asked to do," The student replies.
"So...what is the definition of photosynthesis?" Ben states.
"Uh, I don't know," The student answers.

"Yes. I thought you might not know. You've copied the answers out of the Spanish section of the glossary."

Simply having students pulling data out of the textbook and regurgitating for the sake of completion is an ineffective way of teaching and leads to little learning. Textbooks can be engaging, meaningful tools if employed in engaging, meaningful ways. A crucial element is connecting the student experience to the curriculum. By limiting students to just the words and views of a textbook, a teacher who employs the textbook as the sole means of teaching is limiting the experiences of students to a single perspective that does not reflect or honor the diverse backgrounds in our history and in our classrooms.

Class Activity: Strengths and Weaknesses of Textbooks

In your reflective journal:

- Create a T-chart labeled "Strengths" and "Weaknesses."
- As a class, discuss the strengths and weaknesses of textbooks and list them on the chart.

BEST PRACTICES FOR USING WORKSHEETS

As of this writing when one types the word "worksheets" into an Internet search engine, 215 million hits are listed. Worksheets are one of the most commonly used tools in the classroom. Many worksheets, sometimes called "reproducibles," are often created by textbook companies and used as selling points for their books (Loewen, 1995). There are also free worksheets, created by teachers or companies that can easily be found on the Internet. Many of these free worksheets allow users to type their own information into a template and print them for their classes. No matter where they locate worksheets, many teachers believe that students need something to work with and write on while they are learning. Worksheets provide an easy-to-find document to get students to work, and teachers often do not know much about who created them. It should be noted that these worksheets found on websites like Pintrest or Teachers Pay Teachers have a multitude of problems including bias, inaccurate information, and not being crafted with specific students in mind (Shelton et al., 2020).

As with any other instructional tool, there are some excellent worksheets and some that are extremely poor. For example, some textbook companies produce outstanding reproducibles that include primary source analysis, inquiry, and encourage students to practice important writing, math, and geography skills. Two excellent sources for high quality inquiry-based worksheets and lesson plans are the Stanford History Education Group (Reading Like a Historian) and C3 Teachers. Other worksheets are not as well conceived, such as those that are strictly limited to "word-finds" or based on "fill-in-the-blank" activities.

There are two key elements for appropriate use of worksheets. The first is to only use ones that are worthwhile and meet your educational goals for students. While younger students may enjoy activities such as word searches, this activity is an extremely low-level exercise. Before you distribute any worksheet make sure that you truly believe it will help your students in their overall understanding of social studies. Very few people, adolescents or otherwise, enjoy work without benefit. If the worksheet does not correlate to any of the 10 NCSS themes or C3 Framework, it is probably not worth using. In his first year of teaching, Ben was absent for a day and required his students to complete a word search with the names of all 50 US States. The next day, a parent called to get clarification on the reason for such an assignment. Having no other reason than "to keep the students busy," the parent called him to the carpet; "This assignment isn't worth the time because it has no educational value," the parent said. Swallowing his pride and responding in a way that would change his approach to worksheets for the rest of his career, Ben answered; "You're right. I will work harder to provide assignments that have meaning." To this day, Ben works to remind his preservice teachers that time spent on the worksheets for his class reflect the values of the class itself.

Second, do not rely solely on the worksheets made by others, such as those found on Teachers Pay Teachers. If you are going to use worksheets, more often than not, you are better off making your own than using the ones provided by the textbook company or found on the Internet. There are several reasons for this. First, unlike the people who created the worksheets for the textbook companies, you are the only one that really knows your students and their abilities. You are more likely to create worksheets that meet their capabilities and push your students' understandings further. Second, the challenge of developing a worksheet that is far beyond the traditional fill-in-the-blank or matching approach will make you a better teacher in both your content and pedagogical knowledge. Finally, creating your own worksheets allows you to be in control of the textbook and not the other way around. When a textbook company creates worksheets, it usually does not allow students to question the narrative that it is portraying. However, if you create a worksheet that allows students to compare and contrast the accounts of historical figures or events found in several works, the worksheet is serving its purpose as an educational tool, not functioning as a time-filling crutch or busy work.

The approaches worksheets take are often reflective of the types of information valued in the class. If worksheets seek rote recitation of information, (e.g., names of capitals, the US Presidents in order, true/false statements), then that is all most students will seek and produce. While it may be useful for trivia nights, these types of worksheets truncate opportunities for deeply meaningful learning. Worksheets that seek opinions, analysis, creative responses, or evaluation of sources, on the other hand, can work to stretch students' understanding of complex concepts, events, and trends. Most social studies teachers seek the latter for their students. The quality of the work students produce is often deeply informed at the outset by the quality of the worksheets and other assignments they receive.

It is probably safe to assert that worksheets, in some form, are used by almost every teacher, in every class, in every school in the United States. In social studies courses, while some worksheets can be well made and worthwhile, many only offer only lower level recall activities such as word searches or matching. As a middle-grades social studies teacher, it is important to understand that worksheets, just like any other traditional approach can be a useful tool. However, you should remember that it is the quality of the worksheet that makes it worthwhile.

You should not simply make your students complete several pages in a workbook, or give them numerous handouts, just so that they have something to do. Worksheets should be an integral and valuable part of a larger study or activity.

COLLABORATIVE ACTIVITY: GOOD AND BAD WORKSHEETS

Using the Internet:

- Find a middle level social studies worksheet that you would describe as "good" and that you would use in your class.
- Find one that is "bad" and that you would not use in your class.
- Discuss your reasoning with a classmate.

BEST PRACTICES FOR USING LECTURE

Contrary to the impressions many education majors garner from their professors, the use of lecture is not always an ineffective teaching strategy. Though there is some debate about the concept of "learning styles," many educators know some students who appear to be "auditory learners" and best gain knowledge by listening to others (Toppo, 2019). These students are often able to sit back, listen to their teacher, take a few notes, retain the information that is presented, and answer the questions correctly on their test. In addition, there are also some teachers who are natural storytellers and have the ability to keep all of their students actively engaged in their classes based on their talent for simply being entertaining. To some, the use of lecture in itself is not bad; there are just bad approaches to lecturing (Chapin, 2011; McDaniel, 2010; Singer et al., 2010; Stacy, 2009).

Unfortunately, many teachers are NOT entertaining lecturers, even though many think they are. The most important thing to remember about lecture is that just because you are interested in the subject, and just because you think you are entertaining, does not mean that your students do. Research has proven, especially in examining the best practices for the instruction of middle level students, that lecture should be used sparingly (Chapin, 2011; Dean et al., 2012; Johnson, 2010; Marzano & Pickering, 2011; Singer et al., 2010).

On the other hand, lecture can be used in the social studies classroom. We have found it is most effective at the beginning of classes when you have your students' attention and when it is used to introduce the topic of study for that day. Keep in mind, the average student can only pay attention in the classroom for seven to ten minutes (Rothman, 2016). Therefore, teachers should not lecture for more than 10 minutes in a given class period at the middle school level (Chapin, 2011). These shorter talks are often referred to as mini-lectures (Chapin, 2011). Once the topic has been introduced or explained, the teacher should move on to more student-centered activities.

In addition, at certain intervals during a lecture, students should be given the opportunity for "Brain Breaks," or brief stopping points where they are able to discuss and synthesize what they have just been told. If you lecture, you need to allow students to find a way to work with the subject matter that you just presented. This could include a verbal summarization of what was just said with a peer, a small group discussion or brief debate, or an inquiry assignment (Chapin, 2011; Marzano et al., 2001; Marzano & Pickering, 2011). Regardless of the strategy you use during or after a lecture, the only way most students will remember what you presented will be for them to actively work with the material.

Student Involvement in the Lecture

An important concept within effective lecturing is student involvement. While the common perception is that lecturing is a one-way communication from teacher to student, it does not have to happen that way. Asking students to provide examples of concepts, requesting their opinions on controversial subjects, and integrating students as hypothetical examples into lectures are a few of the many ways of bringing lectures to life.

Having students move during a lecture can also be an effective method to keep students engaged with the content. When discussing the long-term effects of the Triangle Shirtwaist Factory fire of 1911, for example, Ben could simply talk about improved fire codes and labor laws. Instead, he gives students a tour of the school building, looking at different safety features in the architecture. Connecting past events to concepts we see currently turns the lecture into a guided tour of the environment in which students interact every day. This approach has the added effect of getting students out of their seats for some much-needed movement during their curricular day.

As another example of student interaction in lectures involves the use of manipulatives to exemplify concepts. Ben has a large bag of money in his desk. (Yes, you read that right). Foreign currency from around the world allows him to hand cash to students and practice transactions when lecturing on topics ranging from taxation, to political corruption, to the differences between the Articles of Confederation and the Constitution and more. Similarly, he has toy soldiers that he sets on the floor to illustrate Napoleonic infantry tactics. Rather than standing behind a lectern with notes, engaging lectures often involve movement about the classroom, student recitation, and objects to assist in learning concepts.

Student as "First Person" Lecturing

Another way to encourage students to remain active participants during lectures is to encourage them to see themselves as the subject of the lecture. Assigning perspectives, such as leaders of European countries at the start of World War I or as colonists while lecturing about the different pre-revolution taxes, encourages students to empathize with figures from history. When lecturing about the influence of the machine gun on battle tactics during World War I, for example, Ben has his students sit on the floor behind their desks to provide a slight taste of what trench warfare might look like. Though clearly this is no substitute for sitting in a water filled, disease-infested mud hole, it takes students one step closer to visualizing the experiences of the soldiers at the front.

The first-person lecture makes more concrete and more memorable the topics being discussed because the students are encouraged to become enveloped in the time period. Rather than discussing far off places and people who have been dead for centuries, addressing them as though they were the first-person subject holds them more accountable for the information being discussed. However, it should be noted that some first-person experiences are NOT appropriate to be used. Teachers have been fired for conducting first-person experiences related to horrific topic such as slavery and the holocaust (Gonzalez, 2019). If you have any concerns about a teaching approach, we strongly encourage to you talk with your school administrator or a trusted colleague.

COLLABORATIVE ACTIVITY: IMPROVING LECTURE

With a partner discuss the following question and list your answers in your reflective journal:

- What are some simple strategies/tools that you can use to improve a traditional lecture that makes it more worthwhile and memorable to your students?

BEST PRACTICES FOR USING MOVIES

For better or worse, many of our students come into our classes having gathered much of their understanding of social studies concepts, processes, and events from popular Hollywood movies. While they certainly have artistic and, at times historic value, movies such as *Saving Private Ryan*, *American Sniper*, *The Help*, and *300: Rise of An Empire* need academic contextualization to provide a more complete picture of the events and time periods they portray. Because of the power of the movie as a form of media, students often come to class believing that the good guys always win, the bad guys never hit their targets, and the problems are always resolved in about two hours.

While more academically oriented and often more accurate, documentaries and "school movies" also need interpretation and discussion to achieve their full value. Similar to the issues surrounding textbooks, academic movies can often lack the relevance and depth that students need and desire. The stereotype of "hitting play in August, stop and rewind in May" is one that must be extinguished if students are to more deeply appreciate the beauty of studying the social studies.

When discussing the use of film with teachers we are often asked questions to the effect of, "I know showing movies all of the time is bad, but what will help students learn a topic better, me talking about it or letting them see a movie?" This is a very good question. The appropriate use of movies is similar to the appropriate use of the textbook and lecture; they can be effective if used in small doses. As Russell and Waters (2017) argue "Film can be a remarkable learning tool capable of stimulating student interest and increasing student engagement... However, film can also be misused in the classroom..." (Russell & Waters, 2017, pp. 3–4) A teacher should never simply turn on a movie, press play, tell students to take notes, and then go back to his or her desk and grade papers. As with any other strategy, the teacher should use a movie as an interactive tool to help students better visualize the topic being discussed, but not use it as the only source or reference (Metzger, 2010). As with any activity in the classroom, a strong rationale that supports the time used by the movie is a must.

When showing a movie in class (whether it is a documentary or Hollywood feature film), you should explain to your students why they are watching the film, what topic or topics it will help them visualize, and what you hope they will learn from viewing it (Russell, 2012). Be prepared to stop the film, or only show sections, and explain what is going on, ask students questions, and answer any questions that they may have about what they are viewing. It is also appropriate to have students answer guided questions or complete advanced graphic organizers as they watch. Scott has produced several publications about an effective strategy for using film in the classroom called *Hollywood or History?* that address the elements above. The lessons allow teachers to have students use primary and secondary sources to analyze the accuracy of film clips using an inquiry-based approach (Elfer et al., 2017; Roberts, 2014; Roberts & Elfer, 2017, 2018, 2021). Great websites to find films as a whole or broken up into segments include TeacherTube, and Discovery

Education Streaming, and Youtube

It is important to note that when showing any movie, (including clips from internet sites), it is vital that you preview it in its entirety first. Many teachers have been caught off guard by language or scenes that are inappropriate for the classroom setting. What you remember as a casual observer may look very different as you view a movie through the eyes of a teacher of young adolescents. It is better to spend a few hours reviewing a movie and choosing to not use it than spend a few hours with your administrators explaining why you selected a movie with profanity that you forgot was in it. Early in her career, Karrie showed a short fifteen-minute movie when teaching about the abolitionist movement. Despite being on the school's approved streaming site and being rated appropriate for 5th grade and up, the movie showed brief historical footage of the Ku Klux Klan and a very brief historical image of a lynching that took place. Unfortunately, Karrie spent several hours explaining the video to administration and apologizing to parents for the content that was shown. She learned her lesson about previewing videos the hard way. Just because a video is approved for certain ages and grade levels, it does not mean it is appropriate for the classroom setting. Most school districts have policies regarding the use of movies in this regard and these policies are often closely watched and strictly enforced. The moral of the story is do not rely on an external rating system to evaluate the appropriateness of the film for your students.

In summary, films are great educational tools that offer students an opportunity to visualize, and in many cases, become emotionally connected to a historical topic or current issue. However, the use of films should be a structured activity where the teacher serves as a facilitator to help students understand what they are watching and why it is important to their understanding of the topic being discussed. Finally, films are only beneficial when students have opportunity to process what they saw and connect it to what they have already learned.

Individual Activity: Great Social Studies Movies

Locate your state standards (see Table 2.1) then think about some of the best social studies movies and documentaries that you have seen. In your reflective journal:

- Jot down what movies you would show your middle level students.
- Write down the exact scenes you would use and describe how they match up to your state's standards.

WHAT TO TAKE AWAY FROM THIS SECTION

After reading this section you should not take away thoughts that textbooks, worksheets, lecture, and movies are inherently terrible or that these instructional tools should never be used. Rather, there are appropriate times to use all these tools in your social studies classes. For example, when comparing and contrasting historical viewpoints, using textbooks as one of many sources is a great way to incorporate them into your classes (Loewen, 2010). When introducing a topic, trying to set the stage for an activity, or discussing a large amount of information, a mini-lecture is one of the best strategies to use. Worksheets encouraging students to analyze written documents, songs, and images are great assets in social studies instruction. Finally, engaging students in movies and encouraging two-way communication about the media can work to help students relate and connect to a person or group in a far-away land or time long past.

However, almost any strategy and method can be overused. Students, especially those in the middle grades, need constant variety to remain engaged in their classes. This means teachers must be creative to make the learning active and student centered. Variety in teaching methods will help to alleviate complacency within the social studies classroom (Bass, 2018). Even some of the more advanced strategies and activities that we will discuss in later chapters can become dull and boring if used too much. Nonetheless, the singular use of textbooks, worksheets, lecture, and movies has been proven to be quite ineffective in helping students with their academic success. The key to being an effective educator is to use as many tools at your disposal as often as you can. Even better, ask students for feedback on the activities and tools you are using to know what is working for them.

Remember, by the time most of your students walk into your social studies class, they will already have had one, two, three, or more other classes that, more than likely, used textbooks, lectures, worksheets, and/or movies. As a social studies teacher you can make your class the most fun or boring subject depending on your teaching style and the instructional tools you use. The difference between educationally valuable tools and tools that are inadequate often comes down to how they are integrated into your specific classroom setting. Having solid rationales that reflect your students' specific needs can mean the difference between activities and tools that connect with students and ones that are quickly forgotten. Keep these thoughts in mind as you begin developing ideas about how you would like your classroom to operate and what you hope your students will gain from having you as their teacher.

BASIC TEACHING STRATEGIES

There are several basic teaching strategies that teachers can use to help break out of the mode of solely using traditional tools and approaches in their classes (Gallavan & Kottler, 2010; Key et al., 2010). These simple strategies break up the monotony of lessons and allow for more student interaction and enjoyment. We will explain over the next few pages some of these strategies in detail. Though they can be useful for all courses, the ones provided correlate well with the 10 NCSS themes (2010) and the overall nature and purpose of social studies.

Basic Vocabulary Strategies

Social studies is a subject flooded with vocabulary. Almost every person, place, event, or natural feature that students learn begins as a "vocabulary word," or a word that students need to know in order to understand what is being discussed. Words such as "latitude," "equator," "militia," and "market economy" are scattered throughout typical social studies textbooks in bold, italicized, or red ink. Traditionally, when learning vocabulary, students were often told to simply write the word on a sheet of paper and copy the definition from the back of the book or a dictionary. However, for most students, this strategy does not bring that word or concept into their working language, and thus the five minutes it took the student to write down the word, find it in the glossary, and provide a definition, was more than likely a waste of time (refer back to Ben's story of the student copying definitions from the Spanish section of his Science textbook). Ben likes to ask students whether they want their physicians and airline pilots to have simply memorized terms in their training without working to understand what those terms mean and how they are applied. They invariably conclude that simply memorizing vocabulary definitions is not enough.

This section will examine five short and simple strategies to help your students with social studies vocabulary development. These strategies also correspond with the appropriate use of the textbook section. Due to the fact that the standardized tests that your students are required to take are heavy in vocabulary content, these strategies will provide your students with helpful knowledge and will make you feel more confident of their success when they take these tests. Additionally, working with your students' language arts and science teachers may encourage interdisciplinary thought and assist in reinforcing the applicability of the terms learned in your class.

Word Walls

A word wall is one of the easiest ways for students to keep track of the vocabulary that they learn in class, as well as providing a visual reminder of the learning that has taken place throughout the year. A word wall can be a piece of chart paper, a white board, or an entire wall or ceiling where vocabulary words are displayed and used in context. These words can be grouped in various ways such as specific categories like *"Rivers"* and *"Presidents,"* alphabetical order, or by time period. In order for a word wall to be effective, the teacher must frequently refer back to the listed words and use them to compare or contrast other new words or concepts. Word walls can even be used in games, riddles, and sponge activities (Johnson, 2010, p. 225).

Learning Logs

Another way to track and define words that have been used in the classroom is through learning logs. This technique is more interactive than the word wall. Students, working in pairs, locate, record, and define words that they think are interesting in a text or story. Thus, after reading a text and locating a certain number of words, students write the sentences that contained the words. Students then take turns "logging" as many different words or phrases as they can in place of the vocabulary word found in the sentence. For example, if a sentence read "The legislative branch is responsible for creating laws." With the word legislative being selected, students could use words and phrases such as "Congress," "General Assembly," or "Law-Makers," "The Big 535," or as one of Scott's students humorously wrote, "a bunch of idiots" to replace the word "legislative" (see Figure 3.1). No matter what words they use, try to reward students who are creative. The more fun they have with this activity the more these specific words will become part of their working vocabulary.

The legislative branch is responsible for creating laws
The Congress is responsible for creating laws-Lucida
The General Assembly is responsible for creating laws-Bradley
The law makers are responsible for creating laws-Lucida
The big 535 are responsible for creating laws-Bradley
A bunch of idiots are responsible for creating laws-Lucida

FIGURE 3.1. Example of a Learning Log

Concept Definition Maps

A concept definition map is a graphic organizer consisting of several boxes and circles that allow students to "dissect" a vocabulary word (Alexander-Shea, 2011; Johnson, 2010; Ogle et al., 2007). Quite often a student will write the vocabulary word in a shape found in the center of the page and lines to other sections of the page will be connected to the square or circle with the vocabulary word written inside. Above each series of boxes are guiding questions or statements such as "What is the definition?" "What is it like?" and "Examples." Students should fill in each of the boxes to gain a better understanding of what the word is, what words are similar, and what the characteristics of each word are (Alexander-Shea, 2011, p. 98). There are many variations that can be used to adapt and alter this strategy. Figure 3.2 is a student completed concept definition map for the term "Mixed Economy."

Frayer Model

A Frayer Model is a more compact version of a concept definition map (Frayer et al., 1969). Consisting of four squares with a fifth square placed in the middle, this strategy allows students to write down the vocabulary word in the center, along with the definitions, characteristics, and examples in three of the other squares. The thinking level of this activity increases with the last square requiring students to write "non-examples" of the vocabulary word (see Figure 3.3) (Alexander-Shea, 2011).

Teaching Middle Level Social Studies • 67

Concept Definition Map

An economic system combining private and public enterprise

What is it?

Concept: mixed economy

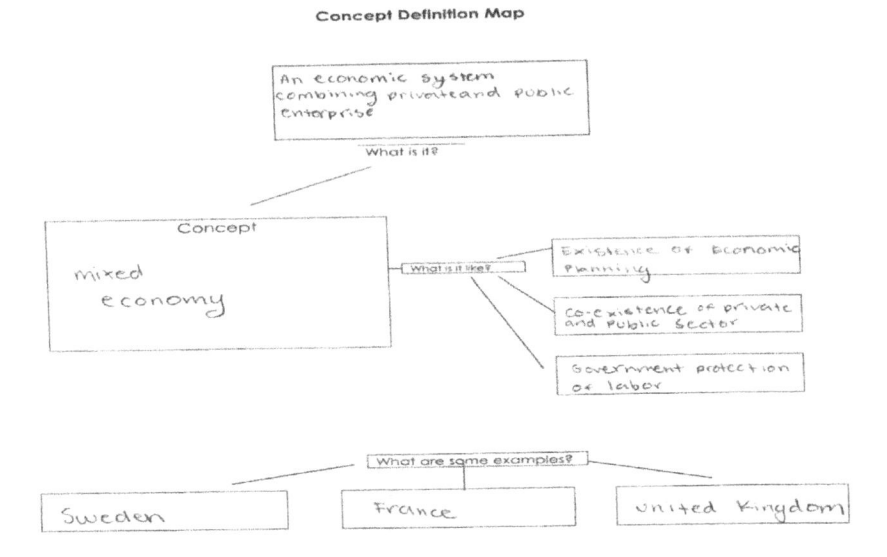

What is it like?
- Existence of Economic Planning
- Co-existence of private and public sector
- Government protection of labor

What are some examples?
- Sweden
- France
- United Kingdom

FIGURE 3.2. Example of a Concept Definition Map

Frayer Model

Definition:

Characteristics:

Government Revenue

Examples:

Non-examples:

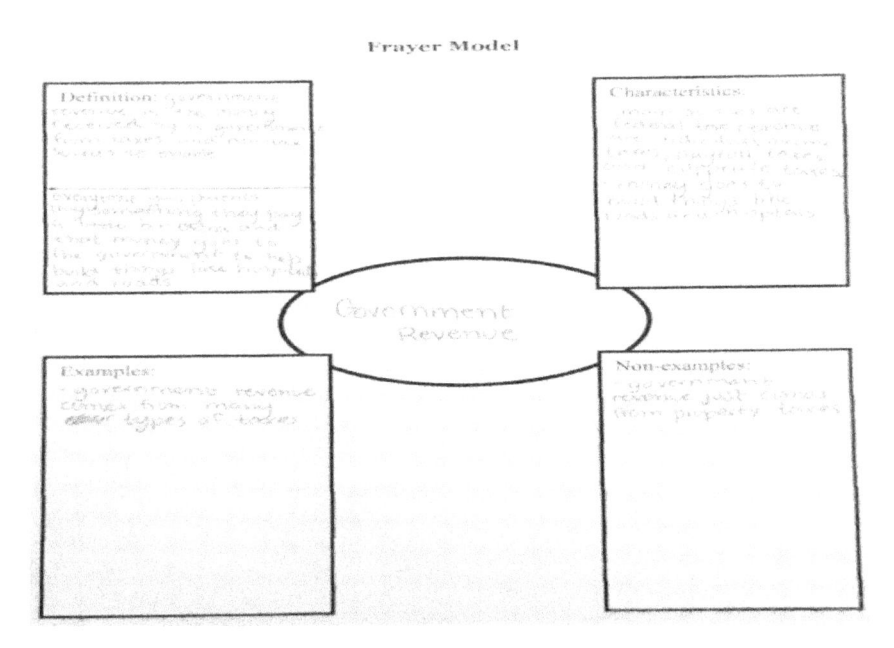

FIGURE 3.3. Example of a Frayer Model

68 • TEACHING MIDDLE LEVEL SOCIAL STUDIES (3RD EDITION)

Prior Knowledge/Predicting ABC Chart

By the time students have made it to your middle level classes many have already heard about or learned some of the same vocabulary that will be required in your class. With the large number of "standards" that social studies teachers are required to discuss in a short time span, it is easier to not have to "reinvent the wheel" and spend a lot of time on any particular person, place, or event that your students have already learned. One way to determine what your students already know while discussing vocabulary is through the use of a Predicting ABC's Chart (see Figure 3.4).

A Predicting ABC Chart is simply a chart with 12 boxes containing two letters each, with the exception of the last box which contains the letters "W" through "Z" (Ogle et al., 2007). Students are given a topic such as "World War II" and must go through the boxes writing down as many vocabulary words they think are connected to the war. Some examples could include: "H" *Hitler, Hiroshima, Home Front* and "P" *Pacific, Patton, Propaganda*. If students begin to run out of words let them use their textbook to "discover" new ones. By incorporating this

A B	C D	E F
G H	I J	K L
M N	O P	Q R
S T	U V	W X Y Z

FIGURE 3.4. Example of a Predicting ABC Chart

activity your students will show you what they remember, and it will allow them to connect important people, places, and events. Additionally, it allows you opportunity to spot misunderstandings that may then be gently adjusted.

A Basic Using Prior Knowledge Activity: The KWL Chart

Like Predicting ABC charts, KWL charts ask students to use their prior knowledge when beginning a new topic or as a tool for pre-reading a social studies text. Introduced by Ogle (1986) the KWL chart is a simple, three column chart where students identify what they *know* about the topic to be discussed or read about (**K**), what they *want to know* about the topic (**W**), and finally, upon the conclusion of instruction, what they *learned* about the topic (**L**). KWL charts are also an easy way for teachers to gain a sense of what their students already know and are a useful guide in planning.

When Scott was in the classroom, it often seemed that he had one group of students who knew a lot more about a topic than most others. Beginning a lesson with a KWL chart allows you to gain a better understanding of your students' prior knowledge and plan each class to meet students' needs. Additionally, allowing students to come up with their own questions in the W section allows for some ownership in the instruction. This is better than telling students all of what they need to know from the start. Make sure to take the time to answer some of the students' questions, or even have them research the answers themselves. Finally, from a multicultural standpoint, a KWL chart allows you to gain a better understanding of your students' biases or misconceptions about a particular social studies topic and to be prepared to discuss some of these perspectives (see Figure 3.5).

While KWL charts are great for all social studies disciplines, world geography is an example of a topic that lends itself well to its use. Some teachers will often add a 4th, 5th, or even 6th column to the KWL chart. These are called "**KWL+**" charts (Ogle et al., 2007). For example a teacher may include a changed column (**C**) and ask their students to list the changes they made from the K section once they learned more about the topic. However, no matter how you use a KWL chart, and the alterations you make to it, there is no better way for a student to organize

What do you think you **KNOW** about Mexico?	What do you **WANT** to know about Mexico?	What did you **LEARN** about Mexico?

FIGURE 3.5. Sample KWL Chart About Mexico

their prior knowledge, develop questions about a topic, and write down the information they learned, than with this quick and easy activity.

A Basic Compare and Contrast Activity: The Venn Diagram

The use of compare and contrast strategies can be one of the most effective ways to help students learn. According to Dean et al. (2012), using strategies that consist of comparing and contrasting "enhances students' understanding of, and the ability to use, knowledge" (p. 15). The most common tool to help students compare and contrast two or more topics is called a Venn diagram. A Venn diagram is simply two interlocking circles. In the center of the two circles, students list the similarities between two topics being studied, and on the outside of the circles the students should list the differences between the two (see Figure 3.6).

Like KWL charts, a Venn diagram is a quick and easy way to allow students to use certain elements of higher order thinking during class. Venn diagrams are great to use after lecturing about two individuals or after students read about two economic systems in their textbooks. Some teachers add a third circle to increase the complexity of the Venn diagram and have students compare three things. For example, a teacher may use a three circle Venn diagram to compare and contrast the three allied leaders during World War II (e.g., Churchill, Roosevelt, and Stalin); however, the simple two circle Venn diagram is effective in helping students learn more about and understand the similarities and differences between two social studies concepts.

A Basic Cooperative Learning Activity: Think-Pair-Share

Most adults do not like to be "put on the spot," and many fear public speaking in general. Yet every day, teachers ask students to answer questions individually and out loud. While the teacher waits for them to answer, the student's peers may

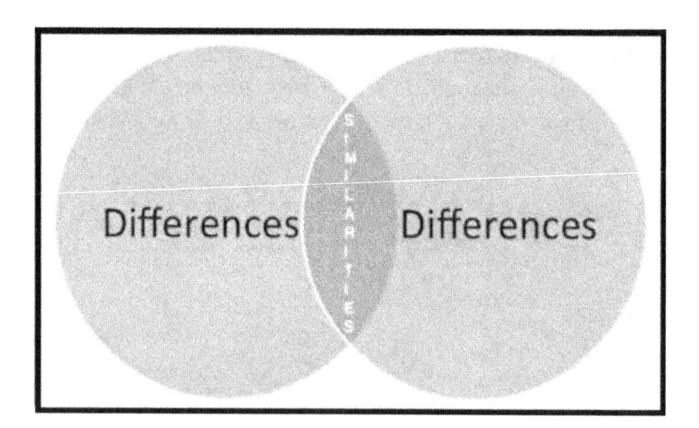

FIGURE 3.6. Example of a Venn Diagram

either laugh at them or try to avoid eye contact with the teacher for fear of being the next one asked. While there are a few students who will raise their hand in order to be called upon, most will not, and many hardly ever speak out during class. Creating and maintaining a classroom where students are not afraid of seemingly random "on the spot" moments is vital if students are to enjoy the learning process. Shifting the focus from a punitive learning approach (in the eyes of the students) to collaborative learning approaches can mean the difference between disengaged citizens and life-long self-advocates.

Collaboration and cooperative learning are two of the most effective strategies to foster student learning and participation (Dean et al., 2012). Many teachers do not utilize these strategies often enough. Some fear that students will not learn anything by talking with each other, while others simply do not want to relinquish authority. Nevertheless, group work and cooperative learning are essential in the middle-grades classroom.

One of the quickest and easiest cooperative strategies to include in a middle level social studies classroom is Think-Pair-Share. In this strategy, a student is asked a question and given some time to think. After the student comes up with an answer or opinion, they write it down. Karrie likes to give the students sticky notes to write their answer down. Students tend to feel less intimidated when it is a small sticky note than if you give them a full piece of paper. Then, the student is given the opportunity to find a partner and discuss their answers together.

This strategy is effective for three reasons. First, it gives all students in the class a chance to actively discuss a topic with a fellow classmate, as opposed to passively sitting and listening to the teacher or another student answer a question or discuss their opinion about the topic. Second, it allows students to think about the material at a deeper level, as they are required to develop a plan about how to explain their thoughts to another student. Finally, making students change their partners daily will allow them to work with, and get to know, others who may not normally be in their social group (Johnson, 2010).

The Think-Pair-Share strategy can also be more structured. One way to ensure students are not working in the same groups all the time is to have them make an "appointment clock." Using the appointment clock strategy students simply list appointment times (e.g., 1:00 pm, 1:10 pm, 1:20 pm) and then go around the room filling in the appointment times with different classmates. When the teacher decides to conduct a Think-Pair-Share activity they simply tell the students to get with their next appointment. Another way to make the Think-Pair-Share more structured is to use a graphic organizer for students to fill out as they question and share with one another (see Figure 3.7). Assigning a listener and talker (that alternate) encourages all students to be actively contributing.

A Basic Review Game: "Trashketball"

Believe it or not, "game-like activities" have been found to be one of the best ways to gain students' attention and motivate them to learn. According to Marza-

Question	My Ideas	My Partner's Ideas	What we will Share

FIGURE 3.7. Think-Pair-Share Graphic Organizer

no and Pickering (2011), "game-like activities help trigger situational interest and provide a foundation for maintained situation interest" (p. 9). VanSickle (1986) found that the average student can rise to above average in classrooms where game-like activities and competition are used. Though gaming can help students learn the course's required information and have fun while doing it, two questions to consider are what types of games to play, and when.

For years many teachers have used quiz type activities based on popular television game shows such as *Jeopardy* for test reviews. More recently, teachers will use *Kahoot!* to assist students in recalling basic information in an exciting and competitive venue. While using these quiz type games is fine and many students enjoy the competition, these games do not provide the kinesthetic component that middle grades students need. Additionally, these games often focus only on lower-order skills such as memorization and recall, not on critique or evaluation. A fun game that incorporates the question and answer components of a quiz-based game with movement is called Trashketball.

Trashketball is a fantastic game because it supports the strengths of both the intellectual and athletically gifted students in a class. Like its namesake, basketball, the objective at some point in the game is for students to throw a plastic ball or any other round object into a "hoop" that is usually a small wastebasket. However, in order to receive the opportunity to shoot, students must correctly answer a question based on the course's content.

Usually, when Scott played the game with his students, he divided the class into three teams. Scott then went around the room asking questions to students about the content they learned that week. If the student answered the question correctly, they received a point. They then had the opportunity to take a shot for additional points. If the student missed the answer, another team could "steal." As not to embarrass any student, he made sure to have three lines where students could choose to shoot from. The one-point line was extremely close to the basket where a nonathletic student or less of a risk taker could easily drop the ball into the basket. The second line was moved back a little further for a two-point shot. Finally, Scott made a line as far back as possible for the three-point shot.

Another idea is to have a designated substitute shooter who can come off the bench if another student does not want to take a shot. Scott often used the position as a reward for students who showed appropriate behavior in class, completed all their assignments, or did well on a quiz or test that was taken prior to the game.

Other students wanted to be official scorekeepers, a position also used as a reward. However, no matter how you structure the activity, you will be amazed at how many students look forward to and will ask if you are playing the game that day. One of the most highly ranked activities in Scott's end of the year student evaluation was "Trashketball Fridays."

Trashketball is but one example of the many game-like activities that a teacher can use in their middle-grades social studies classroom. Students will view game days as a welcome break from the traditional routines of school. Teachers who use this strategy are often surprised at how much their students learn and how well they perform on assessments after participating in game-like activities.

SUMMARY

This chapter offered you a better understanding of how to effectively use some of the more traditional approaches in social studies education (e.g., textbooks, worksheets, lecture, and movies). In addition, several simple, quick, and easy strategies were introduced that can be used immediately in middle level social studies classrooms. Though these strategies are easy to incorporate and appear relatively straight forward, they have been proven to be effective in promoting student learning. They also incorporate the higher thinking skills that are one of the major objectives of social studies. In the next chapter, we will examine more complex methods and strategies that should also be used in middle level social studies classrooms. For more ideas, we recommend articles by Ingold (2018) and Long (2017) for information about the basics of teaching middle level social studies.

Individual Activity: Incorporating Basic Teaching Strategies

Choose four of your state's standards (see Table 2.1) and identify the basic teaching strategies that you think would work well for teaching them. In your reflective journal create graphic organizers you could use for teaching the standards.

Website Resources

- **Archive.org** (https://archive.org/) provides free access to millions of documents and pictures. The "Wayback Machine" option allows users to enter a website URL and see what that site looked like on days in the past.
- **As She Grows** (http://as--she--grows.blogspot.com/2010/02/word-walls-update.html) is a blog spot created by a new teacher documenting her growth as an educator. The blog has great images of activities she used in her classroom. The page listed shows several excellent examples of word walls.
- **C3 Teachers** (https://c3teachers.org/) C3Teachers.org facilitates open collaborative conversations among teachers as they tinker with their own instructional practice as it relates to the C3 Framework.

- **Discovery Education/United Streaming** (http://streaming.discoveryeducation.com) is a website produced by the Discovery Channel that offers teachers videos and other digital media they can use in the classroom. Membership is required to access the website, but many schools have membership rights to the program.
- **Kahoot!** (https://kahoot.com/) is a game-creation website. Teachers can enter questions and students can play individually or as teams.
- **Stanford History Education Group: Reading Like a Historian** (https://sheg.stanford.edu/history-lessons) The Reading Like a Historian curriculum engages students in historical inquiry. Each lesson revolves around a central historical question and features a set of primary documents designed for groups of students with a range of reading skills.
- **Teacher Tube** (http://www.teachertube.com/) is a free website that allows teachers to download free educational movie clips. The program contains "safer" media than YouTube and is usually not blocked by most school districts. We do suggest you review the entire movie clip before showing to students.
- **Youtube** (https://www.youtube.com/) is a website that allows uses to view a variety of video clips including feature films. These clips can be useful when using the *Hollywood or History?* strategy. Please be aware that some material in Youtube videos may be inappropriate in a classroom setting.

REFERENCES

Alexander-Shea, A. (2011). Redefining vocabulary: The new learning style for social studies. *The Social Studies, 102*(3), 95–103.

Alridge, D. P. (2006). The limits of master narratives in history textbooks: An analysis of representations of Martin Luther King, Jr. *Teachers College Record, 108*(4), 662–686.

AZ Quotes. (n.d). *Alfie Kohn.* https://www.azquotes.com/quote/54921

Bass, B. (2018). Action research study of classical teaching methods vs. Active learning methods in the middle school social studies classroom. *Culminating Experience Action Research Projects, 18*(2), 26.

Berkeley, S., King-Sears, M. E., Vilbas, J., & Conklin, S. (2016). Textbook characteristics that support or thwart comprehension: The current state of social studies texts. *Reading & Writing Quarterly, 32*(3), 247–272.

Bimbaum, M. (2010, March 18). Historians speak out against proposed Texas textbook changes. *The Washington Post.* http://www.washingtonpost.com/wp-dyn/content/article/2010/03/17/AR2010031700560.html

Chapin, J. R. (2011). *A practical guide to secondary social studies* (3rd ed.). Pearson.

Dean, C. B., Hubbell, E. R., Pitler, H., & Stone, B. (2012). *Classroom instruction that works* (2nd ed.). ASCD.

Dole, J., Duffy, G., Roehler, L., & Pearson, P. D. (1991). Moving from the old to the new: Research on reading comprehension instruction. *Review of Educational Research, 61*, 239–264

Elfer, C. J., Roberts, S. L., & Fahey, B. (2017). "They're not just for Fridays anymore:" Media literacy, historical inquiry, and Hollywood films. *Teaching History, 42*(2), 83–96.

Frayer, D., Frederick, W. C., & Klausmeier, H. J. (1969). *A schema for testing the level of cognitive mastery*. Wisconsin Center for Education Research.

Gallavan, N. P., & Kottler, E. (2010). Visualizing the life and legacy of Henry VIII: Guiding students with eight types of graphic organizers. *The Social Studies, 101*(3), 93–102.

Goodreads. (2021). *Roger Lewin > Quotes > Quotable quote.* https://www.goodreads.com/quotes/287548-too-often-we-give-children-answers-to-remember-rather-than

Gonzalez, J. (2019). Think twice before doing another historical simulation. *Cult of Pedagogy.* https://www.cultofpedagogy.com/classroom-simulations/

Ingold, J. (2018). *Hacking the middle school social studies code*. http://www.c3teachers.org/hacking-the-middle-school-social-studies-code/.

Johnson, A. P. (2010). *Making connection in elementary and middle school social studies.* Sage.

Key, L., Bradley, J., & Bradley, K. S. (2010). Stimulating instruction in social studies. *The Social Studies, 101*(3), 117–120.

Loewen, J. W. (1995). *Lies my teacher told me: Everything your American history textbook got Wrong.* The New Press.

Loewen, J. W. (2010). *Teaching what really happened: How to avoid the tyranny of textbooks and get students excited about doing history.* Teachers College Press.

Long, E. R. (2017). *Visions of the possible: Case studies of how social studies teachers enact the C3 framework (PhD).* North Carolina State.

Marshall, J. D. (1991). With a little help from some friends: Publishers, protestors and Texas textbook decisions. In M. W. Apple & L. K. Christian-Smith (Eds.), *The politics of the textbook* (pp. 56–77). Routledge.

Marzano, R. J., & Pickering, D. J. (2011). *The highly engaged classroom.* Marzno Research Laboratory.

McDaniel, K. N. (2010). Harry Potter and the Ghost Teacher: Resurrecting the lost art of lecturing. *The History Teacher, 43*(2), 289–295.

McKinley, J. C. (2010, March 12). Texas conservatives win curriculum change. *The New York Times.* http://www.nytimes.com/2010/03/13/education/13texas.html

Metzger, S. A. (2010). Maximizing the educational power of history movies in the classroom. *The Social Studies, 101*(3), 127–136.

Moyer, W. A. (1985). How Texas rewrote your textbook. *The Science Teacher, 52*(1), 22–27.

National Council for the Social Studies. (2010). *National curriculum standards for social studies.* Silver Spring, MD: Author. https://www.socialstudies.org/national-curriculum-standards-social-studies-chapter-2-themes-social-studies

Ogle, D. (1986). K-W-L: A teaching model that develops active reading of expository texts. *The Reading Teacher, 39,* 564–570.

Ogle, D., Klemp, R., & McBride, B. (2007). *Building literacy in social studies: Strategies for improving comprehension and critical thinking.* ASCD.

Roberts, S. L. (2011). Did Georgia (Eventually) Like Ike: Perceptions of 20th and 21st century presidents in Georgia history textbooks: 1951–2005. *The Georgia Social Studies Journal, 1*(1), 1–18.

Roberts, S. L. (2014). Effectively using social studies textbooks in historical inquiry. *Social Studies Research and Practice, 9*(1), 119–128.

Roberts, S. L., & Elfer, C. J. (2017). Hollywood or history?: Inquiring about U.S. slavery through film. In W. Russell & S. Waters (Eds.), *Cinematic social studies* (pp. 255–283). Information Age Publishing.

Roberts, S. L., & Elfer, C. J. (Eds.). (2018). *Hollywood or history? An inquiry-based strategy for using film to teach United States history*. Information Age Publishing.

Roberts, S. L., & Elfer, C. J. (Eds.). (2021). *Hollywood or History? An inquiry-based strategy for using film to teach World History*. Information Age Publishing.

Rothman, D. (2016). *A tsunami of learners called Generation Z*. https://mdle.net/Journal/A_Tsunami_of_Learners_Called_Generation_Z.pdf

Russell, W. B. (2012). The reel history of the world: Teaching world history with major motion pictures. *Social Education, 76*(1), 22–28.

Russell, W. B., & Waters, S. (2017). *Cinematic social studies: A resource for teaching and learning social studies with film*. Information Age Publishing, Inc.

Shaver, J. P., Davis, O. L. Jr., & Helburn, S. W. (1979). The status of social studies education: Impression from three NSF studies. *Social Education, 43*(2), 150–153.

Shelton, C., Koehler, M., Carpenter, J., & Greenhalgh, S. (2020). Taking stock of TeachersPayTeachers.com: Analyzing four million classroom resources. In D. Schmidt-Crawford (Ed.), *Proceedings of Society for Information Technology & Teacher Education International Conference* (pp. 1477–1482). Association for the Advancement of Computing in Education (AACE).

Singer, A., Kirchgaessner, R., Howlett, C., Snyder, C., Vermette, P., Pezone, M., Roberts, S., & Gunn, J. (2010). Does lecture have a place in the social studies classroom? *Social Science Docket,* (Summer/Fall, 2010), 2–7.

Stacy, J. (2009). The guide on the stage: In defense of good lecturing in the history classroom. *Social Education, 73*(6), 289–295.

Stevenson, N. A., & Mussalow, P. R. (2019). The effects of planning, goal setting, and performance feedback on avoidance behaviors for struggling readers. *Journal of Positive Behavior Interventions, 21*(3), 171–180.

Toppo, G. (2019). "Neuromyth" or helpful model? *Inside Higher Ed.* https://www.insidehighered.com/news/2019/01/09/learning-styles-debate-its-instructors-vs-psychologists

VanSickle, R. L. (1986). A quantitative review of research on instructional simulation gaming: A twenty-year perspective. *Theory and Research in Social Education, 14*(3), 245–246.

CHAPTER 4

TEACHING MIDDLE LEVEL SOCIAL STUDIES: ADVANCED STRATEGIES AND METHODS

We only think when we are confronted with a problem.
—*John Dewey (Brainy Quotes, 2021)*

It is nothing short of a miracle that modern methods of instruction have not yet entirely strangled the holy curiosity of inquiry.
—*Albert Einstein (Oxford Reference, 2021)*

Activity List
- Reflecting on Advanced Strategies.
- Student Created Graphic Organizers.
- Develop a Center Based Lesson.
- Bringing Trade Books and Primary Sources into Social Studies.
- Develop a Multiple Source Based Lesson Plan.
- Simulations and Field Trips.
- Reflecting on the Chapter.

COLLABORATIVE ACTIVITY: REFLECTING ON ADVANCED STRATEGIES

Review the strategies listed in Chapter 3. With a partner discuss how you could make them more challenging to your students.

INTRODUCTION

Two primary purposes of education are self-improvement and professional advancement. If you are reading this book it means that you have already successfully advanced through elementary, middle, and high school. You may be close to the next level of educational advancement by becoming a college graduate. Once you find a teaching job, the need for advancement continues. Some teachers go on to earn advanced degrees. Some seek to become master teachers, department heads, or grade level coaches. Others find themselves gravitating toward local school administration. In Scott's case, he actively pursued several advanced degrees, the social studies chair position at both schools he worked in, and eventually moved into a position as a Social Studies Program Specialist in his district's central office, as well as becoming a college professor. Ben followed a similar developmental trajectory, earning degrees in school counseling and teacher education, eventually moving from the middle school classroom to an undergraduate teacher education program. Through his studies, Ben has had the opportunity to study school systems in South America, Europe, Africa, and Asia. One advantage of education is that it offers many opportunities for growth, advancement, and perhaps international travel. We tell you this because we can personally attest to the growth from novice teaching techniques to expert approaches. As we hope for our own students, we strongly encourage you to take the approach that learning never ends.

In the last chapter we introduced basic strategies and methods for teaching social studies. These ideas were simple to create and incorporate while adding richness to your social studies instruction. Now it is time to examine more advanced strategies and methods that you can use in your lesson planning. These strategies are more advanced in the sense that they may take you longer to plan or implement and because of their use of the progressive education philosophy explained in the Preface of the book. The featured advanced strategies have teachers:

- Taking a role in helping students understand who they are;
- Providing students an opportunity to form a critical consciousness about their society;
- Using curriculum and content standards as a guide in the interpretation, understanding, celebration, and critique of the topics and themes of social studies;
- Offering students a variety of choices in their own learning;
- Helping students develop a commitment to community problems and the tools with which to address them; and

- Allowing students to make connections and draw their own conclusions about social studies topics.

Keep in mind you do not have to be an advanced or veteran teacher to incorporate these strategies into your classroom so you should try them from day one.

ADVANCED ORGANIZERS

Chapter 3 was about how to incorporate several simple graphic organizers in your lessons. These included the concept definition map, the Frayer Model, the Predicting ABC chart, the KWL chart, and the Venn diagram. In this section we will discuss more graphic organizers that take longer for your students to complete but offer them the opportunity to think more deeply about the social studies topic that is being examined.

The KWL + and the "Three Circle" Venn Diagram

One way to make your graphic organizers more advanced is to simply add additional columns to them. In the case of the KWL chart, adding a column makes it a KWL+ chart (Ogle et al., 2007). For example, you can change a KWL chart into a KWLS chart. The "S" stands for "still want to know." After students complete their "still want to know" column, you should allow them to research their new questions through the school resources and share their work with one another.

To make the Venn diagram more advanced, an extra circle can be added. Students will then have to determine the similarities and differences between more than two people, places, or events. When they compare three topics, students will often need extra help in filling out the Venn diagram. For example, if students are comparing the government systems of South American countries such as Argentina, Brazil, and Chile they should first list all of the differences of Argentina's government as compared to the two other countries and have them list these in section 1 of the diagram. Then we would have them do the same for Brazil and place them in section 2 followed by Chile and write them in section 3. Then have students compare the similarities between the governments of Argentina and Brazil and place them in section 4. They do the same with Argentina and Chile and write the similarities in section 5 and then Chile and Brazil and place the similarities in section 6. Finally, students should write down all the similarities that the three countries have in section 7 of the diagram (see Figure 4.1).

Venn diagrams can also be used to compare different types of texts or media. In investigating whether "war is worth the sacrifice," the Gettysburg Address, letters from soldiers, and songs with lyrics discussing the cost of war can be compared visually through use of Venn diagrams. Employing different media types, then using Venn diagrams encourage students to find themes, similarities, and differences among them.

80 • TEACHING MIDDLE LEVEL SOCIAL STUDIES (3RD EDITION)

FIGURE 4.1. Example of a Three Ring Venn Diagram

Student-Developed Graphic Organizers

Often, when teachers use a KWL chart, Venn diagram, or any other type of graphic organizer, they predetermine the intellectual task students are to do and simply ask students to fill in the organizer. One way to help students actively participate is to have them create their own graphic organizers. Scott used this strategy in many of his social studies classes throughout the years. For instance, when discussing the major battles of the Revolutionary War, Scott often had his students create their own organizer to remember these events. One student created an organizer labeled "Revolutionary War Battles" with a cannon firing. With each "explosion" the student listed the name of the battle and then drew three "cannon balls" falling from each explosion. These cannon balls were labeled with information about each of the battles (see Figure 4.2). Encouraging students to take the lead promotes ownership of the concept and can often lead to better teacher understanding as well. We have often found that when students have license to explore, they create products better than we anticipated. At lower grades, allowing students to choose the graphic organizer is an effective means of differentiation and enrichment.

Another example of a student developed graphic organizer is based on the three branches of government. One of Scott's students took this concept and created an organizer that was truly based on the visual of three branches. He drew a tree and labeled the branches "legislative" "judicial" and "executive." Once again, though he was simply graphing the balance of power, he had more buy-in with the assignment and retained the material better (see Figure 4.3); in other words, he created a personal connection to the information.

A third example of a student created graphic organizer is the causes of World War One picture map that is shown in the figure below (see Figure 4.4). One of Karrie's students created this visual to help them remember and understand the big causes that lead to the first World War. This student chose to draw a picture of each of the 4 MAIN causes, Militarism, Alliances, Imperialism, and Nationalism.

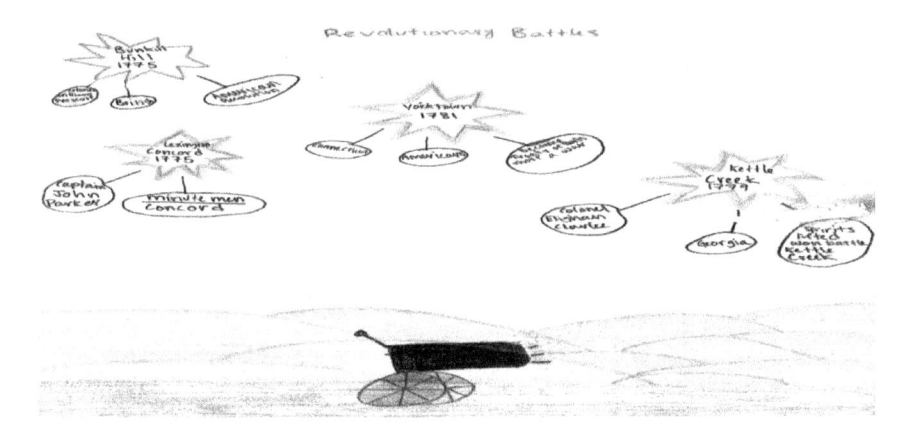

Teaching Middle Level Social Studies: Advanced Strategies and Methods • 81

FIGURE 4.2. Student Developed Revolutionary War Graphic Organizer

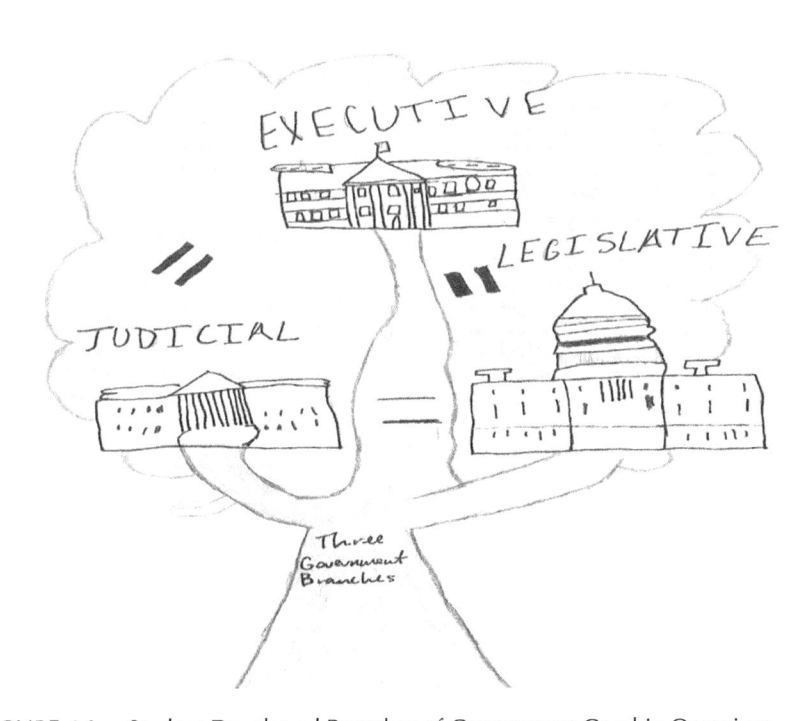

FIGURE 4.3. Student Developed Branches of Government Graphic Organizer

FIGURE 4.4. Student Developed World War I Causes Graphic Organizer

By having students develop picture maps, Karrie gave them a chance to create their own meaning for the unfamiliar vocabulary and also increased the likelihood of students remembering what caused the war.

Individual Activity: Student Created Graphic Organizers

Examine your state's standards (see Table 2.1). In your reflective journal create a list of topics that would lend themselves best to student developed graphic organizers.

LEARNING CENTERS

The use of differentiated instruction (sometimes simply called differentiation) is the idea that educators should teach to each student's individual learning style and background in order to maximize their achievement. Differentiation has been a key issue on many school districts' initiatives for decades now (Westman, 2018). Teachers who use the traditional teaching style of whole group instruction regularly are often concerned about how to teach to the individual needs of each student. One way to do this is through learning centers (Nicholson, 2017).

When developing learning centers there are several factors to keep in mind. These can include timing, incorporating noisy media sources, making sure students participate in both favored and unfavored stations, allowing students to plan out their own centers, and checking student performance. There are many approaches teachers can take to develop effective learning centers; however, the one that we think is the best, due to its connections to the NCSS 10 themes, is the "choice board," "menu," or "buffet," style strategy. Using this approach allows students the opportunity to choose the centers and activities in which they are the most interested in participating, or areas they know they need additional assistance with. Developing students' ability to make appropriate choices incorporates the democratic values stressed by social studies advocates.

A successful choice board or menu/buffet style center activity requires you to develop anywhere from seven to ten learning center options. Each of the centers should have its own unique activity. After you offer a brief introduction to each center, you may give your students a "menu" to keep track of which centers they complete (see Figure 4.5). You should develop centers that will take about the same time to complete, usually 10–15 minutes. However, your students should be given the option to move to a different center once their work is finished.

To check for understanding at each center there are two progress check options that you can use as students move from activity to activity. One is a "ticket" that students must fill out and hand to you once they complete a center. The ticket should include summary questions about the activity or topic that the students

---

Develop a Catchy Name Based on Your School's Mascot such as "The Knight's Table" or "The Comet Café"

Appetizer (Choose 1 of 2)
- Center 1: KWL Chart (The American Revolution)
- Center 2: Predicting ABC Chart (The American Revolution)

Soup and Salad (Free Center: Choose if you need help with vocabulary)
- Center 3: Frayer Diagram

Entrée (Choose 2 of 4)
- Center 4: Propaganda
- Center 5: History vs. Hollywood (Boston Tea Party/Lexington and Concord)
- Center 6: Write Your Own School House Rock Song
- Center 7: Primary Source Analysis (The Boston Massacre)

Dessert (Everyone gets dessert!)
- Center 8: Paired Questions and Answers

FIGURE 4.5. Example of a Learning Center Menu: The American Revolution

Topic:	Center #:	Name:
What I learned from this center:		
What I liked about the center:		
What could make this center better?		

FIGURE 4.6. Sample Learning Center Ticket

were learning about. A "door prize" can be used to encourage student participation. The more centers/tickets that they complete, the better chance they will win (see Figure 4.6). Make sure to have the prize drawing at the end of the class—your students will certainly remind you to if you do not! Another approach is to simply have students write their answers to questions or respond to their peers' answers about the activity on a large sheet of paper located at each center.

During any center-based activity, some centers will prove to be more popular than others. This reflects the different learning styles our students have. It is certainly acceptable to instruct students that they all must go to one or two centers. Scott calls these the "dessert centers" and tells his students that today "everyone gets dessert" (see Figure 4.5). The goal of this approach is to allow students as much choice as possible as they go to the centers that best fit their learning needs. With this in mind, it is also acceptable to have a "free or open" center where students are given the opportunity to work individually on a topic that they have predetermined they need to learn more about. This can also be used as a time for students to make up work, complete missed assessments, or retake and make corrections to tests. See Figure 4.7 for a sample center-based lesson about the American Revolution.

This is but one of the many ways you can incorporate learning centers in your classroom. It should be noted that this type of activity can, at first, result in some off-task behaviors. Make sure that when you have a "center day" that you plan to constantly move around the room and monitor the class. However, once your students get used to the routine of this activity it can become a great opportunity for all your students to effectively take part in the day's lesson. In Scott's classroom he found that no matter how he structured a center-based activity his students had fun. In addition, they were more engaged since they had the opportunity to, at least partially, choose their topic of study. More importantly, they learned the content better as a result of being able to use their dominant learning style for at least one center.

- **Center 1: K-W-L Chart (The American Revolution).** This center will be an introductory activity to determine students' prior knowledge about the American Revolution and what they would like to know about the war. At the completion of the centers, students will be able to fill in the "L" column about what they learned.
- **Center 2: Predicting ABC Chart (The American Revolution).** At this center have students complete a Predicting ABC chart using the Revolutionary War section in textbook.
- **Center 3: Frayer Diagram (Five American Revolution vocabulary words).** This center will allow students to "dissect" and learn the vocabulary that will be asked on standardized tests. Base these words on your state standards about the American Revolution (see Table 2.1).
- **Center 4: Propaganda.** In this center students will analyze several works of propaganda that could include Franklin's Join or Die Poster, (this was actually drawn during the French and Indian War), The Gadsden Flag, and the Pennsylvania Journal and Weekly Advertiser Stamp Act protest. Each of these resources is quickly available at the Library of Congress website (See Website Resources below). Students will then draw a propaganda poster in support of the Patriots and a propaganda poster in support of the Loyalists.
- **Center 5: History vs. Hollywood (Boston Tea Party or Lexington and Concord).** In this center students will read an account about the Boston Tea Party or Lexington and Concord. They will compare the reading to a clip from the Disney film Johnny Tremain (Boston Tea Party). Make sure that students bring in their own headphones or provide some since students will be watching a media clip.
- **Center 6: Write Your Own *School House Rock* Song.** In this center students will watch the School House Rock video "No More Kings") or "The Shot Heard Around the World" (Both are available on Youtube. See Website Resources below). After watching the video put your students in pairs. One should write the words for a song about a topic from the Revolutionary War while the other sketches out a cartoon. Tell your students that they should be prepared to perform the song in front of the class. Make sure that students bring in their own headphones or provide some since students will be watching a media clip.
- **Center 7: Primary Source Analysis (The Boston Massacre).** Students will examine two images of the Boston Massacre, "The Bloody Massacre" by Paul Revere, and "Portrait of Crispus Attucks in Boston Massacre,." (Both are available on the Library of Congress website (See Website Resources below). Tell your students to list three ways the images are similar, and five ways they are different. Ask them to write a paragraph about which image they think is the most accurate and have them explain why.
- **Center 8: Paired Questions and Answers.** In this center students will work on a Paired Questions and Answers activity using the "Causes of the American Revolution" section in the textbook. This will be a "dessert center" since this topic is more than likely a state standard.

FIGURE 4.7. Center Lesson Plan: The American Revolution

COLLABORATIVE ACTIVITY: DEVELOP A CENTER BASED LESSON

Using the center-based learning information above as a guide, work with a partner to create a center-based lesson about a social studies topic. Share copies of your center-based lesson plan with your classmates.

LITERACY STRATEGIES IN SOCIAL STUDIES

In Chapter 3 we examined the appropriate use of textbooks in the classroom and how they should be just one of many tools used in social studies instruction. Due to the influence of recent curricular initiatives such as the Common Core movement, it is safe to assume that literacy will remain an important element in social studies classrooms. Common Core standards, employed in many states, have entire sections dedicated to subject-area literacy. Two advanced strategies for middle grades social studies that perfectly blend with incorporating literacy are the use of trade books and primary sources (see Chapter 11 for a more in-depth examination of the strategies that can be used for building literacy in social studies).

Trade Books

Trade books can be works of fiction or nonfiction that are usually written in a narrative format. Researchers have found that the use of trade books is, overall, beneficial to students who read them in their social studies classes (e.g., Bickford & Clabough, 2020; Fuhler, 1992; Richgels et al., 1993; Vacca & Vacca, 2005) These books are usually easier for students to read than textbooks due to their narrative style, sentence structure, and elaborate depictions of people and events. Trade books usually retain student interest as they are often filled with action, humor, and characters that middle level students can relate to. The NCSS also supports the use of trade books in social studies classes and offers a yearly list of those that they recommend. The lists from several years can be found on their website under the section "Notable Trade Books for Young People."

As with any other teaching tool, trade books have weaknesses and should not be used exclusively. First, they often take a long time to read. Even if a teacher reads a book out loud in class as a book study, they can take several days to finish. Second, trade books often stray from the content of the social studies course and can spend many pages on material that is not in the curriculum. Finally, since many trade books are not written by historians, reviewed by adoption boards, or critiqued in the same way that textbooks are, there is no guarantee that the social studies content is accurate.

Nevertheless, trade books should be used in middle school social studies classes. Some ways to effectively include the use of trade books include assigning trade books to read that match up as close as possible to your state standards (see Table 2.1), have students read the book outside of class on their own, or in your class when other assignments have been completed. To ensure students are reading the book, an alternative assessment you can use is a book club where students post their thoughts and feelings about the book on a blog. Using a blog, students lead the discussion about the book, and you can offer guiding questions, remedy incorrect content, and track students who are reading the book and those who are not. No matter how you incorporate the use of trade books in your classes, it is imperative that you make sure that students can connect what they are reading to the social studies content that is being taught.

Primary Sources

A primary source is simply a firsthand account of historical events or figures that date back to the time period under investigation. These sources can be photographs, speeches, newspaper reports, diaries, maps, census recorders, court transcripts, or autobiographies. In contrast, secondary sources are accounts of historical events written by people who did not witness them. Secondary sources are made possible by someone's research about people or events. There are several examples of secondary sources including textbooks, encyclopedias, Hollywood films, etc. Though some often think primary sources are more reliable than secondary sources, this is not always the case. A primary source can have as much bias, if not more, than a secondary source. For instance, a letter from a slaveholder written in the 1850s may contain many elements of bias based on his or her financial benefit, in addition to the influence of the intense racial bigotry present during that period of U.S. history. An important question used to determine which is appropriate to use is; "What is it I want to know?" If searching for deeply detailed accounts or verbatim wording, primary sources are appropriate. If looking for longer-term, retrospective accounts, secondary sources may be more useful. Often, primary and secondary sources can be used in tandem, providing rich opportunities to find the strengths and weaknesses in each. Spending time early in your course discussing the strengths and weaknesses of these two different types of sources encourages your students to engage more meaningfully with the sources, ultimately working toward deeper analyses and critiques of them.

Much research has been conducted on using primary sources in social studies classes. On the whole, the vast majority of the literature has concluded that primary sources should be used in the classroom and are an effective tool in the study of history and the social sciences (e.g., Brophy & VanSledright, 1997; Kobrin, 1996; Lawrence et al., 2019; Wineberg, 2001). These documents from the past allow students to gain a better understanding and personal connection to history. Though important, primary sources can also be challenging to incorporate in your lesson. To illustrate, the older the primary source is, the more difficult it is likely to be for students to read due to changes in language and the remoteness of events. You could expect to experience little success if you simply gave your students a copy of the Declaration of Independence, had them read it, and then attempted to have them discuss or answer questions about it. However, there are several ways primary sources can be used effectively.

Using Written Sources

When using written primary sources in the middle level classroom, the most important thing to keep in mind is that you want them to add to your students' understanding of a historical topic. You do not want the sources to be so difficult that students are turned off or do not see the benefit of using them. There are several ways that you can incorporate written primary sources in your classes. Three of these include using excerpts from the primary source materials with guiding questions written above the source, altering the language of the document to modern English, and using a "silent discussion" strategy that allows students to work together to analyze, question, and comment on a written document (Cafarella, 2011; Kobrin, 1996; Roberts, 2009; Stanford History Education Group, 2011; Wineburg & Martin, 2009).

When using short excerpts from a larger document, it's important to write guiding questions above or below each excerpt. To make this strategy more effective, ask students to highlight the location in the source where they found the answers to the questions. This approach allows students to practice their reading compression skills by allowing them to show you where they found the answers. This approach also helps you determine if students read the document or if they may be having reading comprehension issues. It may also be helpful to students to read aloud the sources as they follow along. Often seen as an elementary approach, hearing and seeing the text at the same time certainly provides opportunity for students of all ages to more deeply understand what they are looking at. This strategy has the added benefits of allowing you to verbally emphasize words and concepts as well as pronounce unfamiliar words.

In his Georgia studies classes, Scott used this strategy when discussing two important historic Georgia documents. The first was for the Georgia Charter of 1732 and the second was for a letter General William T. Sherman wrote to the Mayor of Atlanta explaining why he was about to destroy the city (Roberts, 2009). Using this strategy allowed his regular and special education students to easily analyze two documents that were well over 100 years old. In turn, it allowed Scott's students to understand the reasons for the founding of Georgia, which was an indicator of achievement on the state's standards, and to determine if Sherman was truly the villainous figure often portrayed in southern history courses and textbooks.

Ben spent time reading aloud portions of the Declaration of Independence to his students. Even integrating hand motions, his animation of the text assisted his students in better understanding the complex vocabulary and concepts. Consider how the following section from the Declaration of Independence can be better understood by students when hearing it read and seeing hand motions acted out:

> In every stage of these Oppressions We have Petitioned for Redress in the most humble terms: Our repeated Petitions have been answered only by repeated injury. A Prince whose character is thus marked by every act which may define a Tyrant, is unfit to be the ruler of a free people.

When saying the word "Petitioned" Ben clasped his hands together as if begging for something. As he approached the work "humble" he bowed down to an unseen ruler. When he got to "repeated injury" he pulled out a large mallet that he used for such cases and pretended to hammer down on the colonists. Working these motions into the speaking adds a dimension of communication that many students find useful and enjoyable. It is also appropriate to alter the language of a primary source and create lessons around these modified sources. Researchers such as Sam Wineburg have determined that altering the language of these documents keeps the primary meaning behind the text, while at the same time allowing students to gain historical understanding by using primary sources (Stanford History Education Group, 2011; Wineburg & Martin, 2009). For example, in their lesson plan about the Battles of Lexington and Concord, the Stanford History Education Group uses two modified sources. One is from a British soldier and one is from a sworn statement by 34 minutemen. These sources were selected to allow students to compare both sides of the conflict and to determine who fired the first shot of the war (Stanford History Education Group, 2011) However, unlike the Stanford group, we would make sure to place the original source next to the altered sources just so students can read both if they choose. Another approach is to have students rewrite a source in their own words before using it as comparison resource. In Ben's classes, students enjoyed re-writing the Declaration of Independence as a breakup letter between (former) middle school sweethearts.

The challenge in studying history is that even primary sources do not paint a complete picture. A colleague of the authors uses the letters of Grace Bedell and the reply from Abraham Lincoln in conjunction with images to form a timeline around Lincoln's election of 1860. Coupled with the story *Mr. Lincoln's Whiskers*, his 4th grade classes challenge the notion that an 11-year old girl convinced Abraham Lincoln to grow a beard (Winnick, 1996).

A final strategy for analyzing a written primary source document is to have students analyze it collaboratively with a silent discussion. Using a large sheet of butcher paper with the document glued to it, you can allow students to read the document together and write their comments, questions, and answers around the document. You can use guiding questions or allow students to take the lead and sort out the document's meaning on their own (Cafarella, 2011). It may be helpful to have multiple copies placed around the classroom to allow students to converse and interact in smaller groups.

Using Primary Images

Most of us have heard the saying "A picture is worth 1000 words," and as clichéd as it seems, whoever originated this adage (the source is unknown) had a great point: you can gain a large amount of insight from carefully examining an image, especially one from the time period being studied. As Foster et al. (1999) explain, images offer elementary students "refreshing accessibility and immediate

90 • TEACHING MIDDLE LEVEL SOCIAL STUDIES (3RD EDITION)

engagement" to historic understanding, and images can also "evoke critical and reflective student thought" (p. 201).

This, of course, is true for students of all ages. When Scott wrote the first edition of this book, he used a photo he had recently purchased from an antique shop to develop a lesson. The photo (which cost him $6) is labeled "Flat Rock School 1901–1902" and shows a very serious looking group of students surrounding a very stern looking male teacher (with the exception of one of the eldest students cracking a smile in the back row). The students, all dressed in their "Sunday best," range in age from what appears to be perhaps 8 to 17. As he looked at the picture (see Figure 4.8) many thoughts came to mind such as "Where is Flat Rock School?" "Did the students dress up because they knew that they were going to be in photo or were they expected to dress like that every day?" "What was the average school day like?" "Was the student who dared to crack a smile a good student or a challenge?" And, as women had limited professional opportunities during this period in U.S. history and often left school early to work at home, "What did the older girls do with their education?"

This image is a great primary source and from it you can infer quite a bit about early 20th century schooling. For example, one can conclude that there were male teachers who must have taught students of all grade levels at the same time. Additionally, you can determine that the school was coeducational, and just like today,

FIGURE 4.8. Primary Source: Flat Rock School

mathematics possibly dominated the curriculum: there are math problems written on both of the blackboards.

Though it has benefits, this image unfortunately offers many more questions than answers. Because no one wrote more information on the back of the photo the teacher and students are regulated to obscurity. More than likely we will never find out who the students and teacher were and what happened to them. In fact, we have no doubt that we may never even be able to determine where the school was located. When Scott asked the owner at the antique store if she knew anything about the photo, she said no. Someone just walked in and sold the image, along with many others, for $1 a piece (Scott guesses he should have been angry about the 600% profit margin she earned from him). Scott is frustrated that he will never know as much about the students in the photo as he would like. Your students may feel the same sense of frustration in using primary source images. This photograph illustrates that just like any other tool, there should be some scaffolding and explanation that takes place when incorporating primary images. Similarly, this photograph serves as an example of the fact that historical inquiry is never completely satisfied with a single source of information.

If we were to use this image in our classes, the first thing we would tell the students would be that the teacher was our great-great grandfather and we have come from a long line of teachers and apparently, we cannot break out of the cycle. Then we would say "just kidding" and remind them that it is important for them to always double-check your sources and not believe everything they are told. After the prank was over, we would become more serious and tell them that while we know very little about these people, the image can be useful in furthering our understanding of the lives of students, education, and other historic events in the early 1900s. Primary sources, like secondary sources, never tell the complete story. Informational holes can, however, stimulate authentic inquiry. Tantalizing clues like those described above can become stems to seek out further information. An internet search with tidbits of information can quickly lead to answers or to more questions. Reflecting what many professional historians do, encouraging your middle school students to seek answers to the mysteries inherent in primary sources can jump start their imaginations.

Even with the missing information, this photograph offers several examples of how to incorporate primary images into the classroom and Scott would then use one or two of the strategies listed below. They include:

- Have students compare and contrast the image to their own school or classroom.
- Have students read their textbook's account of American life in the early 1900s and compare and contrast what they see in the image to the description found in their textbooks.
- Have students choose one of the children in the photograph and write a journal or diary entry from the perspective of the child. We would make

sure that our students included information about historical events from the time period. For example, President Theodore Roosevelt took office during the same year the picture was taken, so they could discuss how their selected child may have felt about his presidency up to that point.
- Have students stand/sit in front of the projected picture and "step way" from this scene to act out what they wrote in the prior suggestion.
- Upload the image to a website such as Blabberize (see Website Resources below) On this website students can write a script and record their voices. With the uploaded image they can create mouths on the photograph that move to their voices.
- Have students recreate the photograph to encourage them to visualize it in three dimensions.

No matter which strategy or strategies you select, this $6 photograph of an unknown school in an unknown state can lead to a great activity where students identify with their peers from over 100 years ago while learning historic content at the same time.

Multiple photographs can be tied together to paint a picture of a place, time, event, or concept. Ben provides his students the opportunity to use the internet to assist in creating "Photoessays" in which they select up to 10 photographs or works of art related to a specific subject. Child labor, for example, serves as a powerful topic with which students can find hundreds of examples, both historically and, unfortunately, in modernity. Students soon discover the powerful work of photographers such as Jacob Riis and Dorothea Lange. Students are required to write rationales for why the photographs were selected from the thousands of possibilities. Additionally, they must craft open-ended discussion questions for their classmates to consider when the photoessays are presented. Going beyond US History, potential photoessay topics include civil rights, social justice, geographic regions, sociological concepts, and democratic principles, to name a few. Considering the powerful images of protests across the United States in recent years, there is a deep well of possibility for employing visual images in social studies classes. Encouraging students to find primary sources that speak to them is a powerful way to connect students to concepts being experienced in your classroom. You may even find that students provide visual primary sources that are more interesting than what you have selected. If this is the case, asking their permission to use their find in your future classes is an empowering event for the student.

Using Other Primary Sources Including Audio Recordings, Music, Art, and Drama

There are other types of primary sources that can be used in the social studies classroom. Video and audio clips are great ways for students to see and hear those who were involved in the historical events. For example, the audio for both Franklin Roosevelt's fireside chats and Martin Luther King Jr.'s "I Have a Dream

Speech" are easy to find on the Internet and can be used to enrich the discussion of these speeches which are often written about in history textbooks and found state standards.

Another great strategy for incorporating primary sources is song analysis (Wellenreiter, et al., 2020). Songs offer students another way to witness the events that shaped our society. Quite often teachers use the protest music of the 1960s as a way to frame their discussion about this time period. However, there are many other songs from different eras that offer students a glimpse of the thoughts and feelings of those who lived during the event (Lindquist, 2007). For example, there may be nothing more heart-wrenching than the lyrics and music to "Brother Can You Spare a Dime" (1932) by Yip Harburg, which describes a war veteran and working man's struggle during the Great Depression (VCU Libraries, 2020). The song allows students to empathize with the anguish and despair that many Americans felt during this chapter in American history.

When you use songs in the classroom, make sure to display the lyrics on the board as students listen to the music. Also, in the same vein as movies, you may want to consider stopping the song at various points. This allows you to discuss what the writer/singer is saying, answer any questions that students may have, or to connect what is being sung about to the curriculum. Other activities can include comparing the themes of songs from the past to those from today and creating a chart where students can analyze several songs from the same time period. If a deeper analysis is to be done, it may also be helpful to provide students paper copies of the lyrics so they can annotate as the song is played.

Using songs in class can encourage students to see ties between the concepts and strategies they are learning in their language arts classes and your social studies class. Working with your language arts colleague, it may be beneficial to students in both classes to discuss imagery, symbolism, themes, and other concepts more frequently discussed outside the social studies curriculum.

Paintings are another great resource to use, especially given the lack of fine arts education in many schools. Since they are often in color, students sometimes appreciate examining them more than black and white photographs. As with other resources, comparing and contrasting two paintings is a great way to promote historical thinking. For instance, in an examination of the impact of the railroad on Georgia's development, Scott often had his students examine two famous paintings, George Innes's Lackwanna Valley (1856) and John Gast's American Progress (1872; National Gallery of Art, 2021; Sandweiss, 2021). His students used these paintings as sources to answer the question "to what extent can all progress be seen as good?" (Roberts, 2009, p. 1). This lesson was created to help students determine both the cost and the benefits of the development of railroads, since many textbooks only discuss the benefit of railroads. Scott's students enjoyed analyzing the paintings and did a good job of using them as a source when they defended their arguments about whether the benefits of the railroads were worth the cost.

Ongoing societal debates regarding the naming of buildings, military installations, streets, and mascots, combined with debates on the maintenance or removal of statues provides students opportunity to explore history and social studies at the local level (Wellenreiter & Noraian, 2020). Students may explore their communities for these references, research the subjects and debate the merits of removal or maintenance of the subject. Indeed, statutes, memorials, and building names say as much about the people who selected them for public display as they do the person of honor (Wellenreiter & Noraian, 2020). Your students may even find that a building name or mascot should be reconsidered in new social and historical contexts.

Finally, dramas from the time period are great primary sources to use in the middle level classroom (movies and television shows can be included as well). Though watching a drama is fine if used appropriately (see Chapter 3), allowing students to read and perform plays, or even recite poetry, provides for kinesthetic learning as they are up moving around as they perform. Using drama also brings about a connection to the characters that they are portraying and the time period from when they lived that cannot be obtained from simply reading from the textbook (Howlett, 2007).

Objects as Primary Sources

Like other primary sources, three dimensional objects can serve as rich primary sources of information. Recent popular television shows in which individuals bring their treasures, (and sometimes trash) for experts to assess attest to the potential interest your students may have when investigating objects. Hand tools, fabrics and clothing, communications technologies, medical technologies, and even old money can serve as interesting points of analysis and discussion. Ben purchased a replica Revolutionary War medical kit to demonstrate battlefield surgical techniques. While not actually performing surgery in class, he certainly had the attention of his students when manipulating the bone saw and describing the tourniquet. When discussing the growth of business and industry in the late 1800s, Ben took the opportunity to conduct an "obsolete technology day" in which he brought into class phonographs, old cameras, a car phone, and other old technologies for students to analyze. Similarly, objects around the school can exemplify concepts taught in your social studies classroom. From building materials to objects required under the Americans with Disabilities Act (ADA), your school is certainly filled with objects worthy of analysis (Wellenreiter, 2018). Shown in Figure 4.9 are questions Ben uses in his class when analyzing objects.

We are surrounded by objects, both cutting edge and obsolete, that exemplify concepts in the social studies. Tying social studies concepts and time periods to the objects we see daily is a wonderful way to encourage students to see how their world of objects today is influenced by objects of the past.

These are just a few of the many ways to incorporate primary sources into your classroom. However, no matter which type of primary source you chose to incorporate in your lessons and which strategy you decide to use with them, make

> - What is the object made of (fabric, wood, metal, plastic, etc.)?
> - Is there any writing on the object, including serial numbers?
> - If the object has buttons, levers, or other manipulatives, what might they do?
> - Is there anything part the object that seems to be missing?
> - Describe the condition of the object.
> - How does this object compare to objects you see in use today?
> - What might the object be?
> - What might make the object obsolete?
> - Anything else about this object that needs mentioning?

FIGURE 4.9. Primary Source Object Analysis Questions

sure that you tell your students what the source is, why you are using it, and how it relates to the topic that you are discussing. Additionally, some primary sources are better than others and you want to be careful about where you find them. Some of the best places to find public primary sources are through agencies such as the Gilder Lehrman Institute of American History, the Library of Congress, the National Archives, the National History Education Clearing House, and the Smithsonian Institution. More information, including their web addresses, are in the Website Resources section at the end of this chapter.

Class Activity: Bringing Trade Books and Primary Sources into Social Studies

As a class, discuss:

- The strengths of using trade books and primary sources into your social studies classes.
- The challenges of bringing these sources into your lesson planning.
- New ways to incorporate trade books and primary sources into your lesson planning.
- Primary source objects you could integrate into your lesson planning.

BRINGING SOURCES TOGETHER

So far, we have described many types of primary and secondary sources and strategies that can be incorporated into your lesson planning. We also mentioned that it is imperative to use several sources and to make sure students compare and contrast them. For example, students can look for similarities and differences between a primary source image and a textbook account of the time period, or they can compare a movie's version of a historic event to a diary of someone who participated in it. Below are three additional strategies that can be used to offer students a more structured approach to reading, analyzing, discussing, and most importantly, comprehending the information that can be found when using several sources.

Jigsaw

The jigsaw approach is a cooperative learning strategy that asks students to become experts on one specific topic or source and then teach their peers about what they learned (Silver et al., 2007). This approach teaches students good research, communication, planning, and collaborative skills. To make this activity more structured, Scott usually includes a chart (see Table 4.1) students must complete together based on what they learned. One of the sources he most often used is the textbook (which he usually assigns to the group's middle level reader). He has also used images, songs, and movies as sources in jigsaw activities. No matter how you use this strategy, students enjoy the collaborative nature of the project and often learn quite a bit about their assigned source as they prepare to teach classmates about it.

This strategy also leads itself to differentiation as you can discreetly group the students into threes by reading ability. In this set up, one member should be a higher-level reader, one a lower-level reader, and one an average reader. Usually the students will not pick up on this fact as they work together to achieve a common goal: completing the chart.

Circle of Knowledge

At first glance, a Circle of Knowledge lesson appears to be very similar to a jigsaw strategy. Students read different sources and then have an opportunity to discuss what they read with one another. However, the Circle of Knowledge is much more complex. For one, students are asked "focus" and "sparking" questions before the activity begins (Silver et al., 2007, p. 224). For instance, in Scott's Georgia studies course a typical focus question was something such as "Who were some of most influential 20th century Georgians." However, the sparking question is the key to the strategy. To add a bit of contention and debate to the lesson the sparking question would become "Who do you think was the most influential 20th century Georgian and why?" Of course, this activity can be used for any group of historic individuals or events.

Once students are given the questions, have time to think about them, and offer their preliminary answers in a whole group setting; they are then divided into small groups. In the case of the Georgia studies lesson example, Scott's students were placed into one of three groups, "Jackie Robinson," "Martin Luther King Jr.," or "Jimmy Carter." Students then read and analyze resources about their historical figure and discuss why their specific person is the best answer to the sparking question using a graphic organizer to write down their thoughts

After this phase the students are then reassigned into new groups made up of one member from each of the original groups. Each group must come to consensus about which figure was the most influential. Finally, a vote is taken in order to determine who the class believed was the best answer to the sparking question.

Teaching Middle Level Social Studies: Advanced Strategies and Methods • **97**

TABLE 4.1. Sample Jigsaw Chart: Historic Figure

Source	Date of Birth	Date of Death	Interesting Facts	Family Life	Jobs	Achievements	Challenges
Source for lower level reader (e.g., a biography written at a lower grade level)							
Source for middle level reader (Textbook)							
Source for higher level reader (e.g., an encyclopedia entry or a higher grade level biography)							

This activity should take a full class period, but you will be astounded by how much each student in the class will learn. Due to the discussion with other group members, most students learn quite a bit about all the people, topics, or events studied. Each group of students should be given several primary and secondary sources to use as they develop their arguments. Scott published a lesson idea for bringing this strategy to the K–3 classroom to help students examine American Symbols that can also be used as a guide for using this strategy (Roberts, 2013).

INQUIRY LEARNING

Inquiry-based learning is one of the most advanced and challenging approaches with which to teach social studies. However, we found it to be the most effective strategy that could be used in the middle level social studies classroom. Simply put, inquiry is a method where students use primary and secondary sources to generate their own conclusion about a specific social studies topic. Though not always the case, an inquiry-based activity is often a culmination of each of the strategies listed above.

To begin an inquiry-based lesson, students should be asked a sparking question that has no definite answer. Some examples include: "Should we explore Mars?" "Do women have equal rights today?" "What is Atlanta's true name?" "Is war worth It?," "Which of the responsibilities of government is the most important?" and "What if the British had won the American Revolution?" After receiving these questions, students are then given the opportunity to analyze and evaluate primary and secondary sources in order to help them develop their own unique answers. Students must back up their answers with the evidence that they found in these sources. All the while, students are using their higher order thinking skills and not only learning but developing a deeper understanding of the district's or state's mandated standards in the process.

Educational experts both in and out of the field of social studies have suggested inquiry-based strategies for a long time. In fact, many of the ideas for using inquiry strategies are based on the works of John Dewey (1902, 1933, 1938). More recently, some of the most influential leaders of social studies education such as Brophy and VanSledright (1997), Levstik and Barton (2005), and Wineburg (2001), to name a few, have all written important works outlining how to bring inquiry into classrooms. Several authors (including Scott) have attempted to put those ideals into practice and created specific lesson plans based on inquiry (for more information about these plans see Barlowe, 2004; Ogle et al., 2007; Roberts, 2009, 2011; Silver et al., 2007; The Stanford History Education Group, 2011; Yell, 2012). Reflecting the increasing support of this approach, the National Council for the Social Studies College, Career, & Civic Life C3 Framework for Social Studies State Standards places great emphasis on inquiry-based learning goals. These goals are currently being integrated and adapted into many states' learning goals. The C3 Framework is discussed throughout the book.

Planning an Inquiry Lesson

Whether it is called inquiry, problem solving, or mystery, all inquiry-based lessons begin with a question. Either teachers or students may develop questions. After the question(s) has been assigned, the next step is for students to examine primary and secondary sources to explore potential answers to the question, problem, or mystery. Once students have had an opportunity to examine, compare, and discuss each of the sources, it's a good idea to use a compare and contrast chart as a scaffolding tool to help students write down and analyze information from the sources. After completing the chart, students use the data to formulate an answer to the question. The key for this lesson to be successful is for students to use the sources to back the rationale behind their answers. In this exercise students should feel free to provide a multitude of answers so long as they explain their logic by using the sources at hand. However, some answers may be better than others as they may be more historically accurate or complete and offer solutions to everyday problems that are lawful, constitutional, and economically feasible. In an inquiry lesson answers can be judged in several ways including by their quality, their correctness, and/or their use of logic and empirical support. It should be noted that due to this intense study of a social studies topic, students are more prone to memorize the specific details about the topic being studied and therefore, in our experience, more likely to perform well on standardized multiple-choice tests.

Going through the process encouraged by inquiry-based lessons is as important as the results students produce. Like professionals in the social sciences and active citizens in our communities, asking pertinent questions, having experience in analyzing sources, and formulating responses based on reliable information is a key part of the student-centered learning process. You will probably find that as students go through the inquiry process, they produce additional questions, leading to a potentially unending process of knowledge seeking.

SAMPLE INQUIRY LESSONS

We believe that inquiry is one of the best strategies to use in middle level social studies courses, so we will offer more specific details about its use. In this section we provide examples of questions we used to set up inquiry-based lessons. We also give a brief description of each lesson, the documents that were used to answer the question, and information about the chart we created to help students organize their ideas about the topics.

Should the United States Explore Mars? (A 5th–8th Grade Lesson)

The first lesson is about the space race of the 1950s and 1960s. At the beginning of this inquiry students were simply asked to answer the question "Should the United States explore Mars? Why or why not?"

After the students had time to share their thoughts, they were then given a chart with the following guiding questions:

- "Why did Americans decide to explore space?"
- "What are the benefits of exploring space?"
- "What were some of the most important inventions created for space exploration?"
- "What are some of the drawbacks (problems) of space exploration?"

Additionally, students were asked to write down facts they found interesting from the sources and new questions they had about them.

After discussing the chart, students were grouped into pairs in order to work collaboratively to analyze the documents. They were given three sources. The first was a reading from their textbook about the space race of the 1960s. The second was a collection of political cartoons with a pronounced anti-NASA bias, mostly discussing the cost of the program and some of the failures the agency was having with the exploration of Mars. The third was an article discussing many of the inventions that have been created due to space exploration. After using these documents to answer the questions, they were then asked to respond to the final question "In three to five sentences answer the following question: Should the USA explore Mars? Why or Why not? Use examples from your sources to explain you answer."

It should be noted that none of these documents contained all the answers to the questions and sometimes had different answers. Students should begin noticing this as they worked on the lessons. Therefore, a secondary benefit to the activity is that students should start commenting about the importance of using multiple sources.

Do Women Have Equal Rights? (A 4th–8th Grade Lesson)

The second example of an inquiry lesson explores women's suffrage. This lesson was centered on the sparking question "Do women have equal rights today?" Like the space race question, students were given time to discuss their answers before beginning the inquiry. The students had prior knowledge of the subject based on their study of the women's suffrage movement. As with the first lesson, students were given a chart to complete with guiding questions. The questions/directions on this chart were:

- "Who were some of the most important women in the women's suffrage movement?"
- "When did women gain the right to vote?"
- "What were some other rights that women did not have before 1920?"
- "List some positive changes for women since 1920. List some inequalities that women still face today."

In order to answer these guiding questions students were given three sources. The first was the textbook while the other two were documents that Scott found in the book, *Bringing Learning Alive: The TCI Approach for Middle and High School Social Studies* (Bower et al., 2005). One was the song "Let Us All Speak Our Minds." The third was an adaptation of the list called "Fact Sheet on Women in the U.S." (Bower et al., 2005, p. 380). Students then analyzed the documents in pairs, filled in the chart, and answered the final questions: "Do women have equal rights today? Why or why not? Make sure to use examples from your chart to support your opinion."

Atlanta vs. Atalanta (An 8th Grade Lesson).

The third example is based on the question, "What is Atlanta's true name?" This lesson was written for Scott's 8th grade Georgia studies class and was a collaborative effort between Scott's two student teachers, Derek Tuthill and Elly Frachiseur, and himself.

The lesson started with a PowerPoint® presentation called "What is history?" and discussed the fact that historians use questions and hypotheses to guide their research. More importantly, the class discussed how historians used multiple primary and secondary sources to study and try to find answers to their questions. They then told our students that Atlanta may not be the city's true name, and that some people claim that the name was really "Atalanta." Next, though the students were older, we still gave them a scaffolding handout that was divided into four boxes. The students used the graphic organizer to summarize their sources and to write about their conclusions concerning their options about Atlanta's "true name."

The first source was the textbook account of the origins of Atlanta's name. The book gave the traditional account of Atlanta's development due to the railroad and two of the names it used in its early history (i.e., Terminus and Marthasville). The book went on to explain that Atlanta received its name because "freight shipped to the city was marked 'Atlanta' (a feminine form of Atlantic in reference to the Atlantic and Pacific Railroads) the town was called Atlanta…" (London, 2005, p. 311). The textbook did not mention that Atlanta's name may have really been Atalanta.

The second source was from the *New Georgia Encyclopedia*. The article discussed the origins of Atlanta's name as well (Ambrose, 2011). Though the source argues for the Western Atlantic story as well, it does allude to the idea that Governor Wilson Lumpkin's daughter Martha's (who Marthasville was named) middle name was Atalanta.

The final source was a newspaper story and map image from an *Atlanta Journal Constitution* article about an antique map dealer, Alex Branch, who found an 1847 map from Mexico where Atlanta's name was spelled Atalanta (Auchmutey, 2007). Branch believed that the map is authentic and proves the fact that Martha Lumpkin was the namesake for the city twice. Her first name being the source of Marthasville and her middle the source for Atalanta. The map dealer also claims that the additional "a" was dropped from the city's name due to human speech patterns. Saying the word "Atalanta" is much more difficult than saying the now accepted pronunciation "Atlanta"

After students analyzed all three documents, they were given the opportunity to write what they thought Atlanta's true name was and why. They then were placed in Think-Pair-Share pairs to discuss their answers. They then moved back and discussed students' answers in a whole group setting. Since Scott used this lesson for many years in his classes, he was able to see its impact first hand and was impressed with the results. Due to the fact that the students were given a chance to analyze and discuss a historical question and then express their own opinion, the vast majority remembered why Atlanta was founded in the first place. They had a better grasp of a few key state standards such as how the development of the railroad affected Georgia. In turn, the students were reminded about the importance of referring to multiple sources for information and that history is not "a bunch of dates and facts" but a mystery to be unraveled from generation to generation. An adapted version of this lesson can be located in the teachers' guide of Scott's textbook *Time Travel Through Georgia* (Hodge & Roberts, 2011). Though this is a Georgia specific example, the idea behind the lesson can be the basis for the study of any local, state, regional, or national "history mystery."

Is War Worth It? (An 8th Grade Lesson)

Because many American and world history classes spend time discussing the various conflicts in which humanity has been engaged, it is important to ask the question; "Is war worth it?" This inquiry based lesson is intended to encourage students to see both the merits and deficits of the concept of armed conflict.

After Ben's classes concluded formal discussions of the American Revolution, the question arose, "When is war worth the cost?" This question opened a can of worms dealing with ethics, morality, entitlement, and even patriotism. Students were provided with primary sources such as Robert E. Lee's farewell address to his soldiers at the end of the US Civil War, Lincoln's Gettysburg address, writings by Mohandas Gandhi and Henry David Thoreau, as well as letters from soldiers during World War II and the Vietnam War. Questions used to guide students included:

- "What are the benefits of armed conflict?"
- "What are the costs of armed conflict?"
- "What alternatives are there to armed conflict?"
- "Under what circumstances is armed conflict acceptable?"
- Under what circumstances, during disagreement, is armed conflict not acceptable?
- What should "rules of war" include?
- What are examples of wars that were necessary?
- What are examples of wars that were not necessary?

Spanning more than just US History, students spent time researching different wars throughout human history. Using Venn diagrams to compare and contrast goals of belligerents, themes often emerged that informed students as to when, in their opinions, war is necessary and when it is not. Students were often conflicted about balancing their own patriotism with the realization that sometimes armed conflict could have been avoided. This inquiry activity provided the added benefit of encouraging students to not just study tactics and strategy, generals and battles, but to go beyond and investigate intent and motive.

It is important to note that students' personal histories may play significant roles in this type of discussion. Those with family members who have or are currently serving in the military may have strong opinions either way. Because of the potentially emotional nature of this topic, it is important to have established a rapport of trust and open-mindedness in your classroom before venturing into such ethical and moral discussions.

Which of the Responsibilities of Government is the Most Important (A 6th–8th Grade Lesson)

Often the Preamble to the Constitution of the United States is overlooked when students learn about the foundations of American government. This inquiry lesson works to connect the concepts outlined in the Preamble with the functions of government and how we see these functions in our daily lives outside the classroom. We first begin by discussing the responsibilities as outlined in the Preamble; to form a more perfect Union, establish Justice, insure domestic Tranquility, provide for the common defense, promote the general Welfare, and secure the Blessings of Liberty to ourselves and our Posterity. Ben's students worked to define and apply the more difficult terms, (posterity can be a difficult concept for 8th graders). Placed into groups, students were then charged with the unenviable task of deciding which of the responsibilities is the most important. After a presentation by each group defending their response, a debate takes place to allow students the opportunity to convince one another that one responsibility wins out.

In developing their presentations, students were encouraged to respond to the following questions;

- "What are some examples of your responsibility we see in our country?
- "What would it be like if the government did not have your responsibility?"
- "What would it be like if the government did not have the other responsibilities?"
- "How are the responsibilities interrelated?"
- Why, ultimately, is your responsibility the most important?

The students found very quickly that the responsibilities of government as outlined in the Preamble rely on one another, and it is therefore difficult to determine which is the most important. Like a house of cards, if one is removed, the other falls. The purpose of this inquiry-based lesson is not necessarily to come to a specific conclusion on which of the responsibilities of government is most important. Rather, it is to go through the process and conclude that they are interdependent and to see how each is exemplified in life outside of the classroom.

What if the British Had Won the American Revolution? (A 4th–8th Grade Lesson)

The final inquiry lesson is based on a counterfactual or alternative history question. Counterfactual history is a literary genre that examines what may have caused historical episodes to diverge from what really happened and how these differences could have changed the present. Though generally dismissed by scholars for much of its existence, counterfactual inquiry is gaining popularity amongst college professors and researchers who believe that it can help their students gain a better understanding of the past. Though there has been little research conducted on its effectiveness in the middle level classroom, Scott used a counterfactual history project with his students for several years. When using this strategy, he witnessed positive results in his students' understanding and interest in the subject of history (Roberts, 2011).

In an article published in *The Social Studies* (Roberts, 2011) Scott outlined a plan that helped the reader construct a counterfactual inquiry. Though similar to the inquiry above, the project was an expanded seven-step process that took several weeks to complete. Additionally, the students played more of a role in developing their own "what if" sparking questions (though What if the British won? was one of the more popular topics) and were responsible for finding their own sources to analyze and used to support their final questions.

Though students were given the opportunity to choose their own counterfactual history questions, the lesson plan includes several structured activities to help students develop their own conclusions. These activities included creating five counterfactual history questions; creating a KWL chart to analyze three of the questions; developing a proposal for the project they planned to use to display the answer to their "what if" questions (e.g., a PowerPoint®, a counterfactual history story, or a poster); creating a map of the alternative world; completing a counterfactual Venn Diagram explaining the difference between their alternative world and what really happened; and finally, giving a presentation and chalk talk discussion about the answers to their what if question (Roberts, 2011, p. 121).

It should be noted that for this type of lesson to be effective you should have familiarity with the topic of counterfactual history before presenting it to your students. Scott was always a fan of the genre and started thinking about how he could incorporate its use in the classroom when he was an undergraduate. Once he started teaching, he developed a counterfactual inquiry lesson that proved to be a favorite of his students.

CHALLENGES OF CREATING INQUIRY LESSONS

Creating inquiry-based lessons can prove challenging. There are several factors involved in the process such as the development of guiding questions that meet state standards, locating primary and secondary source documents, and the large amount of time it takes to complete them. Nevertheless, teachers who have used inquiry-based lessons have nothing but praise for the strategy. Most report that their students loved it, participated, and were actively engaged in their lessons. They also saw positive student results on quizzes and tests.

COLLABORATIVE ACTIVITY: DEVELOP A MULTIPLE SOURCE BASED LESSON PLAN

With a partner:

- Choose one of the multiple source-based strategies introduced above (Jigsaw, Circle of Knowledge, Inquiry).
- Using one of your state's standards (see Table 2.1), develop a lesson plan based on the topic.
- Share this lesson plan with your classmates.

Expanding the Walls of the Classroom

Due to budget cuts, safety concerns, the standards-based focus of current educational policies, and in some cases, lack of parent involvement (especially at the middle school level), students spend a vast majority of their time confined to the school's grounds. However, students should be given the opportunity to explore the world around them, especially in social studies courses. With this in mind, this section offers ideas about how to expand the walls of the classroom and allow your students a chance to get out of their seats and experience true hands-on learning.

Three-Dimensional Learning—Measuring It Out

Often students find it helpful to see, in three dimensions, artifacts discussed in class. Rather than just look at a picture of a Mongolian yurt (Ger), for example, it is easy to find the dimensions of a standard yurt and have students, with the help of measuring sticks, outline a yurt in your classroom or other larger space. A discussion of what it might be like to live in this confined space can encourage students to consider how their lives would be different and similar if they were living on the Mongolian steppe. While you might not have the time, resources, or yurt-building expertise, providing opportunities to visualize this three-dimensional object may help them better understand it. Blending this concept together with visual primary sources can bring to life many of the concepts and objects that you cannot reasonably access.

Ben's students could often be found in the faculty parking lot measuring out various objects from US and World History and Geography. Though they did not actually have the materials to build the objects, drawing their outlines in sidewalk chalk helped students bring these objects from the abstract into the concrete (quite literally). In the fall, they measured out and formed the walls of George Washington's Ft. Necessity from the French and Indian War. In the winter, they measured out and are in awe of the size of Abraham Lincoln's boyhood home in Kentucky. In the spring, they measured out the dimensions of a World War I Curtiss Jenny. For comparison, they then measured the dimensions of a Saturn V rocket lying on its side. The resulting comparison was a stark example of how quickly technology has advanced in the past one hundred years.

Taking opportunities to measure out objects discussed in your class is worthy of time for many reasons. First, your students need the opportunity to move and interact with one another. Adolescents are often confined to their seats for hours a day and this approach is an opportunity to get them moving. Almost as important, it allows students to employ their spatial skills when visualizing the objects they are measuring out. After Ben's students measured out Columbus' ship Pinta, they discussed what it might have been like to be confined to such a small vessel for such a long time. Students described boredom, sea sickness, and annoyance with their classmates as they visualized the ship. The conversations lead Ben's classes to talk about technology of the time, diseases that were common, lifestyle, and even why sailors sing songs. Measuring out objects discussed in your class literally adds a dimension of learning that most students find interesting and deeply beneficial. To continually further the opportunities, Ben encouraged students to come up with other objects that could be measured in similar fashion. This approach built his repertoire of activities and empowered students to remain engaged as valued members of the class.

SIMULATIONS

Simulations are a great way to help students personalize social studies topics and help them gain a better sense of empathy concerning historical or present-day situations. Researchers such as Ronald VanSickle (1977, 1980, 1986) and William B. Russell III (2010) have long concluded that simulations are better for motivation and equal other methods for cognitive outcomes. While many simulations can be held in the classroom others can be taken outside into the hallways, playground, or a nearby athletic field. There are also many computer-based simulations and games that students can participate in (Ray & Coulter, 2010). No matter which medium is used, a simulation can be considered "leaving the traditional classroom" as students are out of their seats and moving around or at the very least taken out of the normal school day routine. It should be noted that some researchers have dismissed or even criticized the use of simulations as being ineffective and offering students an inaccurate portrayal of the topic being discussed (DeLeon, 2008). However, we see the strategy as beneficial in student learning and should be used in your classes. Indeed, no simulation is an exact replica of the topic or event and this itself provides a good discussion venue for the complexity of the real experience.

There are many examples of simulations that can be used in the social studies classroom. Many are used for history instruction, but there are several that can be used with geography, economics, political science, or any of the NCSS themes. Below are four examples of simulations that can be brought into your middle level social studies classes.

How History Is Written

One of Scott's favorite simulations that he used in his 8th grade social studies classes and continues to use with his college students is called "How History Is Written." He used this simulation when he transitioned between the focus on Georgia's geography to studying the state's history. This lesson was based on one that he observed a U.S. history teacher conducting, though he altered it greatly to make it more meaningful to his students. The purpose of the lesson is for students to gain a better understanding of how history is truly written and that there are many perspectives, ideas, and opinions that have been lost over time (Hodge & Roberts, 2011).

In his version of the lesson, before the simulation starts, he has three preselected students write a passage. One is a scathing critique of his class, one is a fairy tale or legend, and one is just a couple of paragraphs describing their day. The simulation begins with Scott asking his students to write about what they did that day. He tells them to include information about what they ate, what they wore, what they listened to, what they saw on the internet, current events along with their opinions about them, and any other information they wanted to include. He usually lets them write for about 10–20 minutes. After they finish their paragraphs, he tells a large majority of the class to tear up their papers. After the initial shock of having to destroy their documents, he explains to students that this is what happens to most historic documents; they are lost soon after they are written or created.

He then tells the remaining students to ball up their papers and pass them up to the front to simulate the damage that happens to many historical documents over time; he makes sure to separate the three preselected student papers ahead of time and place them to the side. Scott then tells students that it is now 30 years later and that he has finally retired from education. He places his paragraph into a plastic sleeve and tells the class that because of his important role as an educator and a student of history he has donated his personal effects to a local college's archives. He explains that this document will be saved for future generations. He then makes the point that in many cases the documents of "important" historical figures such as presidents, generals, statesmen, and civil rights leaders are placed in libraries. He also explains that well educated people such as college professors, historians, and writers send their materials to archives as well. He reminds students that, unfortunately, the documents of most regular people are not usually preserved or may be handed down from one family member to another but are not available for use or study by historians or sold to Pawn shops like on the show *Pawn Stars*.

He then tells the class that it is 100 years later, and a major flood has swept the area. He proceeds to take out a large bucket of water and select a few students to dunk several of the paragraphs. He reminds students that natural disasters like floods, fires, or earthquakes sometimes damage historical documents (Historical example: the Notre Dame fire in 2019).

In the next portion of the activity he explains that it has been 200 years and the country has been attacked by a foreign power. He calls up a few students to act like soldiers (some have even marched) and destroy several of the paragraphs. He then makes clear to his class that throughout history war has destroyed important documents (Historical example: Richmond & Atlanta during the Civil War).

Then Scott declares that it is 50 years later, and a dictator has taken over the country. He explains that this dictator wants complete power and censors anything that may be perceived as questioning authority or hostile to his government. He then explains to the students that this dictator uses schools as a venue to get his message out to youth. He then "discovers" the student's paragraph that critiqued his class. He reads the paragraph to the class (to the shock of many of his students) and destroys it (Historical example: Adolf Hitler, the Vichy French).

Finally, Scott says that it is now 40 years later and the dictator's reign is over and a few more paragraphs have been discovered and sent to various archives throughout the country. Unfortunately, there are some clumsy archivists out there. He then calls a few students up to the front to spill coffee on the remaining paragraphs.

Three paragraphs are left: Scott's, the fairy tale or legend, and the one remaining student paragraph. He explains to students that it is now 500 years later and that a historian is trying to write a book about what student life was like during our lifetimes. He reads his paragraph, the fairy tale, and the student paragraph. He asks students if they think that the fairy tale should be used in the historic record. He reminds them that there are many myths and legends in the historical record and tells students that historians must sort through them to decide if they had any value or not. He also reminds them that sometimes myths and legends (at least certain aspects of them) turn out to be true (Historical example: The city of Troy).

After students make their decision about whether they think that the fairy tale should be kept in the historical record, he writes on the board vast generalizations about the information found in the two remaining paragraphs. After writing he passes out discussion questions about the final paragraph. The questions include:

- What are some of the similarities and differences between your everyday life and the depiction of (year) on the board?

Teaching Middle Level Social Studies: Advanced Strategies and Methods • 109

- Do you think the final description of life in (year) is accurate? Why or why not?
- Think about both the man-made and natural disasters in this simulation. Can you think of any actual historical examples that may have damaged historic documents?
- Other than documents, what are some other ways that people learn about the past?
- Some of the events you have or will learn about in history are based on very few sources. For example, what we know about Hernando de Soto's travels through Georgia is based on a few Spanish diaries. Does this change the way you feel about these people and events you have learned about in school? Why or Why not?

Bringing Water to a Lesotho Village.

An example of a simulation that focuses on world geography and cultures is "Bringing water to a Lesotho village: A classroom simulation" (Ray, 2000). This four-to-five-day simulation sponsored by the U.S. Peace Corps offers students the opportunity to learn about how African communities acquire water and how community health is affected by the availability of water. Highlights of this simulation include students comparing Lesotho to their own community, being assigned different roles and collaboratively working together to determine the best way to bring water to their land-locked community and presenting their proposals to their classmates.

This simulation does not start immediately, as on the first day students have a chance to discuss questions about how communities acquire the water. They then complete a Venn diagram where they list the differences between obtaining water in rural and urban areas. Finally, they are asked to change the name of the rural side to "Lesotho" and the urban to their own community and are asked to conduct research about Lesotho for homework.

After gaining background knowledge, on the second day of the lesson students begin the simulation, which lasts four days. The simulation starts with the class being divided into groups of four. Each group member has a specific job. These include "Spokesperson," "Designer" "Researcher" and "Engineer" (Ray, 2000). Students then are required to collect and analyze information that will assist them in making a plan and design their village's water supply system.

On days three and four, students conclude their information collection and discussion and begin the design phase. They are given examples of water systems that are being used in other African countries. Students are then asked to discuss which example best meets the needs of their village and must come to a consensus about which option they should use.

On the fifth and final day of the simulation students are required to create models or drawings of their solutions for bringing water to the village. Each group is then asked to present their solution to the issue to those gathered in the "village center." After the presentations students then write down the strengths and weaknesses of each plan and what they would do to create a better one. Finally, students are asked a series of discussion questions where they determine if their plan is applicable to communities in the United States.

Separation of Peoples—The Invisible Box

When groups of people are separated from one another for long periods of time, they create different languages, economies, cultures, and even immunities to disease. As a sociological and historical process, isolation of peoples from one another is important to understand if we are to analyze why there are differences between groups.

Ben's students work to understand how thousands of years of separation influenced initial interactions and long term effects when studying the contact between Christopher Columbus and the Taino people of the Caribbean, The "Invisible Wall" simulation begins when students walked into class and the desks were placed on two sides of the room with a blue painter's tape line going down the middle. Ben informs students that the blue tape represents an impenetrable wall that cannot be broken, seen through, heard through, or in any way circumvented.

He then informs students that this wall extends to all six sides of their room and they are now in an impenetrable box from which there is no chance of escape. Air, water, food, and basic hygiene resources are provided but there is absolutely no contact with the world outside the box. They have access only to the resources on their side of the room, (in their box) and they work quickly to establish what resources might be useful.

Ben states that the students have been in the box for one hour. They are then directed to write down what might have happened in that hour. Students look around their side of the classroom to determine what their resources happen to be. One side cheers when it realizes it has a computer, but is brought back to reality when told that it does not have internet access. The other side is thrilled to have the thermostat, only to discover the heating unit is on the other side of the room. It will become apparent to each side that their histories are beginning to diverge as a result of different populations and different economic resources.

Ben then informs students that one month has gone by and repeats the writing process. As the amount of time increases, the two sides develop distinct rules and processes, ultimately leading to different cultures and histories. Ben ends the first day by informing students they have now been in their boxes for one year. Students begin to grow concerned that they might never be able to leave their box.

On the second day of the scenario, Ben informs students that they have been confined to their boxes for ten years. He reminds them to view themselves as 24-year olds and not the teenagers they were. As reality settles in, they begin to realize that they have other members of the clan in their box who know nothing of the world outside their environment. When the students realize their own children are with them, the scenario goes from interesting to fascinating, (and a bit awkward).

Students are provided time at each stage to write their thoughts down regarding government, language, culture, and daily life.

As the scenario progresses and the time frame grows from 10 years to 75, students learn that their generation, the last to know of the world outside the box, grows old and passes away. Before they do, these primary sources to the outside world work desperately to convey the nuances of life outside the box but ultimately fail to provide a comprehensive picture. The second generation must find its own way with the resources available in their world.

Hundreds, then thousands, of years go by and each generation has worked to refine its understanding of the box. From their perspectives, the box may not even exist as it is such an assumed part of their world. After thousands of years, the box is their world.

One day, without warning, a crack in the wall appears and an individual from one side crosses over. Each side is tasked with creating questions to ask one another as they work to learn of the other side. The result is a list of questions about technology, culture, language, and resources.

The box clearly serves as an analogy to the meeting of worlds that happens whenever two previously unknown peoples meet one another. Students are then prompted to explain what the tape on the floor represented (oceans or other geographic barrier), what resources they had on their side, (economic and geographic differences), and how their cultures, languages, and even religions developed differently. As the scenario concludes, students demonstrate visible relief that they are no longer confined to their box and they rejoice at learning that there is a larger world outside their box. A discussion of the human need for exploration and learning often takes place. Ultimately, this scenario encourages students to see from the first person how geography, resources, and culture blend together to define a people's way of life.

Three Branches of Government

The final example of a classroom simulation is a simple lesson based on the three branches of government. This simulation titled "Three Branches of Government" offers students the opportunity to visualize the process of creating laws within the U.S. Congress (Ashcroft & Pettit, 2011). While the lesson is written for 5th graders it can be useful for any middle grades students learning about any level of government.

This lesson, which is broken up into nine steps, begins with students being divided into committees that are responsible for creating laws for their classroom and school. Each committee is then given the task of writing a bill, selecting a speaker, and presenting their bill to the class (a template is provided to the students). Then the whole class has the opportunity to vote on the bill. If the majority of the class agrees then it is given to the president (the teacher) to sign or veto the law. Once the lesson is complete the students fill out graphic organizers describing the different roles of each branch of government during the law-making process.

FIELD TRIPS AND VIRTUAL FIELD TRIPS

Traditionally, field trips have been a major part of children's social studies experiences. Most of us can remember field trips we went on as middle level students. Growing up in Metro Atlanta, Scott will never forget his 4th grade field trip to the Cyclorama (a large painting depicting the Battle of Atlanta), followed by lunch at a landmark drive-in called The Varsity. Ben's childhood in central Illinois naturally led to trips to the Abraham Lincoln landmarks, including the recreated 1850s village in New Salem and Lincoln's home and gravesite in Springfield. Unfortunately, it has been suggested that due to the focus on standardized testing and standards based learning, along with a poor economy and increasing legal liability issues, field trips are being phased out in many public schools (Cassady et al., 2008; Coughlin, 2010). This is a shame, as researchers have determined that field trips can help students learn the basics about historical research, develop chronological understanding, work with and understand primary sources, increase content retention, and develop an overall appreciation of history and historic sites (e.g., Cassady et al., 2008; Coughlin, 2010; Farmer et al., 2006).

It should be noted that field trips ought to be selected based on meeting the content standards and should not be viewed as a way to get out of school for the day. However, as a teacher you are doing your students a disservice if you do not at least attempt to take them on a field trip to a museum, historic site, history center, or university somewhere in the vicinity of your school. If you have a difficult time receiving permission from your administration to take an entire team of students on a field trip, you may want to consider starting or sponsoring a social studies club at your school, with a field trip being the culminating event of the year. Additionally, many museums and historic centers have topic specific artifact boxes that they loan out to schools.

Another option for a field trip is to take one that is "virtual." (Petersen et al., 2020) Virtual field trips are web-based and conducted via the Internet. With a virtual field trip, students can tour a historic home, view museum exhibits, or talk to students from different countries without ever leaving the classroom or spending a dime. Two articles written in 2010, offer the reader several excellent websites that offer virtual field trips. These are "The Beginners Guide to Interactive Virtual Fieldtrips" (Zanetis, 2010) which is geared toward a general audience, and the social studies specific "Using Online Field Trips and Tours in Social Studies" (Risinger, 2010). It should also be noted that many museums, history centers, and state and federal parks offer virtual tours, so you may want to explore their websites on your own to find one that meets your specific curriculum standards.

As with any activity, students should understand why they are going on either the real or virtual field trip. Therefore, before loading the bus or logging on to the computer, you should explain to your students why they are going on the trip and what they should learn from it (you may also want to remind them about appropriate and inappropriate behavior and consequences that will occur if they make poor decisions). This is where a tool such as a KWL chart can be effective, since you should have already taught the students something about the topic that is the purpose for the trip, the students can easily show you what they have already learned in your class and how the trip expanded their knowledge about it.

"Around the School" Field Trips

If you are not able to leave school property for field trips, (and even if you are), your school environments provide countless opportunities to exemplify concepts discussed in your classroom (Wellenreiter, 2018). "Field Trips" around the school provide students the opportunity to see concepts in action, to see how these concepts apply outside your classroom, to get out of their seats, and to better appreciate their school building itself.

Discussing concepts such as taxation or life safety conditions during the Progressive Era, then seeing current conditions in their own school encourages stu-

- **Field Trip 1: The Progressive Era—Seeing Its Influence in Our School Today.** The Triangle Shirtwaist factory fire was the catalyst for changes in the role the government played in protecting citizens. As we go on our field trip, look for examples of building codes and safety features/devices that reflect how the government works to protect its citizens. When we return to the classroom, you will be asked to explain how the examples you find relate to issues raised during the Progressive Era.
- **Field Trip 2: The Preamble—Finding Examples of Promoting the General Welfare.** One of the duties of government is to "…promote the general welfare" (Preamble to the Constitution). Similarly, the 14th Amendment works to ensure all members of the community have equal access to public facilities. As we go on our field trip, look for examples of devices, building features, and grounds planning that assist individuals who have limited mobility. When we return to the classroom, you will be asked to explain how the examples you find relate to issues related to Promoting the General Welfare.
- **Field Trip 3: The First Amendment in Our School**—The First Amendment guarantees freedom of expression. As we go on our field trip, look for examples of expression and the free exchange of ideas. When we return to class, you will be asked to explain how the examples you find relate to the First Amendment.
- **Field Trip 4: The Five themes of Geography**— Human/Environment interaction is one of the major themes of geographical study. As we go on our field trip, look for examples of positive and negative interactions between people and their environment. Additionally, look for architecture designs and grounds designs that are a result of the climate/environment of central Illinois. When we return to class, you will be asked to explain how the examples you find relate to Human/Environment Interaction.

FIGURE 4.10. Around the School Field Trip Prompts Adapted from: Wellenreiter B. R. (2018)

dents to be more aware of how the past influences their present. You can begin with a discussion of the concept, then provide students the opportunity to observe examples of the concept. A discussion of Title IX, the gender equity legislation, can continue in the hallways as students compare trophies and plaques earned by boys' and girls' sports teams; a study of the Americans with Disabilities Act can be enhanced with students looking at sloping sidewalks, handicap accessible water fountains, and parking spaces; and discussion of fire code and the Progressive Era can be reinforced with a tour of the school, looking to see how the building is designed with safety in mind. Figure 4.10 has a few examples of the many ways your school building and grounds can be integrated into your curriculum.

Individual Activity: Simulations and Field Trips

Analyze your state standards (see Table 2.1). In your reflective journal note the following:

- Which standards lend themselves to the use of simulations?
- Which standards lend themselves to field trips?
- In an Internet search locate historical sites and museums in your state to which you could take your students.
- Note if any of these sites offer virtual exhibits.

SUMMARY

This chapter offers ideas about how to use more complex teaching strategies in the middle level social studies classroom. Even though they can be considered more advanced, there is no reason why these strategies cannot be incorporated into your middle level social studies lessons right away. Though these strategies are a bit more difficult, take a little more time to plan, and use more class time, they have been proven again and again by researchers and classroom teachers to be effective in promoting student content learning. Working beyond the traditional views of social studies, we believe these approaches add rich dimensions to the social studies classroom. Incorporating higher level thinking skills that are one of the major objectives of social studies education, these strategies are worth the planning and classroom time devoted to them. In the next chapter, we will discuss how to use all of the strategies provided in Chapters 3 and 4 to develop full middle school social studies lessons and units.

COLLABORATIVE ACTIVITY: REFLECTING ON THE CHAPTER

Review the strategies provided in this chapter and answer the questions below in your reflective journal. Share with a classmate.

- Which strategies did you like the best? Why?

- Which strategies do you think would be the most difficult to use with middle level students? Why do you think this is the case?
- What ways can you adapt the strategies to match your ideal teaching style?
- Which strategies are you going to use immediately? How will you go about doing this?

Website Resources

- **Atlanta History.com** (http://atlhistory.com) is a website devoted to the history of the city of Atlanta. Though the site is primarily for a local audience, information on the site such as Sherman's March and Martin Luther King, Jr. may be useful to U.S. history teachers.
- **Blabberize** (www.blabberize.com) is a web-based program that allows students to upload images and record a script that goes along with it. The site allows students the ability to create a "moving mouth" effect where the person or object in the picture can "talk" about themselves.
- **Central Pacific Railroad Photographic History Museum** (http://cprr.org/) offers teachers outstanding images of life on the railroad from the 1840s to the late 20th century. The site includes several on-line exhibits, a page about Chinese-Americans contributions to the railroad, and a page devoted to railroad maps.
- **Gilder Lehrman Institute of American History** (http://www.gilderlehrman.org/) is a nonprofit organization supporting the study and love of American history through a wide range of programs and resources for students, teachers, scholars, and history enthusiasts throughout the nation. Their website offers teachers access to a wide variety of historical documents, curriculum modules, podcasts, online exhibitions, and an online journal providing teachers with lesson plans.
- **Illinois Historical Digitalization Projects** (https://digital.lib.niu.edu/illinois/lincoln)This website, managed by the Northern Illinois University Libraries, offers a variety of resources for teachers in Illinois and throughout the country. Some of the highlights include the Abraham Lincoln Historical Digitization Project page, The Teaching Future Historians U.S. History Lesson Plans page, Using Primary Documents page, and the American Archives: Documents of the American Revolution page.
- **Library of Congress** (http://www.loc.gov/index.html) offers teachers a wide variety of primary sources to use with their students including prints and photographs, historic newspapers, performing arts, sound recordings, films, maps, and manuscripts. Features such as "Today in History," "Places in the News," and a teacher's resources page are also included.
- **National Archives** (http://www.archives.gov/) offers teachers a wide variety of resources and includes lesson plans and activities, information about using primary sources, and state and regional resources. Opportunities for professional development are offered as well.

- **National History Education Clearing House** (http://teachinghistory.org/) offers K–12 teachers access to primary and secondary sources. The website offers a page of "quick links" to help middle grades U.S. history teachers locate resources and lesson plans.
- **National Gallery of Art Classroom** (http://www.nga.gov/content/ngaweb/education/teachers.html) offers free images to classroom teachers. The page devoted to 19th century America in art and literature offers great primary images of this time period.
- **National Council for the Social Studies** (https://www.socialstudies.org/) The NCSS provides "leadership, service, and support for all social studies educators. Founded in 1921, National Council for the Social Studies has grown to be the largest association in the country devoted solely to social studies education. NCSS engages and supports educators in strengthening and advocating social studies." The NCSS website offers teachers access to the 10 NCSS themes for teaching social studies, information about their annual conference, lesson plans and resources, and position statements.
- **NCSS Notable Social Studies Trade Books for Young People** (https://www.socialstudies.org/notable-social-studies-trade-books) The page listed is the link to their list of notable trade books from 2000–present. The list of the prior years' books is available only to members of the organization.
- **New Georgia Encyclopedia** (http://www.georgiaencyclopedia.org/nge/Home.jsp) is the "first state encyclopedia to be conceived and designed exclusively for publication on the Internet." Though focused on the state of Georgia, the webpage has interesting articles about national events and leaders, written by well-known historians that can be used as a source in any classroom throughout the country.
- **PBS: Africans in America** (http://www.pbs.org/wgbh/aia/home.html) is a website that chronicles "America's journey through slavery" and is presented in four parts. For each era, there is "a historical Narrative, a Resource Bank of images, documents, stories, biographies, and commentaries, and a Teacher's Guide for using the content of the Website and television series in U.S. history courses."
- **Rethinking Social Studies Education** (http://rethinkingsocialstudieseducation.blogspot.com/) is a blog created by professors at the University of Victoria that offers reviews, suggestions, and critiques about recent social studies publications. The reviews do a great job of offering teachers ways to incorporate the topics into their classrooms.
- **Smithsonian Institution** (http://www.si.edu/) "seeks to bring content experts and educators together to help strengthen American education and enhance our nation's ability to compete globally. The Smithsonian serves as a laboratory to create models and methods of innovative informal education and link them to the formal education system." The website offers teachers access to lesson plans developed to align with state standards and

access to a variety of resources from many museums including the Air and Space, American History, and the Portrait Gallery.
- **Stanford History Education Group** (http://sheg.stanford.edu/?q=node/45) This group's Reading Like a Historian curriculum "engages students in historical inquiry. Each lesson revolves around a central historical question and features sets of primary documents modified for groups of students with diverse reading skills and abilities." Their website offers teachers over 75 free inquiry-based U.S. history based lesson plans.
- **Teacher Link** (https://teacherlinkusu.weebly.com/) is a website maintained by Utah State University that provides "free teacher resources such as TeacherLINK's Treasures for Teachers, units, lesson plans, worksheets, multimedia files, etc. Many of these are produced by students in the College of Education and Human Services at Utah State University."
- **TeacherTube** (https://www.teachertube.com/) is a venue for airing instructional and educational videos. Filtered for appropriateness and content, we still recommend these videos be viewed by the teacher before showing them in class.
- **Teaching American History** (https://teachingamericanhistory.org/our-purpose/ is a project of Ashbrook Center at Ashland University. The website offers curriculum, teaching resources, and online resources that can be used by teachers throughout the country.
- **Uchronia** (http://www.uchronia.net/) is a website maintained by Robert B. Schmunk that offers a biography of "3,100 novels, stories, essays and other printed material involving the "what ifs" of history." These types of stories can be used as guides in counterfactual inquiry lessons.
- **U.S. Flag.org** (https://www.chamberofcommerce.org/usflag/) is a website maintained by Duane Streufert that offers information about the history of United States flags including a historical debate about the Betsy Ross legend.
- **U.S. History.org** (http://www.ushistory.org/) is a website created and hosted by the Independence Hall Association in Philadelphia, Pennsylvania. The website offers free online textbooks and pages devoted to Benjamin Franklin, The Declaration of Independence, and the Liberty Bell. The site also includes a "Congress of Websites" with links to over 50 additional American history websites.
- **U.S. Peace Corps** (https://www.peacecorps.gov/) provides educator resources, with a focus on primary source narratives, from people around the world.

REFERENCES

Ambrose, A. (2011). *Atlanta.* http://www.georgiaencyclopedia.org/nge/Article.jsp?id=h-2207&sug=y

Ashcroft, K., & Pettit, L. (2011). *Three branches of government.* http://teacherlink.ed.usu.edu/tlresources/units/byrnes-s2000/Ashcroft %26 Pettit/lesson plan.html

Auchmutey, J. (2007, December 23). Map of mystery. *The Atlanta Journal Constitution.*

Barlowe, A. (2004). *Teaching American history: An inquiry approach.* Teachers College Press.

Bickford, J. H., & Clabough, J. (2020). Civic action, historical agency, and grassroots advocacy Historical inquiry into Freedom Summer. *The Social Studies, 111*(1), 39–49.

Bower, B., Lobdell, J., & Owens, S. (2005). *Bring learning alive: The TCI approach for middle and high school social studies.* Teachers' Curriculum Institute.

Brainy Quotes. (2021). *John Dewey quotes.* https://www.brainyquote.com/quotes/john_dewey_154051

Brophy, J., & VanSledright, B. (1997). *Teaching and learning history in elementary schools.* Teachers College Press.

Cafarella, L. (October, 2011). *Boosting content though vocabulary and reading.* Paper presented at the Georgia Council for the Social Studies Annual Conference, Athens, GA.

Cassady, J. C., Kozlowski, A. G., & Kommann, M. A. (2008). Electronic field trips as interactive learning events: Promoting student learning at a distance. *The Journal of Interactive Research, 19*(3), 439–454.

Coughlin, P. K. (2010). Making field trips count: Collaborating for meaningful experiences. *The Social Studies, 100,* 200–210.

DeLeon, A. P. (2008). Are we stimulating the status quo? Ideology and social studies simulations. *Theory and Research in Social Education, 36*(3), 256–277.

Dewey, J. (1902). *The child and the curriculum.* University of Chicago Press.

Dewey, J. (1933). *How we think* (rev. ed.). D.C. Heath.

Dewey, J. (1938). *Experience in education.* Touchstone.

Farmer, J., Knapp, D., & Benton, G. M. (2006). The effect of primary sources and field trip experiences on the knowledge retention of multicultural content. *Multicultural Education, 14*(3), 27–31.

Foster, S. J., Hoge, J. D., & Rosch, R. H. (1999). Thinking aloud about history: Children's and adolescent's responses to historical photographs. *Theory and Research in Social Education, 27*(2), 179–214.

Fuhler, C. J. (1992). The integration of trade books into the social studies curriculum. *Middle School Journal, 24*(2), 63–66.

Hodge, C. M., & Roberts, S. L. (2011). *Time travel through Georgia: Teachers edition.* Wesmar.

Howlett, C. F. (2007). Guardian of the past: Using drama to assess learning in American history. *Social Education, 71*(6), 304–207, 331.

Kobrin, D. (1996). *Beyond the textbook: Teaching history and using documents and primary sources.* Heinemann.

Lawrence, S. S., Langan, E., & Maurer, J. (2019). Using primary sources in content areas to increase disciplinary instruction. *The Language and Literacy Spectrum, 29*(1), 1–18.

Levstik, L. S., & Barton, K. C. (2005). *Doing history: Investigation with children in elementary and middle schools* (3rd ed.). Lawrence Erlbaum.

Lindquist, D. H. (2007). "Denmark 1943:" Using music to teach Holocaust rescue. *Social Education, 71*(6), 316–321.

London, B. (2005). *Georgia and the American experience*. Clairmont Press.

National Gallery of Art. (2021). *George Inness: The Lackawanna Valley, c. 1856*. https://www.nga.gov/collection/art-object-page.30776.html

Nicholson, S. (2017). *Thrifty teacher's guide to creative learning centers*. Gryphon House Inc.

Ogle, D., Klemp, R., & McBride, B. (2007). *Building literacy in social studies: Strategies for improving comprehension and critical thinking*. ASCD.

Oxford Reference. (2021). *Albert Einstein 1879–1955*. https://www.oxfordreference.com/view/10.1093/acref/9780191843730.001.0001/q-oro-ed5-00003988

Petersen, G. B., Klingenberg, S., Mayer, R. F., & Makransky, G. (2020). The virtual field trip: Investigating how to optimize immersive virtual learning in climate change education. *British Journal of Educational Technology, 51*(6), 2099–2115.

Ray, B., & Coulter, G. A. (2010). Perceptions of the value of digital mini-games: Implications for middle school classrooms. *Journal of Digital Learning in Teacher Education, 26*(3), 92–100.

Ray, D. M. (2000). *Bringing water to a Lesotho village: A classroom simulation*. http://files.eric.ed.gov/fulltext/ED456084.pdf

Richgels, J. D., Tomlinson, C. M., & Tunnell, M. (1993). Comparison of elementary students' history textbooks and trade books. *Journal of Educational Research, 86*(3), 161–171.

Risinger, C. F. (2010). Using online fieldtrips and tours in social studies. *Social Education, 74*(3), 137–138.

Roberts, S. L. (2009). *Georgia economic history: Lessons for implementing the GPS at grade 8*. Georgia Council on Economic Education.

Roberts, S. L. (2011). Using counterfactual history to enhance students' historical understanding. *The Social Studies, 102*(3), 117–123.

Roberts, S. L. (2013). Let freedom ring: Using the "circle of knowledge" strategy to examine American Symbols. *Social Studies and the Young Learner, 25*(4), 23–26.

Russell, W. B. (2010). The Berlin Wall: A simulation for the social studies classroom. *Social Education, 74*(3), 152–154.

Sandweiss, M. A. (2021). *John Gast, American progress, 1872*. https://picturinghistory.gc.cuny.edu/john-gast-american-progress-1872/

Silver, H. F., Strong, R. W., & Perini, M. J. (2007). *The strategic teacher: Selected the right research-based strategy for every lesson*. ASCD.

Stanford History Education Group. (2011). *Reading like a historian*. http://sheg.stanford.edu/?q=node/45

Vacca, R. T., & Vacca, J. L. (2005). *Content area reading: Literacy and learning across the curriculum, 8/e*. Allen and Bacon.

VanSickle, R. L. (1977). Decision making in simulation games. *Theory and Research in Social Education, 5*, 425–454.

VanSickle, R. L. (1980). Instructional simulation of economic processes. *Peabody Journal of Education, 57*(3), 172–182.

VanSickle, R. L. (1986). A quantitative review of research on instructional simulation gaming: A twenty year perspective. *Theory and Research in Social Education, 14*(3), 245–264.

VCU Libraries. (2020). *"Brother, can you spare a dime"—1932*. https://socialwelfare.library.vcu.edu/eras/great-depression/brother-can-you-spare-a-dime-1932/

Wellenreiter, B. R. (2018). Within these halls: In situ primary sources in your own school. *Middle Level Learning, 61*, 18–22.

Wellenreiter, B. R., Henning, M. B., & Lucey, T. A. (2020). On the other side, it did not say nothin': Patriotic art, music, and the promotion of economic loyalty. *Oregon Journal of the Social Studies, 8*(1), 91–104.

Wellenreiter, B. R., & Noraian, M. C. (2020). Preservice teachers' perceptions of the "public displays of history" debate. *The Counselor: A Journal of the Social Studies, 81*(2), 1–53.

Westman, L. (2018, August 23). *Succeeding with differentiation.* https://www.edutopia.org/article/succeeding-differentiation

Wineburg, S. (2001). *Historical thinking and other unnatural acts: Charting the future of teaching the past.* Temple University Press.

Wineburg, S., & Martin, D. (2009). Tampering with history: Adapting primary sources for struggling readers. *Social Education, 73*(5), 212–216.

Winnick, K. B. (1996). *Mr. Lincoln's whiskers.* Boyds Mills Press.

Yell, M. W. (2012). Engaging students in world history with a bog body mystery. *Social Education, 76*(1), 17–22.

Zanetis, J. (2010). The beginner's guide to interactive virtual fieldtrips. *Learning and Leading with Technology, 37*(6), 20–23

CHAPTER 5

PLANNING MIDDLE LEVEL SOCIAL STUDIES LESSONS AND UNITS

The greatest sign for success as a teacher…is to be able to say, "the children are working as if I did not exist."
—*Maria Montessori (Language Magazine, 2020)*

Tell me and I forget. Teach me and I remember. Involve me and I learn.
—*Benjamin Franklin (Brainy Quote, n.d.)*

Activity List
- Reflecting on Creating Social Studies Units.
- Why Do We Have to Create Formal Units and Lessons?
- Using State Standards.
- Intelligences and Learning Styles.
- Chapter Review: Create a Lesson.

COLLABORATIVE ACTIVITY: CREATING SOCIAL STUDIES UNITS

In your reflective journal:

- List what you think are the key components to lesson and unit planning for middle level social studies students. These could include, for example, incorporating standards, setting time frames, and finding resources.
- After reviewing your list, think about and write the challenges that you may face in developing each of the components.
- With a partner discuss these challenges and determine approaches you can use to remedy these issues.

Introduction

In the last two chapters we discussed both basic and advanced strategies for teaching middle level social studies. Now the challenge becomes how to take these strategies, along with several others, to develop cohesive lesson and unit plans (units are simply a series of lesson plans combined to present a certain topic or concept usually based on state standards). In this chapter we will first examine the importance of creating formal lesson and unit plans. Second, we will determine how the 10 NCSS themes and C3 framework should be used as the basis for your unit planning. We will then examine state standards and how they can be used as a guide in creating units and lessons. Finally, we provide ideas about how to create unit and lesson plans that will meet the educational needs of every child in your class.

The Importance of Formal Lesson and Unit Planning

Though important to employ as a general rule, most teachers dislike creating formal lesson plans (Cameron, 2006; Singer, 2003). In turn, some schools do not require that their teachers, especially those who are veterans, create or provide formal written plans and units of study (Singer, 2003). Until the end of his classroom career Scott was one of these teachers and often told his coworkers that, "I come up with my best lessons on the drive over here." It was not until he started publishing lessons and using them in his classroom that he realized the value of well thought out written plans. In his first years of teaching, Ben would write elaborate lesson plans that followed the format he learned as a preservice teacher. Through the years, he realized that going through this process forced him to internalize the process of systematically planning activities for students. Like any skill, writing effective lesson plans takes a great amount of time in the beginning, but becomes more efficient and more effective with practice. The continuing result can be well thought out and well rationalized classroom activities. Writing out unit and lesson plans helps the teacher as well as students understand the direction the lessons are heading and ensures that objectives and goals are met.

Additionally, thorough, well-written lesson plans build confidence with parents, administrators, and colleagues that everything taking place in a classroom is intentional and serves greater purpose. Indeed, we argue that well-articulated lesson plans strengthen the education profession generally.

There are many reasons why all teachers, especially those in their first year, should create formal lesson and unit plans. First, formal written unit plans help you map out your lesson ideas and allow you to have a detailed document showing you what the unit will look like (Chapin, 2011; Singer, 2003). Second, while great lesson ideas may come to mind at any time, having them written down in an organized manner allows you to flesh out your plans and will make your ideas even better to enhance student learning (Johnson, 2010; Singer, 2003). Going through the process can work to stimulate alternate ideas and find potential flaws in your planning. Third, writing lessons and units allows you to save them for future years and offers you the chance to add to and make changes to these lessons based on student performance. Fourth, taking the time to write formal lesson plans and units provides you with the opportunity to find quality primary and secondary sources along with other tools and strategies to use in your classes (Chapin, 2011; Johnson, 2010). As we discuss later, it also allows you to plan ways to incorporate the 10 NCSS themes along with the state and local standards. In addition, creating written lessons and unit plans allows you to consider the individual needs of your students and determine which strategies best meet them.

Finally, following a unit plan ensures that you are using your time effectively and teaching the standards that truly need to be taught. Many units in social studies can cover a lot of information. It is important to use a unit plan to pace the unit appropriately. For example, Karrie teaches the US Civil War to fourth grade students. Since the Civil War encompasses so much, it would be easy for her to spend an entire semester on just the Civil War. However, since she must cover United States History from the Revolution to Reconstruction, it is not practical to spend more than six to eight weeks on the war. This is why it is imperative she utilizes effective lesson planning and a unit plan.

Class Activity: Why Do We Have to Create Formal Units and Lessons?

Imagine that you have just been selected by your principal to serve as the social studies chair for your school. One of the tasks your principal has designated for you is to make your teachers create and share formal lesson plans on your school's webpage. Think about the arguments that your coworkers may have against creating these lessons. Then, using the prior section as well as your own ideas, write down counter arguments to help your teachers understand why lesson planning is important. Discuss these ideas with your classmates.

•••

Incorporating the 10 NCSS Themes Into Your Lessons

In Chapter 2 we discussed the 10 NCSS themes for teaching social studies. Once again, these themes are:

- Theme 1: Culture
- Theme 2: Time, Continuity, and Change
- Theme 3: People, Places, and Environment
- Theme 4: Individual Development and Identity
- Theme 5: Individuals, Groups, and Institutions
- Theme 6: Power, Authority, and Governance
- Theme 7: Production, Distribution, and Consumption
- Theme 8: Science, Technology, and Society
- Theme 9: Global Connections
- Theme 10: Civic Ideas and Practices. (NCSS, 2010)

Some of these themes can and should be incorporated into any given social studies unit. For example, when studying a historical topic such as the Civil War, you should point out other social science disciplines such as geography, government, economics, and technological innovation that were major factors in the decisions of key historical figures. For a unit on this topic, Themes 3, 6 and 10 can be easily incorporated. One lesson could focus on geographical differences between the North and South and how they led to the cultural differences between the two regions. Another lesson could focus on the governmental decisions that were made which led to the war. Finally, a third lesson could focus on how technological and economic factors played a role in the war strategies used by both sides.

Using State and Local Standards

Due to the emphasis on standardized testing stemming from recent education initiatives and legislation, many states have developed state standards for most of their subjects, and social studies, being a core area, is no exception. In Scott's home state of Michigan, the state's Department of Education has social studies standards for all grade levels K-12. In turn, some local districts have their own standards that add to the content found in the state's standards. Karrie's district in Georgia has added their own standards to the state standards to include things that are missing from the standards but curriculum coordinators feel are vitally important. For instance, students in 5th grade are required to learn the states and capitals in Karrie's district.

In Washington, where Jessica and Stephanie teach, along with state standards a mandated Indigenous curriculum entitled *Since Time Immemorial: Tribal Sovereignty in Washington State* has been created. Indigenous curriculums such as this one are needed because research within the field of social studies has repeatedly demonstrated that settler colonial narratives and Indigenous erasures are abundant within the curriculum and standards (Calderón, 2014; Journell, 2009; Keenan, 2019; Sabzalian, 2019; Shear, 2015; Shear et al., 2015; Rogers Stanton, 2014). Recognizing this problem, the NCSS (2018) states that "social studies education has a responsibility to oppose colonialism and systemic racism that impact Indigenous Peoples" (p. 167). Other states such as New Mexico, Oregon, Montana, Alaska and Wisconsin have also created and mandated Indigenous curriculums.

State standards, especially those in social studies education, have been a source of great controversy for politicians, historians, and educators (see the examination of the Texas standards controversy in Chapter 2). In turn, classroom teachers, who are assigned to teach these standards, often feel that the state standards limit their ability to teach what they want and that standards take time away from teaching important topics, current events, or take advantage of teachable moments (Gagnon, 2003; Levinson, 2011; Percy & Duplass, 2011). Teachers often find themselves focused on covering the standards through worksheets or lectures and not creating units that incorporate strategies and methods that provide students with an in-depth examination of the topics being studied (Percy & Duplass, 2011). We whole-heartily disagree with these approaches to state standards and believe that they can and should be the guide to thoughtful and complex lessons that incorporate the 10 NCSS themes and other core purposes of social studies education, such as providing students opportunities to develop higher order thinking skills and building decision-making and problem-solving skills. The C3 framework, discussed throughout the book, also encourages teachers to develop lesson plans based on the four dimensions of the inquiry arc that will help students meet these purposes as well (NCSS, 2013).

At first glance the list of standards you will be assigned to teach may appear daunting. For example, in the 8th Grade Georgia Studies standards, students are required to learn about 63 individuals and groups, five wars, eight battles, five historical documents, 16 acts of legislation and amendments, and three Supreme Court cases. There are also one geography standard, six government standards, and three economics standards that include various topics and vocabulary (Georgia Department of Education, 2020). It should be noted that the state's standardized test for this subject, administered in mid to late April, is based completely on the standards. Therefore, to help guarantee his students' success on the Georgia Milestones assessment, Scott chose to use these standards as a guide in his lesson planning. His goal was to be sure that he taught all the standards in a meaningful way while allowing his students to explore and critique the topics and themes of social studies. Finally, it is vital to remember that a lesson can certainly approach more than one standard at a time. Creative planning and emphasis on interdisciplinary approaches encourage both teachers and students to see that more than one concept may be learned at a time. Keeping this in mind can help make the list of standards less daunting.

"Digging Wells"

Just like many educators, over his career Scott discovered that there were two ways to teach the required state standards (Percy & Duplass, 2011). The first is to spend very little time on each standard and hope that you cover them all by the time the standardized test is given. This approach is sometimes called teaching "an inch deep and a mile wide." However, Scott decided it was much better to select specific standards and go into more detail about them. Scott called this the "digging wells" approach. In this way, Scott chose the topics that he thought to be either the most important for his students to learn or that offered the best opportunities to incorporate the 10 NCSS themes of social studies. This is not to say that he did not teach all the state standards. He just had to decide which ones he was going to go into more depth about and which ones that he would use strategies (both traditional and non-traditional approaches) to quickly present. As you develop your lesson and unit plans there are several ways that you can decide which standards to spend more time on and which ones to briefly examine. Below are some tips for making these decisions.

Analyze the Wording of the Standard

The first approach you should take when deciding which standards to focus on and which can be briefly examined is to analyze the wording of the standards. How a standard is written offers clues to teachers about the potential number of questions, as well as the cognitive level of the questions, that may appear on state tests. For example, in Georgia's 7th grade World Studies Course, a standard concerning Africa states "locate on a world and regional political and physical map: the Sahara, Sahel, savannah, tropical rainforest, Congo River, Niger River, Nile River, Lake Victoria, Great Rift Valley, Mt. Kilimanjaro, Atlas Mountains, and Kalahari Desert." (Georgia Department of Education, 2020).

This standard is simply one that is based on rote memorization. One could assume that if the state standardized test had questions on this standard, they would simply require labeling a map. Students can practice for this standard by taking part in an activity where they label these locations on a map. This could be used as a warm-up activity in the first five minutes of class or a small exercise as part of a larger unit about Africa. We would also include this labeling exercise on quizzes and chapter tests and review it again in preparation for the standardized test.

Another example of a Georgia standard concerning Africa uses more complex language and has greater expectations for students. This standard says, "explain how water pollution and the unequal distribution of water impacts irrigation, trade, industry, and drinking water" (Georgia Department of Education, 2020). This standard requires more time because it requires that students have a complex understanding of water usage patterns and problems across Africa. Even on a multiple-choice question assessment, the questions used to assess this standard will require more than rote memorization. Students will need to use a greater depth of knowledge to understand and explain this concept. When creating a lesson based on this standard, a teacher can incorporate and discuss several of the NCSS themes and have students analyze multiple sources, debate the reasons behind the unequal distribution of water in Africa, and describe what can be done to improve the situation. An excellent example of a lesson that could be incorporated into this unit plan is Ray's (2000) "Bringing water to a Lesotho village: A classroom simulation" discussed in Chapter 4.

Karrie also likes to incorporate the book, *A Long Walk to Water* by Linda Sue Park when teaching about the water problems in Africa. Students love hearing the true story of Salva Dut and how he is giving back to Africa through his company, *Water for South Sudan*. After reading and discussing the novel, Karrie assigns her students a project that requires them to research one of the water issues plaguing Africa and develop ways the problem could be lessened or eliminated.

Examine Standards from Prior Grade Levels

Another approach in using standards to plan lessons and units is to examine those from prior grade levels. If students have learned about similar topics before, you can spend less time on those topics and more time on standards with which they are less familiar. For instance, out of the 63 individuals and groups students are required to learn about in the Georgia Studies course, 18 are historical figures that they've learned about in at least one prior grade level.

In order to determine what students remember from past grade levels, you can assess their prior knowledge using a KWL or Predicting ABC chart. If students demonstrate a good understanding of the topic, you can focus on standards less familiar to them. Often, if students have not learned about the topic in a prior grade level, then you will need to spend more time developing student-centered lessons to help them master the material. It is important to keep in mind that many of your students may come from outside your school district, state, or country and thus, their background knowledge may be significantly different than their classmates.

Know Your State

Another approach to determine which standards to spend more time on in your lesson planning is to know your state. Often, any topic that has a direct connection to your state will appear on your standardized tests, no matter if its state history, U.S. history, or world geography. There are several examples of this in the 4th, 5th, and 8th grade history courses in Georgia. For instance, one of the more influential cities in Georgia is Savannah. Based on the city's prominence in colonial history, Scott guessed that there would be several questions about this time period on the standardized test, so he made sure he focused on this topic in more detail during the year. Scott assumed the same to be true about other topics including Sherman's March through Georgia, the Civil Rights Movement, and even Georgia's "capitals of the world" such as Dalton, (the carpet capital) and Gainesville (the poultry capital). Karrie did the same thing in 4th grade. When teaching about the Civil War, she put more emphasis on battle sites in Georgia and how the war affected the state. In Michigan, the Great Lakes, The War of 1812, and Henry Ford are important topics that teachers should spend more time discussing in their classes. Similarly, the prairie biome, Abraham Lincoln, Ronald Reagan, and agriculture are important topics of study for students in Illinois.

Make Educated Guesses

No matter how many strategies you use, it is difficult to truly prepare lesson and unit plans solely for an end-of-the-year state-mandated exam. Standardized tests typically offer only a limited number of questions. It is easy to see that every standard will not have a question on the test. Sometimes you must simply make an educated guess about what topics will be covered. How to do this was alluded to in the "analyzing the wording of the standard" and "understanding your state" sections. There are other ways to make educated guesses about which standards may appear on the test and which should be the focus in your lesson and unit planning. For instance, look at the number of subsections or "indicators of achievement" attached to each standard and use your content knowledge to choose topics that you think will be more important (for example, spending more time on the Civil War than the War of 1812 in Georgia, and vice versa in Michigan or Illinois).

Find Commonalities and Connections in Standards

Another approach is to use strategies that help students find commonalities and connections between several standards. One way to go about pinpointing commonalities with your students is a categorized word wall that can be used to help students make these connections. Periodically discussing such connections on your word wall is an easy way to achieve this goal.

One strategy to use is called "concept attainment" (Ogle et al., 2007; Silver et al., 2007). For this type of exercise students are given two images about individuals, events, vocabulary, etc., and are asked to determine if the two images have a connection or not. Then students write the word "yes" or "no" on a handout of the slides. After going through each of the image pairs, students are then asked to write in a few sentences about why they think there is a connection or not. For example, if you were to show images of Christopher Columbus and Martin Luther King Jr. your students could write either yes or no. In their explanation one student may support his or her "yes" answer because both historic figures have a holiday in their honor. Another student may say no because Columbus enslaved a group of people, while MLK fought for civil rights. This type of activity will help students find the similarities and differences between several topics and thus help them be better prepared for standardized tests. With concept attainment, there is no right or wrong answer so long as students can support their answer with sound reasoning and evidence.

Go Beyond the Standard

The most important concept to remember about using standards to write lesson and unit plans is to consider how you can use specific standards as a centerpiece to incorporate important social studies themes and skills. For instance, in a unit plan about the Revolutionary War, Scott created one lesson plan focusing on what he considered to be a relatively unimportant standard that students were required to learn and took it to a different level that incorporated some of the overarching goals of social studies education.

The standard concerned Nancy Hart, a Revolutionary War hero, whose exploits during the war moved the Georgia Legislature to name a county in her honor. Her most famous action was single-handedly capturing and eventually executing several British loyalists who invaded her remote cabin in the Georgia frontier. This standard requires students to know that Nancy Hart is the only woman from Georgia with a county named after her. While this fact could have been taught to his students by simply telling them to write it down during a lecture, Scott felt that this standard offered more elements that should be discussed in greater detail.

Scott developed this idea from simply examining several sources about Nancy Hart. In each story there were several different details about what happened on that fateful day. Some of the discrepancies included a different number of loyalists who barged into her cabin, the manner in which she captured them, the number that she shot or hanged, and whether she gave the loyalists that she captured a fair trial or not. Based on these differences, Scott created a lesson that gave students an opportunity to analyze multiple sources, use the sources to develop their own version of the story, and to discuss how they could use what they learned from the lesson regarding the use of multiple sources in their everyday lives (Hodge & Roberts, 2011). Scott has taken this inquiry-based approach and has developed articles and lesson plans using this same concept concerning the topics of Civil War films (e.g., Roberts, 2014; Roberts et al., 2014).

Later Scott added a discussion element to this lesson asking students if they think it is fair that only one woman has a county named after her and if they could think of any other women that they had learned about in Georgia history that might also have deserved this honor. If students believed that there should be another county named after a woman, they had to find the county's name that they would change and offer arguments as to why they believed that the original honoree should have his name removed (Roberts, 2013). Scott has since changed this topic to focus on important women in the states of Michigan and Iowa (Roberts & Block, 2019, 2020).

This lesson took at least a full period. Due to the length of time it took, his coworkers often asked Scott why he chose to take so much time covering only one indicator in a Revolutionary War unit. Scott explained that, for one, students learned about the Revolutionary War in the 4th grade and already knew some of the more traditional information in the standards. He also told them that his students would not have a problem recalling Nancy Hart on the standardized test. Scott concluded by explaining that more importantly the multiple skills and worthwhile discussions that students had about the Hart justified the extra attention given to this standard as well as the purpose of teaching social studies: citizenship skills. Essentially, standards should be neither the ultimate beginning nor the ultimate end of your classroom activities. They serve to inform, but they are not capable of directing how you interpret them. In this case, Scott's growth of the concept embedded in the standard took the students to new levels of understanding even though the standard stayed the same.

Individual Activity: Using State Standards

Using Table 2.1, locate your state's standards for two or three middle level social studies courses:

- Read through the standards and determine which would be ideal for the approaches listed above.
- Select one of the standards and describe in your reflective journal the strategies you will use to teach it.

Teaching All Students

When creating lesson and unit plans you must keep in mind that students have different ways of learning. As discussed in other chapters, you should incorporate as many strategies and methods into your plans as possible. Taking the time to create formal written lesson plans will offer you the opportunity to do this. However, it will be difficult to create lesson and unit plans without knowing some of the different theories about how students learn. In the following section we examine some of these theories in more detail and show how you can use them to create lesson and unit plans that cater to a classroom based on differentiated instruction.

Gardner's Theory of Multiple Intelligences

In 1983, Howard Gardner introduced his theory of multiple intelligences. Simply put, he states that there are eight "intelligences" that people may have (see Figure 5.1). Though we use many of these intelligences simultaneously, everyone has a dominant intelligence that allows him or her to be successful at various activities. While Gardner's (1983) theory of multiple intelligences has many critics, many in the field of education view it as a valuable guide for lesson planning and pedagogical development.

Knowing your students' intelligence types can help your lesson planning. Talented, professional educators plan lessons and units that appeal to all types of learners rather than relying on strategies that favor just one form of intelligence. There are several free tests that you can give your students to help both you and them determine their own intelligences. One example of a free multiple intelligence test can be found on the VeryWell Mind website, available in the Website resources section at the end of this chapter. It is called, "What Kind of Intelligence Do You Have."

1. **Bodily-Kinesthetic Intelligence**—having control over bodily motions and movements along with the ability to work with objects skillfully. Students with this type of intelligence learn best in classes where there is physical movement and that incorporate "hands-on' activities.
2. **Interpersonal Intelligence**—having the ability to understand and respond appropriately to the moods and motivations of other people. Students with this type of intelligence learn best in classes where they are allowed to work with others and participate in discussions or debates.
3. **Intrapersonal Intelligence**—having the ability to self-reflect and understand one's own strengths and weaknesses and how to use them productively. Students with this type of intelligence learn best in classes where there are opportunities to work alone and are provided time for reflection about the topic being learned.
4. **Linguistic Intelligence**—having the ability to work with words and language. Students with this type of intelligence learn best in classes where there are opportunities to read, write, and take notes. They enjoy lecture but also the opportunity to talk and discuss what they have learned.
5. **Logical-Mathematical Intelligence**—having the ability to work with numbers or logical sequences and exercises. Students with this type of intelligence learn best in classes where they have the chance to look for patterns, use the scientific method, and perform calculations.
6. **Musical Intelligence**—having the ability to produce rhythms and identify pitch along with being able to express ideas in a musical form. Students with this type of intelligence learn best in classes where they are given the opportunity to incorporate song and that have an auditory focus.
7. **Naturalistic Intelligence**—having the ability to understand, classify, and work with living things and in their natural surroundings. Students with this type of intelligence learn best in classes where they are given the opportunity to take field trips, work outside, and organize and classify objects.
8. **Spatial Intelligence**—having the ability to visualize and understand the visual-spatial world. Students with this type of intelligence learn best in classes where they are given the opportunity to create artistic projects and solve puzzles.

*It should be noted that these definitions and examples are about children who have a preponderance of one type of intelligence or a preference for one type. Also, it should be understood this theory as critics and detractors.

FIGURE 5.1. Gardner's Multiple Intelligences

Learning Styles

The concept of learning styles is based on Gardner's (1983) theory of multiple intelligences along with work conducted by Dunn and Dunn (1978), Fleming and Baume (2006), Fleming (2011), and Sternberg (1996). Fleming (2011), with his VARK model, has simplified the theory of multiple intelligences by arguing that there are three major types of learning styles. These are visual, auditory, and kinesthetic or tactile. Visual students learn best by using graphic organizers, viewing visual images, and receiving both visual and written instructions. Auditory students learn best by hearing and listening. This group of learners responds well to lecture-based courses and should also be given opportunities to verbalize information out loud. Sometimes you will hear auditory learners reading instructions to themselves; this is not only okay for them to do but should be allowed even during tests. Kinesthetic/tactile students learn best by touching and doing. These learners respond well to inquiry based, hands-on lessons. Simulations also work well with these students.

Employing concepts from Gardner's (1983) theory of multiple intelligences, there are several free inventories your students can take in order to find out their learning styles (Cherry 2017; Pennsylvania Higher Education Assistance Agency, 2019). Knowing how your students learn best will help you plan your lessons and units. Some of these can be found on the Education Planner webpage "Self-Assessments."

Differentiated Instruction

Thinking about how to teach a group of students with several different intelligences and learning styles presents a daunting mountain to climb. However, one of the easiest ways to meet the learning needs of all students is to create lessons based on differentiated instruction. Kirchner and Inman (2005) define differentiated instruction as "designing and implementing curriculum, teaching strategies, and assessment to meet the needs, interest, and abilities of all students" (p. 10). Parsons et al. (2018) stated that adapting instruction is "a cornerstone of effective instruction" (p. 206) and "considered the gold standard teachers should strive for" (p. 206). However, it is not an easy task. There are several authors and researchers who have written guides about how to use differentiated instruction in the classroom, with the most prominent being Carol Ann Tomlinson (2001).

There are several strategies you can use when creating a lesson or unit plan to meet the needs of a diverse classroom. Many of the basic and advanced strategies that were discussed in Chapters 3 and 4 including the think-pair-share strategies for your interpersonal and auditory learners, Venn diagrams for your intrapersonal, naturalist, and visual learners, and simulations for your kinesthetic learners. Other ideas that you could include in an integrated social studies unit include writing poetry or songs, creating statues, paintings, or diagrams, making a commercial or radio interview, or creating and analyzing surveys. The center approach discussed in Chapter 4 is another example of differentiation.

Individual Activity: Intelligences and Learning Styles

Take the intelligences and learning styles inventories listed above and answer the following questions in your reflective journal:

- What is your dominant intelligence and learning style?

- How do you think it will impact your teaching style and lesson planning?
- Now that you know your learning style, what approaches can you use to ensure that you will teach to meet the needs of all of your students?

SUMMARY

Though not always required by schools or school districts, writing formal lesson and unit plans is an important practice you should consider. Writing plans in a formal manner allows you to map out your units, make sure you use a variety of teaching strategies, develop good ideas into great ones, and save lessons in order to make changes based on student performance. More importantly, formal, written lesson and unit planning allows you to find multiple resources and incorporate many different strategies into your lessons.

When creating formal unit and lesson plans you can base your lessons around the 10 NCSS themes, the C3 framework, as well as your state and local standards. Standards can and should be used as guides in the development of units and lesson plans. When incorporating standards in your lessons, you should keep in mind that you can go deeper into the standard as opposed to simply covering it. Additionally, in order to choose which standards you should focus on more in a unit, analyze the wording of the standard, examine standards from prior grade levels, know the history, culture, and political preferences of your state, and make educated guesses about which topics may be discussed on your state's standardized test. The most important approach that you can take when using standards to guide your unit and lesson planning is to find those you deem to be the most applicable for incorporating the themes and skills advocated by social studies experts.

Finally, when developing lesson and unit plans you should consider the different intelligences and learning styles of your students. Though a daunting challenge, one of the best ways to meet the needs of all students is to incorporate differentiated instruction in your planning (see Figure 5.2). Many of the strategies discussed in previous chapters provide ideas of ways to include differentiation in your lesson and unit planning.

Use the lesson plan template (Figure 5.3) to create a formal written lesson about a social studies topic.

- First choose the grade level, state standard (see Table 2.1), NCSS theme and one of the approaches your plan to use for incorporating state standards in your lesson planning. This will help you to determine the scope of your lesson.
- Complete each box (instructions are in italics).
- Using the Web Resources links in the book find materials to use in the lesson.

•••

1. Know and use your state or local standards as the basis for your unit.
2. Identify the most important/least important standards.
3. Determine a realistic number of days it will take to discuss the most important topics in detail while touching on the least important.
4. Identify and incorporate elements of the 10 NCSS themes that correlate with the standards and topics.
5. Know the student learning styles and intelligences of each class period you teach.
6. Use a variety of strategies and sources in your lessons that meet these learning styles (do not exclusively use any).
7. Include opportunities to discuss how the information may be assessed on a standardized test.

FIGURE 5.2. Tips for Developing an Outstanding Social Studies Unit Individual Activity: Chapter Review-Create a Lesson

Lesson Name:		
Create a lesson title that encompasses the topic of the lesson.		
Grade	Subject	Topic
Unit Name		Estimated Time Needed for Lesson
State Standard	Description	
Standard Number	Detailed description of each standard you are discussing.	
NCSS Theme	Description	
Theme Number	Detailed description of each NCSS theme you are incorporating.	
Handouts/Materials/ Textbook Pages/Web Links		

FIGURE 5.3. Lesson Plan Template (Note: This lesson plan template was developed based on our examination of a variety of sources including: Docstock.com; Gwinnett County Public Schools, Lesson Plan Depot.com; Lesson Plan Template.net; Roberts, 2009; Roberts, 2018, and Teacher Planet.com)

Planning Middle Level Social Studies Lessons and Units • **135**

List all of the materials that you will be using in the lesson. List pages in textbooks and online links.

Guiding Questions
What will be the focus of the lesson?

Lesson Objectives
What should students know or understand at the completion of the unit or lesson?

Vocabulary
List all of the important vocabulary words (important people, places, and events) that students will need to know at the conclusion of the lesson.

Assessment Strategies
Describe the assessments that will be used during the unit.

Required Background Knowledge for Students (Optional)
What background information will students need to have to be successful the lesson's activities.

Teaching Strategies

Describe all the teaching strategies that you will be using in this lesson. In the squares calculate the percentage of the lesson that the strategy will take. For example in an hour lesson, lecture should take no more than 25% (15 minutes) of the lesson

(continues)

Sparking Strategy/Warm-Up

Sparking Strategy (Lesson introduction)

Lesson Procedures

In a numerical list provide a step-by-step outline of what you plan to do in the lesson. Include questions you will ask the students and materials you will use.

Differentiation

Think about your students' skill levels, intelligences, and learning styles. How are you going to make this lesson meet the needs of all of your students?

Scaffolds:

ELL Interventions:

Extensions/Interventions:

Summarizing Strategies/Synthesizing Activity

What strategies are you going to use to allow students to summarize what they learned in the lesson?

Additional Information (Optional)

Any other ideas that will be beneficial to students or other teachers.

Citations (as needed)

FIGURE 5.3. Continued

WEBSITE RESOURCES

- **Edutopia** (http://www.edutopia.org/) is an educational foundation funded by George Lucas. According to their website their mission is "We are dedicated to transforming kindergarten through 12th-grade (K–12) education so all students can thrive in their studies, careers, and adult lives. We are focused on practices and programs that help students acquire and effectively apply the knowledge, attitudes, skills and beliefs to achieve their full potential."
- **Education Planner** (http://www.educationplanner.org/students/self-assessments/learning-styles-quiz.shtml) is a website that offers readers with inventories that allow users to learn their own learning strengths and styles.
- **Very WellMind** (https://www.verywellmind.com/what-kind-of-intelligence-do-you-have-3867398) is a website that offers readers with inventories that allow users to learn their own learning strengths and styles.

REFERENCES

Brainy Quote. (n.d.). *Ben Franklin quotes.* https://www.brainyquote.com/quotes/benjamin_franklin_383997

Calderon, D. (2014). Speaking back to manifest destinies: A land education-based approach to critical curriculum inquiry. *Environmental Education Research, 20*(1), 24–36.

Cameron, L. (2006). Picture this: My lesson. How LAMS is being used with pre-service teachers to develop effective classroom activities. In R. Phillip, A. Voerman, & J. Dalziel (Eds.), *Proceedings of the First LAMS Conference 2006: Designing the Future of Learning* (pp. 25–34). LAMS Foundation. http://lamsfoundation.org/lams2006/papers.htm

Chapin, J. R. (2011). *A practical guide to middle and secondary social studies: Third edition.* Allyn and Bacon.

Cherry, K. (2017). *What kind of intelligence do you have?* https://www.verywellmind.com/what-kind-of-intelligence-do-you-have-3867398

Dunn, R., & Dunn, K. (1978). *Teaching students through their individual learning styles: A practical approach.* Reston Publishing Company.

Fleming, N. (2011). *VARK: A guide to learning styles.* https://vark-learn.com/

Fleming, N., & Baume, D. (2006). Learning styles again: VARKing up the right tree! *Educational Developments, 7*(4), 4–7.

Gagnon, P. (2003). *Educating democracy: State standards to ensure a civic core.* The Albert Shanker Institute.

Gardner, H. (1983). *Multiple intelligences: Theory into practice.* Basic Books.

Georgia Department of Education. (2020). *Grade 8 social studies Georgia standards of excellence.* https://www.georgiastandards.org/Georgia-Standards/Pages/Social-Studies-Grade-8.aspx

Hodge, C. M., & Roberts, S. L. (2011). *Time travel through Georgia: Teachers edition.* Wesmar.

Johnson, A. P. (2010). *Making connections in elementary and middle school social studies* (2nd ed.). Sage.

Journell, W. (2009). An incomplete history: Representation of American Indians in state social studies standards. *Journal of American Indian Education, 48*(2), 18–32.

Keenan, H. B. (2019). Visiting Chutchui: The making of a colonial counterstory on an elementary school field trip. *Theory & Research in Social Education, 47*(1), 52–75.

Kirchner, J., & Inman, T. (2005). Differentiation tips for teachers: Practical strategies for the classroom. *The Challenge, 14*, 10–11.

Language Magazine. (2020). *Last writes.* https://www.languagemagazine.com/last-writes-11/

Levinson, M. (2011). Democracy, accountability, and education. *Theory and Research in Education, 9*(2), 125–144.

National Council for the Social Studies. (2010). *National curriculum standards for social studies.* Author. https://www.socialstudies.org/national-curriculum-standards-social-studies-chapter-2-themes-social-studies

National Council for the Social Studies. (2013). *Social studies for the next generation: Purposes, practices, and implications of the College, Career, and Civic Life (C3) Framework for social studies state standards.* NCSS.

National Council for the Social Studies. (2018). Toward responsibility: Social studies education that respects and affirms Indigenous peoples and nations. *Social Education, 82*(3), 167–173.

Ogle, D., Klemp, R., & McBride, B. (2007). *Building literacy in social studies: Strategies for improving comprehension and critical thinking.* ASCD.

Parsons, S. A., Vaughn, M., Scales, R. Q., Gallagher, M. A., Parsons, A. W., Davis, S. G., Pierczynski, M., & Allen, M. (2018). Teachers' instructional adaptations: A research synthesis. *Review of Educational Research, 88*(2), 205–242. doi:10.3102/0034654317743198

Pennsylvania Higher Education Assistance Agency. (2019). *What's your learning style: 20 questions.* http://www.educationplanner.org/students/self-assessments/learning-styles-quiz.shtml

Percy, M., & Duplass, J. A. (2011). Teaching history: Strategies for dealing with depth and breadth in the standards and accountability age. *The Social Studies, 102*(3), 110–116.

Ray, D. M. (2000). *Bringing water to a Lesotho village: A classroom simulation.* http://files.eric.ed.gov/fulltext/ED456084.pdf

Roberts, S. L. (2009). *Georgia economic history: Lessons for implementing the GPS at Grade 8.* Georgia Council on Economic Education.

Roberts, S. L. (2013). Women of action and county names: Mary Musgrove County-Why not? *Middle Level Learning, 48*, M12–M16.

Roberts, S. L. (2014). Effectively using social studies textbooks in historical inquiry. *Social Studies Research and Practice, 9*(1), 119–128.

Roberts, S. L., & Block, M. K. (2019). "Remember the ladies:" An inquiry-based approach for examining important women in your state's history. In J. Hubbard (Ed.), *Extending the ground of public confidence* (pp. 109–122). Information Age Publishing.

Roberts, S. L., & Block, M. K. (2020). Using "open" and "inquiry-focused" standards to study important women in Iowa's history. *The Iowa Journal for the Social Studies, 28*(2), 107–123.

Roberts, S. L., Elfer, C. J., & Fahey, B. (2014). *Hollywood or history: Little Round Top.* Lesson plan developed for the Ivey Center for the Cultural Approach to History-Columbus State University. http://culturalapproach.org/resources/resources-by-type/category/lesson-plans-and-supplemental-material

Rogers Stanton, C. (2014). The curricular Indian agent: Discursive colonization and Indigenous (dys) agency in US history textbooks. *Curriculum Inquiry*, *44*(5), 649–676.

Sabzalian, L. (2019). The tensions between Indigenous sovereignty and multicultural citizenship education: Toward an anticolonial approach to civic education. *Theory & Research in Social Education*, *47*(3), 311–346.

Shear, S. B. (2015). Cultural genocide masked as education. In P. T. Chandler (Ed.), *Doing race in social studies: Critical perspectives* (pp. 13–40). Information Age Publishing.

Shear, S. B., Knowles, R. T., Soden, G. J., & Castro, A. J. (2015). Manifesting destiny: Re/presentations of indigenous peoples in K–12 US history standards. *Theory & Research in Social Education*, *43*(1), 68–101.

Silver, H. F., Strong, R. W., & Perini, M. J. (2007). *The strategic teacher: Selected the right research-based strategy for every lesson.* ASCD

Singer, A. J. (2003). *Social studies for secondary schools: Teaching to learn, learning to teach* (2nd ed.). Lawrence Erlbaum Associates.

Sternberg, R. J. (1996). *Successful intelligence: How practical and creative intelligence determine success in life.* Plume.

Tomlinson, C. A. (2001). *How to differentiate instruction in mixed ability classrooms.* ASCD.

CHAPTER 6

ASSESSMENT: FORMAL AND INFORMAL

One thing I never want to see happen is schools that are just teaching the test because then you're not learning about the world, you're not learning about different cultures, you're not learning about science, you're not learning about math. All you're learning about is how to fill out a little bubble on an exam and little tricks that you need to do in order to take a test and that's not going to make education interesting.
—*President Barack Obama (Strauss, 2011)*

The educational process has no end beyond itself; it is its own end.
—*John Dewey (Ward, 2017)*

Activity List
- Reflecting on Assessment.
- The Importance of Formal Assessments.
- The Differences between Norm-Referenced and Criterion-Referenced Tests.
- Additional Tips for Preparing for Standardized Test.
- Document Based Questions.
- School and District Created Tests.
- Standards-Based Grading.
- Chapter Review: Create a Project.

COLLABORATIVE ACTIVITY: REFLECTING ON ASSESSMENT

Respond to the following questions and statements in your reflective journal and discuss your answers with a classmate:

- What is the purpose of assessment?
- Describe some positive assessment experiences you had as a student.
- Describe some negative assessment experiences you had as a student.
- What are some examples of the most authentic types of assessments?
- What are some examples of the least authentic types of assessments?
- What can you learn from students' scores on multiple-choice assessments?
- What can you determine from projects?

INTRODUCTION

If you were to write down 10 words characterizing your middle school experience, we are certain that at least one would deal with a form of assessment. Specifically, you probably would write tests, quizzes, or projects, and perhaps something about taking assessments such as "scantrons" or number two pencils. In any event, testing and school are almost synonymous and have been for many years. Today, with federal or state initiatives tying assessments to funding, testing can sometimes appear to be the only reason why students go to school.

Assessments are important. Used correctly, assessments, both informal and formal, are vital in evaluating the development of your students, what they are learning in your classes, and how you can improve your instruction to help them achieve at the highest levels. From the chapter test that may be the cause of your students being grounded by their parents due to a low test score, to the LSAT that may determine their entry into law school, whether we like them or not, assessments will affect our lives. Due to their importance, creating high quality assessments is an essential skill for social studies teachers to develop. We believe it is a responsibility of teachers to educate students and the general public about healthy, research-based uses for, and limitations of, assessments.

With that said, the question becomes "how do you develop worthwhile assessments that simultaneously serve as a formative tool, help prepare students for the state-mandated year-end tests, and are authentic enough to show you what they actually learned in your class?" While no single assessment will help you meet these goals, using a variety of formal and informal assessments will help you come as close as possible. As with differentiated instruction, differentiated assessment can assist each student in meeting her or his potential.

The Importance of Formal Assessments

Formal assessments are often thought of as tests that produce mathematical data such as percentages, standardized scores, or formal letter grades. Formal assessments are developed to measure what students have learned in a course.

Though these assessments have many critics (e.g., Johnson, 2010; Marzano, 2010; Wiggins, 1998) they can be useful in informing your instruction, when used properly. For example, if a majority of your students performed poorly on a particular topic it may be that the test questions were bad, but it may also mean that you need to go back and review how you taught the material because your students did not learn from your approach the first time. Either way, assessment encourages you to consider what takes place in your classroom, ultimately improving the student experience.

It needs to be made clear that your principal or district may measure your effectiveness as a teacher based on your students' scores on formal assessments. Though the specific number fluctuates because of changing federal guidelines (Close et al., 2020), many states require student test scores or indications of student growth in teacher evaluation tools. Right or wrong, it is up to you to make sure that you teach the state mandated standards to help your students do well on assessments. You should make it a point to teach your students how to take these tests. As mentioned in the introduction, formal assessments are going to be part of your students' lives for a long time. If they understand tricks of taking tests students will perform better on them. For example, one way to prepare students for taking a state-mandated standardized test is to use questions from older versions that have been released by the state. Going over these questions with your students helps them learn how test questions are written and what information to keep in mind as they take these tests.

COLLABORATIVE ACTIVITY: THE IMPORTANCE OF FORMAL ASSESSMENTS

In addition to the reasons listed above, what are some other reasons that formal assessments are important to your students? Discuss your answers with a partner.

Types of Formal Assessments

For a test to be considered formal there is usually a process that typically involves panels of teachers or testing experts writing, critiquing, and trying out batteries of test items written to assess specific curriculum standards. This means that teacher generated tests and quizzes are not truly formal assessments. State mandated formal assessments usually come in two forms, Norm- Referenced and Criterion-Referenced. This section will provide you with more information about these types of tests and how they are being used in schools.

State Mandated Standardized Tests

Beginning with the No Child Left Behind Act of 2001 (US Department of Education, n.d.), the US Department of Education has had a series of initiatives requiring states to collect assessment data in order to receive much-needed funding. With positive-sounding names such as "Race to the Top" (IES-NCEE, n.d.), "Every Student Succeeds Act" (US Department of Education, n.d.), these initiatives include numerical data to determine student, school, and state education effectiveness (US Department of Education, 2017). We have little doubt that regardless of the name, the US Department of Education will—right or wrong—continue to include formal test scores as a foundational measure of success of schools. With this focus on standardized testing, it would be imprudent to simply inform you about the strengths and weaknesses of standardized tests and recommend that you ignore the "elephant in the room" until you begin preparing your students "two weeks before the standardized test occurs" (Johnson, 2010, p. 71).

Fair or not, you may well teach in a school system(s) where these tests may make or break you professionally. Teachers with higher test scores, or who have scores showing more improvement, may breathe a sigh of relief, and possibly be recognized or rewarded for their student performance. On the other hand, those who do not have high test scores or meet an improvement standard will, more than likely, be urged to take staff development courses or even be asked to resign (Stronge et al., 2006).

To some this may seem like a bleak and unfair system, while others see it as a way to reward better teachers and help ineffective teachers become better (Stronge et al., 2006). No matter your opinion, you will more than likely be working in this type of system. While many agree that associating student test scores with teacher performance has problems (Ballou & Springer, 2015) due to the importance placed on this concept by most school districts, it is more important for us to offer a detailed accounting of the two types of standardized tests. More critically, it is our responsibility to offer you some tips about how you can prepare your students for the state standardized tests while also incorporating the many themes and purposes for teaching social studies at the same time.

Norm-Referenced Tests

Over the course of your academic career you have doubtlessly taken several norm-referenced tests such as the Iowa Test of Basic Skills (ITBS) the Scholastic Aptitude Test (SAT) and the Graduate Record Examination (GRE). With these examples you can probably determine that the definition of a norm-referenced test is one that "describes student performance relative to a norm group" (Johnson, 2010, p. 68). This basically means that your performance is compared to the other groups who took the same test. If you rank in the 95% percentile (and we are certain all our readers do) then you have a score that is higher than 95% of the students in the norming groups.

If you teach grades 5 or 8 your students may take the ITBS, a norm-referenced standardized test that ranks your student's "performance to the average scores of [other] students of each grade level" (Johnson, 2010, pp. 68–69). If you have an 8th grade student scores at a 10.5 grade equivalency, it means they performed better on the test than a 10th grader with five months of schooling on that same test. It is important to note, however, that the score does not imply the student is ready for 10th grade work. Other factors must be accounted for, such as maturity and other characteristics not reflected in the score. In addition to grade equivalency, the ITBS provides a National Percentile Rank (NPR) that is an important score for some schools as they have used their percentile rank on the mathematics and reading portion of the test for the entire school as benchmarks.

Criterion-Referenced Tests

Unlike norm-referenced tests, criterion-referenced tests do not compare one student's score to another, but how an individual student performs on a given criterion (Johnson, 2010). Some state mandated tests such as the State of Texas Assessments of Academic Readiness (STARR) are criterion-referenced. It should be noted that these types of tests do not report their results in a 0–100 grade equivalency. For example, after all students take the test, testing administrators may examine the scores and determine that in order to meet the criteria students should answer 30 out of 60 correct. Therefore, if this was based on a percentage the student would have "failed" the test; however, since 50% was the cut off score any student who made at or above 50% would meet the standard. Students who perform a certain percentage over 50% such as at the 60% range may score in the "exceeds" category. However, neither the student nor the teacher will ever know how many questions it took to receive a 'meets' or 'exceeds' score as the percentage is scaled. Because of this, student scores on state criterion-referenced tests often do not measure up to nationally normed tests such as the National Assessment of Educational Progress (NAEP).

COLLABORATIVE ACTIVITY: THE DIFFERENCES BETWEEN NORM-REFERENCED AND CRITERION-REFERENCED TESTS

In an interactive journal answer the following questions and discuss your answers with a partner:

- Draw a T-chart listing the differences between a Norm-Referenced and Criterion-Referenced test.
- Explain which type of test you think offers the more authentic measure of student knowledge.

Tips for Preparing Students for State Standardized Tests

Determining the best way to help prepare your students for standardized tests is difficult. On one hand, virtually all teachers want their students to do well on these tests whether their own teaching performance is judged by these scores or not. On the other, you do not want to spend hours a day going over mock tests and test taking strategies. Nor do you want to feel the need to "cover" all the topics and revert to the sole use of ineffective teaching strategies such as lectures and worksheets.

It is important to talk with your students about the purpose(s) of standardized tests, their strengths, their weaknesses, the teachers' role and the students' role.

To be expected to both try hard while putting these tests into perspective, students need to be informed consumers and active participants in what takes place in your classroom. Discussing with students well in advance of the tests works to avoid student confusion or animosity toward the test on the day(s) it is given. Additionally, many states and school districts have laws and policies about students refusing or "opting out" of standardized tests (Marland et al., 2020). As with many other concerns, it is good practice to consult with your administrators. As with everything else we discussed in the book, the answer about how to prepare for these tests is to find the balance between competing interests or goals. The difficult part is figuring out this balance.

Figure 6.1 provides tips that you can use to help you achieve this equilibrium. These ideas were successful for Scott as his students consistently led his department in standardized test scores over his eight-year classroom teaching career. We would highly recommend that you try these as you begin preparing for mandated tests your students will take.

Class Activity: Additional Tips for Preparing for Standardized Tests

As a class research and discuss other ways that you can prepare students for taking standardized tests. Write your classmates' responses in your reflective journal.

- **Tip 1: Teach the Standards**. Fact: your students will be tested on the state mandated standards and not the topics that you think are important. If you use the standards as a guide and do not add additional people, places, and events to your instruction then your students should perform at a higher level.
- **Tip 2: Go Deep Into the Standards.** Just because you must teach the standards does not mean your students cannot learn important social studies themes and skills. Additionally, the deeper you go into a standard and the more interactive, higher order, and hands on activities you create for it, the more lower-level fact-based information your students will retain.
- **Tip 3: Examine Standards From Lower Grades/Give Pretests.** Go through the standards from lower grade levels and compare them to your own. If any of the same people, places, events, and concepts appear on your grade level's standards, give your students a pretest to find out how much they remember. If they remember the pertinent information, quickly review it and then move on to those standards that are new to your students.
- **Tip 4: Don't Teach Lessons That Are an Inch Deep and a Mile Wide.** With the large amount of material that teachers are asked to present or cover over a year, it is easy to spend a few minutes on a topic and then move on to something else without allowing students to work with the concept. This approach should be avoided as students need to apply these concepts in order to remember them.

FIGURE 6.1. Ten Tips for Preparing Students for State Mandated Tests

- **Tip 5: Don't Revert to Traditional Methods Such as Lecture and Worksheets.** When attempting to cover all the standards, especially toward the end of a nine week or semester period, teachers spend the last few days or weeks reverting to the sole use of traditional methods in order to teach the standards. While you may feel good about covering the standards by constantly lecturing, your students will more than likely not learn the material. Consider using more progressive methods like center work or concept attainment strategies in order to allow students to learn a large amount of material in a short amount of time.
- **Tip 6: Make Your Warm-Up Questions a Test Taking Skill Discussion.** Open each day's class with a quick multiple-choice warm-up question based on a topic recently covered or one that your students did not perform well on previously. Make sure you not only go over the right answer, but also let your students explain why they think it is the right answer. Also, have your students explain why the distractors are incorrect and try to point out some of the tricks that may be used to write the question or the distractors that may cause students to get it wrong.
- **Tip 7: Make Weekly Quizzes Test Preparation Sessions.** Using an approach like warm-up questions, your students will get more out of a quiz than just showing their content knowledge if you make them interactive sessions. A recommendation is to find questions that resemble the end of the year standardized test and use them frequently on the quizzes. Conduct quizzes using a whole group approach. This can be accomplished by displaying the questions, and having students answer them while you read them aloud at least two times. It is okay to summarize, define words, and offer other explanations of what the question is asking during the quiz. Often, students know the content but are thrown off by how the questions are written. After the quiz is complete, go over the correct answers with students and have them write or discuss why the distractors were incorrect, as well as the rationale behind why the correct answer was "right." If your school has them, use "student response clickers" instead of the traditional paper and pencil test. Not only do students get instant feedback about what they missed, the software used for the clickers will grade their quizzes for you. They also provide the percentages about how many students in your classes answer the question correctly.
- **Tip 8: Retest, Retest, Retest!** There is absolutely nothing wrong with retesting students or allowing them to make corrections and returning them to regain points (Dueck, 2011; Wormeli, 2011). Sometimes it takes students a few times before the concept "clicks." When students see a poor grade, they are often willing to go back and make corrections. In his classes, Scott made sure that not only did students change the correct answer, they had to write a two to three sentence summary about each question they missed, why they thought they missed it, and why their new answer was correct. Due to the amount of work it took for his students to complete the task (either at home or during center-based activities); he gave them full credit for anything they missed.

(continued)

> While some of Scott's coworkers and administration questioned this practice and sometimes called it "grade inflation," these approaches gave students the incentive to make the corrections and work with the material one more time. This proved to be effective in their standardized test scores.
> - **Tip 9: Make the Last Two Weeks Before the Test a Content Review.** Johnson (2010) argues that content reviews for standardized tests should take place two weeks before testing and that these reviews should be relatively short. While we agree with the two-week window, based on standardized tests' influence over your career and your students' promotion, the last two weeks before a standardized test should be devoted to an intense review. A poor approach to reviewing is to simply give study guides to students, tell them to complete it before the test, without reviewing the answers in class. Instead, multiple strategies should be used to review for the tests. Several of the strategies we have discussed work well for review, including games, center-based activities, concept attainment, and even showing movie clips to help students visualize the topics they may need to know.
> - **Tip 10: Have Students Use Several Small But Organized Notebooks.** Middle grades students learn a lot more in a given day, week, month, or year than just social studies. This information can be difficult to keep track of. It is even more difficult when students try to keep all of their completed work in one spiral notebook, or even one notebook per subject for the year. One of the easiest approaches Scott found for students to prepare for standardized tests was to make sure they kept four social studies notebooks (one per nine-week period). These spiral notebooks were based on the TCI (2010) "interactive notebook model" and held only the material that was given for the nine weeks. Any handouts that he provided were glued in the notebook during class. At the end of each nine weeks Scott took up the notebooks and kept them so students would not lose them before the end of the year. During their review days, he had students go back and look through their notebooks (one per day) and rate their favorite and least favorite activity of the nine weeks. Then his students were able to discuss which ones they liked the best/least in groups of three. While discussing the lessons, they were also reviewing the material amongst themselves. During this activity Scott often heard "oh yeah!" and "I remember that!" Students told Scott after the test that discussing what they learned for prior activities helped them perform better on the standardized test. They were also allowed to keep their notebooks and use them as study guides.

FIGURE 6.1. Continued

Teacher Created Formal Assessments

As mentioned above, formal assessments do not usually include teacher-generated tests. However, this does not mean that you cannot prepare your students to take formal assessments by creating teacher-made tests that closely resemble standardized tests. This can be a challenge because even though as teachers we have taken formal assessments for most of our lives, writing assessments that resemble formal ones is not easy.

When writing these types of assessments there are two important factors to take into consideration including making the test valid and authentic. A valid assessment is one that measures what it intends to measure (Johnson, 2010). Sometimes teachers inadvertently include questions on their self-made tests that were not covered in their lessons. For example, though a teacher may view it as reviewing prior material, a test about the Civil War that includes questions about the Revolutionary War may not be considered valid, as it does not test what the students learned for that specific unit. Also, questions that are written to be intentionally tricky may also cause the test to lose its validity (Salend, 2011). Trick questions by nature do not measure what is intended. Ben remembers a time in his own high school career when he was given a series of true/false questions. He was instructed to place an "F" in front of the true statements and a "T" in front of the false statements. Contrary to past practice, this switching of letters was intended to test direction-reading, not the material covered in the test.

An authentic test is one that can be considered to be worthwhile and authentic. Though multiple-choice tests are not often viewed as authentic, there are approaches to making your multiple-choice tests that way. These include incorporating primary source document analysis, skills-based questions, or writing questions based on Norman Webb's (2002) Depth of Knowledge strategies.

Creating Authentic Assessments

Norman Webb's (2002) work assigns levels of understanding students need to have in order to answer a test question. The four levels are: 1) Recall and reproduction; 2) Skills and concepts; 3) Strategic Thinking; and 4) Extended Thinking. Many states and school districts are using Webb's framework to improve their standardized tests. Webb (2002) explains that lower level skills, such as fact recall, considered to be "Level 1" questions, make your assessments less authentic. However, the higher the thought process and the more mental steps it takes to answer a question increases the level of authenticity (Hess, 2005; Webb, 2002). Most multiple-choice test questions are at Level 1, which asks for basic fact recall. For example, a test that asks, "What is the capital of the United States? (Washington D.C.) and one that asks, "What is the capital of Ukraine? (Kiev)" are basically asking the same question, though an American may think the first question is easier.

Level 2 questions are a bit more complex. These types of questions are based on skills such as compare and contrast, convert information, give examples, show cause and effect relationships, and classify or sort information. An example of a Level 2 question would be to explain the causes of the Revolutionary War and what effects the war had on England and the United States. Though difficult to write, these types of questions can be incorporated into a multiple-choice format.

For instance, charts and graphs attached to a multiple-choice question are often used.

Level 3 questions are even more complicated, both for the students to answer and for the teachers who are trying to write multiple-choice questions at this level. A Level 3 question is based on skills such as problem solving and making connections between topics. However, many standardized tests will include Level 3 questions, so it is important to develop them for your chapter and unit tests. A question about population migrations in U.S. history and the factors that led to and resulted from these migrations would be Level 3.

Level 4 questions require students to make connections across concepts and even across traditionally-defined subject areas. Employing deep problem-solving skills and merging concepts, students might, with supporting data, propose solutions to global warming that take into consideration economic, social, and political concepts.

Creating Chapter/Unit Tests

Due to the pressures imposed by mandated standardized tests, multiple-choice items usually dominate today's teacher generated chapter and unit tests. Traditionally, teacher-made tests also included fill-in-the-blank, matching, and true false items. They also often contained short answer and essay questions. The number of questions on a chapter or unit test usually ranges from 25 to 50, thus allowing the test to cover several topics or standards.

When writing test questions, teachers often base the number of items for each topic on how much time they spent teaching it. Teachers frequently find themselves spending more time presenting subjects that they are interested in and more quickly covering other topics. Due to this approach, some districts and schools have created curriculum calendars (also called pacing guides or curriculum maps) that provide teachers with information about what they should be teaching during a specific timeframe. These curriculum calendars are useful in the creation of unit tests as they help guide teachers in determining the number of questions that should be written about each topic.

Though there is no tried and true approach to writing test questions, there are some helpful ideas to keep in mind. In the case of multiple-choice questions, it is best to model them after those that may be found on a state's standardized test. There are many coach books that are written to help students prepare for these tests and many states release questions from older assessments. Also, Webb's (2002) Depth of Knowledge protocols should be used to help write test questions at different levels of understanding.

Another approach in writing test questions is to use document-based questions (often referred to as DBQs) that require students to analyze and interpret one or more primary or secondary source documents in order to answer a series of questions. The questions typically require higher order thinking that involves the application of concepts and skills. It has been suggested that many exams for all subjects under the nationwide Common Core Standards will be modeled on document-based questions. There are several sources to find information about writing these types of questions. For example, the DBQ Project (2011) is a commercial organization that has created a program using document-based activities, the Stanford History Education Group (2011) offers free DBQ lessons on their website, and Peter Pappas (2012) of Edteck offers several free examples of document based assessments for grades 4, 5, 6, and 8. Please refer to the Website Resources section at the end of this chapter for additional information on these great resources.

Class Activity: Document Based Assessments

Go to the Edteck website (found in the Website Resources section) and examine the Document Based Questions provided for grades 4, 5, 6, and 8. In your reflective journal:

- Rank the assessments in order from best to worst.
- Explain the rationale behind your rankings.
- As a class share each students' best and worst assessments and compare and contrast the answers and in your reflective journal answer the following question: What does this activity tell you about creating assessments?

In addition to curriculum guides and content maps many schools and districts use common assessments (tests) created by the district that all teachers are required to use, usually around the same time of the school year. There is some debate about the usefulness of these tests. On one hand they keep teachers on the same schedule and help students prepare for state-mandated standardized tests. However, they also deter teachers from focusing on specific topics in which their students may be more interested, and most certainly limit teachers' academic freedom. No matter how you feel about them, if you are a teacher in a school or district that uses common assessments then there is a possibility that you may never write your own chapter or unit tests.

Whether you, your school or your district writes the tests you use, you should consider them to be the diagnostic tools that they are meant to be. Though tests are not the only indicator of student success or your capabilities as a teacher, they do offer a gauge about how well your students might perform on a state mandated standardized test. If your students are doing well, or even average, on your tests then they will most likely perform at a high level on the state test (as many standardized tests are not as difficult as district or teacher created unit tests). If students are continuing to struggle on unit tests, then they may need extra help and review to perform well on those mandated by the state. Since students in many states need to pass specific standardized tests for promotion (in some cases including social studies) it is important that students are prepared for them.

COLLABORATIVE ACTIVITY: SCHOOL AND DISTRICT CREATED TESTS

In your reflective journal:

- Write about what you think are the strengths and weaknesses of using mandatory school-or district-generated tests.
- What is your opinion about having to use them in your classes?
- Share your ideas in a small group of three or four.

The Importance of Informal Assessments

Informal assessments are those that are used by teachers to gain insight into how well students understand the topic being explored. Sometimes these assessments may count as a grade, such as those based on completion of assignments or homework. Often, however, informal assessments are quick—but well-considered and systematic—checks of student understanding. The "informal" nature of these assessments refers to the recording and reporting of results, rather than the rigor or thoughtfulness of the assessment. Informal assessments are important because they provide you with constant information about what your students are learning as opposed to periodic snapshots offered by formal assessments. As a professional, you will find yourself constantly informally assessing student understanding through their verbal responses, their non-verbal gestures, even the look in their eye as they respond.

Types of Informal Assessments

Some informal assessments serve as venues for students to display an in-depth understanding of the material. These assessments, such as student projects or writing assignments, can offer other approaches in determining what they learned and understand about your class. As we discussed in the last chapter, students have different learning styles and intelligence types, so alternative assessments can also be used to help reach all students and allow them a chance for success (Marzano & Heflebower, 2011). Below are some examples of informal assessments.

Progress Checks

No matter how hands-on, fun, or interesting an assignment is, sometimes students still will not want to work or participate in the activity and will find ways to be off task. An informal assessment that you can use to keep this from happening is the daily progress check. A progress check is simply a tool to determine how far along a student is in a project or activity. Progress checks can be written down on a checklist or grading roster, or by simply walking around the class, examining the students' work and letting them know if they are on track. When Scott used a progress check he simply put a check or an "x" in his grade book to make sure that he knew who was heading in the right direction at that point of the assignment. Sometimes he used this information as a daily grade.

Daily Grades

Daily grades are informal assessments often used to determine if a student participated in class by finishing an assignment during a specific time period. Sometimes teachers use daily grades to assess a student's overall participation during a specific class period. Daily grades make up a percentage of students' overall grade, usually counting anywhere from 10–30%. As with progress checks, sometimes teachers use daily grades as a method of keeping their students on task. No matter how they are used, daily grades are a good way to keep students engaged and for you to judge if they have learned the material for that day. Scott never used letter grades for a daily grade, students who were doing their work or had the assignment completed earned a 100. If a student's work was partially complete or if they were sometimes on task, they received a 50. If they did not finish or were completely off task, then they received a zero. With the large number of daily grades Scott recorded during a semester a zero or 50 did not affect their average very much and for the most part, his students all received passing grades in this category.

Ticket Out the Door

A ticket out the door strategy, also known as "exit tickets," is a summary exercise that allows students to show you what they learned during the class as they walk out of the room. The ticket out the door can be a pre-generated handout or graphic organizer such as a 3-2-1 activity where students write down 3 things they learned, 2 things that they found to be interesting, and 1 question that they still have about the lesson. However, a ticket out the door can also be as simple as a three to five sentence summary about the topic studied in class and what they learned. No matter how they are used, they give students the chance to cement what was taught as they leave the class and offer you a quick snapshot of the concepts that they understood and what you may need to re-teach.

Student Led Informal Assessments

Students should also be given the opportunity to be involved in informal assessments. This can include using their own checklists to grade their work or their performance for that day. They can also be given the opportunity to anonymously evaluate their peers' projects or presentations, the participation shown by their group members in a collaborative activity, or even what they learned from your lesson that day by grading your performance and offering you feedback. Different than students formally grading the work of one another, feedback can be used by students to gain insight into their own work. It needs to be noted that in many states it is a violation of privacy laws to have students grade one another's work or to be informed of grades. Having students shout out their grades or the grades of classmates to expedite your record-keeping is not advised for this reason, in addition to the potential for embarrassment and angry phone calls or emails from parents.

Quizzes

Quizzes are often used by teachers to provide a snapshot of what their students have learned over a specific time period. They are usually short informal assessments that can include multiple-choice, true false, or fill in the blank responses, and make up a small percentage of students' course averages. Some teachers choose to separate their test and quiz grades, while others choose to combine them. It is important to note that quizzes, specifically pop quizzes, should not serve as forms of punishment if the teacher feels discipline is lacking or to "call students out" if you feel many of them are not completing work. Blending learning with discipline may encourage students to see education as a punishment. Ultimately you want your students to love the subject you hold so dearly, not feel fear and resentment toward it.

When Scott was teaching 8th graders, he attempted to give short weekly quizzes. Initially they consisted of 10 multiple-choice questions and two bonus questions. The questions were developed from coach books that were provided by his school. They contained questions that resembled those that may be found on standardized tests. His quizzes were usually created with PowerPoint®. In administering the quiz, he read each question aloud from the back of the room and gave students several minutes to answer each one. Reading from behind the students limited their ability to cheat or find ways to get into trouble, as they could not see where he was or who he was looking at. Scott chose to read the questions aloud in order to use the opportunity to discuss any vocabulary words that students did not understand and to help students think about approaches to use in trying to answer each question. He then allowed students to grade their own tests (making sure they used a marker or highlighter he provided to avoid cheating) and told them the correct answers and discussed the distracters in each question. These quizzes counted toward their quiz average at the end of the grading period.

These quizzes not only provided Scott with the opportunity to determine what students had learned during the week and what topics he had to re-teach, but also gave him the opportunity to go over test taking skills to help prepare students for the state-mandated test. Later, he realized that he needed to incorporate higher order thinking and writing skills into his weekly quizzes and added questions that asked students to compare and contrast, analyze documents, and summarize the material they learned that week. For example, a question might require students to write a persuasive or expository essay based on documents or images being displayed on the screen.

In summary, when developing quizzes, keep in mind that they should be only a few questions and based on the material covered over a short time period, usually a week. They should be used as a diagnostic tool of what students learned for that week and help you determine what material needs to be reviewed. They should have at least one question that involves higher order thinking. Finally, quizzes may be used to prepare students for the standardized test they will be required to take at the end of the school year.

Projects

For many "former adolescents," some of their fondest memories about school are the projects that they created. Projects have the potential to bring standards and the concepts therein to life in ways paper tests, quizzes, and homework cannot. From active volcanoes in science classes to scale replicas of the Great Pyramids in social studies, most of us can easily recall a favorite project we created in school. What we probably do not remember was that many of these projects were really a rubric based assessment used by our teachers to determine what we learned about a specific topic.

Though there are inherent weaknesses of assigning projects as assessments, such as the fact that they are time consuming, usually focus on one content standard and not several, and require homework and time outside of class, the benefits of using them certainly outweigh their drawbacks. One such benefit is that projects allow your artistic and creative students an opportunity to use their strengths. They also allow students who do not perform well on multiple-choice tests to have the chance to increase their averages and gain a sense of accomplishment. Finally, working on these intensive and in-depth projects can help students develop important skills while building greater interest in the topics being studied. All these benefits support the progressive ideas for teaching social studies that have been presented throughout the book.

All projects are not equal, and it is up to you to develop ones that students will find fun while incorporating the content knowledge and skills-based goals you have for them. When developing projects, we recommend creating detailed rubrics that explain to students what they must do in order to achieve their desired grade. Students can also be involved in creating the rubrics to be used (Marzano & Heflebower, 2011; Roberts, 2011). Additionally, you should try to offer your students as much choice as possible with the project to ensure buy-in and increase participation. When administering projects, Ben has found that the more latitude students are given for making the projects their own, the better the results and the deeper the learning. Finally, you need to make certain that your project has some elements of higher order thinking involved. Some questions to consider when developing projects are found in Figure 6.2.

Project Examples

Multiple times a year, Ben has his students complete a "Top Ten in History" project. In this activity, students are given a broad topic such as the Civil War,

> - What is the purpose of this project?
> - What content knowledge do I hope my students gain from completing this project?
> - How much class time will I allow for students to work on this project? How much time will be needed at home?
> - To what extent can parents help?
> - Will students be able to work in groups or individually? What do I do if I assign this project to a group and a student wants to work individually? What if a group complains that one person did not do his or her share of the work?
> - What if a student does not have the financial ability or technology at home to complete this project?
> - How much of a student's grade should this project be worth?
> - Will I allow late work? And if so, what penalties, if any, will I specify?

FIGURE 6.2. Questions for Developing Projects

the Industrial Revolution, or Immigration, and are required to select the top ten events, people, places, or concepts related to the topic. Students often select subtopics of interest to them such as the "Top Ten Songs during the Civil War" or "Top Ten Fashion Trends of Colonial America." Students create their lists, providing rationales for why the elements on the list belong there. For example, a group may put the discovery of gold at Sutter's Mill, California at number 8 in a Top Ten event in American expansion. They would then have to defend this event on the list as well as why it deserves the number 8 spot. Providing students with opportunities to select subtopics that are interesting to them produces better results and work to cover information and concepts that are often not found in traditional social studies courses. Requiring them to provide rationales for their decisions encourages them to think deeply about the topic and how it relates to others.

Karrie assigned her gifted students the task of teaching the class one of the standards in her seventh grade World Geography class. The project was open ended so students had the opportunity to develop a lesson and a student activity in the way they felt suited the information best. She met with students individually as they worked on the project to ensure they were on the right track. Then students presented their projects by taking over the class for one class period to teach their peers one of the required standards. Karrie became one of the students during their presentations. This was a popular project with the students who were presenting the lesson and the students doing the learning. They loved the opportunity to learn from someone new and had the added benefit of enjoying seeing their teacher as a peer.

As a Georgia Studies teacher Scott assigned four major projects a year, one for each nine-week period. Because the course was a truly integrated social studies class with standards focusing on history, geography, government, and economics, he made sure to have at least one project based on each of these disciplines. With each of these projects he attempted to not only cover the standards and incorporate higher order thinking skills, but also to allow students to have an opportunity for choice. Each of these projects was graded based on a rubric often co-created with students, and all counted as the equivalent of a test grade. While he would not be telling the truth if he claimed that all of his students turned in their projects (there will always be a few who do not) most of them enjoyed these assessments and consistently listed them as their favorite assignments for the school year. These projects, called the "create your own colony project," "historic figure statue project," "Georgia-based business project," and the "counterfactual history project" are described in more detail below.

Create Your Own Colony

The first of Scott's projects was an in-class and collaborative assignment called "create your own colony" (Hodge & Roberts, 2011). It was based on students' study of Georgia's colonial past, though it could also be used to study any state's origins, and served as an assessment of his students' knowledge of this era in Georgia history. While participating in the project students were required to study Georgia's colonial history and then develop a new English colony to be founded anywhere on Earth. Students then compared the geography, governance, and economics of their colony to that of Georgia.

To help guide students through the lesson the project was divided into four parts. Scott allowed students to work with partners to complete the activities and asked each student to have an equal share in the work. The assessment was developed to meet different learning styles with writing and art being important components of the assignment.

The first part of the assignment was for students to write a proposal to King George III explaining the economic, political, and social reasons that led to the desire to establish a colony The second part of the project was for students to create a map (either hand drawn or computer generated) showing where their colony would be located. Students were required to include latitude and longitude, a scale, a Compass Rose and the land areas and bodies of water nearby). Students also had to write a list of directions for how one could travel to the colony by ship, or if required, over land. The third section was a persuasive flyer or newspaper advertisement that was to persuade potential colonists to choose their colony instead of Georgia. The final portion of the assignment was to write a comparative essay or create an in-depth Venn diagram that explained how their colony was both similar to and different from Georgia using specific examples from the *Georgia Charter of 1732*, the textbook, and the other sources we used in our study of Georgia's colonial history. A rubric was used to grade each section of the project with the sum of all four equaling their final score.

The Historic Figure Statue Project

The project Scott assigned during the second nine-week period required students to create their own historic figure statue (see Figure 6.3). Using this assessment as a review/preview assignment, he told students that they could base their statue on any person in the state standards or textbook that they have already learned about or will learn about later in the year. Students were then given a list of the historic figures and were told to pick the three that they were the most interested in. In order to avoid having 30 Abraham Lincolns in a 31-person class, he held a "lottery" where only three students per class could research the same person. By telling everyone to choose three individuals, he never had a situation where a student did not receive at least one of their choices.

Once students selected their historic figures, they were required to work individually on the project. Students were only given two days in class to conduct research or to build their statues. Scott also made sure he was available before and after school to assist students. Like the create your own colony project, the

FIGURE 6.3. Example of a Historic Figure Statue Project. Note: Because Scott's name was in their Georgia history textbook as a reviewer, one of his students chose to make a "historic figure statue" of him. After the student did this, Scott made a rule allowing students to only choose figures from the state standards. This just shows how middle level students can take your directions literally while offering a glimpse of how funny they can be. Images of real historic figure statues can be found in Chapter 7.

statue assessment was graded using a rubric and was broken up into specific parts (something that you should consider doing with all projects). The first activity was a lower level exercise where students had to research the person and find five interesting facts about them. The next step was to create a name plate with the person's name, dates, and five facts. Students were also required to locate a quote that the person said or wrote. Students had to put the quote in context and describe what the individual was saying in their own words.

Upon finding their information, students determined how to build their statues. They could use any materials they wanted. With this rule, Scott had students make projects using materials such as cardboard and poster paper, clay, and wood. The best project he ever received was a stuffed, 6 feet 7-inch-tall Abraham Lincoln, complete with a beard made out of the fur of the student's shaved dog. The statues were required to be at least one foot high (to prevent the use of Barbie dolls and GI Joe figures) and had to be placed on a base with a nameplate. Another requirement was for the statue to look as much like the historic figure as possible.

To include at least one higher order thinking process, the figure needed to hold a symbol in his or her hand that represented what they were most well known for. The symbol could not be a flag or gun as the flag only represented which country they were from and guns were not symbolic but a tool that military figures used. This proved to be most difficult for my middle grades students to conceptualize, but once we discussed different types of symbols and the meaning behind them, they began to develop interesting symbols including broken chains for abolitionists and hawks for military leaders and war proponents.

Students were required to present their project on the last two days of school before winter break in a museum walk format, and their peers were required to fill out a graphic organizer writing down at least one fact that their classmates shared. The class then selected the projects that they thought were the best. The winners were displayed in the school media center for the remainder of the school year and into the following year if students chose not to take them home. This project became such a tradition at one of the schools where Scott worked, that by his third year he had students asking me when they were going to get to begin working on the projects like their brothers and sisters did. The media specialist also began asking him when they would have new projects to display.

The State-Based Business Project

Most states are homes to businesses that have become national or international corporations. The state of Georgia has several, including Coca-Cola, Delta, The Home Depot, and Georgia Pacific. These specific companies, along with several economic concepts such as entrepreneur, opportunity cost, and profit, are standards in Georgia (Georgia Department of Education, 2016). With this in mind Scott developed a project that required students to choose, research, and contact a Georgia-based business (see Figure 6.4). Students were allowed to work in groups of three and could choose any company they wanted as long as

---

Directions:
Choose a business based out of GA. (ex. Home Depot, Coke, Chick-Fil-A etc.) You will be given a list.
- Pick a team of up to four people.
- You will present your project in a museum walk format.

Project Must Haves:
- Made with display board
  - Company
  - Timeline
  - Innovations
  - Business Letter
- Identify if public or private and explain why it is or is not.
- If public, trace stock prices for a week and create a graph to place on the display board.
- Color photos
- Founders of company (Entrepreneurs)
- Discuss the risks the founders took to start the company.
- Facts about the company
- Lesser known companies will receive 5 bonus points

FIGURE 6.4. Requirements for the Georgia-Based Business Project

it had its headquarters in the state. Most students choose larger and well-known companies, usually restaurants such as Chick-Fil-A or Waffle House. However, many also chose small businesses that their parents owned or worked for. Students were then able to display what they learned about the company while incorporating economic concepts into their projects. Students placed the information they found about their companies on a display board and once again Scott used a museum walk to have students present their projects. This lesson was a Georgia Council on Economic Education award winner and was later published by the Council (Roberts, 2009).

The Counterfactual History Project

The counterfactual history project was the last project that Scott assigned at the end of the year and a favorite among his students. This project, which was discussed in the sample inquiry lesson found in Chapter 4, was a multistep project that allowed students to use research and higher order thinking skills to develop an answer to a "what if" question of their own choosing. The project consisted of seven steps which were "teacher introduces the topic;" "students create five counterfactual history questions," "students create a counterfactual KWL chart," "students create a proposal/rubric"), "students create a map of an alternative world," "students create a counterfactual Venn diagram," and "students present their final projects." However, the most important elements of this project was that students ultimately had the ability to choose their own topic of interest, present their "what if" answer in any way they chose, and developed their own rubric for Scott to use to grade their assignments (Roberts, 2011, p. 121).

Thoughts About Projects

Projects, just like unit tests and quizzes, are assessments; they just happen to be more hands-on and offer students the ability to use higher order thinking skills and not just recall facts. Still, student content knowledge is important in the development of projects. While projects are viewed as effective assessments, time restraints in the middle level classroom sometimes prevent their use. Nevertheless, a teacher should assign a project once or twice during each nine-week period. The most important things to remember about using projects as a method of assessing student knowledge is to make sure that you are especially clear with the requirements for the project, offer students step by step instructions to help them keep track of what they are supposed to accomplish, use a rubric that outlines exactly how they will be graded, offer students as much choice as possible to maintain buy-in, and include various lower and higher level concepts within the parameters of the assessment.

Standards-Based Grading

Determining a student's success, failure, or aptitude with demonstration of a specific skill is a deeply complex process. At first glance, whether a student is an "A" student, a "C" student, or a "D" student may seem straightforward, but summarizing vast cognitive processes and knowledge into a single letter grade masks the multifaceted nature of the learning process. For generations, teachers have used percentages (92%, 70%, 50%, 0%, etc.) on assessments to then rate student products as A, B, C, D, or F. Unfortunately, this approach is very arbitrary and does not reflect such concepts as effort or even strong connection to learning objectives. More broadly, most teachers did not describe strong connections between a student's performance in class with the external state standards required for that class. If a student "earned" a B in a geography class, for example, what standards were met by the student and which need further attention? Essentially, a deep flaw with the percentages and letter grades approach is that it is not clear what each actually means (Zimmerman, 2020).

Though teachers have certainly been doing it informally for years, a recent movement in assessment—Standards-Based Grading (SBG) has grown significantly in popularity. With this approach, students provide data that is then used to justify a rating on a scale of performance reflecting a specific standard. Often a 0–4 or a 1–5 rating system is used. First, a standard is selected and then performance indicators are described at various levels of achievement. A top rating of 4 or 5—depending on scale—reflects a student's deep internalization, ability to

Level	Informal Description
0	Student does not demonstrate adequate understanding or application of skill or concept. "Student is 'lost'."
1	Student demonstrates basic understanding or application of skill or concept. Deficits exist, or understanding or application are uneven or rudimentary. "Student is emerging. Just beginning to 'get it'"
2	Student demonstrates adequate understanding of application of skill or concept. Student may demonstrate understanding or application slowly, with hesitation, or in a novice way. "Student gets it, but with some effort."
3	Student demonstrates solid understanding of skill or concept. Student demonstrates with ease and confidence. "Student clearly gets it and can apply skill or concept effectively and efficiently"
4	Student demonstrates deep understanding of skill or concept. Student demonstrates with ease and confidence and can create applications or examples beyond what they have been instructed. "Student clearly gets it and can teach others or can alter, adapt, or create new applications of skill or concept."

FIGURE 6.5. Generic, Informal Descriptions of Levels of Performance for SBG

apply, and even ability to teach a specific standard to others. A lower rating of 0 or 1—again depending on scale—demonstrates deep deficit in knowledge, inability to apply, or misapplication of a concept. The product a student provides, whether it is written, verbal, or otherwise, is then placed compared to the indicator to determine level of performance. Figure 6.5 provides generic, informal descriptors that may be used with most any standard. Figure 6.6 applies the SBG concept to a C3 standard in the area of geography (NCSS, 2013).

Though it may be argued that the Levels of Performance are easily transcribed into the letter grades of the past, (an A equals level 4 performance, for example), the strength of SBG lies in the performance descriptors that connect a student's product with the standard. Rather than "Sally earned a solid B, 87% in the course," we can now more confidently say; "Sally's work effectively explains how changes in transportation and communication technology influences spatial connections and affects diffusion of ideas and cultural practices." The connection between Sally's work and the standard is more articulate and detailed. Consequently, the reporting process to students and parents is much lengthier but demonstrates clearer connection between the assessment and the standard. Many report cards are now multi-page documents, indicating to what level a student performed for multiple standards.

SBG is not without its challenges. Increased work for teachers as they sift through student-created data (homework, projects, tests, etc.) to determine levels of performance is very time consuming. Parents who may not be familiar with standards or rubrics may complain that they do not know; how their child is "ac-

Level	Performance Indicator
0	Student does not explain relationship between transportation and communication technologies and spatial connections and the diffusion of ideas and cultural practices.
1	Student explains relationship between communication OR transportation and diffusion of ideas and cultural practices. Specific student-created examples are not provided.
2	Student explains how transportation OR communication technology influences diffusion of ideas and cultural practices.
3	Student explains how changes in transportation and communication technology influences spatial connections and affects diffusion of ideas and cultural practices.
4	Student creates multiple hypothetical examples—in multiple historical eras—of relationships between human migration and transportation and communication technologies.

FIGURE 6.6. Example of C3 Standard Levels of Performance C3 Standard, D2.geo.7.6-8. Explain how changes in transportation and communication technology influence the spatial connections among human settlements and affect the diffusion of ideas and cultural practices,(NCSS, 2013)

tually" doing (Townsley et al., 2019). Similarly, many teachers may resist the philosophical and practical shift from traditional letter grades to SBG.

Another challenge with SBG is the fact that many of the indicators used to determine levels of performance are interpreted differently by different teachers (a concept known as "interrater reliability") (Townsley & Buckmiller, 2020) Finally, the culture of the "Straight-A student" may be deeply challenged as students realize top-level performance is very difficult and requires a much higher level of understanding than what might previously have been an "easy A."

Despite the challenges of SBG, including increased time needed for assessment, initial student and parent confusion while transitioning to SBG, and interrater reliability, teachers report the SBG process to improve their connection of standards with classroom activities and assessments (Knight & Cooper, 2019). We encourage you to explore the SBG options, its challenges, and articulate your thoughts on the shift from traditional grading to the SBG approach.

COLLABORATIVE ACTIVITY: STANDARDS-BASED GRADING.

List some project ideas in your reflective journal. With a partner examine your state's standards (see Table 2.1), select a standard, and create indicators for 5 different levels of performance.

Summary

Whether we like them or not, informal and formal assessments are a major part of education. While some states do not have formal state-mandated social studies assessments that count for students' promotion, they may still have year-end tests that may be used to judge your effectiveness as a teacher. This does not mean that you must revert to traditional approaches to teaching or "teach to the test" for your students to perform well.

This chapter provided you with several key concepts about assessments. We examined what informal and formal assessments are, how to develop them, and how they can be used to frame your instruction. We then considered the differences between criterion-referenced and norm- referenced testing and how students' scores are calculated. More importantly, we offered several tips and strategies that you can use to prepare your students to do well on state-mandated tests. In the standards-based and high-stakes testing world in which we live, we hope that this chapter offered you some real-world examples about testing and how to prepare for them. Finally, we provided several ideas about using projects in your classes and four samples of projects you can use for students in grades 4–8. In the next chapter we shift gears and begin our discussion about the best practices for teaching specific middle level social studies courses.

COLLABORATIVE ACTIVITY: CHAPTER REVIEW: CREATE A PROJECT

- Use the lesson plan template (Figure 5.2) to create a project about a social studies topic.
- Choose the grade level, state standard (see Table 2.1), and NCSS theme that you plan to use and one of the approaches to incorporate state standards in your lesson planning.
- Use the sample project ideas above as a guide to create your project.
- Share your lessons with your classmates.

WEBSITE RESOURCES

- **The DBQ Project** (http://www.dbqproject.com/) "is committed to helping teachers implement rigorous writing and thinking activities with students of all skill levels." This commercial company has developed several document-based materials for middle and high school students. Their website offers free samples of their products along with ordering information.
- **Edteck: Document Based Questions** (http://www.edteck.com/dbq/testing/dbq.htm) is a website by educator Peter Pappas. The site includes a blog, a showcase for all of his projects and sample lesson plans. The page listed includes 14 sample document-based questions lesson plans.
- **Stanford History Education Group** (http://sheg.stanford.edu/?q=node/45) This group's Reading Like a Historian curriculum "engages students in

historical inquiry. Each lesson revolves around a central historical question and features sets of primary documents modified for groups of students with diverse reading skills and abilities." Their website offers teachers over 75 free inquiry-based U.S. history-based lesson plans.
- **TCI** (https://www.teachtci.com/ and http://www.scribd.com/doc/35466600/Basic-Training-2010-LessonB) is a K–12 commercial publishing company established by teachers. Their website includes free lesson plans, ordering information for their products, and a blog for members of their site. The second link shown offers free information about their interactive notebook model that helps students better organize and use the information and handouts their teachers give them.
- **The White House** (https://www.whitehouse.gov/)is the official website of the U.S. President and his or her advisers. The website offers a large about of information ranging from economic forecasts, blogs, podcasts, live video streaming, and the President's perspectives on legislation. The link provided offers a factsheet about the Race to the Top program.

REFERENCES

Ballou, D., & Springer, M. G. (2015). Using student test scores to measure teacher performance: Some problems in the design and implementation of evaluation systems. *Educational Researcher, 44*(2), 77–86.

Close, K., Amrein-Beardsley, A., & Collins, C. (2020). Putting teacher evaluation systems on the map: An overview of state's teacher evaluation systems post-Every Student Succeeds Act. *Education Policy Analysis Archives, 28*, 58.

Dueck, M. (2011). How I broke my own rule and learned to give retests. *Educational Leadership, 69*(3), 72–75.

Georgia Department of Education. (2016). *Social studies 6–8.* https://www.georgiastandards.org/Standards/Pages/BrowseStandards/SocialStudiesStandards6-8.aspx

Hess, K. (2005). *Applying Webb's Depth-of-Knowledge levels in social studies.* http://www.nciea.org/publications/DOKsocialstudies_KH08.pdf

Hodge, C. M., & Roberts, S. L. (2011). *Time travel through Georgia: Teachers' edition.* Wesmar.

IES-NCEE. (n.d.). *Race to the top: Implementation and relationship to student outcomes.* https://ies.ed.gov/ncee/pubs/20174001/

Johnson, A. P. (2010). *Making connections in elementary and middle school social studies* (2nd ed.). Sage.

Knight, M., & Cooper, R. (2019). Taking on a new grading system: The interconnected effects of standards-based grading on teaching, learning, assessment, and student behavior. *NASSP Bulletin, 103*(1), 65–92.

Marland, J., Harrick, M., & Sireci, S. G. (2020). Student assessment opt out and the impact on value-added measures of teacher quality. *Educational and Psychological Measurement, 80*(2), 365–388.

Marzano, R. J. (2010). *Formative assessment and standards-based grading.* Marzano Research Laboratory.

Marzano, R. J., & Heflebower, T. (2011). Grades that show what students know. *Educational Leadership, 69*(3), 34–39.

National Council for the Social Studies. (2013). *Social studies for the next generation: Purposes, practices, and implications of the College, Career, and Civic Life (C3) Framework for social studies state standards.* Author.

Pappas, P. (2012). *Document based questions.* http://www.edteck.com/dbq/testing/dbq.htm

Roberts, S. L. (2009). *Georgia economic history: Lessons for implementing the GPS at Grade 8.* Georgia Council on Economic Education.

Roberts, S. L. (2011). Using counterfactual history to enhance students' historical understanding. *The Social Studies, 102*(3), 117–123.

Salend, S. J. (2011). Creating student friendly tests. *Educational Leadership, 69*(3), 34–39.

Stanford History Education Group. (2011). *Curriculum.* http://sheg.stanford.edu/?q=node/45

Strauss, V. (2011). *Obama bashes his own education policies.* https://www.washingtonpost.com/blogs/answer-sheet/post/obama_bashes_his_own_education_policies/2011/03/29/AFKbDlyB_blog.html

Stronge, J. H., Gareis, C. R., & Little, C. A. (2006). *Teacher pay & teacher quality: Attracting, developing and retaining the best teachers.* Corwin Press.

Teacher Curriculum Institute. (2010). *The interactive student notebook.* http://www.scribd.com/doc/35466600/Basic-Training-2010-LessonB

The DBQ Project. (2011). *Frequently asked questions.* http://www.dbqproject.com/faq.php

Townsley, M., & Buckmiller, T. (2020). Losing As and Fs: What works for schools implementing standards-based grading? *Educational Considerations, 46*(1), 1–10.

Townsley, M., Buckmiller, T., & Cooper, R. (2019). Anticipating a second wave of standards-based grading implementation and understanding the potential barriers. Perceptions of high school principals. *NASSP Bulletin, 103*(4), 281–299.

US Department of Education. (n.d.). *Every student succeeds act* (ESSA). https://www.ed.gov/essa?src=rn

US Department of Education. (n.d.). *No child left behind.* https://www2.ed.gov/nclb/landing.jhtml

US Department of Education. (2017). *Revised State Template for the Consolidated State Plan: The Elementary and Secondary Education Act of 1965, as amended by the Every Student Succeeds Act.* OMB Number: 1810-0576.

Ward, L. R. (2017). *Theology & liberal education in John Dewey.* https://theimaginativeconservative.org/2017/08/theology-liberal-education-john-dewey-leo-ward.html

Webb, N. (2002). *Depth of Knowledge levels for all four content areas.* Unpublished paper.

Wiggins, G. (1998). *Educative assessment: Designing assessments to inform and improve student performance.* Jossey-Bass.

Wormeli, R. (2011). Redos and retakes done right. *Educational Leadership, 69*(3), 22–36.

Zimmerman, J. K. (2020). Implementing standards-based grading in large courses across multiple sections. *PRIMUS, 30*(8–10), 1040–1053.

CHAPTER 7

BEST PRACTICES FOR TEACHING STATE HISTORY

If some countries have too much history, we have too much geography
—*Mackenzie King (Statistics Canada, 2009)*

The great social adventure of America is no longer the conquest of the wilderness but the absorption of fifty different peoples.
—*Walter Lippman (Brainy Quote, 2021)*

Activity List
- Do You Remember State History?
- What is the Purpose of State History?
- When Should State History Be Taught?
- Benefits and Drawbacks of State History
- Reflecting on the Chapter

Teaching Middle Level Social Studies: A Practical Guide for 4th–8th Grade (3rd Edition),
pages 167–189.
Copyright © 2022 by Information Age Publishing
www.infoagepub.com
All rights of reproduction in any form reserved.

COLLABORATIVE ACTIVITY: DO YOU REMEMBER STATE HISTORY?

You may have been taught the history of your state at some point during your K–12 career. If you were, think back to this class and write your answers down in your reflective journal. Then discuss them with a classmate:

- What do you remember about your state history class?
- What were similarities and differences between your state history class and other history courses you have taken?
- Do you think the course offered you a balanced portrayal of your state's history? Why or why not?

INTRODUCTION

Arizona offers state history in the 4th grade, while Georgia mandates it be taught in the 8th. New Hampshire covers their state's history in all grades, K–12, and Texas students take the course in the 7th grade. No matter the state, if you teach at the middle level there is a possibility that you will be assigned to teach a state history course. State history is a subject that is often taught between the 3rd and 8th grades. In some states it is taught at more than one grade level (Stern & Stern, 2011).

In most states, state history is not simply a U.S. history course with some discussion about the state, but it is an independent history course that focuses primarily on the people and events that shaped the state. While major events in U.S. and world history are often included, the emphasis is usually on the impact individuals from the state had on these events or how the events affected the state directly. State history is unique in many ways and is also the only history course whose very purpose is often questioned (Isern, 1990; Moore, 1969; Roberts, 2013a; Roberts & Block, 2019; Roberts et al., 2020; Tyron, 1936). If taught correctly, however, state history can be a useful course as it allows teachers to discuss important concepts of history and incorporate the 10 NCSS themes at a local level. This local connection can help students gain a better link to the people and events of the past. It also provides many potential opportunities for your students to connect to history in ways more convenient than US or World history. However, if taught poorly, state history courses can easily provide students with an inaccurate and "ethnocentric belief in the superiority of the state's culture and disparagement of 'outside' contributions" (Moore, 1969, p. 267).

Individual Activity: What is the Purpose of State History?

In your reflective journal answer the following questions:

- Why do you think states mandate that their history be taught in schools?
- What is the purpose of these courses?

- What do you think are three reasons for teaching state history and what can students learn from it?

The History of State History

State history has been offered mostly to adolescents (ages 10–14) in many states throughout the nation since the early 1820s and 1830s (Isern, 1990; Tyron, 1936). Offering and maintaining a course in state history has been important to most states. Traditionally, there was a regional difference concerning when states choose to teach their state history/social studies courses. Many southern states taught their history in higher grades (6–8) while states in the north and west offered state history to their students at earlier ages (grades 3 or 4). Today, this tends to not be the case with several southern states including Alabama, Arkansas, Florida, and Tennessee teaching state history in the earlier grades (Stern & Stern, 2011).

COLLABORATIVE ACTIVITY: WHEN SHOULD STATE HISTORY BE TAUGHT?

Should state history be taught at the elementary, middle, high school, or in all grade levels? In a collaborate group of four:

- Choose a state that teaches state history in the grade level you think it should be taught. Research the state history standards of that state (see Table 2.1). Group members should be examining a different grade level/state.
- Examine the standards for that grade level/state and discuss if you think the content is appropriate for students taking the course.
- After discussing the standards, as a group write a pro and con sheet about the teaching of state history at each grade level.
- As a group come to a consensus about at what grade level state history should be taught and why.

The Similarities and Differences between State and U.S. History

There are several similarities between teaching U.S. and state history. In many cases there is overlap between the topics that are discussed in state history standards and those of U.S. history, with most state history standards including major wars (e.g., The Civil War), important national legislation (e.g., the 13th, 14th, and 15th amendments), and key national figures (e.g., Martin Luther King, Jr.). In turn, the methods and strategies used to teach U.S. history can most certainly be adapted to teach state history. As we have seen through discussion of the C3 Framework (NCSS, 2013), the process of inquiry, information analysis, and conclusion-making is broad enough to include state history events and concepts.

However, as previously mentioned, state history usually focuses on the individuals and events of a state and their impact on the United States, not necessarily the United States' impact on the state. Though state history can lead to a limited and biased view of history, this more local perspective can be useful in allowing students to gain a local understanding of major events. Some examples include a study of local women who worked in a factory during World War II, a discussion about how a Senator used their experience living in a state to impact the development of national policy, or an investigation of a battle that took place in the area and how its outcome impacted a war (Roberts & Clabough, 2021).

Additionally, the inherent nature of state history leads to a large amount of discussion of lesser known topics or relatively minor figures or events. In some cases, this can be interesting or beneficial. For example, the study of women in state standards brings up several important topics such as the lack of attention to women in the study of history, a discussion of stereotypical gender roles in American society, and the importance of using multiple sources (Ellsworth et al., 2019; Roberts, 2013b; Roberts & Block, 2019; Roberts et al., 2020).

Occasionally, however, this local focus can be a detriment. For example, as a Georgia studies teacher Scott spent a significant amount of time studying inaccurate portrayals of U.S. Presidents based on their connections to his state. In concurrence with the work of political scientist Thomas Cronin (1974), Scott believes that the over-idealized image of the native presidents in state history courses may be a factor in lack of civic participation in local and state elections. This is due to the fact that students are both directly and indirectly taught that the presidential election is all that matters as the president from their state made things better for the country and did little wrong during their term(s) (Roberts & Butler, 2012).

Another situation that Scott found while teaching this subject is that students often become confused with the importance of certain events and individuals and rank them on par with arguably more important national and world topics. For example, he had several high school teachers ask him; "Can middle school teachers stop overemphasizing the Battle of Kettle Creek (a small skirmish in Georgia that was one of the few Patriot victories in the state. The Battle was a state standard in two grade levels) in the 8th grade? My students rank it as high as the Battle of Yorktown." This situation brings up an important point about state history and the relative nature of historical events in general. Since state history is often providing building blocks for further U.S. history instruction, it is important for teachers to make sure that they are aware of what they are teaching and how it fits within the national perspective. For example, a teacher could develop an inquiry-based lessons where students are encouraged to explain how the Battle of Kettle Creek can be viewed in the larger context of the American Revolution. Obviously, if not taught in the correct fashion, state history can lead to skewed or inaccurate understandings in our national memory. It may be beneficial to students to discuss with them how localness to a historic event can influence their perception of its importance.

Individual Activity: Benefits and Drawbacks of State History

In your reflective journal answer the following questions:

- Other than those listed above, what are the benefits and drawbacks of the subject of state history?
- What are some positive or negative consequences of its study?

Critiques of State History

In 2010, a 4th grade Virginia state history textbook made national headlines for a blatant misrepresentation of history. A passage claimed that "thousands of African-Americans fought for the South during the Civil War," a claim that is "rejected by most historians but used by groups to play down slavery's role as a cause in the conflict" (Sieff, 2010, para.1). Though state and local curriculum committees adopt state history textbooks, there has been a lack of national research conducted about the books and standards used in state history instruction. This example demonstrates the possibility of state history courses offering students inaccurate depictions of the past and illustrates the need for more careful study of the textbooks and other materials used to teach state history.

Though the standards and materials used in state history courses have not often been examined, there have been a few studies about the textbooks used in them. In one of the oldest state history critiques, Moore (1969) explained why there was a lack of analysis on these courses and their corresponding textbooks. He claimed that state history courses are "often considered sacrosanct since they are required by state legislatures and presumably dear to the natives of the state" (p. 268). Moore went on, however, to offer several critiques of state history textbooks, including that they "rarely satisfy . . . the requirements of scholarship, the curiosity of students, or the needs of society" (p. 275). Subsequent reviews of state history textbooks, including those by Scott and his colleagues, have gone on to find similar issues with the writing found in both state history textbooks and state history standards (e.g., McLaurin, 1971; Hilburn & Fitchett, 2012; Roberts, 2013a; Roberts & Block, 2019; Roberts et al., 2020). Though further study is needed, it will be up to you as a state history teacher to spend time analyzing the content in both the textbooks and standards and develop lesson plans that make the subject more beneficial to your students. You may go one step further and analyze directly the standards and mandated curriculum with your students. Discussing why specific topics are required may make transparent to your students political and special-interest influence on legislators and subsequent law. Rather than facilitating cynicism about the law-making process, this approach uses standards and mandated curriculum as case studies on the relationships between various voices in your community and subsequent law and policy. For the remainder of the chapter several ideas will be offered that will help you develop strong state history lessons based on both your state's standards as well as the 10 NCSS themes.

Using the 10 NCSS Themes and C3 Framework to Teach State History

Though state history standards relate to the people, places, and events of a state's unique past, any state history lesson should also meet at least one of the NCSS 10 themes of social studies education. Incorporating these themes into your state history standards will help make even the most seemingly irrelevant topic worthwhile in your students' understanding of important social studies concepts. Indeed, we have yet to locate a topic or event that cannot be used as a case study for historical thinking, geographic thinking, economic thinking, or civic thinking. Ben often told his students that "everything is representative or reflective of something bigger" Below are 10 lesson ideas Scott developed based on state history standards that incorporate at least one of the 10 NCSS themes (2010) and focus on elements of the NCSS C3 Framework (2013). In each section we provide a definition of the theme along with the corresponding topic. We will then describe how these lesson ideas connect to the theme, other social studies goals, and state history specifically. For additional lesson ideas for teaching state history effectively please read Colby (2009), Clabough and Bickford, (2018), Denenberg (2011), McCall and Ristow (2003), Muetterties and Haney (2018), Neumann (2017) and Scheuerell (2019).

Theme 1: Culture (Local Riots)

The first NCSS (2010) theme states that social studies programs "should include experiences that provide for the study of culture and cultural diversity" (p. 14). One state history topic that can be used to discuss this theme is riots that are based on racial tensions and oppression. Many cities both large and small throughout the nation have had a riot based on the region's culture, racial demographics, and economy. Some of these cities include San Francisco in 1851 and 1856, New York City in 1863, Chicago in 1964, and Los Angeles in 1965 and 1992.

In Georgia there was a massive, two-day riot in Atlanta in 1906. Though Atlanta has traditionally been viewed as a relatively tolerant southern city where progressive racial practices helped produce many successful African-American business leaders, the 1906 Atlanta Riot tarnished this image. The riot led to the deaths of at least 25 African-Americans as well as significant economic damage to blacks and whites alike. The causes of the riot have been linked to economic competition in the city between blacks and whites looking for jobs, false newspaper accounts of African-American men raping white women, and two white supremacist gubernatorial candidates accusing each other of being too progressive toward African-Americans' civil rights.

Based on this event Scott created a lesson called "'The Least Likely Place for a Race Riot:' The Economic Consequences of Discrimination" (Roberts, 2009). This lesson used a biographical study of Atlanta businessman Alonzo Herndon, a former enslaved person who rose from being a sharecropper to one of the richest

African-Americans in the United States. After learning about Herndon through a biography and being introduced to the race riot through Herndon's story (two of his employees were killed during the riot), students watched a video and read an interview with an expert on the race riot. They then used a chart to compare the two accounts. In this lesson students not only learned about the importance of economics in the decisions made by citizens, they also learned that different sources can offer both similar and different accounts of the same event. Using their sources, students then wrote their own interpretation of the Atlanta race riot and its causes.

Developing a historical inquiry lesson based on the dimensions of the NCSS C3 Framework (2013) to study riots in state history courses provides students with the chance to use several overarching social studies skills as they examine these tragic events using multiple sources. More importantly, these riots are part of history in many cities, and this type of lesson helps students wrestle with some of the more unpleasant aspects of race and culture in U.S. history. Examining a local riot does not allow students to believe that racial violence is something that happens somewhere else and lets them see that these events can and have happened in their own backyards

Theme 2: Time, Continuity, and Change (City Origins)

The second NCSS (2010) theme states that social studies programs "should include experiences that provide for the study of the ways human beings view themselves in and over time" (p. 15). One way to provide this experience is to explore changes that have happened in your local community across decades and generations. Influenced by changes in communication and transportation technologies, the people of the community may view themselves as well-connected or isolated from others.

From 1907–1953 an interurban railway bisected the community where Ben taught. Passengers were able to board trains to larger communities. With the growth in personal car ownership, the interurban line fell into decline and the rail line itself was eventually covered with street pavement or turned into a bike trail. Gradually, knowledge of the interurban line became less well known as generations passed.

Evidence of the interurban continues to exist, however. Working to answer the broad question: "Why is Morton, Illinois laid out in the way it is?," Ben and his students employed Google Maps to gain a birds-eye view of the street layout of the community. Through the center of town, a distinct line exists where the interurban railway existed. Indeed, students were familiar with a strange "hump" on several streets in town where the track bed once rested. Ben and his students then explored the transportation opportunities and limitations with the interurban and compared them to personal car ownership and interstate travel of today. Through this experience, students were encouraged to observe and identify idiosyncrasies in their community (the "hump" in the streets, for example), form hypotheses (something was there that now is gone) and speculate as to what changes have transpired across generations. A major goal of social studies experiences is to work to explain how things came to be. Through exploration of local community attributes, students are encouraged to be more observant of their surroundings and to compare the lives and perspectives of past community members.

The overall social studies connection of this type of lesson is that it encourages students to realize that people's views of themselves, as well as their achievements and failures, and change over time. In fact, as time goes on, people often forget about what happened in the past. Additionally, this lesson helps teachers understand that their state and local history students should master important concepts about learning history, such as the use of primary and secondary sources, and assessing the validity of these sources (in this lesson the primary source, characteristics of the town as viewed through Google Maps images may be interpreted incorrectly). This type of lesson helps students pinpoint both obvious and covert biases in historical sources and subsequent interpretation as described in the C3 framework (2013).

The connection to state history is that the interurban network connected many communities in Central Illinois. It allows students to answer questions such as: "How did the interurban rail line bring people and commerce together?" Learning about the history of any local community is a great way to incorporate the theme of *Time, Continuity, and Change* in state history courses. With a little research, you should be able to find out the stories and historical controversies about the founding of your state's towns and cities.

Theme 3: People, Places, and Environments (Who has lived here in the past?)

The third NCSS (2010) theme states that social studies programs "should include experiences that provide for the study of people, places, and environments" (p. 16). A state history lesson idea that corresponds to this theme is one called "Who has lived here in the past?" Virtually all locations in the United States have seen changes in populations throughout time. By exploring the cultures and histories of local populations throughout time, students gain a deeper understanding of the fact that change is the only constant in local and state history. Exploring thousands of years of rich history then bringing in "recent" history of the past 500 years provides your students with a broader perspective on the land that is now their community.

A deeply rich example of this change across history is Cahokia. What was once the largest city north of Mexico, this settlement was located in what is currently southwestern Illinois, near St. Louis Missouri (Baltus & Baires, 2020). With a rich history dating back to 1050 CE, the history of the rise and decline of Cahokia presents students with a case study in geography, politics, economics, history, and culture. Layers of artifacts throughout the Cahokia region provide students the opportunity to explore a history of people who had a thriving civilization 500 years before the arrival of Columbus in the faraway Caribbean. Though local students are aware of this history, students statewide may not be as familiar. Ben, again using Google Maps© and Google Earth© explored this region with his students, integrating photographs of artifacts and archaeological descriptions of economic activity. Creating a timeline to assist students in understanding the length of time this civilization existed before the first European settlers entered the area, Ben worked to demonstrate the relative recency of more modern settlements of St. Louis, Peoria, and what was to become Chicago. These explorations naturally, (and with encouragement from Ben), led to the question; "to whom does this land belong?" Working to assist students in breaking away from broad, modern conceptualizations of land "ownership," Ben turned the question to; "Who does the land currently host?"

Exploration of the lives, cultures, and histories of indigenous peoples, the assumption upon the land of European and American colonizers, and modern communities such as East St. Louis and St. Louis reinforces not only a longer, broader history not often taught in schools, but encourages students to think about this history of the land on which their communities rest as longer, more-complex, and more controversial.

As discussed above, this theme invites students to analyze maps in order to better understand people, places and environments. This theme can be addressed in the curriculum is by including important information about the original inhabitants of the land upon which we reside today, Indigenous peoples. For example, a unit of study could begin by studying maps to investigate whose ancestral land the school resides upon. This information can be located by using searchable maps such as the one found on the website Native Land. For instance, if students search for Knoxville Tennessee, the map indicates that Knoxville is the ancestral land of the Eastern Band of Cherokee Indians (EBCI). This knowledge may prompt students to ask who the EBCI are and what ties they might have to Cherokee Indians. These questions are an excellent basis for an inquiry lesson.

This investigation will lead students to explore how human actions changed the environment and how those actions influenced human lives. More specifically, students will learn about President Andrew Jackson, The Indian Removal Act of 1830 along with the Trail of Tears where 16,000 Cherokee (approximately 100,000 natives in total) were forced to march westward to new homelands. Of particular importance in their investigation will be that approximately 4,000 Cherokee died during this forced relocation. This background knowledge is necessary, yet their inquiry to discover the potential connection between the Cherokee Indians and the EBCI persists. An important next step in this inquiry would be for students to examine both tribal webpages. The Cherokee webpage describes that during the Trail of Tears "a thousand Cherokees, including those who stayed in in the mountains or made their way back from the Trail of Tears, became the ancestors of today's Eastern Band of Cherokee Indians. Today, the Eastern Band of Cherokee Indians is a sovereign nation with over 14,000 members (Cherokee Historical Association, n.d.).

A deep study to understand the Cherokee Indians and the EBCI along with the effects of their forced removal could lead to many critical thinking activities such as cause and effect charts, compare and contrast charts, creating timelines, family trees, and mapping to name a few. Such critical thinking activities should not merely focus on memorizing when events took place but should instead focus on NCSS' third theme which seeks to understand "how human actions change the environment and how the environment influences human lives" (p. 34). For example, a cause-and-effect chart could ask students to hypothesize what the environment might look like if the Cherokee had not been forced to move from the land. Similarly, students can investigate how the culture, foods, language, celebrations and ways of living changed for the Cherokee. For instance, did the Cherokee adapt family recipes due to the different soil and crops in their new environment? Children's literature such as the book *Fry Bread* by Kevin Noble Millard, can scaffold classroom discussions about how food evolved due to forced relocation.

The Trail of Tears is a familiar topic in many social studies textbooks; therefore, the above example might be used in districts across the United States. However, to provide a local context, we recommend that each school-in partnership with tribal nations- also teach specific information about forced removal and or assimilation practices about the native people on whose ancestral land the school resides. Doing so will provide students with local knowledge of how the people and land around them has changed over time due to human actions, thus attending to NCSS's third theme.

Theme 4: Individual Development and Identity (Teaching Local Governments)

The fourth NCSS (2010) theme states that social studies programs "should include experiences that provide for the study of individual development and identity" (p. 17). A way to incorporate this theme into state history is to provide students with an examination of local governments. One lesson Scott used in his state history courses was called "'In This Life Nothing Is Certain but Death and Taxes' Funding Georgia's Government" (Roberts, 2009). This lesson was about state funded public programs and helped students understand the various forms of revenue the state collects and its uses. More importantly, the lesson mirrored the "Great Recession" that started in 2007 as students were given a budget, along with a description of several government programs, and asked to cut funding to the programs based on the lack of revenue over a given year. The purpose was to allow students to make their own decisions about which state-supported programs to save and which to cut and to explain why they made these decisions.

This lesson's overall social studies connection was that it provided students with an activity that was relevant to their daily lives. What made this lesson ideal for a state history course was that students, who have a closer connection to the topics being discussed, were given the opportunity to understand why state officials were making cuts that affected them or their families. In state history courses, civics or government standards embedded into the curriculum offer teachers a valuable opportunity to allow their students to analyze their own feelings and beliefs about current controversial and important political topics and events. In turn, state history teachers should use local and state political examples to help students understand that civic participation is needed at all levels of government, not just during presidential elections. It should be noted that similarly to historical analysis, the C3 Framework offers dimensions for each social studies discipline including Economics and Civics that work well with this type of lesson.

Theme 5: Individual Groups and Institutions (Local Civil Rights Movements)

The fifth NCSS theme (2010) states that social studies programs "should include experiences that provide for the study of interactions among individuals, groups, and institutions" (p. 18). In response to this theme, Scott created a lesson called "'The City Too Busy to Hate:' The Atlanta Business Community's Response to the Civil Rights Protest" (Roberts, 2009). This lesson offers an example of teaching the civil rights movement in state history by examining the impact that Atlanta's business leaders had. It also incorporated documents that discussed the economic strategies local civil rights groups used, including the document "An Appeal for Human Rights" (which outlined the boycotts and sit-ins that the students of the Atlanta University Centers planned to help gain their civil rights). Finally, students evaluated how individuals, groups, and institutions worked together to peacefully end government-sponsored segregation in Atlanta.

As mentioned above, the Civil Rights movement is an overarching topic that is taught in all U.S. and state history courses. However, state history teachers from all regions of the country can incorporate elements from this lesson to determine and discuss those who were involved in the civil rights movement in their state (Stiff-Williams & Strutz, 2012). In addition, they can examine how their city responded and how its actions compare to other cities such as Birmingham or Atlanta. A great resource you can use to study the national civil rights movement and incorporate it into your state history course is the Birmingham Civil Rights Institute's website.

Theme 6: Power, Authority, and Governance (Connecting U.S. and State History)

The sixth NCSS (2010) theme states that social studies programs should "include experiences that provide for the study of how people create and change structures of power, authority, and governance" (p. 19). This theme highlights one of the more interesting, and in some cases confusing, aspects of teaching state history. Though focused on the history of the state, there are standards that have been selected and placed in the curriculum which focus solely on national or world events. Therefore, it should be noted that state history teachers not only need a large amount of content knowledge about their state's unique past, but they also need to know how to incorporate studies of national or international events into their classes.

One of the most important changes in power, authority, and governance in U.S. history is the monumental shift from the Articles of Confederation to the U.S. Constitution. In a lesson Scott created on the economic weaknesses of the Articles of Confederation, he attempted to merge the NCSS theme, a national event, and a Georgia standard in one cohesive lesson (Roberts, 2009, 2016). The lesson began with a student WebQuest about the Articles of Confederation using the Library of Congress' website *The Articles of Confederation*. He then provided his students with a short, 10-minute lecture about the Articles of Confederation.

Once the lecture was complete, students then watched films about trade during the Confederation period and how the Articles of Confederation limited the nation's interstate trade After students answered questions about the film, they were then given "Articles of Confederation Problem Slips," that provided students with problems found in the Articles including "one vote per state" and the "national government could not levy taxes." Students were then provided with an "Articles of Confederation Decision Tree" where they had to develop three alternatives to correct the problems, determine the negative and positive impacts of each, and then agree on one solution (Burke, 2010; Worksheet Library, n.d.).

After students completed the decision tree, Scott made sure to incorporate the Georgia standards by playing a game called "Are you smarter than Abraham Baldwin" (one of the Georgia signers of the Constitution who is a state standard)? The game consisted of a whole group discussion where he went over the students' solutions to the problem and told them what the Constitutional solution was. If students came up with the same solution as the Constitution or one that class thought was better, they were given the title of being smarter than Abraham Baldwin.

While playing the game students filled out a chart that consisted of four columns. Column one was a list of all six problems that each group of students analyzed; the second was "Your Solution," where students wrote down their classmates' solutions to the problems. Next there was a column called the "Constitutional Solution," where students wrote down what actually happened, and then they filled in the last column called "Similar or Different?" where they wrote if their solutions were similar or different than those of the founders. Finally, along with the Articles of Confederation the state standard included an analysis of the changes to the Georgia constitutions of 1777 and 1789. Students used their knowledge of the changes to the Articles of Confederation to determine the impact the U.S. Constitution had on the state's second constitution. Venn diagrams were used to discuss the similarities and differences between the four constitutions listed in the standards.

The overall social studies connection of this lesson was that students learned about the changes that have taken place in the government of the United States. They learned about how economic forces can cause major changes in the structures of power, authority, and governance. In addition, students learned about the decision-making process. Even though the Articles of Confederation and the Constitutional Convention were national events, Scott made sure to incorporate the study of the state by including a historical figure who signed the U.S. Constitution and allowed students to compare national and state constitutions. There are many similar topics in national history that state history teachers can use to incorporate this theme into their courses.

Theme 7: Production, Distribution and Consumption (Local Business Projects)

The seventh NCSS (2010) theme states that social studies programs "should include experiences that provide for the study of how people organize for the production, distribution, and consumption of goods and services" (p. 20). Creating a lesson that meets this theme can be quite easy in state history as most states are home to numerous well-known companies that can be used as examples in analyzing the components of the theme (Malczewski et al., 2011). In Scott's state history course, he wrote a lesson called "'When Old Coke Became New Coke: The Georgia-based Company Economic Project" (Roberts, 2009).

However, it should be noted that along with meeting the goals of Theme 7, this project has an important connection to overall social studies instruction and state history specifically. The lesson illustrates how to provide students with the opportunity to examine their own state's companies in order to learn about key economic concepts such as production, distribution, the consumption of goods and services, supply and demand, profits, and incentives.

Theme 8: Science, Technology, and Society (Impact of the Railroad)

The eighth NCSS (2010) theme states that social studies programs "should include experiences that provide for the study of relationships among science, technology, and society" (p. 21). In hopes of incorporating this theme into his state history course, Scott adapted a lesson he co-authored with one of his student teachers, Drew Schoen. The lesson, titled "'All Progress is Precarious...' The Growth of Georgia 1790–1840" (Roberts, 2009), examined both the cost and benefits of progress by focusing on how the railroad, and more specifically Atlanta, developed.

Portions of this lesson were discussed in Chapter 4, primarily the use of two paintings about railroads (George Innes' *Lackawanna Valley* and John Gast's *American Progress*) to analyze two different perspectives about the impact of the technology. The lesson began with students coming up with their own definition of the word "progress" and then being asked to list three modes of transportation prior to the railroad. They then moved on to the painting analysis. After discussing the paintings as a whole group and answering questions, Scott gave students notes about the history of the railroad and more information about the artist of each painting. Due to the state standards, Scott also discussed the introduction of railroads to Georgia and the impact they had on the state. Students watched a movie clip from the *Georgia Stories* series about the economic impact railroads had on Georgia and answered questions about the film Finally, students wrote an essay describing the costs and benefits of the railroad and if they thought the benefits outweighed the cost or vice versa.

In national history textbooks, progress is usually portrayed as a positive event (Loewen, 1995). Often, textbooks treat concepts such as westward expansion, Manifest Destiny, and industrialization as inherently beneficial, while minimizing the cost or negative aspects of the very same concepts. In turn, most state history standards and textbooks follow suit. However, this lesson provided students with the understanding that people must make choices about what they are going to do and that they should understand that there is always a cost involved in every choice. Due to the impact that railroads have had on most states (refer back to Ben's lesson on the interurban railroad), this lesson can be easily adapted to meet the standards and provide an opportunity to study the costs and benefits of "progress."

Theme 9: Global Connections (The Economic Impact of Special Events)

The ninth NCSS (2010) theme states that social studies programs should include experiences that "provide for the study of global connections and interdependence" (p. 22). It should be apparent that all states have multiple connections to the rest of the world. From sister city partnerships with other countries, to international trade, to university research, every state is an interdependent member of the global family. In order to incorporate this theme into his state history course, Scott chose to write a lesson that discussed the impact one major global event had on Georgia: the 1996 Summer Olympic Games.

The lesson titled "'We Finally Won Something!' How Special Events and the 1996 Olympics Contributed to Georgia's Economic Growth" discussed the economic impact that the Olympics had on the state (Roberts, 2009). The primary focus was the interdependence that Georgia had with other nations to make this event successful. In turn, students learned how Georgia's international reputation was enhanced by the event and how this eventually impacted Georgia's foreign trade (e.g., the building of a KIA motors plant in the state and the relocation of Porsche's North American headquarters to Atlanta.)

For any state, a lesson like this one will enhance the study of global connections and interdependence. Scott used Atlanta as an example to examine the impact that special global events, such as hosting the Olympic Games, can have on both the short- and long-term economy of a state. Even if your state has not hosted an Olympics, every state has global partnerships and connections with other countries and these connections should be explored in state history courses.

Theme 10: Civic Ideals and Practices (The Interaction of Local, State, and Federal Governments)

The 10th NCSS (2010) theme states that social studies programs "should include experiences that provide for the study of the ideals, principals, and practices of citizenship in a democratic republic" (p. 23). In order to bring this theme into his Georgia Studies course, Scott created a lesson that examined one of the many questions teachers hear almost daily: "Why do we take so many tests?" He decided to use this question as a teachable moment to help describe the influence that varied levels of government (e.g., local, state, federal) have on students' everyday lives and what they can do to participate in the political system.

This lesson, titled "'Why Do We Take So Many Tests?' How the Federal, State, and Local Government Fund Your School," offered students the opportunity to "explore how schools are funded and to critically analyze the current educational climate" (Roberts, 2009, p. 1). The lesson began with students receiving an adapted article about the No Child Left Behind Act.

After reading the article students were required to answer questions about it in pairs. Students participated in a WebQuest using the National Center for Educational Statistics concerning education funding in 2006 to answer questions about how much schools throughout the United States received in local, state, and federal support.

Students calculated and drew several pie charts showing the various percentages of spending for public schools by the different levels of government. After discovering how relatively few federal dollars actually support education, the students answered a series of questions concerning which level of government they believed had a better understanding of the needs of students, whether the federal government should have a say in local education based on the amount of financial support they provide, and if funding were cut which school programs would they support and which would they drop? Students were then asked to discuss what they could do to make changes in educational policy now and when they become adults.

This state history lesson has a connection to the 10th theme of social studies because it gives students the opportunity to explore the intricacies of how their education is funded and allows them to critically analyze the current educational climate in a balanced discussion about the "No Child Left Behind Act" and the impact this has had on their state and local school systems. While NCLB has been repealed, there are numerous other acts and laws about education passed by the federal government that can be studied instead.

Hands-on Projects

All state history curriculums require students to learn about people, groups, and events that influenced the course of its history and middle level students need more than just reading assignments to gain and retain this information. Further, the instruction provided is likely to be students' first contact with these local individuals, groups, or events, so teachers must take extra steps to put learning in appropriate contexts and offer activities that are genuinely engaging. For example, when Scott taught Georgia Studies there were over 60 individuals and groups that students were required to learn. Of these, there were only 18 individuals that they had learned about in prior grades. Understanding that background, Scott knew he had to develop fun, hands-on projects that would help his students learn and retain knowledge about these historic figures. In Chapter 6, Scott introduced the historic figure statue project, which is a great way for students to learn more about those individuals who impacted the state (see Figure 7.1). A second activity he incorporated to help his students remember the material was creating state historic figure and event baseball cards.

FIGURE 7.1. Sample Historic Figure Projects: Ulysses S. Grant and Harriet Beecher Stowe

State Historic Figures and Event Baseball Cards

The historic figures and events baseball cards project is simply an updated version of flash cards, cleverly disguised to help ensure student buy-in and participation (see Figures 7.2 & 7.3). There are several on-line templates that teachers can use to develop these projects (list websites). When Scott used this lesson in his classroom, he gave students a list of historic figures and events (based on the number of figures and events in the state standards for that particular unit) and told them that they would be making baseball or trading cards. Students were given time to research the people and events and create either hand drawn or computer-generated cards. The students had to find a picture of the individual or event for the front of the card. On the back of the card students were required to list information about the person or the event. For a historic figure they were required to write the figure's birth and death dates along with three important facts about the person. For the event students were required to write a definition and list two important facts about the event.

Those students who finished all their cards participated in a trading day. Using the cards as a review before a test, the students would go around the room and try to create a complete set of cards that were not their own. The twist to the game was that students had to verbalize what the person did or say one fact about the event in order to make a trade. For example, during an important 'women in Georgia's history' unit, before making a trade, a student would have to say, "I will trade you my Mary Musgrove card, about the multi-racial woman, who translated for James Oglethorpe for your Charlayne Hunter-Gault card, about the first African-American women who attended the University of Georgia." In order to finalize the trade the other student had to say the sentence in the reverse order: "I will be glad to trade you my Charlayne Hunter-Gault card, about the first African-American women who attended the University of Georgia for your Mary Musgrove card, about the bi-racial woman, who translated for James Oglethorpe." Students who completed their sets first and who then could tell at least one fact about each of their cards won a prize.

When Scott was a Social Studies Program Specialist, he shared this project with his district's teachers. Several used the lesson in their classes and said that their students enjoyed it. However, as all good teachers do, many changed the lessons to meet the needs of their students. Some told Scott that they used the cards in a match game where students match the pictures to the definitions and facts and then glue the cards together. Other teachers had pictures preprinted in order to allow students to spend more time focusing on the information and less time researching and finding images. No matter how teachers decided to allow students to create the cards, they all found that the trading portion of the assignment was beneficial in helping students learn a large amount of unfamiliar information.

FIGURE 7.2.   Sample Historic Figures Baseball Cards: (Front Side)

FIGURE 7.3.   Sample Historic Figures Baseball Cards: (Back Side)

Field Trips

In Chapter 4 we reviewed the importance of field trips, whether they be real or virtual. If you are teaching state history, there are many field trip opportunities due to the very nature of the subject. While you probably won't be teaching close to such famous places as Bunker Hill or Gettysburg, there are plenty of local history sites in every state. For example, at one school where Scott taught, there was a nature trail a block away where artifacts made by Paleo Indians were found. Next to the nature trail stood the oldest house in the county, complete with a working farm. Near Ben's community is Fort Crevecoeur, an early French settlement. Learning further that the name of the fort translates roughly to "brokenhearted," Ben's students explored the challenges faced by both indigenous people and French explorers of the time. Learning that there is controversy as to the where the actual, original location of the fort, Ben's students explored not only the park dedicated to the fort, but the immediate geography and discussed why it might have been chosen as a location for settlement (Ross, 2011). Within a short distance both Scott and Ben's students could experience history firsthand. If you do teach state history, find out about the local history of your school district, create lesson plans that match up to the state standards, and try to take your students to these locations.

SUMMARY

In this chapter we discussed a subject that is taught throughout the country but receives little attention by researchers or in methods textbooks. Though state history is similar to U.S. and world history courses and many of the same strategies can be used, due to the content and inherent nature of the subject, teaching state history can be quite different. As Moore (1969) points out, as a state history teacher you should be aware of the possibility of biases and inaccurate information found in the materials due to the lack of professional study and criticism. The local nature of the subject, though, can make history more relatable to your students and provide them with a deeper connection to the past.

When writing lessons that relate to state history, it is important to match them to your state standards, the NCSS 10 themes of teaching social studies, and the C3 Framework. This chapter provided several lesson ideas that combined state history with the NCSS standards. Additionally, creativity is an important component and makes the subject meaningful for your students. In sum, the value of state history depends on how you teach it. If you teach it poorly it can be almost worthless, and as Moore (1969) and Scott have warned, one of the more potentially damaging social studies courses (Roberts, 2013a). However, if taught well, state history can bring important themes, skills, and concepts to your students. Years after you taught them, you may be amazed when your former students tell you it was their favorite social studies class.

In the next chapter we will examine the best practices for teaching U.S. history. Though many of the strategies discussed in this chapter can be adapted to teaching the subject, the next chapter offers more information about both traditional and progressive strategies that can be used for teaching the history of the United States. These include the use of timelines, primary sources, comparing and contrasting, cause and effect, historical inquiry, and projects.

Individual Activity: Reflecting on the Chapter
Return to your answers about the importance of teaching state history. In your reflective journal answer the following questions:

- After reading this chapter how have your ideas changed about the purposes of teaching state history?
- What steps will you take in order to ensure that you include the NCSS standards and C3 Framework into a state history course?
- What are some strategies discussed in the chapter that you think would help meet this goal?

WEBSITE RESOURCES

- **The Birmingham Civil Rights Institute** (https://www.bcri.org/) offers teachers a variety of resources concerning the modern civil rights movement in Birmingham and throughout the nation. The website offers online resources such as images and oral history videos, an interactive timeline, and curriculum guide. The institute also focuses on modern international civil and human rights movements.
- **Cherokee Historical Association** (https://www.cherokeehistorical.org/) is an organization who "tells our Cherokee story through a diversity of offerings which are authentic, educational, sustainable and enhances public awareness of human rights."
- **Civil Rights Movement Archive** (http://www.crmvet.org) "is of, by, and for Veterans of the Southern Freedom Movement during the years 1951–1968. It is where we tell it like it was, the way we lived it. With a few minor exceptions, everything on this site was written or created by Movement activists who were direct participants in the events they chronicle." The website offers important images, documents, web links, timelines, and a bibliography about the modern civil rights movement. The "Appeal for Human Rights" can be found on this site.
- **Georgia Stories** (https://www.gpb.org/georgiastories) is a series of documentaries produced by Georgia Public Broadcasting for use in 8th grade Georgia Studies classes. The videos correspond with the Georgia Standards of Excellence and cover all periods of Georgia's history up to the 1990s. Though the videos have a Georgia focus some of the free video clips can be

used in other state history and U.S. history courses such as "Archaeology," "Cherokee Myths and Legends," and "King Cotton and the Cotton Gin."

- **Illinois Adventure** (http://illinoisadventuretv.org/) "Shot on location throughout the state, Illinois Adventure shows viewers the many interesting places to visit and things to do just a few hours from home. From fishing on Lake Michigan to searching out tree frogs in the Cache River swamp to visiting long-forgotten towns that are vital parts of Illinois' history, there's something for everyone here."
- **Library of Congress** (http://www.loc.gov) offers teachers a wide variety of primary sources to use with their students including prints and photographs, historic newspapers, performing arts, sound recordings, films, maps, and manuscripts. Features such as "Today in History," "Places in the News," and a teacher's resources page are also included.
- **National Center for Educational Statistics** (http://nces.ed.gov/) is the primary federal entity for collecting and analyzing data related to education in the U.S. and other nations. NCES is located within the U.S. Department of Education and the Institute of Education Sciences. Their website offers teachers a vast array of data about education that can be used in the social studies classroom.
- **Native Land** (https://native-land.ca/) is a website "strives to create and foster conversations about the history of colonialism, Indigenous ways of knowing, and settler-Indigenous relations, through educational resources such as our map and Territory Acknowledgement Guide. We strive to go beyond old ways of talking about Indigenous people and to develop a platform where Indigenous communities can represent themselves and their histories on their own terms. In doing so, Native Land Digital creates spaces where non-Indigenous people can be invited and challenged to learn more about the lands they inhabit, the history of those lands, and how to actively be part of a better future going forward together."
- **Worksheet Library** (http://www.worksheetlibrary.com/subjects/graphic-organizers/decisiontrees/) offers teachers free worksheet templates such as the "Decision Tree" Graphic Organizer discussed in this chapter. Heinemann Publishing also offers a free "Decision Tree" Graphic Organizer at (https://www.heinemann.com/shared/companionresources/e02157/burkewtbichapter3/decisiontree_fig3.19blank.pdf)

REFERENCES

Brainy Quote. (2021). *Walter Lippmann quotes*. https://www.brainyquote.com/quotes/walter_lippmann_151317

Baltus, M. R., & Baires, S. E. (2020). Creating and abandoning "homeland": Cahokia as place of origin. *Journal of Archaeological Method and Theory, 27*(1), 111–127.

Burke, J. (2010). *What's the big idea?* Heinemann.

The Cherokee Historical Association. (n.d.) *The Cherokee Historical Association.* https://www.cherokeehistorical.org/

Clabough, J., & Bickford, J. H. (2018). Birmingham and the human costs of industrialization: Using the C3 Framework to explore the "Magic City" in the Gilded Age. *Middle Level Learning, 63,* 2–10.

Colby, S. (2009). Finding citizenship and place in state history: Connecting to students through diverse narratives. *Social Studies and the Young Learner 22*(2), 16–18.

Cronin, T. E. (1974). The textbook presidency and political science. In S. Bach & G. T. Sulzner (Eds.), *Perspectives on the presidency* (pp. 54–74). D.C. Heath.

Denenberg, D. (2011). Changing faces: Your state hero in the U.S. Capitol. *Social Studies and the Young Learner, 23*(4), 4–9.

Ellsworth, T. M., Stigall, J., & Walker, A. (2019). Remembering the ladies: Connect to local women's history using storytelling. *Social Studies and the Young Learner, 31*(3), 14–18.

Hilburn, J., & Fitchett, P. G. (2012). The new gateway, an old paradox: Immigrants and involuntary Americans in North Carolina history textbooks. *Theory and Research in Social Education, 40*(1), 35–66.

Isern, T. D. (1990). Teaching Kansas state history: The state of the state. *Teaching History: A Journal of Methods, 15*(1), 21–28.

Loewen, J. W. (1995). *Lies my teacher told me: Everything your American history textbook got wrong.* The New Press.

Malczewski, J., Plafker-Gutt, D., & Cophen, R. (2011). Teaching about Starbucks and consumer literacy. *Social Education, 75*(3), 142–143, 148.

McCall, A. L., & Ristow, T. (2003). *Teaching state history: A guide to developing a multicultural curriculum.* Heinemann

McLaurin, M. (1971). Images of Negroes in Deep South public school state history texts. *Phylon, 32*(3), 237–246.

Moore, J. R. (1969). State history text: Essays in ethnocentrism. *Social Education, 33*(1), 267–278.

Muetterties, C., & Haney, J. (2018). How did slavery shape my state? Using inquiry to explore Kentucky history. *Social Studies and the Young Learner, 30*(3), 20–25.

National Council for the Social Studies. (2010). *National curriculum standards for social studies: Chapter 2—The themes of social studies.* https:// www.socialstudies.org/standards/strands

National Council for the Social Studies. (2013). *College, career, and civil life (C3) Framework for social studies state standards.* http://www.socialstudies.org/c3

Neumann, D. (2017). Cold War homefront: Making connections through local history. *Social Education 81*(6), 362–367.

Roberts, S. L. (2009). *Georgia economic history: Lessons for implementing the GPS at Grade 8.* Georgia Council on Economic Education

Roberts, S. L. (2013a). "Georgia on my mind:" Writing the new state history textbook in the post-Loewen world. *The History Teacher, 47*(1), 41–60.

Roberts, S. L. (2013b). Women of action and county names: Mary Musgrove County—Why not? *Middle Level Learning, 48,* M12–M16

Roberts, S. L. (2016). "Keep'em guessing:" Using student predictions to inform historical understanding and empathy. *Social Studies Research and Practice, 11*(3), 45–50.

Roberts, S. L., & Block, M. K. (2019). "Remember the ladies:" An inquiry-based approach for examining important women in your states' history. In J. Hubbard (Ed.). *Extending the ground of public confidence* (pp. 109–122). Information Age Publishing.

Roberts, S. L., & Butler, B. M. (2012). Idealizing and localizing the presidency: The president's place in state history textbooks. In H. Hickman & B. J. Porfilio (Eds.) *The new politics of the textbook: Critical analysis in the core content areas* (pp. 287–305). Sense Publishers

Roberts, S. L., Butler, B. M., Elfer, C. J., Kendrick, D. T., & Widdall, V. (2020). "Isn't it peachy:" The successes and pitfalls of teaching complicated topics in eighth grade Georgia studies. In T. Flint & N. Keefer (Eds.), *Critical perspectives on teaching in the southern United States* (pp. 143–160). Lexington Books

Roberts, S. L., & Clabough, J. (2021). Using the C3 Framework to evaluate the legacy of Southern segregationist Senators. *The Social Studies.* https://doi.org/10.1080/00377996.2021.1871580

Ross, R. A. (2011). The controversy over the location of Forth Crevecoeur, 1846–1923. *Journal of Illinois History, 14*(4), 277–292.

Scheuerell, S. (2019). Using primary sources to investigate local history: Pawnee County Kansas 1877–1880. *Social Education, 83*(1), 43–50.

Sieff, K. (2010, October 20). Virginia 4th-grade textbook criticized over claims on black Confederate soldiers. *The Washington Post.* http://www.washingtonpost.com/wp-dyn/ content/article/2010 /10/19/ AR20101019079 74.html

Statistics Canada. (2009). *Geography.* https://www150.statcan.gc.ca/n1/pub/11-402-x/2008/4017_3119/ceb4017_3119_000-eng.htm

Stern, S. M., & Stern, J. A. (2011). *The state of state U.S. history standards 2011.* The Fordham Institute.

Stiff-Williams, H., & Strutz, J. P. (2012). Interviewing the "Lost Generation" from Prince Edward County's closed school era. *Social Education, 76*(2), 77–81.

Tyron, R. M. (1936). The teaching of local and state history. In NCSS (Ed.), *Elements of the social studies program: 1936 sixth yearbook* (pp. 132–143). McKinley Publishing Company

CHAPTER 8

BEST PRACTICES FOR TEACHING UNITED STATES HISTORY

The American experiment is the most tremendous and far-reaching engine of social change which has blessed or cursed mankind.
—*Charles Francis Adams (Notable Quotes, 2021)*

We used to root for the Indians against the cavalry, because we did not think it was fair in the history books that when the cavalry won it was a great victory, and when the Indians won it was a great massacre.
—*Dick Gregory (Brainy Quote, n.d.)*

Activity List
- Reflecting on Teaching American History.
- Reflecting on the National Center for History in Schools Standards.
- Cause and Effect.
- Compare and Contrast.
- Reflecting on Classroom Discussion.
- Reflecting on the Chapter.

COLLABORATIVE ACTIVITY: REFLECTING ON TEACHING AMERICAN HISTORY

United States history is the cornerstone of most middle level social studies courses. Answer the following questions in your reflective journal and discuss them with a classmate:

- Why do you think U.S. history is a primary focus in middle grades social studies courses?
- How can other social studies disciplines be integrated into a U.S. history course?
- What do middle level students gain from its study?

INTRODUCTION

U.S. history is a major component of the social studies curriculum in the middle grades. The subject is taught at the middle level in every state, usually in grades 4, 5 and 8 (Stern & Stern, 2011). The courses are often broken up into two segments. The first segment usually covers the Pre-Colonial period until the Civil War, with the second segment discussing Reconstruction to the present. In these courses teachers are often surprised by the large number of people, events, and other topics found in many states' history standards, especially those who teach in the 4th and 5th grades, where they are often given a shorter time to teach the material due to the responsibility of teaching all subject areas, not just social studies. With that said, due to the introduction of the C3 framework, states have reduced the number of people and events, an approach that also has positives and well as drawbacks. (Roberts & Block, 2019; Roberts et al., 2020).

Much has been written about the challenges educators face when teaching U.S. history and the issues that students have grasping historic concepts. With the large amount of material that teachers are required to cover in these courses, they often revert to traditional teaching methods. To remedy this there have been books, curriculum guides, and individual lesson plans written to aid teachers in the development of lessons based on the subject (e.g., Brophy & Van Sledright, 1997; Levstik & Barton, 2004; Wineberg, 2001). Also, the National Center for History in Schools (NCHS) has written standards for teaching U.S. history at the middle and high school level that go into more depth than just teaching students a bunch of dates and facts. The NCHS also offers ideas on how to meet their standards (See Website Resources section for more). Figure 8.1 offers a summary of these standards.

Individual Activity: Reflecting on the National Center for History in Schools' Standards

Find the middle level U.S. history standards for your state (see Figure 2.1). In your reflective journal answer the following questions:

Era 1: Three Worlds Meet (Beginnings to 1620)
- Standard 1: Comparative characteristics of societies in the Americas, Western Europe, and Western Africa that increasingly interacted after 1450.
- Standard 2: How early European exploration and colonization resulted in cultural and ecological interactions among previously unconnected peoples.

Era 2: Colonization and Settlement (1585–1763)
- Standard 1: Why the Americas attracted Europeans, why they brought enslaved Africans to their colonies, and how Europeans struggled for control of North America and the Caribbean.
- Standard 2: How political, religious, and social institutions emerged in the English colonies.
- Standard 3: How the values and institutions of European economic life took root in the colonies, and how slavery reshaped European and African life in the America.

Era 3: Revolution and the New Nation (1754–1820s)
- Standard 1: The causes of the American Revolution, the ideas and interests involved in forging the revolutionary movement, and the reasons for the American victory.
- Standard 2: The impact of the American Revolution on politics, economy, and society.
- Standard 3: The institutions and practices of government created during the Revolution and how they were revised between 1787 and 1815 to create the foundation of the American political system based on the U.S. Constitution and the Bill of Rights.

Era 4: Expansion and Reform (1801–1861)
- Standard 1: United States territorial expansion between 1801 and 1861, and how it affected relations with external powers and Native Americans.
- Standard 2: How the industrial revolution, increasing immigration, the rapid expansion of slavery, and the westward movement changed the lives of Americans and led toward regional tensions.
- Standard 3: The extension, restriction, and reorganization of political democracy after 1800.
- Standard 4: The sources and character of cultural, religious, and social reform movements in the antebellum period.

Era 5: Civil War and Reconstruction (1850–1877)
- Standard 1: The causes of the Civil War.
- Standard 2: The course and character of the Civil War and its effects on the American people.
- Standard 3: How various reconstruction plans succeeded or failed.

FIGURE 8.1. NCHE Standards for U.S. History: Grades 5–12 (continues)

Era 6: The Development of the Industrial United States (1870–1900)
- Standard 1: How the rise of corporations, heavy industry, and mechanized farming transformed the American people.
- Standard 2: Massive immigration after 1870 and how new social patterns, conflicts, and ideas of national unity developed amid growing cultural diversity.
- Standard 3: The rise of the American labor movement and how political issues reflected social and economic changes.
- Standard 4: Federal Indian policy and United States foreign policy after the Civil War.

Era 7: The Emergence of Modern America (1890–1930)
- Standard 1: How Progressives and others addressed problems of industrial capitalism, urbanization, and political corruption.
- Standard 2: The changing role of the United States in world affairs through World War I.
- Standard 3: How the United States changed from the end of World War I to the eve of the Great Depression.

Era 8: The Great Depression and World War II (1929–1945)
- Standard 1: The causes of the Great Depression and how it affected American society.
- Standard 2: How the New Deal addressed the Great Depression, transformed American federalism, and initiated the welfare state.
- Standard 3: The causes and course of World War II, the character of the war at home and abroad, and its reshaping of the U.S. role in world affairs.

Era 9: Postwar United States (1945 to early 1970s)
- Standard 1: The economic boom and social transformation of postwar United States.
- Standard 2: How the Cold War and conflicts in Korea and Vietnam influenced domestic and international politics.
- Standard 3: Domestic policies after World War II.
- Standard 4: The struggle for racial and gender equality and the extension of civil liberties.

Era 10: Contemporary United States (1968–Present)
- Standard 1: Recent developments in foreign and domestic politics.
- Standard 2: Economic, social, and cultural developments in contemporary United States

FIGURE 8.1. Continued

- Compare the state's standards to those of the National Center for History in Schools. Which standards are similar? Which are different?
- Based on your findings, how much attention did state standards developers' pay to the national standards? Why do you think this is the case?

The NCSS has also written a list of expectations that all teachers should have for themselves as they teach U.S. history. These expectations are similar to the NCSS's 10 Themes and include "assist learners in utilizing chronological thinking so that they can distinguish between past, present and future time" and "enable readers to develop historical understanding through the avenues of social, political, economic, and cultural history" (as cited in Johnson, 2010, pp. 256–257). The entire list of expectations for history educators can be found in the NCSS book *Expectations of Excellence: Curriculum Standards for Social Studies* (2010). The NCSS also provides two articles that can assist the middle level U.S. history teacher incorporate the themes into their classroom (Golston, 2010; Herczog, 2010).

The material that follows includes many of the teaching strategies and lesson ideas found in this book. Many of the strategies found in Chapters 2 through 7 can be adapted to meet U.S. history standards and can be used in your classroom regardless of the discipline you teach. Along with all of those already presented, this chapter offers more details about some of the best strategies to use in U.S. history instruction.

"Whose" History to Teach?

Though debate has existed for decades regarding which events, groups, individuals, processes, and concepts should be explored by students, recent dialogue has brought to the forefront the question; "Whose history should be taught?" As discussed in Chapter 2, the recent 1619 project (1619 Project, 2019) and the 1776 Commission (Exec. Order No. 13958, 2020; The President's Advisory 1776 Commission, 2021) suggest very different views on foundational events in American history. Consider these two excerpts related to the founders of the United States:

> It is not incidental that 10 of this nation's first 12 presidents were enslavers, and some might argue that this nation was founded not as a democracy, but as a slaveocracy. Jefferson and the other founders were keenly aware of this hypocrisy. And so in Jefferson's original draft of the Declaration of Independence, he tried to argue that it wasn't the colonists' fault. (1619 Project, 2019, p. 18)

> The most common charge levelled against the founders, and hence against our country itself, is that they were hypocrites who didn't believe in their stated principles, and therefore the country they built rests on a lie. This charge is untrue, and has done enormous damage, especially in recent years, with a devastating effect on our civic unity and social fabric (The President's Advisory 1776 Commission, 2021, p. 10).

Varying—and often conflicting—perspectives such as these are reflected in state standards, curricular materials, and spoken and unspoken expectations of administrators, school boards, and parents. As the social studies expert, community members look to you for interpretation and implementation of "the facts" of US history and to determine, at least in part, whose voices get your students' study. To do this, we encourage you to talk with colleagues, work to strongly tie your lessons and experiences to standards, and—above all else—maintain a classroom culture of respect for a large variety of perspectives. Indeed, we encourage you to explore both documents with your students as case studies of the fact that history is more about which facts get focus and how to interpret them than it is about "coverage of material." Broadly, we view the standards above and the historical examples below as open to interpretation. This adds to both the complexity and the opportunity for deep history exploration by you and your students.

As you consider the strategies below, consider what content, voices, and perspectives your students will be spending time with. Consulting with other teachers and administrators can provide valuable insights into selecting the type and content of the materials you use in your classrooms. Ensuring a wide variety of perspectives, we believe, enriches the student experience and provides them opportunity to explore the many varied voices that inform the broad tapestry of US history.

STRATEGIES FOR TEACHING MIDDLE LEVEL U.S. HISTORY: OVERVIEW

As presented in Chapter 3, there are four basic/traditional approaches that have been used to teach U.S. history at the middle level. These include the use of lecture, textbooks, worksheets, and movies. After describing the strengths and weaknesses of each approach we reviewed the best ways they could be used in the middle level social studies classroom. In Chapters 3 and 4, we provided several strategies that could be used to enhance learning in your classrooms. In Chapter 7, we offered several progressive lesson ideas for state history that can be adapted to meet U.S. history standards that incorporated the 10 NCSS themes for teaching social studies and the four motifs for teaching middle level learners. However, there are some specific strategies that are suggested by the NCSS (2010) the NCHS (2012) and the National Council for History Education (2020) that are geared specifically to teaching U.S. history. More information about these strategies is provided below.

Timelines

One of the themes found in both the NCSS and NCHS is for students to learn how to think chronologically. Though this may seem relatively simple to many adults, especially those involved in social studies education, teachers are often shocked when they discover that some of their students think the Civil War happened after World War II or that the Vietnam War occurred in the 1800s. This absence of a mental timeline is common, and teachers should be prepared to help students gain this knowledge (Wineberg, 2001). One of the best approaches is the employment of timelines. Timelines can be about a single subject or any number of historical figures, events, or topics.

Though timelines are often thought of as a traditional strategy, teachers can add more to a timeline assignment than simply having students draw a line in the center of a sheet of paper in order to list dates and events. There are several ways to make timelines more useful, meaningful, and fun for students. These include creating personal timelines, using an ongoing timeline throughout the course, creating reverse chronological timelines, using technology to enhance timeline creation, "off the wall timelines to engage students' spatial abilities, and thematic timelines to emphasize the fact that a multitude of events may be happening simultaneously.

Taking timelines off worksheets and employing them in your classroom, hallways, and even outside open spaces can assist students in better comprehending the chronological "distance" and relationship between events. Ben was well known around his school for taking students into the hallways and outside to create timelines which would not fit well on paper. In his school, the tiles on the floor were 1-foot square, which provided natural timeline markers. His class created a timeline in which each foot was equal to 10 years, creating a timeline 25 feet long for US history, 700 feet long for human history, and the potential for a miles-long timeline for evolutionary history. Depending on the event or length of time, the scale can be adjusted to fit your students' needs.

Personal Timelines

As noted in Chapter 1, middle level students can often be self-centered. This is one of the attributes that can be used in a positive way in a middle level U.S. history course. Early in the year, perhaps on the first or second day of the course, you should discuss the importance of the study of history and how people and events from even hundreds of years before influence our lives today. Examples can include how the immigration of different groups have led to our modern regional accents and cultures, and how the agricultural-based economy of the southern states, which developed during the colonial period, has affected the region's current educational system and income levels. Tell students that one of the best ways to organize these important people and events is to use a timeline. Explain that to better understand timelines they are going to create a timeline about themselves.

Briefly review what might be included in their personal timelines and have students bring in pictures from home, old magazines and newspapers, or Google™ images, that will help them illustrate their personal timelines. After students have made a timeline about their own lives, ask them to search for historic events that happened during their lifetimes and add these events to their timelines. This will help them make a connection to history and gain a better understanding of the importance of our national memory. Examples of websites with a focus on contemporary U.S. history include The Virginia Center of Digital History, PBS Teachers, the Library of Congress, and 1990s Flashback.

Your students are not the only ones who can make personal timelines. They will be thrilled to see you make one about yourself as well. Involve other faculty and staff at your school of all ages, including the principal, the guidance counselor, the cafeteria staff, the custodian, and parent volunteers. To ensure deeper understanding of scale, be sure to encourage all students and adult participants to construct their timelines to the same scale. A teacher who is 60 years old should have a timeline 4 and 1/2 times longer than a 13-year-old, for example. Display the adult timelines alongside your students' timelines for direct comparison. Have your students discuss the common events that everyone has shared or been a part of. Then have your students examine the other important events the adults in the building listed on their timelines. Ask students to determine how many of the events listed are the same and how many are different. Ask students why they think this may be the case. Ask students to think about which events they may keep or remove as they get older. Keep the timelines displayed in your room and as the year progresses have students add or remove any details about their lives or the historic events they listed on their timelines.

Ongoing Timelines

In order to provide students with a constant reminder about which events have been discussed in your class and to help them develop their chronological understanding, keep an "ongoing" timeline throughout the course. The timeline can be on a large poster in the classroom or in a hallway with images, vocabulary words, and student thoughts. This ongoing timeline can also be something that the students keep in an interactive notebook and to which they may frequently refer. Finally, it can be used as a reflection guide where students consider several questions about the timeline including why certain events are featured and why others are neglected, what makes some events worthy of representation, and would different nations or groups of people feature different events. Jessica encourages students to create multiple timelines regarding voting rights. Though a timeline investigation about African American voting rights, Asian American voting rights, Indigenous peoples' voting rights, and women's voting rights, students may—for good reason—question why different disenfranchised groups have different voting rights timelines (Ferreras-Stone, 2020). Karrie creates a visual timeline around the classroom. As each event is discussed in class, it is added to the timeline for students' reference. Students often refer to the timeline throughout the year and it helps to give them an idea of both the passage of time in their studies and how events relate to one another chronologically.

Reverse Chronological Timelines

A reverse chronological timeline is simply a timeline where students begin with present events and work their way backwards through history. Creating timelines in this manner can help students understand the whys behind events and their impact on our current society. This activity can be used as a review at the end of a U.S. history course where students not only place events in the correct chronological order but also have to offer explanations about how and why one event led to today's society.

Technology-Generated Timelines

With today's technology, timelines do not have to be solely a pencil and paper activity. There are several ways to incorporate technology into the development of timelines. As mentioned before, students should make their timelines visual and use the internet to find images they can incorporate into them. However, you can provide students with an opportunity to develop more interactive timelines. Two of the programs that you can use include, Timetoast, and Microsoft Movie Maker.

Timetoast is a free and simple timeline builder that can be embedded or linked to a blog. This program allows students to add dates, descriptions, and media (e.g., movies clip, images, documents) to their timelines. You can use the program for multiple types of timelines. This site also provides access to timelines that have already been created.

Microsoft Movie Maker is a program that is usually part of a school's Microsoft Office Suite. This program is very similar to a PowerPoint® presentation. However, the program allows students to insert images and text and place them in an order that tells a story, or in this case shows a timeline. Probably the best part about the program is the ability for students to incorporate their own music into the presentation as the images pan across the screen. Though this program can take some time to use, allowing students time to work on an ongoing timeline through each unit is worthwhile. You can also use this program to incorporate primary sources by explaining to your students that the only songs they can incorporate in the movie are those from the time period being studied.

"Off the Wall" Timelines

To encourage students to see how "long" history can be, in addition to an ancillary lesson on scale, Ben takes his students to the school yard to measure out a timeline of human history where one foot is equal to one century. This timeline is different than the one described above because the student serve as the markers, making it one dimension more interactive. When he runs out of students as markers, they then use some of the stuffed animals and other toys he keeps in his desk drawer as indicators of major events. Ben has his students measure out the timeline from the approximate crossing of Beringia by migrant peoples, (approximately 25,000 BC), to today. He stops at important events in world history such as the building of the Pyramids, the life of Jesus, the crossing of the Atlantic by Columbus, the Civil War, and finally the birthdates of his students. Once complete, students can see that their entire existence is a fraction of an inch on a timeline hundreds of feet long. A humbling experience even for the most egocentric adolescent.

Thematic Timelines

Often students view history as one event happening after another. In reality, countless events are happening at the same time. To encourage students to see that developments, events, and trends often happen simultaneously, Ben has students select a topic of choice, (sports, fashion, technology, wars, to name a few) and asks them to create timelines with major events related to the topic. Placing the finished timelines side by side allows students to see how fashion changes while America expands, how technology grows while wars happen, and how social change and major sporting events might be interrelated.

Cause and Effect

Historical analysis and interpretation are important activities for middle level students to participate in during U.S. history courses. Building from timelines, which are simply a list of events in chronological order, students should begin to focus more on understanding the cause-and-effect relationships between historical figures and events. Students should be able to use a variety of sources to learn about these relationships. In addition, there are many strategies that you can use to help your students gain knowledge of them. Some of these ideas include graphic organizers, infer-o-graphs and deduct-o-graphs, and How To Books.

Cause and Effect Graphic Organizers

Typing the phrase "cause and effect worksheets" into a Google™ search provides 16,700,000 results at the time of this writing. Certainly, you will not be without options if you choose to incorporate a cause-and-effect graphic organizer into your lessons. Many of the worksheets contain shapes such as arrows pointing to boxes with the words cause and effect over them. Though simplistic, these organizers provide students with a visual concerning how particular events lead to other events. However, simple tweaks can be made to these worksheets to make them higher level and more rewarding, such as having students draw darker arrows for causes and effects that they think are more important or stringing together multiple causes for an event. No matter what you add to them, these types of worksheets can be used as quick and easy guides for students to answer questions such as "What events led to the Civil War?" and "What were the results of the Montgomery Bus Boycott?"

Infer-o-graphs and Deduct-o-graphs

Another strategy to include the study of cause and effect into U.S. history is the use of infer-o-graphs and deduct-o-graphs (Johnson, 2010). Both activities allow students to think about answers without having it provided to them. Each graph consists of three boxes. For the infer-o-graph, the first box is labeled "The Event Cause," the second box is labeled "Clues or Important Information" with space for students to write it down, and the third box is labeled "Possible Effect." The deduct-o-graph is similar, but the first box is labeled "The Event Effect" and the last box "Possible Cause" (Johnson, 2010, p. 52).

In order to use the graphs, teachers should choose an event or topic and provide it to the students. Students are then provided with text, images, or other documents that they can use to fill the boxes. For example, students could be given an event such as "Hitler's rise to power." Then students could be given the infer-o-graph where they write down the cause of the event, the four clues or important information they found in their sources describing Hitler's rise to power, and then guess what they think the effect of Hitler's rise was. In the deduct-o-graph the students would be given the effect of Hitler's rise to power, they would list four clues or important information about what Hitler did after taking power, and then determine a possible cause about why Hitler was able to take control of Germany. See Figures 8.2–8.5 for examples of infer-o-graphs and deduct-o-graphs.

Inferring The Possible Effect

The Event Cause:
Clues or Important Information
1.
2.
3.
4.
Possible effect:

FIGURE 8.2. Sample Infer-o-Graph

Inferring The Possible Effect
The Event Cause: Depression/Hyperinflation
1. Clues or Important Information:
2. Germans lost their life's' savings.
3. Germans blamed Jewish people for losing the war and causing the hyperinflation.
4. The retribution punishment by the allies was a cause of the inflation and people began to dislike the allies even more.
5. Hitler promised to get Germany out of the crisis and to help Germany become a major power again.
Possible effect: People elected Hitler and other members of the Nazi party into office

FIGURE 8.3. Completed Infer-o-graph (Hitler's Rise to Power)

"How To" Books

A great in-depth activity that can be used to discuss cause and effect is the use of "How To" books. These books allow students to write about a topic or event as if they are living during a specific time period and are writing a book to explain how to do something. Jones and Daisey (2011), who developed this activity, offer examples of some of the how to books that they used in their world history classes, which included *How to Form a Feudalistic Government in Europe Around 800 CE* and *How to Decrease the Spread of Bubonic Plague* (p. 49). To write these "how to" books, students will need to understand complex cause and effect relationships. For example, in the feudalism book the student author had to describe what caused the need for a feudalistic government and explain what ef-

Deducting the Possible Cause
The Event Effect:
Clues or Important Information
1.
2.
3.
4.
Possible cause:

FIGURE 8.4. Sample Deduct-o-Graph

Deducting the Possible Cause
The Event Effect: Hitler becomes Chancellor of Germany
Clues or Important Information 1. Germans lost their life's savings 2. Germans blamed Jewish people for losing the war and causing the hyperinflation 3. The retribution punishment by the allies was a cause of the inflation and people began to dislike the allies even more 4. Hitler promised to get Germany out of the crisis
Possible cause: Hyperinflation/Depression

FIGURE 8.5. Completed Deduct-o-Graph (Hitler's Rise to Power)

fect their new type of government had on Europe in 800 CE. These types of books can be easily adapted to describe cause and effect relationships in middle level U.S. history such as "How to End the Great Depression" or "How to Become a Robber Baron."

COLLABORATIVE ACTIVITY: CAUSE AND EFFECT

Think of some topics in United States history where you can incorporate cause and effect strategies in your classes. In your reflective journal write answers to the following questions and share your ideas with a classmate.

- Why are cause and effect strategies important for middle level students to use in U.S. history courses?
- Do you think it would be okay to teach middle school students about events that had debatable causes and effects?

Compare and Contrast

Using strategies that allow students to compare and contrast various topics or concepts in U.S. history is vital to helping students increase their historical understanding. While comparing and contrasting appears to be a relatively simple idea for adults, students need guided practice to help them make fair comparisons that eventually lead to making better decisions. As mentioned in Chapters 3 and 4, usually when teachers think of comparing and contrasting, they fall back on the Venn diagram, which is an effective, but overused, tool for students to explain the similarities and differences. Other tools that can be used to help students document the comparing and contrasting of different subjects are guided comparison and T-charts. More complex approaches include the Bright Idea and Comprehension Cube strategies.

TABLE 8.1. Sample Cause and Effect Comparison Chart: Sharecropping, Tenant Farming, Yeoman Farming

Choice	Who Owned Land?	Who Chose Crop?	Who Owned Crop?	Who Owned Equipment?	Types of Crops Grown?
Sharecropping	Landowners	Landowners	Landowners	Landowner	Cotton
Tenant Farming	Landowners	Landowners	Landowners	Farmer	Cotton
Yeoman Farming	Farmer	Farmer	Farmer	Farmer	Cotton, other fruits and vegetables the farmer would eat or sell

Guided Comparison Charts

As the name suggests, a guided comparison chart adds more structure to the comparison task. In the first column, list the people, places, or events being analyzed. In the corresponding columns, have a series of questions for students to answer about the topics and have them fill in each corresponding row. Once students have completed the chart, allow them to summarize in their own words, using the chart as a guide, the similarities and differences between the topics being examined. See Table 8.1 for an example of a comparison chart concerning sharecropping, tenant farming, and yeoman farming.

T Charts

A T-chart is a two-column comparison chart. To integrate this strategy into a U.S. history lesson, have students draw a large T shape on their paper. This divides the paper into two parts, with the cross of the T serving as an area to write two headings. After completing the T design, students are given two people, places, or events to compare and contrast. Provide students with the two topics and have them write down notes about them in the appropriate columns. Once students have taken notes about the topics, they should be asked to use the chart to help them compare and contrast the two in a written format. Another approach would be to compile the whole class's T-charts on a smart board to compare and contrast students' answers. Students could then attempt to come to a class consensus about which examples to keep on the chart and which ones to remove.

Bright Idea

The bright idea strategy is a fun way for students to compare and contrast historical topics in a whole group setting (Hines & Vincent, 2005). Before the lesson, choose five or six historic topics and write them on a large sheet of paper. Have students draw and cut out light bulb shapes or prepare them yourself before class. Then place one of the topics on the board. For example, one topic could be inventors such as Thomas Edison. Ask students a series of questions that compare and contrast him to other historical figures. One question could be, "Who else was like Thomas Edison?" Students would then write names of famous inventors who were similar to Edison such as Elon Musk, Steve Jobs, or Henry Ford on their light bulb, and rush up to stick answers to the board (it is okay to make a competition out of it). Students will then explain their answer to the class about why they think that their historic figure was like Thomas Edison such as they both worked with machines. This can be followed by the question "Name an inventor who was not like Thomas Edison" and go through the same process. Students may select an inventor like George Washington Carver "because he worked with peanuts not machines."

Comprehension Cubes

A comprehension cube is another entertaining way for students to compare and contrast topics in U.S. history. The cube is a large paper dice with specific headings and questions on each side (Hollas, 2005). In order to use the cube to compare and contrast, you will have to develop questions based on your topic of study. Some of the headings you can use include "Describe It," Compare It," and "Contrast It" (Hollas, 2005, p. 109). Place students in groups of three or four, provide them with strips of paper with topics to draw from, and then have them roll the cube and answer the question on it. Some historical examples you could use in this activity include Booker T. Washington/W.E.B. Dubois, The Panama Canal/ the Northwest Passage, Korean War/Vietnam War, and The Industrial Revolution/ The Information Age.

COLLABORATIVE ACTIVITY: COMPARE AND CONTRAST

Think of some topics in United States history where you can incorporate compare and contrast strategies in your classes. In your reflective journal write your answer to the following questions and then share your ideas with a classmate.

- Why are compare and contrast strategies important for middle level students to use in history courses?
- What do you think: How can you compare to topics without oversimplifying the similarities or differences between the two?

Primary Sources

In Chapter 4 we detailed the incorporation, use, and analysis of primary sources in the middle level social studies classroom. In U.S. history courses the use of primary sources is a key factor for your students' historical development and understanding (De La Paz & Felton, 2010; Westhoff, 2009; Wineburg & Martin, 2009). One of the difficulties about using primary sources is finding them. However, as mentioned in Chapter 4 there are some great websites to find these sources. These organizations' primary focus is American history and are extremely beneficial in teaching the subject. Again, these are Gilder Lehrman Institute of American History, the Library of Congress, the National Archives, the National History Education Clearing House and the Smithsonian Institution

Historical Inquiry

Historical inquiry as described in the NCSS C3 framework (2013) is by far the best way for students of all ability levels to learn history. This is especially true for U.S. history courses due to the large amount of primary and secondary sources that are available. An example is the work of the Stanford History Education Group (2011) that has provided several free inquiry-based U.S. history lesson plans ranging in focus from the Colonial period to the Civil Rights Movement.

Classroom Discussion

School offers students ample opportunity to engage in discussion. Students have opportunity to talk, debate, problem-solve, and make comparisons about their everyday lives in the hallways, cafeteria, and on the bus, often with minimal adult supervision. However, students are often presented very few chances to hone their discussion skills in an academic setting (Roberts, 2013). Using classroom discussion is important and the approach offers students the opportunity to engage in academic discussions that they do not often do on their own. In turn, students can, and often do, learn better through talking to their peers in class rather than being lectured to by the teacher (Cazden, 1988).

Parker (2003) contends that classroom discussion is different from overall discourse as it is "a shared inquiry...which relies on the expression and consideration of diverse views." (p. 129). Buchanan (2011) summarizes discussion as "shared dialogue between individuals; it may include multiple perspectives, and may or may not include a classroom teacher," and can assist students in "developing their own ideas and learn from each other while engaging in the classroom content" (p. 19).

The Importance of Incorporating Classroom Discussion

Classroom discussion is a critical element of social studies instruction. If teachers choose to use discussion as a strategy, it has been recommended that they should serve as facilitators in a multi-layered conversation between all members of their classrooms. The common consensus is that the use of discussion promotes many of the objectives of social studies education, especially in terms of studying controversial issues, promoting critical thinking, learning democratic values, and gaining content mastery (Roberts, 2013). Discussion also builds tolerance among individuals, and makes social studies classes more engaging (e.g., Henning et al. 2008; Hess 2009; North 2009; Parker 2003). If we are to expect our students to engage in informed and civil discourse as adults, they need to practice in safe environments.

Hess (2009) points out that social studies, by its very nature, is a subject that lends itself to the study of controversial issues, topics, and themes. Current issues such as abortion or immigration and historic topics such as the causes of the Civil War or the use of Japanese internment camps during WWII are just a few examples of topics that may be brought up in a social studies classroom on any given day. According to social studies researchers, teachers should not shy away from analyzing these topics in their classroom, nor should they be the sole provider of information about these issues (Hess, 2009; Parker, 2003; Passe & Evans, 1996). Students should have the opportunity to think about and discuss these issues themselves. Though they may never come to a consensus about the topic or issue, what students learn from taking part in the discussion itself is invaluable to the functioning of a democratic society (Hess 2009; Parker 2003, Roberts, 2013). Indeed, some of the most interesting and engaging topics are ones on which students will never agree. Ben's class discussions regarding the role of religion in public schools, the amount of privacy one can expect in the age of technology, and whether we are achieving "liberty and justice for all" are some of the most stimulating for students. He often states that: "If we all agreed, we would not be asking the question." Karrie likes to encourage students to utilize evidence from primary and secondary sources as evidence to back up what they are saying during class discussions or debates. She usually accomplishes this by having students first think about what they want to say and then they can pair with another student to discuss it before sharing the idea with the entire class.

When discussing controversial topics Jessica likes to pair students and assign them opposing viewpoints. Students must then find evidence to support the viewpoint they were assigned in order to engage in meaningful discussion. Jessica does this for two main reasons: 1) it encourages students to see and research perspectives they may not initially agree with and 2) it creates a safe environment where students do not need to disclose their personal point of view but rather the one they were assigned.

The Difficulties of Classroom Discussion

Though viewed as ideal, many classroom teachers, along with teacher educators, find it difficult to hold discussions in their classes. No matter the age level of the students involved, educators are confronted with many challenges when they conduct this type of activity. These can include a lack of student participation or interest, uncomfortableness with a specific topic, a lack of content preparation, talking out of turn, or students who simply do not want to reflect on the specific topic being discussed. Another challenge in using discussion that many classroom teachers may face are class clowns who are more interested in making their classmates laugh than making serious contributions to the topic being examined (Flynn, 2009; Kohlmeier, 2006; Roberts, 2013; Washington & Humphries, 2011). As a middle grades teacher, you need to be cognizant of the maturity level of your students. While some topics such as racism may be appropriate in a 5th grade classroom, a visual image of a lynching to set the discussion may be too disturbing for a student of that age. On the other hand, a middle level student in the 8th grade may be able to handle both the discussion and the image in a more mature fashion. It is vitally important that you teach and model expectations of appropriate discussions and behavior in order to make the most of class discussions. Karrie establishes class norms for discussions during the first week of school. These norms are modeled and referred to frequently. The culture of your classroom in the weeks and months leading to a class discussion can have a significant impact on how that discussion unfolds. Establishing norms is a great way to begin to build class culture.

One frequent problem Ben sees in his classroom discussions is the tendency for students to speak only to him. While he certainly appreciates the attention, students often neglect one another's comments in lieu of his attention. To counteract this, Ben will often instruct students to address one another's comments directly. He also will require students to summarize, then agree or disagree with each other's statements. Through repeated practice, the culture of the class shifts from filtering all comments through the instructor to a setting in which a free-flow of ideas between students is expected. As the school year progresses, Ben finds himself NOT speaking for significant amounts of time as students grapple with one another's comments. Paradoxically, it is during these times that he feels most effective and productive.

Another problem faced in many classroom discussions is the urge for the teacher to comment on each statement made by each student. In addition to inadvertently encouraging students to filter their comments through the teacher, this approach can short-circuit students' formation of their own opinions. Ben sometimes has a difficult time allowing students' comments to rest on their own merits and works to bite his tongue when he hears flaws in logic or fact. The advantage to withholding comment is a climate in which students are held more accountable for listening to one another and a setting in which the students are on a more equitable footing with the teacher. Karrie likes to arrange classroom desks or chairs in a circle for discussions. This way, when her students are sitting in a circle they are facing one another rather than a teacher at the front of the room.

Classroom Discussion Strategies

The bottom line when it comes to using classroom discussion, especially at the middle level, is that you must find ways for students to feel that they can have the freedom to say what they want while also keeping a structure. One strategy is to use a silent discussion called a chalk talk (Baron, 2011; Tidwell, 2007). A chalk talk is a silent discussion where the teacher writes a question on the board and asks students to write their answers and share their independent work by posting and drawing connections. While there are weaknesses to this strategy, some of these can be solved in a silent discussion using Google™ docs, blogs, or having students work in groups writing on a piece of paper, which allows all students to participate in the discussion at the same time (Henning et al., 2008; Kissling, 2011; Roberts, 2013). Other strategies that can be effective in fostering discussions where students speak to one another include the paired questions and answers or a Circle of Knowledge. Using these approaches allows students to participate in discussions about important topics in U.S. history while not having to do it in front of the entire class. It also shortens the wait time for those students who want to speak.

To encourage students to know they have been heard, it is important to intentionally listen and interact with students and their comments. Summarizing, paraphrasing, probing, using appropriate wait time, and asking students to substantiate your understanding of what they have said are important strategies to employ to encourage meaningful discussion. One side effect of these approaches may be students who do them with one another. On more than one occasion, Ben has seen students spontaneously summarize one another's statements, ask for clarification, and provide examples that build upon concepts mentioned by one another.

Though it may seem inconsequential to the discussion, the teacher's physical location can send strong non-verbal messages to students. Planting yourself behind your desk or at a lectern may send the message of division with your students. Ben makes it a priority to sit in student desks as much as he can. It is interesting that at the beginning of the year students find this approach uncomfortable, perhaps because it is a violation of social norms. As the year progresses, it becomes more acceptable and comfortable to students. Ben believes that sitting among the students sends the message that "we are all in this together" when it comes to class activities. As an added benefit, it may also reduce student inattentiveness and distracting behavior as proximity to the teacher implies teacher attention.

Class Activity: Reflecting on Classroom Discussion

Pair up with a classmate and attempt to recall one or more of the best discussions you ever had in your own secondary schooling experience. Discuss the following questions:

- What made these discussions memorable?
- How might you conduct the same or similar discussion with your middle level students once you are in charge of a classroom?

After the discussion form larger groups and list the dos and don'ts on chart paper or create slogan type bumper stickers to promote discussion in the middle level classroom.

Projects

The use of projects was discussed in detail in Chapters 6 and 7. Once again, the project ideas that were discussed can easily be adapted to a U.S. history course. As a reminder, if you do use projects in your classes, make sure that the project is meaningful and provides students with a deeper understanding about the topic they are working on, and not simply a time filler or just something fun for your students to do at the end of the semester or year.

An important project that you can have your students participate in is through the National History Day program. Each year more than half a million students participate in National History Day contests at the local, state, and national level. Students select topics based on themes and conduct research of both primary and secondary sources to develop a variety of final projects such as websites, exhibits, and documentaries about their topic. Historians and educators judge the competitions. State winners go on to the Kenneth E. Behring National Contest held every June at the University of Maryland.

SUMMARY

This chapter offered information about teaching U.S. history in the middle level classroom, a subject that is taught in at least two middle grade levels in every state. In this chapter several strategies were discussed. Some have been mentioned previously in the book while others such as timelines, comprehension charts, how to books, and classroom discussion, were introduced. As with all social studies strategies, these can be altered and used in all social studies courses, though these are extremely useful in U.S. history courses specifically. In the next chapter we discuss the best practices for teaching another common discipline in the middle level classroom: world geography and cultures. Additional articles by Cole and Padgett (2018), Saye (2017, 2018), and Devine (2017) are also helpful for teaching US History at the middle school level.

Class Activity: Reflecting on the Chapter

Pair up with a classmate and examine the middle level U.S. history standards for your state (see Table 2.1). Develop a U.S. history lesson plan that incorporates at least two of the strategies introduced in the chapter. Present and share your lesson plans in small groups.

WEBSITE RESOURCES

- **1990s Flashback** (http://www.1990sflashback.com/) is a website that offers a large amount of information about the decade of the 1990s. Some of the pages include a discussion about the economy/prices, entertainment, and news of each year in the decade. This website can offer students information about contemporary U.S. history for creating timelines.

- **Authentic History Center** (http://www.authentichistory.com/) is a website that "endeavors to tell the story of the United States primarily through popular culture. It was created to teach everyday objects in society have authentic historical value and reflect the social consciousness of the ear that produced them." The site contains sources from 1600-present.
- **Cornell University Collection of Political Americana** (http://cidc.library.cornell.edu/political/) provides a large collection of primary sources concerning American political history
- **TimeToast** (https://www.timetoast.com/)is a free website that allows users to create interactive timelines with images, music, and movie clips. Additionally, the website hosts thousands of free timelines that have been created by other users.
- **Gilder Lehrman Institute of American History** (http://www.gilderlehrman.org/) "is a nonprofit organization supporting the study and love of American history through a wide range of programs and resources for students, teachers, scholars, and history enthusiasts throughout the nation." Their website offers teachers access to a wide variety of historical documents, curriculum modules, podcasts, online exhibitions, and online journals that provide lesson plans and ideas.
- **Historical Thinking Matters** (http://historicalthinkingmatters.org/) is a website "focused on key topics in U.S. history that is designed to teach students how to critically read primary sources and how to critique and construct historical narratives." The site provides four interactive lessons with step-by-step instructions about how to complete each investigation.
- **Internet Archive: Digital Library of Free Books, Movies, Music, and Wayback Machine** (http://www.archive.org/) is a vast database of videos, educational films, music, and a variety of other media available for download.
- **Library of Congress** (https://www.loc.gov/) offers teachers a wide variety of primary sources to use with their students including prints and photographs, historic newspapers, performing arts, sound recordings, films, maps, and manuscripts. Features such as "Today in History," "Places in the News," and a resources page are also included.
- **National Archives** (http://www.archives.gov/) offers teachers a wide variety of resources including lesson plans and activities, information about using primary sources, and state and regional resources. Opportunities for professional development are offered as well.
- **National Center for History in Schools** (http://www.nchs.ucla.edu) "has a threefold mission: to develop and provide teachers with curricular materials that will engage students in exciting explorations of U.S. and World History; professional development for K–12 history teachers; and to collaborate with schools in building their history curricula." The website offers

teachers a wide variety of free resources including interactive lessons for U.S. history as well as books such as *Bringing History Alive* for purchase.

- **National Council for History Education** (https://ncheteach.org/) "provides professional and intellectual leadership to foster an engaged community committed to the teaching, learning, and appreciation of diverse histories. Through historical inquiry, NCHE empowers learners to research and interpret the past. Using History's Habits of Mind, our members investigate the past, engage in the present, and are empowered to shape the future."

- **National Council for the Social Studies** (https://www.socialstudies.org/) provides "leadership, service, and support for all social studies educators. Founded in 1921, National Council for the Social Studies has grown to be the largest association in the country devoted solely to social studies education. NCSS engages and supports educators in strengthening and advocating social studies." The NCSS website offers teachers access to the 10 NCSS themes for teaching social studies, information about their annual conference, lesson plans and resources, position statements, and a list of notable trade books.

- **National History Day** (https://www.nhd.org/) "is a highly regarded academic program for elementary and secondary school students" that allows them to create history projects that can be entered into local, state, and national contests. The website offers teachers information about the program, how to get their students started with the program, guidelines for projects and how to enter them, teacher resources, and opportunities to attend workshops and institutes.

- **National History Education Clearing House** (http://teachinghistory.org/) offers teachers access to primary and secondary sources. The website offers a page of "quick links" to help middle grades U.S. history teachers locate resources and lesson plans.

- **PBS American Experience** (http://www.pbs.org/wgbh/americanexperience/) is a website that provides a collection of PBS's American Experience documentaries along with a page created for teachers featuring timelines, primary source documents, maps, and teachers guide that correspond to episodes in the series.

- **PBS Teachers: Primary Sources & Contemporary U.S. history** (http://www.pbs.org/teachers/thismonth/primarysources/index1.html) offers middle level teacher resources and lesson ideas for teaching contemporary U.S. history. The website includes eight lessons and web links that can be used in middle level U.S. history classrooms. Two contemporary topics on the site include the War in Iraq and The Age of Technology.

- **Picturing America** (http://picturingamerica.neh.gov/) is a website sponsored by the National Council for the Humanities that uses great works of

art "as a catalyst for the study of America." The website offers educators a free resource book and images for the classroom.
- **Picturing U.S. History** (http://picturinghistory.gc.cuny.edu/) is a "digital project based on the belief that visual materials are vital to understanding the American past. The website provides online lessons in 'looking,' a guide to Web resources, forums, essays reviews, and classroom activities to help teachers incorporate visual evidence in their classrooms."
- **Smithsonian Institution** (http://www.si.edu/) "seeks to bring content experts and educators together to help strengthen American education and enhance our nation's ability to compete globally. The Smithsonian serves as a laboratory to create models and methods of innovative informal education and link them to the formal education system." The website offers teachers access to lesson plans developed to align with state standards and access to a variety of resources from many museums including the Air and Space, American History, and the Portrait Gallery.
- **Stanford History Education Group** (http://sheg.stanford.edu/?q=node/45) is directed by Sam Wineburg who is one of the most well-known researchers of history education in the country. The group's "Reading Like a Historian" curriculum "engages students in historical inquiry. Each lesson revolves around a central historical question and features sets of primary documents modified for groups of students with diverse reading skills and abilities." Their website offers teachers over 75 free inquiry-based U.S. history lesson plans.
- **The Virginia Center for Digital History: The Contemporary United States** (http://www.vcdh.virginia.edu/solguide/VUS14/VUS14.html) offers 12 lesson plans containing several primary sources about contemporary U.S. history. Topics include "women in the work force," "immigrants' impact on culture," and "GPS systems."

REFERENCES

The 1619 Project. (2019). *The 1619 Project.* https://www.nytimes.com/interactive/2019/08/14/magazine/1619-america-slavery.html

Baron, D. (2011). Using text-based protocols. *Principal Leadership, 7*(8), 43–45.

Brainy Quote. (n.d.). *Dick Gregory quotes.* https://www.brainyquote.com/quotes/dick_gregory_105750

Brophy, J., & VanSledright, B. (1997). *Teaching and learning history in elementary schools.* Teachers College Press.

Buchanan, L. B. (2011). Discussion in the elementary classroom: How and why some teachers use it. *The Georgia Social Studies Journal, 1*(1), 19–31. http://www.coe.uga.edu/gssj/archives/vol-1-no-1-2011/

Cazden, C. B. (1988). *Classroom discourse: The language of teaching and learning.* Heinemann

Cole, W. G., & Padgett, G. (2018) Through their eyes: Perspective taking activities for social studies classes. *The Councilor: A Journal of the Social Studies, 79*(2), 1–7. https://thekeep.eiu.edu/cgi/viewcontent.cgi?article=1119&context=the_councilor

De La Paz, S., & Felton, M. (2010). Reading and writing from multiple source documents in history: Effects of strategy instruction with low to average high school writers. *Journal of Contemporary Educational Psychology, 35*(3), 174–192.

Devine, C. (2017). Implementing best practice literacy instruction into a middle school social studies classroom. *School of Education Student Capstone Projects, 105*, 2–82. https://digitalcommons.hamline.edu/hse_cp/105

Ferreras-Stone, J. (2020). Women's suffrage: Teaching voting rights using multiple perspectives and timelines. *Social Studies and the Young Learner, 33*(2), 25–32.

Flynn, N. K. (2009). Toward democratic discourse: Scaffolding student led discussion in the social studies. *Teachers College Record, 111*(8), 2021–2053.

Golston, S. (2010). The revised NCSS standards: Ideas for the classroom teacher. *Social Education, 74*(4), 210–216.

Henning, J. E., Nielsen, L. E., Henning, M. C., & Schultz E. U. (2008). Designing discourse: Four ways to open up a dialogue. *The Social Studies, 99*(3), 122–126.

Herczog, M. M. (2010). Using the NCSS national curriculum standards for social studies: A framework for teaching, learning, and assessment to meet state social studies standards. *Social Education, 74*(4), 217–222.

Hess, D. (2009). *Controversy in the classroom: The democratic power of discussion.* Routledge.

Hines, J. I., & Vincent, P. J. (2005). *Teach the way they learn.* Chrystal Springs Books.

Hollas, B. (2005). *Differentiating instruction in a whole groups setting: Taking the easy first steps into differentiation.* Chrystal Springs Books.

Johnson, A. P. (2010). *Making connections in elementary and middle school social studies* (2nd ed.). Sage.

Jones, K., & Daisey, P. (2011). The value of writing "How-to" books in high school world history and geography classes. *The History Teacher, 45*(1), 45–63.

Kissling, M. (2011). A call for Wikipedia in the classroom. *Social Education, 75*(2), 60–64.

Kohlmeier, J. (2006). "Couldn't she just leave?:" The relationship between consistently using class discussions and the development of historical empathy in a 9th grade world history course. *Theory and Research in Social Education, 34*(1), 34–57.

Levstik, L. S., & Barton, K .C. (2005). *Doing history: Investigation with children in elementary and middle schools* (3rd ed.). Lawrence Erlbaum.

North, C. (2009). The promise and perils of developing democratic literacy for social justice. *Curriculum Inquiry, 39*(4), 555–579.

Notable Quotes. (2021). *Charles Francis Adams quotes.* http://www.notable-quotes.com/a/adams_charles_francis_sr.html

Parker, W. C. (2003). *Teaching democracy: Unity and diversity in public life.* Teachers College Press.

Passe, J., & Evans, R. W. (1996). Discussion methods in an issues-centered curriculum. In R. W. Evans & D. W. Saxe (Eds.), *Handbook on teaching social issues,* (pp. 81–88). National Council for the Social Studies.

The President's Advisory 1776 Commission, (2021, January). *The 1776 Report.* White House.

Roberts, S. L. (2013). The chalk talk 2.0: Using Goggle Docs to improve silent discussion in social studies. *The Social Studies, 104*(3), 130–136.

Roberts, S. L., & Block, M. K. (2020). Using "open" and "inquiry-focused" standards to study important women in Iowa's history. *The Iowa Journal for the Social Studies, 28*(2), 107–123.

Roberts, S. L., Butler, B. M., Elfer, C. J., Kendrick, D. T., & Widdall, V. (2020). "Isn't it peachy:" The successes and pitfalls of teaching complicated topics in eighth grade Georgia studies. In T. Flint & N. Keefer (Eds.). *Critical perspectives on teaching in the southern United States* (pp. 143–160). Lexington Books.

Saye, J. W. (2017). Disciplined inquiry in social studies classrooms. In *The Wiley handbook of social studies research* (pp. 336–359). John Wiley & Sons Inc. doi: 210.47.10.86

Stanford History Education Group. (2011). *Reading like a historian.* http://sheg.stanford.edu/?q=node/45

Stern, S. M., & Stern, J. A. (2011). *The state of state U.S. history standards 2011.* The Fordham Institute.

Tidwell, M. (2007). *Chalk talk.* http://pulse.pharmacy.arizona.edu/11th_grade/industrialization/language_arts/chalk_talk.html

Washington, E. Y., & Humphries, E. K. (2011). A social studies teacher's sense making of controversial issues discussions of race in a predominantly white, rural, high school classroom. *Theory and Research in Social Education, 39*(1), 92–114.

Westhoff, L. (2009). Lost in translation: The use of primary sources in teaching history. In R. Ragland & K. Woestman (Eds.), *The teaching American history project: Lessons for history educators and historians* (pp. 62–78). Routledge.

Wineburg, S. (2001). *Historical thinking and other unnatural acts: Charting the future of teaching the past.* Temple University Press.

Wineburg, S., & Martin, D. (2009). Tampering with history: Adapting primary sources for struggling readers. *Social Education, 73*(5), 212–216.

CHAPTER 9

BEST PRACTICES FOR TEACHING GEOGRAPHY

War is God's way of teaching Americans geography.
—*Ambrose Bierce (Brainy Quote, n.d.)*

The study of geography is about more than just memorizing places on a map. It's about understanding the complexity of our world, appreciating the diversity of cultures that exists across continents. And in the end, it's about using all that knowledge to help bridge divides and bring people together.
—*Barack Obama (Klieman, 2019)*

Activity List
- Reflecting on Why Geography is Important.
- Reflecting on the NCSS Expectations for Teachers of Geography.
- Comparing National and State Standards.
- Using Interactive Maps.
- Reflecting on the Chapter.

COLLABORATIVE ACTIVITY: WHY IS GEOGRAPHY IMPORTANT?

Geography as a discipline is often integrated into other social studies courses such as history or world cultures. Discuss the answers to the following questions with a classmate and write down your answers in your reflective journal:

- What types of topics or concepts come to mind when you think of "geography class"?
- Do you think the study of geography is important? If so, what should middle level students gain from its study?
- Why do you think geography is usually integrated into other subjects and not taught as a separate course?

INTRODUCTION

Courses that focus solely on geography are not common in middle level social studies education. Often, school districts use an integrated approach to teaching geography by incorporating map and globe skills into the study of history. An example of this is in California, whose state standards require US geography be integrated into a study of US history in 8th grade (California Department of Education, 2017). However, there may be a chance that you will teach a course primarily about world geography and cultures, sometimes called Human Geography. For example, in the state of Georgia, this course is required in both the 6th and 7th grades, with different regions of the world being examined in each grade level (Georgia Department of Education, 2011). The study of economic and political systems is also incorporated into this course. No matter if you teach geography and/or world cultures as a separate course or as part of an integrated social studies course, you will need to understand the themes and purposes of geography and strategies that you can use to teach it effectively.

GEOGRAPHY STANDARDS

Geography is important in social studies courses to help students learn about people, places, and cultures across the globe. As with history, economics, civics, and all other social studies disciplines, several groups have written about the importance of geography and why it should be studied in schools. In turn, they have written several themes and expectations that encompass the goals of its study and offer educators direction for teaching it.

NCSS Standards

In Chapter 2 we discussed the 10 NCSS themes for teaching social studies and identified several themes as having a connection to geography. These included: Theme 1: Culture; Theme 3: People, Places, and Environments; and Theme 9: Global Connections (NCSS, 2010). The NCSS also developed 18 "Expectations for Teachers of Geography" (Figure 9.1, NCSS, 2002) that focuses specifically on the teaching of geography. Some of the more important expectations that teachers of geography should strive to meet include guiding learners in the use of maps and other resources to acquire, process, and report information from a spatial perspective, helping students understand the characteristics of places, challenging learners to examine how the forces of cooperation and conflict among peoples

1. These expectations, along with the other 14 standards, help explain that the study of geography is not simply about memorizing features of maps and globes, but more about understanding a complex subject that incorporates elements of all social studies disciplines (see Figure 9.1). In other words, though learning how to use latitude and longitude or identifying countries and their capitals is important, understanding the human impact on the earth (both positive and negative) is much more crucial. As a middle-grades social studies teacher you should keep these standards in mind as you begin developing integrated lesson plans for your classes. As with the other disciplines nested within the social studies, our goal is to take students beyond memorization and identification into the realms of analysis, critique, and evaluation of geographic concepts and information.
2. Guide learners in the use of maps and other geographic representations, tools, and technologies to acquire, process, and report information from a spatial perspective. Enable learners to use mental maps to organize information about people, places, and environments in a spatial content.
3. Assist learners to analyze the spatial information about people, places, and environments on Earth's surface.
4. Help learners to understand the physical and human characteristics of places.
5. Assist learners in developing the concept of regions as means to interpret Earth's complexity.
6. Enable learners to understand how culture and experience influence people's perceptions of places and regions.
7. Provide learners opportunities to understand and analyze the physical processes that shape Earth's surface.
8. Challenge learners to consider the characteristics and spatial distributions of ecosystems on Earth's surface.
9. Guide learners in exploring the characteristics, distribution, and migration of human populations on Earth's surface.
10. Help learners to understand and analyze the characteristics, distribution, and complexity of Earth's cultural mosaics.
11. Have learners explore the patterns and networks of economic interdependence on Earth's surface.
12. Enable learners to describe the processes, patterns, and functions of human settlement.
13. Enable learners to use mental maps to organize information about people, places, and environments in a spatial content.
14. Help learners to understand the physical and human characteristics of places.
15. Assist learners in developing the concept of regions as means to interpret Earth's complexity.
16. Enable learners to understand how culture and experience influence people's perceptions of places and regions.
17. Guide learners in exploring the characteristics, distribution, and migration of human populations on Earth's surface.
18. Help learners to understand and analyze the characteristics, distribution, and complexity of Earth's cultural mosaics.

FIGURE 9.1. NCSS 18 Expectations for Teachers of Geography (2002).

influence the division of the Earth's surface, and helping students see how human actions modify the physical environment (NCSS, 2002, pp. 39–40).

COLLABORATIVE ACTIVITY: REFLECTING ON THE NCSS EXPECTATIONS FOR TEACHERS OF GEOGRAPHY

Examine three of the NCSS Expectations for Teachers of Geography and compare them to the answers you wrote in the last activity. In your reflective journal answer the following questions:

- How are your answers similar and/or different to the expectations?
- Do these expectations change your view about how geography should be taught?
- With a classmate review the three standards you chose and discuss state, U.S., or world history topics that you could integrate with these expectations.

AAG/NCGE Five Themes of Geography

Two groups, the Association of American Geographers and the National Council for Geographic Education, whose primary focus is on the study of geography, developed five themes for teaching geography (see Figure 9.2).

These themes were the building blocks for the NCSS' 18 expectations and should also be the foundation for geography instruction of any social studies

---

1. **Location:** describes where something is on the Earth's surface. There are two ways to describe location. Absolute location describes a point on the Earth's surface based on latitude and longitude. Relative location describes a point on the Earth's surface when it is compared to something else. For example, California is south of Oregon.
2. **Place:** refers to what it is like for a person to live in a certain area. This theme includes both the physical characteristics of the Earth's surface and cultural elements such as the economy, government, language, and religion of a place.
3. **Human Interactions with Environments:** how humans interact with their environment. In other words, how humans have used, cultivated, and altered (both positively and negatively) the environment in which they live.
4. **Movement:** is the travel of commodities and people from place to place. The geographic theme of movement also incorporates the dispersion of ideas and technology from place to place.
5. **Regions:** is the study of areas of the Earth that have similarities based on the physical features or environments as well as social, political, and economic similarities.

FIGURE 9.2. The AAG and NCGE's Five Themes for Teaching Geography

Element I: The World in Spatial Terms

- **Standard 1:** How to use maps and other geographic representations, tools, and technologies to acquire, process, and report information from a spatial perspective.
- **Standard 2:** How to use mental maps to organize information about people, places, and environments in a spatial context.
- **Standard 3:** How to analyze the spatial organization of people, places, and environments on Earth's surface.

Element II: Places and Regions

- **Standard 4:** The physical and human characteristics of places.
- **Standard 5:** That people create regions to interpret Earth's complexity.
- **Standard 6:** How culture and experience influence people's perceptions of places and regions.

Element III: Physical Systems

- **Standard 7:** The physical processes that shape the patterns for Earth's surface.
- **Standard 8:** The characteristics, distribution, and migration of human populations on Earth's surface.

Element IV: Human Systems

- **Standard 9:** The characteristics and spatial distribution of ecosystems on Earth's surface.
- **Standard 10:** The characteristics, distribution, and complexity of Earth's cultural mosaics.
- **Standard 11:** The patterns and networks of economic interdependence on Earth's surface.
- **Standard 12:** The processes, patterns, and functions of human settlement.
- **Standard 13:** How the forces of cooperation and conflict among people influence the division and control of Earth's surface.
- **Standard 14:** How human actions modify the physical environment.

Element V: Environment and Society

- **Standard 15:** How physical systems affect human systems.
- **Standard 16:** The changes that occur in the meaning, use, distribution, and importance of resources.

Element VI: The Uses of Geography

- **Standard 17:** How to apply geography to interpret the past.
- **Standard 18:** How to apply geography to interpret the present and plan for the future.

FIGURE 9.3. NCGE's National Geography Standards Source: National Council for Geographic Education

teacher. As stated previously, usually geography is integrated with other social science disciplines, and these important themes can be used in any social studies course to offer students a better understanding of historical, economic, or political events.

NCGE's National Geography Standards

In 1994, the National Council for Geographic Education developed 18 standards to help teachers of geography gain a better understanding of what should be taught in geography courses, or those social studies courses that incorporate its study (see Figure 9.3). Updated in 2012, these standards are grouped into six essential elements. They begin with basic map and globe skills such as "how to use maps and other geographic representations" and "how to use maps to organize information about people, places, and environments," to more complex concepts such as "using geography to interpret the past" and "plan for the future" (National Council for Geography Education, 1994).

Individual Activity: Comparing National and State Standards

Examine your state's geography standards for a middle level (grades 4–8) social studies course (see Table 2.1). Answer the following questions in your reflective journal:

- Compare the state's standards to those of the National Council for Geography's. Which standards are similar? Which are different?
- Based on your findings how much attention do those who developed state standards pay to national educational organizations? Why do you think this is the case?

STRATEGIES FOR TEACHING MIDDLE LEVEL GEOGRAPHY

As noted in Chapter 1, at this age level students are just beginning to move from the Concrete to the Formal Operation stage where visualization and abstract thinking skills are just beginning to become possible. Geography with its study of lands, people, and cultures both close to home and far away allow students to use this new mode of understanding. Students can now be exposed to ethical questions and questions of beauty such as "What makes this place look like it does?" "How do you know whether the people who live here are rich or poor?"

On the other hand, middle level students also need time to work with engaging active lessons. Because of the hands-on and collaborative nature of the subject itself, there are many geography-based activities that meet their needs (McCall, 2011). These include the use of activities such as working with globes, using interactive digital maps, or working on community projects.

Map and Globe Skills

Though the use of GPS systems is commonplace, research suggests overreliance on GPS devices may contribute to decreased use of spatial skills (Ruginski et al., 2019). Important skills in all sorts of settings, spatial awareness and recognition relates to an individual's ability to visualize objects in 3-dimensions, compare physical relationships between objects and places, and to mentally manipulate 3-dimensional objects. With the broad goal of assisting students in understanding their place in the world and how they relate to others, employment and refinement of spatial skill is an important aspect of geography education. Essentially, though GPS devices are handy, deep spatial skill—honed through experiences with maps and globes—assists students in understanding where they are, where other people and things are, and how objects and places interact.

Fundamental to refining spatial skill is the use of maps and globes. When teaching map and globe skills, there are obvious concepts that you must include and review with your students to help them learn to read maps. Some of these include absolute and relative location, cardinal directions, latitude and longitude, the Prime Meridian and Equator, using scale to determine and measure distances and understanding symbols and legends. There are many worksheets provided by textbook companies and found on the Internet that teachers can use to allow their students to practice these skills. These worksheets use all kinds of maps, including historical, topographical, and political. (See the Website resources section below for more information). The types of activities are useful in helping students prepare for standardized tests and can be incorporated into center-based lessons and warm-ups. Though important, these traditional approaches should not be the only strategies used when teaching basic geography skills.

I Want to Live Here!

Today's technology may make the use of globes seem obsolete, but these models of the planet still offer students one of the more realistic, interactive, and hands on-tools for studying the Earth than the sole use of flat maps. We have found due to the distortion of maps, many of our students thought that Greenland is the world's largest island and do not understand why Antarctica is not the largest continent. The use of the traditional globe helps provide students with a more accurate view of the earth. Another way to demonstrate the superiority of globes over flat maps is to analyze the "Great Circle Route" phenomenon. Flights which travel great distances, when viewed on a flat map, appear to be going far out of their way in large arcs. Ben experienced this on a recent trip from San Francisco to Taiwan. On a flat map, it did not make much sense he would travel over the Aleutian Islands and Southern Japan. With a globe and a piece of string, however, it becomes apparent that this arc becomes a straight line between the two points on a globe. Indeed, the globe is, for a lot of reasons, the best tool to represent Earth. That said, Ben was never able to convince his junior high school social studies department chair to purchase a four-foot diameter, bejeweled globe for his classroom, worth many thousands of dollars, (He never got the full suit of armor he requested, either).

One fun activity Scott used with his students to help them gain a better understanding of physical geography, as well as learn many of the geography skills listed above, was to play a game called "I want to live here." In groups of three, students were given a globe and told to spin it as fast as they could. Taking turns, they had to say, "I want to live here" and then place their finger down on the spinning globe. Once they stopped it, they had to move their finger to the closest land area. Using their selected country as a guide, they had to determine the country's absolute location using latitude and longitude, its distance from their state using the scale, and use the symbols on the legend to determine their country's major cities and population density. If they did not know much about the country, they were told to predict what they thought the country's major language(s), religion(s), trading partner(s), allies and rivals would be based on the countries that surrounded it. Students were then offered extra credit points to research cultural, political, and economic information about their country.

While this activity has similarities to standard research reports, the game of chance adds a fun element to a geography study. Scott was often surprised at how interested his students were in their country simply due to its random selection and how many took him up on the extra credit offer because they wanted to know more about the country. This activity is a great way to review geography skills without relying on traditional worksheets.

Ben finds globes to be vital tools in teaching about the seasons and the rotation and revolution of the Earth around the sun. Most globes are tilted at 23½ degrees, reflecting the tilt of the Earth as related to its positioning with the sun. Ben holds the globe level and, with a bright projector on a cart in the middle of the room, he demonstrates how the seasons work. Working through the revolution of the Earth around the sun, students see how the tilt remains the same, but the relative positioning of the Northern and Southern hemispheres change. Once students have a solid understanding of this process, Ben then adds a tennis ball to serve as a moon to demonstrate eclipses-both solar and lunar- and a simplified description of how tides work. Many students deeply enjoy being "Atlas" as the holder of the Earth throughout its yearly journey.

Interactive Maps

Though globes are useful tools in the study of geography, there are several commercial interactive maps and satellite-based programs that teachers can incorporate with the study of geography (Alibrandi et al., 2010; Milson et al., 2012). These programs offer fantastic historical, political, and topographical maps that teachers should use in any social science course. To our dismay, however, in some schools these interactive maps have completely taken the place of globes and pull-down maps. We argue for the use of both to get the best of technology and hands-on tactile experience.

There are also many free interactive mapping websites that teachers can use in their classes. Two of these sites are Zeemaps and Google Earth. Zeemaps allows students to create interactive maps that include locations, descriptions, web links, audio files, and movie files. Teachers can use this program to allow students to create projects that trace important events in history, trace the travels of historic figures, or gain content knowledge about the settings of historic trade books.

Google Earth is a free software download that allows students to explore any point on the Earth. One thing that students love to do with this program is type in their address and view a satellite image of their own homes, school, and community. The program also has a trip function that features concepts such as regions, allows students to explore places or even show the factors of production (e.g., making heavy machinery). In some cases, people have already placed these saved trips on one or more websites. If you find that these pre-generated trips are valuable examples and exist on stable websites, you could link out to them on other programs. Another way to use this program in your classes is to include it as an additional step in the "I want to live here" activity.

Another aspect of Google Earth students enjoy is the "street view" that is available in many places around the world. Students may enter the street view of Times Square in New York, the Pyramids at Giza in Egypt, and the Forbidden City in Beijing. Additionally, students may enter many buildings through this option. Students can explore the interiors of locations such as the Palace at Versailles and the White House in Washington D.C. In the United States, most students will be able to view their own neighborhoods, though many rural areas have yet to be photographed from this perspective.

The Classroom as a Map

One of the inherent advantages of teaching geography is that you can use any space to assist students in developing their spatial awareness skills. Turning your classroom floor, (or any floor for that matter) into a map on which students can walk and interact will provide a unique opportunity for them to practice skills so often overlooked in schools.

Ben was fortunate to have a classroom where the floor was covered with one square foot tiles. This natural grid system could be used with students to demonstrate grid systems, specifically latitude and longitude. Using nothing more than masking tape and a marker, Ben had his students create a Mercator projection of the world on his classroom floor. Certainly, this concept can be adjusted in scale to allow students to create representations of the United States, the State of Illinois, or even the local community. Students can use various colors of tape or trinkets to represent different landmarks. At other times, Ben had students create a map of the United States, Mexico, and the Caribbean to demonstrate how hurricanes move. Students were thrilled to be the hurricane as they spun with their arm, slowly approaching the coast.

As a side note, the use of a grid-system floor approach can also be employed by your mathematics teacher to demonstrate graphing on the X and Y axis. For the third dimension, a string can be pinned to the ceiling and taped to the floor to represent the Z axis. One of the first things Ben notices about a classroom is whether it has a grid system on its floor or not. He always points this out to preservice teachers with whom he works.

If you do not have a ready-made grid system as a floor, using string, masking tape, or painter's tape can achieve the same goal. Though it will take a bit more work, the reaction of students when they walk into your classroom will be worth the cost in tape and bruised knees. If you feel adventurous and you have a willing administrator, this activity can be done in as large a space as you can find, potentially decreasing the scale of your map.

COLLABORATIVE ACTIVITY: USING INTERACTIVE MAPS

In your reflective journal follow the steps below and share your ideas with a classmate:

- Go to one of the free interactive maps on the websites listed above and explore all of the features.
- With a partner discuss all of the different ways that you could incorporate these programs into history, economics, and government lessons.
- Create a list of locations around a school that could be turned into maps.

Human Geography Projects

As mentioned before, the use of projects allows students to have the opportunity to be creative and cement their knowledge of the social studies topics being learned. The subject of geography lends itself to the use of projects, since it's often viewed as being better learned with hands-on activities. Students are often required to manipulate traditional and computer-generated maps and globes to learn more about the world we live in. Below are two examples of projects that can be used in the middle level classroom in the study of geography.

Create Your Own Map

A project that allows students to practice their geography skills is to ask them to create their own maps (see Figure 9.4). Like the "I want to live here game," this project helps maintain students' interest in learning and working with their geography skills. In the case of this project, it allows students to make their own choices in their learning. When Scott used this project in his classes, he allowed students to choose any place they wanted to make a map about. It could also be an imaginary place such as Springfield from *The Simpsons* television program or

Best Practices for Teaching Geography • 227

Overview: This lesson allows students to learn basic geography skills with an approach that they will find to be both fun and relatable...creating a map about their favorite place.

Time: 2 hours

Materials Needed
- Pen/Pencil -Markers/Color Pencils -Atlas -Copy Paper
- *"Maps and Cartography: The Elements of a Map"* Ball State University Library (https://lib.bsu.edu/collections/gcmc/tutorials/pdfs/mapscartography-mapelements.pdf)
- Worksheet: Create Your Own Map Worksheet/Rubric

Procedures:

Ask students to write down, in their own words, the definition of the following terms -Geography -Latitude -Longitude -Equator -Prime Meridian -Hemispheres

Key/Legend
1. Compass Rose -*Cardinal Directions* (Tell them to remember the phrase "Never Eat Soggy Waffles") -Intermediate Directions -Scale
2. Have students share their answers with a partner. Tell students that before they report the information to you, they must be in agreement about their definitions.
3. Have students explore the "Maps and Cartography: The Elements of a Map" presentation from Ball State University. This presentation was chosen because it has wonderful examples of all sorts of maps. Explain to them that they will also be using the "elements of a map" information to create their own maps later in the day.
4. Pass out the directions for the *Create Your Own Map Activity* and have students spend the rest of the class working on the activity. If students finish in time, make them answer each other's questions. If not, continue this activity the next day.

Create Your Own Map Rubric

Directions:
- Create a map of your favorite place. It could be your room, your house, a state, a country, or even an imaginary place. Your map should show that you have an understanding of how maps work.

Requirements:
1. The map should be colorful and creative.
2. The map must contain a key/legend.

FIGURE 9.4. Basic Geography/Create Your Own Map Lesson Plan (continues)

> 3. The map must contain a scale to show distance.
> 4. The map must contain a compass rose with both cardinal and intermediate directions.
> 5. If you choose to draw a map of a state or country, you must include lines of longitude and latitude.
> 6. You must explain what type of map you constructed.
> 7. Upon completion of your map, you should come up with five questions on a separate piece of paper that can be answered by looking at your map. There should be one question concerning the key/legend, one concerning the scale, one concerning the compass rose, and two questions of your choice.
> 8. A third piece of paper should contain an answer key for your questions.
>
> **Rubric Scoring:**
> - Map (25 points) _____
> - Key/Legend/Title (15 points) _____
> - Scale (15 points) _____
> - Compass Rose (10 points) _____
> - Colorful/Creative (15 points) _____
> - Questions (15 points) _____
> - Answer Key (5 points) _____

FIGURE 9.4. Continued

it could be a real location such as their bedroom, their school, or their home state and country (see Figure 9.5). Ben encouraged his students to map their neighborhoods or a themed island based on their favorite movie.

When creating these maps, students were required to include a compass rose, a legend with symbols, a scale, and latitude and longitude for states and countries. More importantly, students were asked to demonstrate their knowledge about these skills as they were required to write five questions about their map. They then switched their maps and questions with other students to allow their peers to interpret their maps. If their classmates missed a question, the creator of the map was required to explain why they missed the question. A lesson plan, rubric, and examples for this project are listed in Figures 9.4 and 9.5.

Place-Based Education Projects

Place-based education is pedagogy that focuses on students using their local communities as the stage for learning about history, the environment, culture, and literature (Yavuz Akbaş & Çakmak, 2019). Essentially, Place-Based education projects take "deep dives" into students' own communities that serve as case studies of larger geographic, historic, economic, and cultural concepts. A leading proponent of Place-Based projects is Professor David Sobel of Antioch Univer-

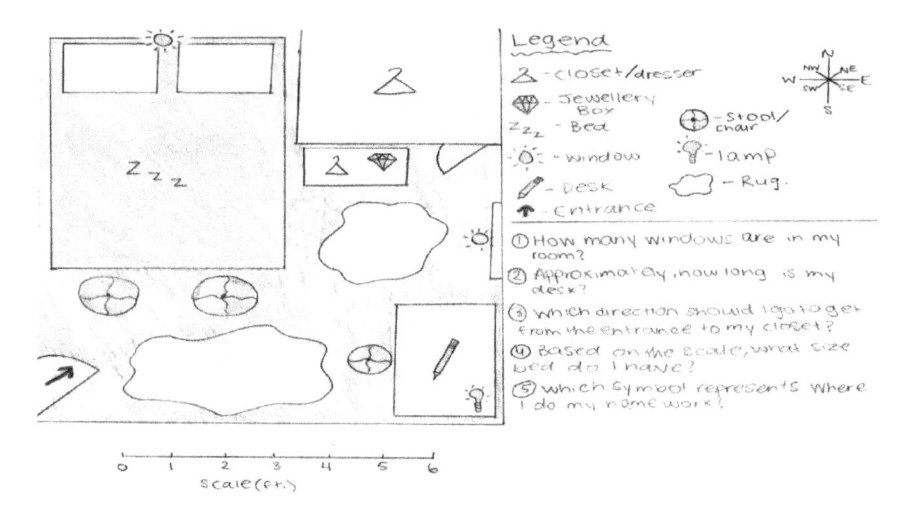

FIGURE 9.5. Sample Map: Student's Room

sity. Through Units of study with titles such as "Using the River as a Textbook" and "The Town Becomes the Classroom," (Sobel, 2020) the approach has potential to be life and community-changing through authentic, action-based research approaches by students.

Though Place-Based education is seeing a recent resurgence in interest, it has been around in several different forms since at least the early 1970s (Elfer, 2011). While the merits of the approach have been debated and the ability to fully use a place-based education philosophy can appear impossible in today's standards based educational system, elements from place-based education can certainly be used in the geography classroom.

An example of a place-based project would be for students to use a GPS system to map their own community. However, once students used the technology resource to map the community, they would then go out into the community where they would take their own pictures of geography features, landmarks, and the people that live in the area. They would then interview residents of the community to gain a better understanding about the beliefs and cultures of those who live there. Students would use the data collected from all sources to write about their discoveries. More information about place-based education can be found on the Center for Placed Based Learning and Community Education website.

Similar in concept is the use of specific locations to serve as examples of concepts explored in your geography class. Grocery stores, with their vast collections of food from all around the world can serve as examples of global interdependence and culture. Having your students find examples of foods from different regions or countries can concretely connect them to the far-off places they are studying. If your community has ethnic-based organizations such as Lebanese-American Associations or German-American Associations, you can invite members from these organizations to talk with your students when studying these areas. Local Chambers of Commerce are willing to provide information that may serve as stems for learning about cultural history, economics of the area, or resources for which the area is known. Essentially, the Place-Based Education approach embraces the physical, historical, economic, and cultural geography of students' own environments as venues for exploration.

SUMMARY

This chapter offered information about teaching geography in the middle level classroom, a subject that is often not taught independently in most middle schools but usually as part of an integrated social studies course. In this chapter we discussed the standards and themes suggested by the NCSS and the NCGE. We also discussed several strategies to teach geography that emphasized both traditional and technology-based tools. As with all social studies strategies, these can be altered to meet the needs of your students and school. For more information about inquiry-based approaches for teaching geography see Brown Buchanan et al. (2016), Kenna and Russell (2017), McPherson (2019), Thacker et al.(2017), Widdall et al. (2018) In the next chapter we discuss the best practices for teaching economics and government in the middle level classroom.

Individual Activity: Reflecting on the Chapter

Return to your answers about the importance of teaching geography in the middle schools. In your reflective journal answer the following questions:

- After reading this chapters, how have your ideas changed about the purposes of teaching the subject.
- What steps are you going to take in order to ensure that you meet the NCSS expectations and the NCGE standards?
- What are some tools and strategies discussed in the chapter that you think will help meet the goals?

WEBSITE RESOURCES

- **The Center for Place-Based Learning and Community Education** (https://promiseofplace.org/) is a "unique public private partnership that works to advance the state of the art in place-based education by facilitating collaborative efforts in research, program design, technical assistance, resource development and dissemination." The website offers links to individual lesson plans, curriculum guides, research and evaluation, and a teachers' forum about place-based education. The website also provides several "stories from the field" where teachers who used the placed-based program candidly describe what they did and the successes and failures in

using the approach. Though in many school districts using a full "place-based" model will not be feasible, many of the ideas found on the website can be incorporated into geography classes.
- **Education.com** (http://www.education.com/worksheets/middle-school/geography/) is a website that offers teachers and parents thousands of free reproducible worksheets over a variety of subjects and topics. Of course, worksheet quality varies, so it will be up to you to review them and use the ones that meet the needs of your students. Even if they do not directly match your curriculum, some of the worksheets may offer you ideas to develop your own worksheets.
- **Google Earth** (https://www.google.com/earth/) is a web-based program that according to the website allows students to "put the world's geographic information at their fingertips. Educators around the globe have created engaging classroom activities that go beyond geography to teach literature, history, math, environmental science, and more." The site also offers a "Google Earth for Educators Community" that "provides all of the tips and tricks for using Google Earth as a teaching tool. On this site, you can view lesson plans for a variety of grade levels and subjects, discuss Google Earth teaching tactics with fellow educators, see student-created work, and read how other teachers are using Google Earth in the classroom." This site is a free download and is well worth exploring. It can be a helpful tool in teaching geography along with many other social studies subjects.
- **Middle School.net** (http://middleschool.net/) is a website that offers links to free worksheets, curriculum guides, and other resources specifically designed for middle grades learners. The website claims that all of the worksheets are created by teachers. In the social studies portion of the site there are links to three other sites with geography worksheets.
- **Zeemaps** (http://www.zeemaps.com/) is a website that allows students to create custom made interactive maps that can be published on a blog or websites. Students can add features to their maps including video clips, music, and text. They can also highlight physical features and save their maps in pdf and jpeg images.

REFERENCES

Alibrandi, M., Milson, A. J., & Shin, E. K. (2010). Where we've been; Where we are; Where we're going: Geospatial technologies and social studies. In R. Diem & M. J. Berson. (Eds.), *Technology retrospect: Social studies place in the information age: 1984–2009* (pp. 109–132). Information Age.

Brainy Quote. (n.d.). *Ambrose Bierce quotes.* https://www.brainyquote.com/quotes/ambrose_bierce_164710

Brown Buchanan, L., Tschida, C. M., & Brown, S. N. (2016). Integrating mapping and ELA skills using giant traveling maps. *Social Studies and the Young Learner, 29*(2), 21–27.

California Department of Education. (2017). *An overview of the new History-Social Science Framework for California public schools: The middle grades.* Author.

Elfer, C. (2011). Place-based education: Making the case for an investigation of historical precedents. *Curriculum History.* https://www.researchgate.net/publication/308079626_PLACE-BASED_EDUCATION_MAKING_THE_CASE_FOR_AN_INVESTIGATION_OF_HISTORICAL_PRECENDENTS

Georgia Department of Education. (2011). *Social studies 6–8.* https://www.georgiastandards.org/Standards/Pages/BrowseStandards/SocialStudiesStandards6-8.aspx

Kenna, J. L., & Russell, W. B. (2017). Keeping it animated: Utilizing animated films to teach geography. *Social Education, 81*(3), 154–158.

Klieman, K. (2019). *The importance of geography—Applications beyond K–12 classrooms.* https://blog.socialstudies.com/the-importance-of-geography-in-the-classroom-applications-beyond-k-12

McCall, A. L. (2011). Promoting critical thinking and inquiry through maps in elementary classrooms. *The Social Studies, 102*(3), 132–138.

McPherson, K. (2019). The fifty states project: Learning about America, one care package at a time. *Social Studies and the Young Learner, 32*(2), 3–9.

Milson, A. J., Kerski, J. J., & Demirci, A. (2012). The world at their fingertips: A new age for spatial thinking. In A. Milson, A. Dermirci, & J. J. Kerski. (Eds.), *International perspectives on teaching and learning with GIS in secondary schools.* Springer.

National Council for Geography. (1994). *Geography for life: National geography standards.* http://www.ncge.org/geography-for-life

National Council for the Social Studies. (2002). *National standards for social studies teachers.* NCSS.

National Council for the Social Studies. (2010). *National curriculum standards for social studies.* NCSS.

Ruginski, I. T., Creem-Regerh, S. H., Stefanucci, J. K., & Cashdan, E. (2019). GPS use negatively affects environmental learning through spatial transformation abilities. *Journal of Environmental Psychology, 64,* 12–20.

Sobel, D. (2020). Place based education: Connecting classroom and community. *Community Works Journal.* https://magazine.communityworksinstitute.org/place-based-education-connecting-classroom-and-community/

Thacker, E. S., Hicks, D., & Friedman, A. M. (2017). It might not be a matter of life or death, but does soccer really explain the world? *Social Education, 81*(4), 234–238.

Widdall, V., Alqahtani, M., & Kraly, T. (2018). The measurement and meaning of landmarks: Integrating social studies and math in fifth grade lessons. *Social Studies and the Young Learner, 31*(1), 26–32.

Yavuz Akbaş, Y., & Çakmak, S. (2019). The effect of place-based education integrated project studies on students' problem-solving and social skills. *Asian Journal of Education and Training, 5*(1), 183–192.

CHAPTER 10

INCORPORATING ECONOMICS AND GOVERNMENT IN MIDDLE LEVEL SOCIAL STUDIES

Too many people think that economics is this subject that should wait until the university level. But it can't wait that long.
—*Robert Duvall (Quote Fancy, n.d.)*

Economics, politics, and personalities are often inseparable.
—*Charles Edison (Brainy Quote, n.d.)*

Activity List
- Reflecting on Economics and Government.
- Reflecting on the NCSS Expectations for Teachers of Economics.
- Comparing the NCSS Expectations and the CEE Standards.
- The Economic Way of Thinking.
- Using the CEE Economic Lesson Plan Database.
- Reflecting on the NCSS Expectations for Teachers of Civics and Government.
- Museum Walk about the National Standards for Civics and Government.
- Key Government Ideals and Concepts.
- Using the CCE Civics and Government Website.
- Reflecting on the Chapter.

Teaching Middle Level Social Studies: A Practical Guide for 4th–8th Grade (3rd Edition),
pages 233–254.
Copyright © 2022 by Information Age Publishing
www.infoagepub.com
All rights of reproduction in any form reserved.

COLLABORATIVE ACTIVITY: REFLECTING ON ECONOMICS AND GOVERNMENT

Economics and political science/government/civics are disciplines that are often integrated into other social studies subjects such as history or world cultures. In your reflective journal write your answers to the questions below and then discuss them with a classmate.

- Do you think the study of economics and government is important?
- If yes, what should middle level students gain from their study?
- Why do you think economics and government are usually integrated into other subjects at the middle grade level and not taught as separate courses?

INTRODUCTION

History can be characterized as the recording of the decisions made by individuals and groups from the past, and nothing has driven those decisions more than economics and government. Though these two social science disciplines have been important in both past and present events, at the middle level they are not often taught as separate courses but integrated in a general social studies class. The authors have increasingly found that it is impossible to separate the various disciplines of the social studies from one another. Rather, we embrace the interdisciplinary nature of these areas of study and blend them together to craft our classes. The reality remains, however, that many social studies classes are described as "single discipline" courses such as US History, World Geography, or Civics. No matter which social studies course you teach at the middle level, it is important to continuously bring economics and government into your classes.

Bringing Economics into Middle Level Social Studies Classes

Economics can be defined as the study of the production, distribution, and consumption of goods and services. However, as most of those who have taken an economics course know, the true study of economics and the impact that it has on the past and our daily lives is much more complicated than that simple definition. The decision to drill for oil in the pristine arctic regions of Alaska; Spanish, English, and French exploitation of the western hemisphere; the role government should play in banking regulation and the minimum wage; cost of living and inflation across decades; and the influence of technology on the cost of consumer products all serve as example of interrelationships between economic, geographic, political, cultural, and historic concepts. Because of its influence on the decision making of historic figures, our leaders today, and us as individuals, economics is a topic that should be incorporated as often as possible in any social studies class. It should serve as a foundation in your students' understanding of our world today.

Incorporating Economics and Government in Middle Level Social Studies • 235

1. Productive resources are limited. Therefore, people cannot have all the goods and services that they want; as a result, they must choose some things and give up others.
2. Effective decision-making requires comparing the additional costs of alternatives with the additional benefits. Most choices involve doing or having a little more or a little less of something; few choices are all-or-nothing decisions.
3. Different methods can be used to allocate goods and services. People, acting individually or collectively through government, must choose which methods to use to allocate different kinds of goods and services.
4. People respond predictably to positive and negative incentives.
5. Voluntary exchange occurs only when all parties expect to gain. This is true for trade among individuals or organizations within a nation, or among individuals or organizations in different nations.
6. When individuals, regions, and nations specialize in what they can produce at the lowest cost and trade with others, both production and consumption increases.
7. Markets exist when buyers and sellers interact. This interaction determines market prices and thereby allocates scarce goods and services.
8. Prices send signals and provide incentive to buyers and sellers. When supply and demand change, market prices adjust, affecting incentives.
9. Competition among sellers lowers costs and prices, encouraging producers to produce more of what consumers are willing and able to buy. Competition among buyers increases prices and allocates goods and services to those people who are willing and able to pay the most for them.
10. Institutions evolve in market economies to help individuals and groups accomplish their goals. Banks, labor unions, corporations, legal systems, and not-for-profit organizations are examples of important institutions. A different kind of institution, clearly defined and enforced property rights, is essential to a market economy.
11. Money makes it easier to trade, borrow, save, invest, and compare the value of goods and services.
12. Interest rates, adjusted for inflation, rise and fall to balance the amount saved with the amount borrowed, thus affecting the allocation of scarce resources among present and future leaders.
13. Income for most people is determined by the market value of the productive resources they sell. What workers earn depends, primarily, on the market value of what they produce and how productive they are.
14. Entrepreneurs are people who take the risks of organizing productive resources to make goods and services. Profit is an important incentive that leads entrepreneurs to accept the risk of business failure.
15. Investment in factories, machinery, new technology, and in the health, education, and training of people, can raise future standards of living.

(continues)

FIGURE 10.1. NCSS 20 Expectations for Teachers of Economics (2002)

> 16. There is an economic role for the government to play in a market economy whenever the benefit of a government policy outweighs its cost. Government often provides for national defense, addresses environmental concerns, defines and protects property rights, and attempts to make markets more competitive. Most government policies also redistribute income.
> 17. Costs of government policies sometimes exceed benefits. This may occur because of incentives facing voters, government officials, and government employees; because social goals other than economic efficiency are being pursued.
> 18. A nation's overall levels of income, employment, and prices are determined by the interaction of spending and production decisions made by all households, firms, government agencies, and others in the economy.
> 19. Unemployment imposes costs on individuals and nations. Unexpected inflation imposes cost on many people and benefits some others because it arbitrarily redistributes purchasing power. Inflation can reduce the rate of growth of national living standards because individuals and organizations use resources to protect themselves against the uncertainty of future prices.
> 20. In the United States, federal government budgetary policy and the Federal Reserve System's monetary policy influence the overall levels of employment, output, and prices.

FIGURE 10.1. Continued

Economics Standards

As with the teaching of geography, several organizations have developed standards and expectations for economics instruction. Though produced by different organizations, many of these themes and expectations have similarities to one another. These themes should be at the forefront of your mind as you plan lessons for teaching economics.

NCSS Teacher Expectations for Teachers of Economics

In Chapter 2 we discussed the 10 NCSS themes for teaching social studies and identified several themes as having a connection to economics. These included: Theme 1: Culture; Theme 2. Time Continuity and Change; Theme 3: People, Places, and Environments; Theme 5: Individual Groups and Institutions, Theme 7: Production, Distribution, and Consumption; Theme 8: Science, Technology, and Society; and Theme 9: Global Connections (NCSS, 2010). The NCSS has also developed 20 "Expectations for Teachers of Economics" (NCSS, 2002) that focus specifically on the teaching of economics. Some of the more important expectations that any teacher of economics must strive to meet include guiding learners to understand that productive resources are limited, that voluntary exchange only happens when all parties expect a gain, and that investment in material, technology, and people can raise future living standards (NCSS, 2002, pp. 43–44).

Incorporating Economics and Government in Middle Level Social Studies • **237**

These expectations, along with 17 others, help explain that the study of economics is not simply about money or concepts such as supply and demand, but a complex subject that incorporates elements of all social studies disciplines (see Figure 10.1). In other words, though learning about specific entrepreneurs such as Madam C. J. Walker, Henry Ford, J. D. Rockefeller, and Elon Musk is important in the study of economics, understanding how economic concepts play a role in decision making is much more crucial. As a middle-grades social studies teacher you should keep these standards in mind as you begin developing integrated lesson plans for your classes. While exploring the expectations, we encourage you to think about both specific examples as well as ways to integrate these expectations into broader social studies courses.

COLLABORATIVE ACTIVITY: REFLECTING ON THE NCSS EXPECTATIONS FOR TEACHERS OF ECONOMICS

Examine three of the NCSS Expectations for Teachers of Economics and compare them to the answers you wrote in the last activity. Answer the following questions in your reflective journal.

- How do your answers compare to the expectations?
- Do these expectations change your view about how economics should be taught?
- With a classmate review the three standards you chose and discuss how these standards could be integrated into common state, U.S., or world history topics.

Council for Economic Education: Voluntary National Content Standards in Economics

In 2010, The Council for Economic Education (CEE) released an updated version of their 1997 "Voluntary National Content Standards in Economics." Like the NCSS Expectations for Teachers of Economics, there are 20 standards. Unlike the NCSS, the CEE offers teachers an understanding of economic concepts, as well as what students will understand from the study of each standard and how they will be able to apply this knowledge to their everyday lives. A free PDF download of the complete list of standards along with benchmarks and lesson activities can be found on their website (CEE, 2010). Table 10.1 offers a summary of all 20 of these standards as well as students' understanding and applications of these standards.

Individual Activity: Comparing the NCSS Expectations and CEE Standards

In your reflective journal:

TABLE 10.1. Council for Economic Education's Voluntary National Content for Standards in Economics (2010)

Standard #/Theme	Student Understanding	Student Application
1: Scarcity	Productive resources are limited. Therefore, people cannot have all the goods and services they want; as a result, they must choose some things and give up others	Identify what they gain and what they give up when they make choices.
2: Decision Making	Effective decision making requires comparing the additional costs of alternatives with the additional benefits. Many choices involve doing a little more or a little less of something: few choices are "all or nothing" decisions.	Make effective decisions as consumers, producers, savers, investors, and citizens.
3: Allocation	Different methods can be used to allocate goods and services. People acting individually or collectively must choose which methods to use to allocate different kinds of goods and services.	Evaluate different methods of allocating goods and services, by comparing the benefits to the costs of each method.
4: Incentives	People usually respond predictably to positive and negative incentives.	Identify incentives that affect people's behavior and explain how incentives affect their own behavior.
5: Trade	Voluntary exchange occurs only when all participating parties expect to gain. This is true for trade among individuals or organizations within a nation, and among individuals or organizations in different nations.	Negotiate exchanges and identify the gains to themselves and others. Compare the benefits and costs of policies that alter trade barriers between nations, such as tariffs and quotas.
6: Specialization	When individuals, regions, and nations specialize in what they can produce at the lowest cost and then trade with others, both production and consumption increase.	Explain how they can benefit themselves and others by developing special skills and strengths
7: Markets and Prices	A market exists when buyers and sellers interact. This interaction determines market prices and thereby allocates scarce goods and services.	Identify markets in which they have participated as a buyer and as a seller and describe how the interaction of all buyers and sellers' influences prices. Also, predict how prices change when there is either a shortage or surplus of the product available.
8: Role of Prices	Prices send signals and provide incentives to buyers and sellers. When supply or demand changes, market prices adjust, affecting incentives.	Predict how changes in factors such as consumers' tastes or producers' technology affect prices.

TABLE 10.1. Continued

Standard #/Theme	Student Understanding	Student Application
9: Competition and Market Structure	Competition among sellers usually lowers costs and prices and encourages producers to produce what consumers are willing and able to buy. Competition among buyers increases prices and allocates goods and services to those people who are willing and able to pay the most for them.	Explain how changes in the level of competition in different markets can affect price and output levels.
10: Institutions	Institutions evolve and are created to help individuals and groups accomplish their goals. Banks, labor unions, markets, corporations, legal systems, and not-for-profit organizations are examples of important institutions. A different kind of institution, clearly defined and enforced property rights, is essential to a market economy.	Describe the roles of various economic institutions and explain the importance of property rights in a market economy.
11: Money and Inflation	Money makes it easier to trade, borrow, save, invest, and compare the value of goods and services. The amount of money in the economy affects the overall price level. Inflation is an increase in the overall price level that reduces the value of money.	Explain how their lives would be more difficult in a world with no money, or in a world where money sharply lost its value.
12: Interest Rates	Interest rates, adjusted for inflation, rise and fall to balance the amount saved with the amount borrowed, which affects the allocation of scarce resources between present and future uses.	Explain situations in which they pay or receive interest and explain how they would react to changes in interest rates if they were making or receiving interest payments.
13: Income	Income for most people is determined by the market value of the productive resources they sell. What workers earn primarily depends on the market value of what they produce.	Predict future earnings based on their current plans for education, training, and career options.
14: Entrepreneurship	Entrepreneurs take on the calculated risk of starting new businesses, either by embarking on new ventures similar to existing ones or by introducing new innovations. Entrepreneurial innovation is an important source of economic growth.	Identify the risks and potential returns to entrepreneurship, as well as the skills necessary to engage in it. Understand the importance of entrepreneurship and innovation to economic growth, and how public policies affect incentives for and, consequently, the success of entrepreneurship in the United States.
15: Economic Growth	Investment in factories, machinery, new technology, and in the health, education, and training of people stimulates economic growth and can raise future standards of living.	Predict the consequences of investment decisions made by individuals, businesses, and governments.

TABLE 10.1. Continued

Standard #/Theme	Student Understanding	Student Application
16: Role of Government and Market Failure	There is an economic role for government in a market economy whenever the benefits of a government policy outweigh its costs. Governments often provide for national defense, address environmental concerns, define and protect property rights, and attempt to make markets more competitive. Most government policies also have direct or indirect effects on people's incomes.	Identify and evaluate the benefits and costs of alternative public policies and assess who enjoys the benefits and who bears the costs.
17: Government Failure	Costs of government policies sometimes exceed benefits. This may occur because of incentives facing voters, government officials, and government employees, because of actions by special interest groups that can impose costs on the general public, or because social goals other than economic efficiency are being pursued.	Identify some public policies that may cost more than the benefits they generate and assess who enjoys the benefits and who bears the costs. Explain why the policies exist.
18: Economic Fluctuations	Fluctuations in a nation's overall levels of income, employment, and prices are determined by the interaction of spending and production decisions made by all households, firms, government agencies, and others in the economy. Recessions occur when overall levels of income and employment decline.	Interpret media reports about current economic conditions and explain how these conditions can influence decisions made by consumers, producers, and government policy makers.
19: Unemployment and Inflation	Unemployment imposes costs on individuals and the overall economy. Inflation, both expected and unexpected, also imposes costs on individuals and the overall economy. Unemployment increases during recessions and decreases during recoveries.	Make informed decisions by anticipating the consequences of inflation and unemployment.
20: Fiscal and Monetary Policy	Federal government budgetary policy and the Federal Reserve System's monetary policy influence the overall levels of employment, output, and prices.	Anticipate the impact of federal government and Federal Reserve System macroeconomic policy decisions on themselves and others.

Incorporating Economics and Government in Middle Level Social Studies • 241

- Draw a Venn diagram comparing the NCSS expectations to those of the CEE. Which are similar? Which are different?
- Select three "student understanding" statements and create an example for each.
- How can you use the CEE standards in your social studies lesson planning?

THE TOP 10 KEY ECONOMIC TERMS AND CONCEPTS FOR MIDDLE LEVEL LEARNERS

After examining the NCSS expectations and the CEE standards you may see that there are several economic terms and concepts that middle grades students are expected to learn in their social studies courses (see Figure 10.2). When examining these terms and concepts, continue to think about how they can be incorporated into middle level social studies courses, with focus on specific examples students may find relevant and applicable to their lives outside school.

Strategies for Bringing Economics into Social Studies Courses

Throughout the book we have provided examples of economics-based lessons that can be incorporated into the middle level social studies classroom. These included the "State Based Business Project" (Chapter 6) and the "Impact of Railroads" (Chapter 7). As mentioned before, while the subject of economics is not

---

1. **Economic Growth and Development:** An increase in the capacity of the economy to satisfy the desire for goods and services by consumers.
2. **Entrepreneurs:** Individuals who take financial risks in order to create a business in hopes of making a profit.
3. **Free Trade:** International trade that is free of tariffs or quotas.
4. **Goods and Services:** What people buy and sell. Goods are tangible things that can be consumed. While Services are actions people perform.
5. **Government Revenue:** Money that the government takes in.
6. **Government Spending (Expenditures):** The money the government spends for goods and services for its citizens.
7. **Incentives:** Any factor (monetary or nonmonetary) that causes a person to do something.
8. **Opportunity Cost:** One's second best option. What a person gives up in order to do something else.
9. **Productive Resources:** Materials, labor, and/or capital (money) used to produce goods and services.
10. **Scarcity:** When there are unlimited wants but limited resources. The less there is of something the more valuable it is.

FIGURE 10.2. The Top 10 Key Economic Terms and Concepts for Middle Level Learners (In Alphabetical Order)

taught as a separate course at the middle level, economic concepts are part of the standards for many states. Below are some of our ideas to help you incorporate economics into your social studies classes. Additional articles by Agnello et al. (2019), Gandy (2016), Gilbert et al. (2018), Knapp and Hopkins (2018), Manfra and Saylor (2016), and Potter (2019) are also helpful for teaching economics and financial literacy at the middle level.

The Economic Way of Thinking

A useful tool in helping students gain a better understanding of economic concepts and how these concepts influence decision making is a list of steps called "The Economic Way of Thinking." These steps have been presented in slightly different ways, but all offer the same concepts (e.g., NCEE, n.d.; Roberts, 2009; Schug et al., 2006). To paraphrase, these steps are:

- People make choices.
- Every choice has a cost (opportunity cost).
- Incentives influence people's choices.
- People create rules that affect their choices (economic systems).
- People benefit when they trade (voluntary trade).
- There are costs and benefits for every choice that affect the future for better or worse (consequences).

When Scott taught, he found these six principles to be the simplest way for his 8th grade students to think about the economic aspects of the history and geography we studied. His students were required to glue the Economic Way of Thinking principles inside the front cover of their interactive notebooks, and whenever we discussed a historic figure and the decisions that he or she made, his students used the list to dissect the individual's actions. Students had to use the correct vocabulary (e.g., opportunity cost, economic systems, incentives, etc.) when writing or discussing their answers.

Individual Activity: The Economic Way of Thinking

In your reflective journal:

- Write about a choice you had to make recently using the Economic Way of Thinking as a guide. Discuss the cost of our choice, what rewards you received for making your choice, how societal or institutional rules affected the choice you made, what you gained from your choice, and how your choices brought about cost and benefits that affected your future.
- Write about a historic or political topic that may lend itself to the use of the Economic Way of Thinking.

Balancing a Budget

One of the most important aspects of economics is personal finance. Due to concern about Americans' limited savings, overspending, high levels of credit card debt, high levels of unemployment, and housing foreclosures, many states have mandated that personal finance be taught in schools. Many middle grades students understand the concept of scarcity and that they cannot always have everything they want. However, when they watch their parents use credit cards regularly for the purchase of goods and services, or when they hear about the amount of debt our federal government has, they have a difficult time understanding the importance of keeping a balanced budget and not spending beyond their means (Jorgensen et al., 2019).

There are many ways to help students understand the importance of budgeting and being financially responsible you can incorporate into your classes. One example is the lesson we discussed in Chapter 7, "There is Nothing Certain…But Death and Taxes," where students were instructed to reduce the state's budget because of its balanced budget amendment. Another example is having students choose specific careers, have them research how much their salary will be, and create a budget based on the annual income. No matter how you incorporate a study of budgeting, it is important that students are taught the concepts of scarcity, needs and wants, savings, investing, and opportunity costs.

It has been Ben's experience that when creating budgets, students frequently overestimate earnings and underestimate expenditures. One way to avoid this is to have students work with their parents on budgeting activities. While some parents may be reluctant to share with their children elements of their own family budget, they are often more willing to talk with them when the budget is simulated. Though it is often overlooked in school curriculums, budgeting and personal finance concepts are some of the most important for students to learn and apply in their lives outside the classroom.

Inquiry and Simulations

The study of economics lends itself to the use of simulations, inquiry-based strategies, or a combination of both. These are easy to find with a simple Internet search. For example, the Council for Economic Education offers a variety of these types of lessons on its resources webpage. Some of the lessons include learning about entrepreneurship, financial literacy, and trading around the world.

COLLABORATIVE ACTIVITY:
USING THE CEE ECONOMIC LESSON PLAN DATABASE

Working together with two or three of your other classmates:

- Choose a grade level (4th–8th) and find the state social studies standards for that grade (see Table 2.1).

- Using the CEE economic lesson plan database identify lessons that correlate to the standards and share these lessons with your group.

INCORPORATING GOVERNMENT INTO SOCIAL STUDIES COURSES

The study of government involves learning about governmental structures and processes. Stemming from the discipline of political science, the study of government is often called civics. Civics can be defined as the study of civic affairs and the rights, duties, and responsibilities of citizens. Though not often taught as a separate course in the middle grades, civics and government are incorporated into all social studies classes. Many states require middle school students to pass a US and/or state Constitution test.

It should be noted that one of the primary objectives of teaching social studies is to help students learn the ideals and practices of being responsible citizens and contributing members of our society. Through experience in social studies, students should learn about their rights and responsibilities at the local, state, and national levels. They should learn about the role that each branch of government plays in their daily life and, as adolescents, about the differences between adult and juvenile laws. While all of this may appear to be a daunting task, as with economics, the study of government and civics can easily be incorporated into a history, geography, or any integrated social studies course.

CIVICS AND GOVERNMENT EXPECTATIONS AND STANDARDS

Like several other social studies disciplines, two organizations have developed standards and expectations for teachers of civics and government. These standards and expectations should be the guidelines of instruction for any social studies teacher, as government is an important part in any integrated course. Though produced by different organizations, many of these themes and expectations are similar and should be at the forefront of your mind whether you are teaching history or geography.

NCSS Expectations for Teachers of Civics and Government

While each of the 10 NCSS themes may be easily tied to instruction about civics and government, Theme 6: Power, Authority, and Governance and Theme 10: Civic Ideals and Practices most directly center on this area of social studies (NCSS, 2010). The NCSS has also developed six "Expectations for Teachers of Civics and Government" (NCSS, 2002) that focus on the teaching of civics and governmental concepts. Some of the more important expectations any teacher of civics must strive to meet include guiding learners in understanding the relationship of the United States to other nations and world affairs, assisting learners in understanding citizenship rights and responsibilities, and ensuring that learners are aware of the many ways to participate as citizens in our democracy (NCSS as cited in Johnson, 2010, p. 276).

These expectations, along with the other three standards, help explain that the study of government is not simply about the three branches of government and voting but is a complex subject that incorporates elements of all social studies disciplines (see Figure 10.3). In other words, while learning about the Bill of Rights is important, understanding how the Bill of Rights directly affects students in their everyday lives is much more crucial. As a middle-grades social studies teacher, you should keep these standards in mind as you begin developing integrated lesson plans for your classes.

- Assist learners in developing an understanding of civic life, politics, and government, so that the learners can explore the origins of governmental authority, recognize the need for government; identify the crucial functions of government, including laws and rules; evaluate rules and laws; differentiate between limited and unlimited government; and appreciate the importance of limitations on government power;
- Guide learners as they explore American democracy, including the American idea of constitutional government, the impact of the distinctive characteristics of American society on our government, the nature of the American political culture, and the values and principles that are basic to American life and government;
- Help learners understand how the government of the United States operates under the constitution and the purposes, values, and principles of American democracy, including the ideas of distributed, shared, and limited powers of government; how the national, state, and local governments are organized; and the place of law in the system;
- Enable learners to understand the relationship of the United States to other nations and to world affairs;
- Assist learners in developing an understanding of citizenship, its rights and responsibilities, and in developing their abilities and dispositions to participate effectively in civic life.
- Ensure that learners are made aware of the full range of opportunities to participate as citizens in the American democracy and of their responsibilities for doing so.

FIGURE 10.3. NCSS Expectations for Teachers of Government (2002) Source: NCSS, 2002

ACTIVITY: Reflecting on the NCSS Expectations for Teachers of Civics and Government

Examine three of the NCSS Expectations for Teachers of Civics and Government and compare them to the answers you wrote in the Reflecting on Economics Activity. In your reflective journal:

- Write down how your answers compare to the expectations. Do these expectations change your view about how civics and government should be taught?
- With a classmate, review the three expectations you chose and discuss state, U.S., or world history topics that you could integrate with these expectations.

Center for Civics Education's National Standards

The Center for Civics Education (1994) also developed national standards for the teaching of civics and government (see Figure 10.4). The standards are written in the form of overarching questions and are followed by a series of sub-questions related to the larger topic. The center then offers teachers a detailed explanation for each question. Below are the five questions and 21 sub questions. To view the full document, visit the Center for Civics Education's website.

Class Activity: Museum Walk about the National Standards for Civics and Government

Form into groups of three or four and choose one of the CCE standards.

- On a piece of poster paper create a T-Chart with your group members' names heading up the left column and CCE heading the right-hand column.
- As a group discuss and answer each sub question found below the larger standard on your side of the chart. Then open the standards on the CEE website and read their answers to the questions.
- On the other side of the chart list any answers that you did not have. At the bottom of the page make a list of ways you could combine the ideas in a study of history, geography, and/or economics.
- After you are finished, post your paper on the wall.
- Once everyone has completed their poster, walk around the room and read your classmates' answers to their standards.
- Feel free to add to the poster if additional answers are needed. Add any ideas or topics that can be used to teach the standard as well.
- After one rotation each group should present what they have on their posters.

I. What are Civic Life, Politics, and Government?
   A. What is civic life? What is politics? What is government? Why are government and politics necessary? What purposes should government serve?
   B. What are the essential characteristics of limited and unlimited government?
   C. What are the nature and purposes of constitutions?
   D. What are alternative ways of organizing constitutional governments?
II. What are the Foundations of the Political System?
   A. What is the American idea of constitutional government?
   B. What are the distinctive characteristics of American society?
   C. What is American political culture?
   D. What values and principles are basic to American constitutional democracy?
III. How Does the Government Established by the Constitution Embody the Purposes, Values, and Principles of American Democracy?
   A. How are power and responsibility distributed, shared, and limited in the government established by the United States Constitution?
   B. What does the national government do?
   C. How are state and local governments organized and what do they do?
   D. Who represents you in local, state, and national governments?
   E. What is the place of law in the American constitutional system?
   F. How does the American political system provide for choice and opportunities for participation?
IV. What is the Relationship of the United States to Other Nations and to World Affairs?
   A. How is the world organized politically?
   B. How has the United States influenced other nations and how have other nations influenced American politics and society?
V. What are the Roles of the Citizen in American Democracy?
   A. What is citizenship?
   B. What are the rights of citizens?
   C. What are the responsibilities of citizens?
   D. What dispositions or traits of character are important to the preservation and improvement of American constitutional democracy?
   E. How can citizens take part in civic life?

FIGURE 10.4. CCE National Standards for Civics and Government: 5th–8th Grades. Source: Center for Civic Education (2014)

KEY CIVICS AND GOVERNMENT IDEALS AND CONCEPTS

One of the primary purposes of social studies is to prepare students to be active and responsible citizens. Woven throughout your discussions of historical, economic, and geographical concepts should be this theme of active and responsible citizenship (Risinger, 2009; Rubin, 2010). While there are several key ideas and

1. **The Bill of Rights**—The first 10 amendments to the U.S. Constitution. The Bill of Rights is a document that should continuously be referred to in social studies classes as it lists some of the most important rights of American citizens (e.g., freedom of speech, freedom of religion, trial by jury).
2. **The Common Good**—The concept that examines what governmental laws and actions, along with those decisions made by other sectors, provide the most good for the most people. For example, while a business owner may make a lot of money while inadvertently polluting a river, the large number of people who live downriver from the business may suffer. If this is the case, the concept of the common good would dictate that the business clean up or cease its operation.
3. **Democracy vs. Republic**—Though sometimes used interchangeably, there is a distinct difference between a democracy and a republic. Technically a democracy is a form of government where citizens make decisions based on the concept of majority rule. Though we do have some forms of a democratic process, our governmental system is based on the republic system where the citizens elect representatives to make decisions for them. Students should be taught this difference in order to have a better understanding of how the American political system works and what role they play in it. This discussion has the added benefit of encouraging students to consider the roles and importance of local and state governments.
4. **Diversity**—An important part of any society. A vibrant and successful nation will have a diverse group of individuals who find ways to use their differences as a positive good in decision-making and compromise.
5. **Equal Rights**—Though landowning white males had their civil rights protected in the U.S. Constitution, it took many years and much conflict for poor whites, blacks, women, and other marginalized groups to fully secure theirs. Today, there are still groups fighting for their civil rights to be recognized. The struggle for equal rights and discussion about what rights should be protected is a critical element of all social studies courses.
6. **Justice**—An ideal that they will be consequences for those who break laws or deny the rights of individuals or groups. The concept of justice includes the ideals of fairness, moral rightness, and that every citizen receives equal protection under the law, both legal and natural. It is the responsibility of local, state, and national governments to ensure that justice is administered.
7. **Life, Liberty, and the Pursuit of Happiness**—A core concept not found verbatim in the U.S. Constitution but in the Declaration of Independence, written before the Constitution. Though not often lived up to, this ideal is the cornerstone of American society and culture. In theory, no individual, corporation, or government has the authority to take these rights away. However, as social studies teachers, it is up to you to remind each new generation about these inalienable rights.

FIGURE 10.5. The Top 10 Key Civics and Government Ideals and Concepts for Middle Level Learners (In Alphabetical Order)

> 8. **Majority vs. Minority Rights**—One of the constant struggles in American politics and society. Many of the framers of the Constitution believed that in a true democracy the rights of the majority would always win out over those of the minority. However, the U.S. Constitution and subsequent amendments were written to protect the rights of the minority. Though controversial, discussion and debate based on this concept should be a part of your middle level instruction.
> 9. **Responsibility**—Citizens not only have rights but they have responsibilities. In some cases, these responsibilities are mandated, such as paying taxes and serving on juries. In other cases, citizens are not forced to act responsibly but should to maintain and improve upon our society. Voting, volunteer work, constructive critique of government policy and leaders' decisions, thoughtful analysis of news, and informed decision-making are activities that exemplify the responsible citizens. Students should be taught that rights and responsibilities go hand in hand and are the cornerstone of our society.
> 10. **Voting**—Students should understand that voting is one of the most direct ways, though not the only way, for citizens to have their wishes heard. Students should be encouraged to vote (and run for office) later in life, especially in local and state elections where elections are more frequent, and the results often affect them more directly. However, they should understand that this is one of many responsibilities they have as citizens. They should also understand that voting is not the only way to have their voices heard. Non-violent protest, boycotts, and petitions historically have worked just as well as going to the ballot box.

FIGURE 10.5. Continued

vocabulary that can be discussed in your classes, below are—in our opinion—the top 10 that should be discussed regularly.

Individual Activity: Key Government Ideals and Concepts

Review the Top 10 Key Government Ideals and Concepts (see Figure 10.5) and write your answers to the following questions in your reflective journal:

- Which ones do you think are the most important and which ones are the least important to teach middle level learners?
- Are there any concepts you would add to the list or use to replace one or more? If so which ones and why?

BRINGING CIVICS AND GOVERNMENT INTO SOCIAL STUDIES

In addition to incorporating civic and government ideals and concepts into the study of history, economics, and geography, there are many ways to teach these concepts on their own. Below are several ideas and strategies you can use in your classroom that specifically focus on these concepts. Using these ideas will help your students gain a better understanding of civics and government and will hopefully lead to civic minded and responsible adults. Additional articles by Adams (2015), Harris et al. (2016), Martin et al. (2019), Massey (2017), and McGuire et al. (2019) are also helpful for teaching civics and government at the middle level.

In the Classroom

There are several ways you can incorporate civic ideals and practices into your classroom. One example many teachers employ at the beginning of the year is allowing their students to help create a classroom bill of rights and responsibilities (Johnson, 2010). When introducing this type of activity, you should explain to your students that they are being given an important opportunity to develop some (but not all) of the rules for the class. Remind students that this is a major responsibility, as they will not have this right outside of the classroom until they are 18. When introducing this project, make sure you introduce some of the key concepts in the "Top 10 Key Civics and Government Concepts and Ideals" listed above, such as minority vs. majority rights, or explain to them why we have freedom of speech, while at the same time we cannot yell fire in a crowded movie theater or say false things about people without getting into trouble with the law.

Outside the Classroom

One of the most important roles a citizen can play is as an active participant in their communities (Filipovitch & Ozturk, 2012). As a social studies teacher, your colleagues and administration will often look to you to spearhead school-wide mock elections, head the student council, and organize events such as Veteran's Day celebrations. As a social studies teacher you should welcome these opportunities to show leadership and urge your students to take part in these events.

Along with the activities listed above, you can encourage your students to join school organizations such as environmental or debate clubs. You can take student volunteers to elementary schools or retirement communities to read for individuals who cannot. You can have your homeroom students organize a food drive during the holiday season or create a volunteer group to clean up around the school and surrounding community. No matter how you choose to teach civic responsibilities to your students, actions speak louder than words, and as a social studies teacher, you should demonstrate outstanding citizenship. A broad goal of social studies teachers is the active, engagement of students' in their local, regional, national, and global communities.

Inquiry and Simulations

Like economics, civics and government courses lend themselves to hands-on inquiry-based lessons and simulations. One such activity "The Three Branches of

Government" (Ashcroft & Pettit, 2011) was introduced in Chapter 4. Additionally, the CCE offers many free lesson plans that examine many of the key concepts listed in Figure 10.5. These include "What is a Republican Form of Government" which helps students learn about America's governmental system along with civic virtue; "How Citizens can Participate" which allows students to learn about how they can be active participants in their communities; and a lesson that also integrates economics "How can You Decide Among Competing Responsibilities."

COLLABORATIVE ACTIVITY: USING THE CCE CIVICS AND GOVERNMENT WEBSITE.

With the same two or three classmates that you worked with on the economics lesson plan collection, continue the same exercise with civics and government lesson plans. Here are the revised instructions: *Choose a grade level (4–8) and find the state social studies standards for that grade. Using the CCE Civic and Government lesson plan database, identify civics- and government-based lessons that correlate with the standards. Share these lessons within your group.*

SUMMARY

This chapter offered information and ideas about teaching economics, civics, and government in the middle level classroom. These subjects are often not taught independently in most middle schools, but, like geography, are taught as part of an integrated social studies course. In this chapter we discussed the standards and themes suggested by the NCSS, the CEE, and the CCE. We also discussed several strategies to teach economics and government that emphasized both traditional and technology-based approaches. We also provided a collection of websites that offer free lesson ideas for both subjects. Of course, these lesson ideas can be altered to meet the needs of your students and school. In the next chapter we examine an important topic in the middle grades: building literacy in social studies classes.

Individual Activity: Reflecting on the Chapter

Return to your answers about the importance of teaching economics and government in middle schools and write your answers to the following questions in your reflective journal:

- After reading this chapter, how have your ideas changed about the purposes of teaching economics and government?
- What steps are you going to take in order to ensure that you meet the NCSS expectations and the CEE and CCE standards?
- What are some tools and strategies discussed in the chapter that you think will help meet the goals?

WEBSITE RESOURCES

- **Ben's Guide to U.S. Government for Kids** (https://bensguide.gpo.gov/) is a website for K–12 students that offers "student friendly" definitions for several elements of government including "branches of government," and "how laws are made," along with games and activities. Additional links to government themed websites for students are provided as well.
- **Center for Civic Education** (http://www.civiced.org) offers civics-based resources, materials, and standards to K–12 social studies teachers. The website includes information about the "We the People" and "Project Citizen" programs along with literacy links, professional development, and grant opportunities.
- **The Choices Program** (http://www.choices.edu/) is a "national educational initiative program developed at Brown University's Watson Institute for International Studies." Their website provides "teaching resources on historical and current issues, offers professional development for classroom teachers, and sponsors programs that engage students beyond the classroom."
- **Constitutional Rights Foundation** (http://crf-usa.org/) is a "non-profit, non-partisan, community-based organization dedicated to educating America's young people about the importance of civic participation in a democratic society." Their website offers teachers hundreds of lesson plans about a variety of civics/government topics.
- **Council for Economic Education** (www.councilforeconed.org) offers economic based resources, materials and standards to K–12 social studies teachers. The website also includes information about their annual conference, on-line teacher training, a free online personal finance video game, and offers teachers K–12 lesson plans and videos. Most states have their own Councils for Economics Education that offer similar information including Colorado (http://www.ccee.net/), Georgia (http://gcee.org/), Indiana (http://www.econed-in.org/), Michigan (https://michiganecon.org/), Nebraska (https://business.unl.edu/outreach/econ-ed/nebraska-council-on-economic-education//), Oklahoma (http://www.econisok.org/), Texas (https://economicstexas.blogspot.com/), and Virginia (http://www.vcee.org/).
- **Econedlink** (http://www.econedlink.org/) is a website sponsored by the Council for Economic Education that offers tools to both students and teachers to use in economic education. All lessons and interactive games are "online" and focus on basic economics concepts, current events, and personal finance.
- **iCivics** (http://www.icivics.org/) is a program founded by Justice Sandra Day O'Connor to help prepare "young Americans to become knowledgeable, engaged 21st century citizens" by creating "free and innovative edu-

cational materials." These include several educational video games about the U.S. government.
- **Law Focused Education, Inc.** (http://www.texaslre.org/) is committed to "planning, promoting, and supporting civic education and engagement programs throughout Texas." The company has partnered with the Law Related Education Department of the State Bar of Texas that is "dedicated to developing and advancing quality law-related and civic education programs across the state." The website offers teachers lessons plans and curriculum, games, special programs for teachers and students, and links to other civic education sites. It should be noted that the many states have similar websites including Georgia (http://www.gabar.org/forthepublic/forteachersstudents/lre/teacherresources/index.cfm) Florida (http://www.flrea.org/), Ohio (http://www.oclre.org/), and Utah (http://lawrelatededucation.org/).
- **National Issues Forums** (http://www.nifi.org/) is a network of "civic, educational, and other organizations and individuals whose common interest is to promote public deliberation in America. For educators the site provides lesson plans, curriculum standards, and book materials.
- **Street Law** (http://www.streetlaw.org/en/home) is a non-profit organization that "creates classroom and community programs that teach people about law, democracy, and human rights worldwide." The website offers teachers programs that "empower students and communities to become active, legally-savvy contributors to society" as well as a "full range of resources and activities to support the teaching of landmark Supreme Court cases, helping students explore the key issues of each case."

REFERENCES

Adams, E. (2015). Civics in the grocery store: A field trip of awareness and agency. *Social Studies and the Young Learner, 27*(4), 16–18.

Agnello, M. F., Laney, J. D., & Lucey, T. A. (2019). Grabbing a tiger by the tale: Using stories to teach financial literacy. *The Social Studies, 110*(5), 198–206.

Ashcroft, K., & Pettit, L. (2011). *Three branches of government.* http://teacherlink.ed.usu.edu/tlresources/units/byrnes-s2000/Ashcroft %26 Pettit/lesson plan.html

Brainy Quote. (n.d.). *Charles Edison quotes.* https://www.brainyquote.com/quotes/charles_edison_220632

Center of Civic Education. (1994). *National standards for civics and government.* http://www.civiced.org/index.php?page=stds_preface

Council for Economic Education. (2010). *Voluntary national content standards for economics* (2nd ed.). Council for Economic Education

Filipovitch, A. J., & Ozturk, T. (2012). Teaching the social studies through your local community. *Social Education, 76*(2), 85–87.

Gandy, S. K. (2016). The Erie Canal: From public works to national wealth. *Middle Level Learning, 56,* 10–16.

Gilbert, S. S., Huddleston, T. R., & Winters, J. J. (2018). Design, build, and test a model house: Using the C3 Framework to explore the economics of constructing a dwelling. *Social Studies and the Young Learner, 30*(4), 24–27.

Harris, C. A., Kharecha, P., Goble, P., & Gobel, R. (2016). The climate is a-changin': Teaching civic competence for a sustainable climate. *Social Studies and the Young Learner, 25*(3), 17–20.

Johnson, A. P. (2010). *Making connections in elementary and middle school social studies* (2nd ed.). Sage.

Jorgensen, B. L., Allsop, D. B., Runyan, S. D., Wheeler, B. E., Evans, D. A., & Marks, L. D. (2019). Forming financial vision: How parents prepare young adults for financial success. *Journal of Family and Economic Issues, 40*(3), 553–563.

Knapp, K. A., & Hopkins, A. (2018). What's the buzz? A K–5 school uses the C3 Framework. *Social Studies and the Young Learner, 30*(3), 9–18.

Manfra, M. M., & Saylor, E. E. (2016). Which woman should appear on U.S. currency? Using primary sources to explore important historical figures. *Social Studies and the Young Learner, 29*(1), 27–32.

Martin, A. S., Pang, V. O., Ginsberg, E. J., Pang, J. M., Duesbery, L., & Dial, E. W. (2019). Citizenship in action: Students create anti-bullying public service announcements. *Middle Level Learning, 64*, 8–16.

Massey, J. (2017). Dialectical discussion: A method at the heart of our democratic process. *Middle Level Learning, 59,* 2–8.

McGuire, M. E., Nicholson, K., & Rand, A. (2019). Live it to learn it: Making elections personally meaningful. *Social Studies and the Young Learner, 32*(2), 19–25.

National Council for the Social Studies. (2002). *National standards for social studies teachers.* NCSS. https://www.socialstudies.org/sites/default/files/NCSSTeacher-StandardsVol1-rev2004.pdf

National Council for the Social Studies. (2010). *National curriculum standards for social studies.* NCSS

National Council on Economic Education. (n.d.). *Advanced placement economics teacher resource manual.* National Council on Economic Education.

Potter, L. A. (2019). Starting conversations with students about personal spending, investing, and stewardship with historical receipts. *Social Education, 83*(2), 72–76.

Quote Fancy. (n.d.). *Robert Duvall quotes.* https://quotefancy.com/quote/1170801/Robert-Duvall-Too-many-people-think-that-economics-is-this-subject-that-should-wait-until

Risinger, C. F. (2009). Citizenship education: The goal of education. *Social Education, 73*(7), 330–332

Roberts, S. L. (2009). *Georgia economic history: Lessons for implementing the GPS at Grade 8.* Georgia Council on Economic Education.

Rubin, B. C. (2010). Using civic identity development in the U.S. history course. *Social Education, 74*(3), 144–147.

Schug, M. C., Caldwell, J., & Ferrarini, T. H. (2006). *Focus: Understanding economics in U.S. history.* National Council on Economic Education.

CHAPTER 11

BUILDING LITERACY IN MIDDLE LEVEL SOCIAL STUDIES

No skill is more crucial to the future of a child, or to a democratic and prosperous society, than literacy

—*Los Angeles Times (1998)*

Writing comes from reading, and reading is the finest teacher of how to write.

—*Annie Proulx (Quote Fancy, n.d.)*

Activity List
- Reflecting on Literacy in Social Studies.
- Finding Quality Books.
- Critical Literacy.
- Reflecting on the Create Strategy.
- The Compare and Contrast Strategy.
- Using Images from the Past and Present.
- Reflecting on the Inquiry Strategy.
- Reflecting on the Chapter.

Teaching Middle Level Social Studies: A Practical Guide for 4th–8th Grade (3rd Edition), pages 255–277.
Copyright © 2022 by Information Age Publishing
www.infoagepub.com
All rights of reproduction in any form reserved.

COLLABORATIVE ACTIVITY: REFLECTING ON LITERACY IN SOCIAL STUDIES

Due to the high stakes testing environment in which schools operate today, the learning of social studies content has been significantly reduced as schools focus more directly on mathematics and Language Arts achievement. However, you do not have to teach Language Arts OR social studies. It is possible to teach Language Arts AND social studies. With this in mind, answer the following question in your reflective journal and then discuss with a classmate:

- What do you think is your role as a social studies teacher in helping your students with reading and writing?
- What literacy benefits do you think are possible when teaching Language Arts and social studies together?
- What social studies benefits do you think are possible when teaching Language Arts and social studies together?
- What challenges do you think might occur when teaching social studies and Language Arts?

INTRODUCTION

Have you ever heard students describe their social studies textbooks as a page turner? Probably not. Of course, not all students love to read but at least some have admitted to enjoying a book. In fact, on several occasions Jessica has even heard her students admit that they not only liked a book but they "liked the book better than the movie." Bringing authentic literature into the social studies curriculum is an opportunity for students to actually enjoy what they are reading and learning. This is particularly important because most students describe social studies textbooks as boring (Loewen, 2008).

INTEGRATING SOCIAL STUDIES AND LITERACY

Despite the long-standing tradition of teachers teaching subjects in isolation from one another, integrating subjects across the curriculum demonstrates to students how knowledge from multiple disciplines are used to solve real world problems. As a social studies educator you play a major role in how students identify and solve problems. Solving real world problems is the heart of social studies. More specifically, "The primary purpose of social studies is to help young people make informed and reasoned decisions for the public good as citizens of a culturally diverse, democratic society in an interdependent world" (NCSS, 2010, para 1). Experts in the field of literacy also voice their support for integrated instruction stating, "knowledge alone is of little value if one has no need to or cannot apply it" (National Council of Teachers of English and International Reading Association, 1996, p. 12). Similarly, the Common Core State Standards insists on a shared responsibility between subjects (National Governors Association Center for Best

Practices & Council of Chief State School Officers, 2010). Integrating literacy and social studies can and should teach students how reading about the past can help them examine and make informed decisions in the present and future.

The integration of social studies and literacy is beneficial for many reasons. One reason is that it ensures social studies is honored by consistently being taught in schools. As a middle level social studies teacher, you may be seen as a generalist that teaches all content areas, or a specialist that focuses on a particular content. Those who are seen as generalists may see integration as a way to ensure social studies is consistently taught in their classroom. With the passage of recent federal mandates, high stakes' tests have come to have a major influence in determining the school curriculum. These standardized assessments disproportionately focus on mathematics and literacy, thus forcing schools to put social studies on the "back burner" (Winstead, 2011). Intertwining social studies with literacy is a way to increase social studies instruction. Thus, increasing the opportunities for students to learn how to become problem solvers that contribute to their increasingly diverse communities. When Karrie taught fourth grade, she taught all subjects as a generalist. She was only allotted about 20 minutes of dedicated social studies instruction each day. By integrating social studies into other subjects, Karrie was able to ensure she was covering the Georgia Standards of Excellence for social studies.

Whether you become a generalist or specialist, this book will help you learn the importance of social studies. This chapter will help you understand that your role as a social studies educator is intimately tied to literacy, defined by the International Literacy Association as "the ability to identify, understand, interpret, create, compute, and communicate using visual, audible, and digital materials across disciplines and in any context" (para. 1). Indeed, recent societal discussion of fake news and "deep fake" videos demand our students experience and explore, analyze, critique, and interpret many sources of information. Monte-Sano (2010) explains that social studies teachers should seize the opportunity to help their students learn literacy skills. For example, writing persuasive essays is a great way for social studies educators to teach literacy. While many literacy teachers invite students to write persuasive essays about any topic, there are unique aspects when literacy and social studies are integrated with persuasive writing. For instance, this type of integrated instruction affords students with opportunities to take informed action by writing persuasive essays to lawmakers regarding social inequities. This type of integrated instruction enhances both social studies and literacy.

Literacy Expands the Eurocentric Curriculum

Perhaps the single most important reason to conduct integrated instruction of literacy and social studies is to expand the Eurocentric curriculum. This Eurocentric curriculum tells a single sided story that omits the perspective and voices of historically marginalized groups such as ethnic groups of color. Many have reviewed social studies textbooks and standards and concluded that social studies textbooks do not tell a complete story and instead tell a sanitized version of history (Brown & Au, 2014; Calderón, 2014; Journell, 2009; Keenan, 2019; Monforti & McGlynn, 2010; Sabzalian, 2019; Shear, 2015; Suh et al., 2014).

The omission of valuable perspectives in the social studies curriculum is especially harmful for middle level learners who are at a stage of development when they are discovering not only who they are but how they fit into the world around them (Brighton, 2007). For this reason, it is especially important that students hear a history that is inclusive of diverse groups. Learning in this way helps students from marginalized communities and non-marginalized communities alike to understand that all people hold knowledge and truth that are worth learning about. In order to disrupt this Eurocentric curriculum and teach social studies in ways that are culturally responsive (Gay, 2018; Ladson-Billings, 2003) all units of study, must include historically marginalized voices.

Finding Quality Books

Knowing that textbooks typically present a Eurocentric perspective, when you seek high quality literature to include in your social studies curriculum you should also seek literature with perspectives that expand this Eurocentric narrative. Table 11.1 presents valuable resources to help you select such texts. You might be surprised to find outstanding picture books in these resources. Yet, the audience for picture books extends beyond young children. In fact, both Jessica and Steph frequently use picture books in their social studies methods courses with preservice teachers and have found that this is when college students are most engaged. Some college students have even told Jessica, "wow I never knew that" or "I can't believe how much I learned from a picture book." In addition to picture books, this list also provides you with strong middle level readers as well as books for your advanced readers, thus allowing you to differentiate your instruction to meet the needs of your learners. This level of differentiation is another benefit your textbook can not afford and thus is a benefit of integrating social studies and literacy.

Individual Activity: Finding Quality Books

In your reflective journal answer the following questions:

- Are there any books you remember reading that you might be able to use for integrating social studies and literacy?
- Examine the resources above to find two books that interest you. Read online reviews to find out more about the book. Then, explain how you think this book might be used to teach some literacy and social studies concepts.

Critical Literacy

Integrating literacy into social studies means more than merely reading about historical figures. One strategy that helps teachers move beyond reading compre-

TABLE 11.1. Resources of Locating High Quality Social Studies Literature

Resource Name	Web Address	Short Description
Database of Award-Winning Children's Literature	http://www.dawcl.com/search.asp	This is a database of approximately 158 book awards and contains over 14,000 book titles. This is a very functional site that allows you to filter by (among other categories) suggested age level and historical period and your own selected key word search. A list of award-winning books that meet your criteria will appear along with a brief summary of each book.
International Literacy Association—Teachers Choice Award	https://www.literacyworldwide.org/get-resources/reading-lists	Each year the Teachers Choice list identifies approximately 30 books rated by teachers around the United States as outstanding books for curriculum use. Many (though not all) books listed include social studies content.
Lee and Low Social Studies books for Middle school	https://www.leeandlow.com/middle-school/social-studies-and-history	Lee & Low's focus on diverse books for middle school students that support culturally responsive teaching by including a wide range of perspectives on history, including those that are historically underrepresented.
National Council for The Social Studies Notable Trade Books for Young People	https://www.socialstudies.org/publications/notables	This annual list provides notable social studies books published each year. Each book listed has a short summary, recommended graded levels as well as social studies themes addressed.
School Library Journal	https://www.slj.com/?subpage=BookLists	This organization puts together numerous books lists each year. Although you'll have to sift through may books lists you find great lists such as the yearly "Best Middle Grades Books" and "Commemorate Holocaust Remembrance Day with these Middle Grade and Young Adult Titles."
Social Justice Books	https://socialjusticebooks.org/booklists/	More than sixty book lists are provided on this site. Within these lists books are classified as elementary, middle or young adult readers. Some lists that will be appealing to social studies educators include: Public Policy, World History, Immigration and Emigration, War, Slavery, Democracy and Citizenship and much, much more.
University of Delaware Literature with Social Studies Themes	https://www1.udel.edu/dssep/literature.html	This university webpage lists Social Studies books divided into four categories: History, Geography, Economics, and Civics. Within each category books for middle level learners are listed.
University School of Nashville—Middle School: What should I read	https://usn.libguides.com/recommended/rec-middle	This site provides many links to award winning books. Although not all lists are social studies specific many will be helpful for social studies educators. One example is the Middle School Native American Books- this list includes fiction and nonfiction middle school readers by and about Native American people.
We Need Diverse Books	https://diversebooks.org/resources/where-to-find-diverse-books/	This site provides links to books focusing on historically marginalized groups. A hyperlinked list of awards allows you to easily find out the focus of each award and see the book recipient of each award. Sample awards include the Coretta Scott King Book Award, Carter G. Goodson Book Award, and the Arab American Book Award.

hension questions is critical literacy. Students who engage in critical literacy ask questions to better understand power, systemic inequities and injustice in human relationships (Demoiny & Ferraras-Stone, 2018). To develop this critical lens teachers must select strong texts and encourage students to challenge them deeply.

Meller et al. (2009) suggest that such texts should:

1. Explore differences rather than make them invisible
2. Enrich understandings of history and life by giving voice to those traditionally silenced or marginalized
3. Show how people can begin to take action on important social issues
4. Explore dominant systems of meaning that operate in our society to position people and groups of people as "others"
5. Don't provide 'happily ever after' endings for complex social issues (p. 77).

Now that you have some guidance to find strong texts, you need a framework for developing questions. McLaughlin and DeVoogd (2004) provide helpful questions you can use when engaging in critical literacy. It is important to note that these questions can be adapted to better fit the context of your classroom and the text. Their recommended questions are:

1. Whose viewpoint is expressed?
2. What does the author want us to think?
3. Whose voices are missing, silenced, or discounted?
4. How might alternative perspectives be represented?
5. How would that contribute to your understanding the text from a critical stance
6. What actions might you take on the basis of what you have learned today?

These questions are higher order thinking questions and many of these questions could have multiple correct answers. The key is to ensure students can support

TABLE 11.2. The C3 Framework

C3 Framework Dimensions	Critical Literacy Practices
Dimension: Developing Questions & Planning Inquiries	Teachers develop questions about perspective, power, and justice.
Dimension 2: Applying Disciplinary Tools & Concepts	Critical literacy books content may focus upon historical event, a civic action, a geographic location and or effects of the economy
Dimension 3: Evaluating Sources & Using Evidence	Students will be able to seek multiple perspectives from various books, including critical literacy picture books.
Dimension 4: Communicating Conclusions & Taking Informed Action	Students will respond to the book readings through reflection, discussion, journaling and social justice projects.

their reasoning and explain their answers logically. Student responses can be shared in classroom discussions or journals. An essential element to keep in mind is that students need a safe space to explore multiple correct answers. Although you might think these questions are too complex for middle level learners, this is not the case. In fact, Jessica and Steph have both engaged in critical literacy with primary-grade students (and informally with their own young preschool-age children).

One of the biggest assets of critical literacy is that it promotes active citizenship which aligns to the four dimensions of the C3 Framework. Table 11.2 describes how critical literacy fosters each of these four dimensions (Demoiny & Ferraras-Stone, 2018). Table 11.3 offers resources that expand on the use of critical literacy in social studies and many even provide sample lesson plans.

So far, this chapter has:

- Provided a rationale for the integration of literacy and social studies
- Proclaimed the need for including historically marginalized voices in social studies
- Reviewed resources for finding high quality literature that can be used in social studies
- Presented questions to use in critical literacy lessons
- Described how crucial literacy aligns to the four dimensions of the C3 Dimensions Guide
- Provided resources for finding examples of critical literacy

Individual Activity: Critical Literacy

In your reflective journal answer the following questions:

- What excites you about creating critical literacy lessons in social studies?
- What fears do you have about creating critical literacy lessons in social studies?
- What are some ways you can adapt a critical literacy stance to your own context?
- Do you ever recall a time when you were taught through critical literacy? If so, how would you describe your learning and feelings? If not, how do you think you would have reacted to this type of instruction?

Five Strong Strategies for Building Literacy in Social Studies

Promoting active citizenship through critical literacy is not the only way to integrate social studies and literacy. The remainder of the chapter will introduce five strong strategies for building literacy in social studies. While many of these strategies have already been mentioned throughout the book, this section offers a more detailed exploration of each strategy and lesson ideas corresponding to each one. You may find them to be useful as you begin your career in education. Remember, one of the benefits of integrating literacy with social studies is that it expands the

TABLE 11.3. Critical Literacy Resources

Resource Type	Title/ Citation
Article	Behrman, E. H. (2006). Teaching about language, power, and text: A review of classroom practices that support critical literacy. *Journal of Adolescent & Adult Literacy, 49*(6), 490–498.
Article	Delaney, C. (2007). World war II and beyond: Middle school inquiry and critical literacy. *The New England Reading Association Journal, 43*(2), 30–5.
Article	Demoiny, S. B., & Ferraras-Stone, J. (2018). Critical literacy in elementary social studies: Juxtaposing historical master and counter narratives in picture books. *The Social Studies, 109*(2), 64–73.
Article	Harshman, J. (2018). Developing global citizenship through critical media literacy in the social studies. *Journal of Social Studies Research, 42*(2), 107–117.
Article	Keegan, P. (2021). Critical affective civic literacy: A framework for attending to political emotion in the social studies classroom. *Journal of Social Studies Research, 45*(1), 15–24.
Article	Muetterties, C., & Darolia, L. J. (2020). Considering different perspectives in children's literature: An inquiry approach that promotes civic learning. *Social Studies and the Young Learner, 33*(1), 22–27.
Article	Reidel, M., & Draper, C. A. (2011). Reading for democracy: Preparing middle-grades social studies teachers to teach critical literacy. *The Social Studies, 102*(3), 124–131.
Article	Soares, L. B., & Wood, K. (2010). A critical literacy perspective for teaching and learning social studies. *The Reading Teacher, 63*(6), 486–494.
Article	Wolk, S. (2003). Teaching for critical literacy in social studies. *The Social Studies, 94*(3), 101–106.
Book	Morgan, W. (2002). *Critical literacy in the classroom: The art of the possible.* Routledge.
Book	Stevens, L. P., & Bean, T. W. (2007). *Critical literacy: Context, research, and practice in the K–12 classroom.* Sage Publications.
Book	Vasquez, V. (2003). *Getting Beyond" I Like the Book": Creating Space for Critical Literacy in K–6 Classrooms.* Kids InSight, K–12.
Podcast— Critical Literacies In Practice (CLIP)	http://www.clippodcast.com/ episode 51 describes the key tenets of critical literacy episode 4 describes what critical literacy mean is episode 11- details what gets in the way of critical literacy

Eurocentric curriculum. As such, you should seek out texts that honor historically marginalized voices when implementing these strategies. Doing so will help you attain the primary principle of social studies which is to help young people make informed and reasoned decisions for the public good as citizens of a culturally diverse, democratic society in an interdependent world" (NCSS, 2010, para 1).

Modeling

The strategies used in reading literary and informational texts differ significantly. As social studies teachers it is our job to teach our students how to read like histo-

TABLE 11.4. Five Strong Strategies for building Literacy in Social Studies

Strategy	Description	Resources
1. Modeling	There is a difference between reading historical text and fiction/literature. There are keywords that students should look for while reading these texts. As a teacher you should be modeling these skills with your students. This activity shows you how to do this.	Article: "On the Reading of Historical Texts." Sam Wineburg Book: Building Literacy in Social Studies: Strategies for Improving Comprehension and Critical Thinking. Website: Outline of Sam Wineburg's On the Reading of Historical Texts (see Website Resources)
2. Create	After students have read, written about, and discussed important people, events, and concepts they should be given the opportunity to create something with their newly found knowledge. There are many ways to do this including creating web pages, historic figure statues, podcasts, plays, etc.	Article: "History boring?" Stuff it! (see Website Resources). Website: Blabberize (see Website Resources) Website: Voice Thread (see Website Resources)
3. Compare and Contrast	A skill that is extremely important in both the social studies and language arts. There are several tools that students can use to compare and contrast important people, places, and events. You can even have students compare perspectives included in the textbook and those that were not.	Book: Building Literacy in Social Studies: Strategies for Improving Comprehension and Critical Thinking. Book: The Strategic Teacher: Selecting the Right Research-Based Strategy for Every Lesson
4. Past and Present Images	An activity that allows students to use primary images to compare and contrast life in the past to today. Students gain a better understanding and personal connection to history.	Book: Document Based Assessment Activities Website: Gilder Lehrman Institute of American History (see Website Resources) Website: The Library of Congress (see Website Resources) Website: National Archives (see Website Resources) Website: National History Education Clearing House (see Website Resources) Website: Smithsonian Institution (see Website Resources)
5. Inquiry Based/ Problem Solving	A strategy similar to compare and contrast. Students answer questions using primary and secondary sources. Students have the opportunity to develop their own conclusions based on evidence from the documents.	Book: Teacher: Selecting the Right Research-Based Strategy for Every Lesson Book: Building Literacy in Social Studies: Strategies for Improving Comprehension and Critical Thinking. Website: Stanford History Education Group (see Website Resources).

rians and social scientists, not as passive, uncritical sponges, simply soaking up the information provided. You should model how to read informational texts with a critical eye by reading and thinking aloud to your students, identifying the language and key phrases that can be used to read like a social science expert (Ogle et al., 2007).

Before modeling your own thinking process with your students, first self-evaluate your own reading of informational texts. Pick up your grade-level textbook or any article of historical reading, and as you read, ask yourself what strategies you are employing to make sense of the text. What questions are you asking? What inferences are you drawing? What keywords are you paying attention to? It is these very strategies that you will model for your students. For example, ensuring students make connections between the past and present is an important aspect of social studies education and likely is a strategy you already utilize without knowing. By thinking aloud as you read and modeling for students how to make connections between, let's say, biased language in both historical and present-day news articles on immigration, you help foster this kind of critical reading in your students.

As another example, specific keywords and phrases are used in informational texts to signal specific text structures (Ogle et al., 2007). While these context clues may be apparent to adult readers, they are often not easily recognized by students. There are several clue words that students should use to help them understand the meaning of a text. These types of clues are those that point out examples (e.g., "like," "for instance," "as you can see here"), a definition or restatement (e.g., "or," also known as," "in other words"), cause and effect (e.g., "therefore," "consequently," "and then"), comparison (e.g., "like" "related to," "also"), contrast (e.g., "but," "on the other hand," "although"), and chronological order (e.g., "first," "then," " in 1861') (Ogle et al., 2007, p. 44).

To help you consider differences between how you and your students might approach reading informational text, it may also be helpful to also examine the comparison chart developed by Professor Judy Lightfoot, based on Sam Wineburg's "reading like a historian" suggestions. The chart lists several differences between how experts and novices read historical texts. For example, when a novice reads a historical text, they typically seek to acquire content whereas an expert seeks to discover context *and* acquire content. As another example, a novice typically assumes neutrality and objectivity in texts whereas an expert assumes bias.

Create

Activities that allow students to create something based on what they've studied are a great way to assess learning and position students as experts. Chapter 6 examined one example of a "create activity:" the historic figure statue. This hands-on, creative project helps to build important literacy skills as students are required to research and write about their chosen figure and create a statue that displays what they have learned.

Earlier, this chapter discussed the Eurocentric nature of social studies textbooks and how incorporating high quality children's literature can expand the people students learn about to include historically marginalized voices. Tying the use of this create strategy and children's literature, students can, after reading a children's book, create a paragraph to add important content omitted in the social studies textbook. To do this, students will need to summarize what they learned in the children's book, ask additional questions about the person/historical period, research and draw conclusions, then add a paragraph (or more) to the social studies textbook. Engaging in an activity like this is important for social studies learning because it helps students learn about historically marginalized characters as well as notice the biased nature of textbooks. This type of activity also involves important literacy skills such as critically reading, summarizing, researching, and editing text for publication.

Creating new content for textbooks can be done with almost any content. One example is with the teaching of the 19th amendment. Most textbooks will include historical figures such as Susan B. Anthony, Elizabeth Cady Stanton, Alice Paul and or Lucy Stone. To diversify the people they learn about, students can read the picture book *Lillian's Right to Vote* by Jonah Winter. Reading this book will present students with important information about the 15th Amendment, Ida B. Wells, poll taxes, literacy tests and the Voting Rights Act of 1965. Students can then research this information or ask new questions to research. After completing their investigation students can create a paragraph (or more) to add to the social studies textbooks for future classrooms to read. This type of activity is also great to pair with persuasive writing since students might be excited to write a persuasive essay to the textbook authors inviting them to include more perspectives.

Chapter 7 discussed another example of creating, which was developing historical figure baseball cards. With this project, not only are students involved in creating a hands-on project using literacy and research skills, they also have to verbalize what they learned about each figure to cement their knowledge during their "trade day." Figure 11.1 displays a sample lesson plan for the historic figure baseball card project.

There are many other ways to have students use hands-on activities to incorporate this Create strategy. For instance, there are many web-based programs that allow students to research individuals or events, write a script, and record their scripts on the Internet. One such program that allows students this opportunity is called Blabberize. This program allows students to create talking images using photographs or their own drawings. Another program is called Voice Thread. This program allows students to create collaborative, multimedia slide shows.

Individual Activity: Reflecting on the Create Strategy

In your reflective journal answer the following questions:
- What do you think are the strengths of the create strategy?
- What are some weaknesses?
- What are some ways you can adapt the strategy?
- How would you use a create activity in your classes?

> You will be responsible for creating baseball cards about five famous abolitionists. They are:
> - Fredrick Douglass
> - William Lloyd Garrison
> - Harriet Beecher Stowe
> - Sojourner Truth
> - Harriet Tubman
>
> You are then to make five "baseball" cards about each historic figure. The front and the back of the card will look like this:
>
> **Picture Goes Here**
>
> (Front)   (Back)
>
> Name   "Stat" 1 (Most Important Fact about Person)
> Date of Birth/Death   "Stat" 2 (2nd Most Important Fact about the Person)
> Place of Birth   "Stat" 3 (3rd Most Important Fact about the Person)
>
> **Directions:**
> You are to write three of the most important "stats" (facts) about each person as well as include a photograph or image of them (you can find these on the web or draw your own). Explain your rationale for selecting this fact and make a connection to present day. For
>
> **Rubric:**
> - Pictures (20 pts)
> - Relevant Facts (20 pts)
> - Rationale and connection to present day (30 pts)
> - Location (10 pts)
> - Card Design and Creativity (10 pts)
> - Participation in "Trade Day" (10 pts)

FIGURE 11.1.   Sample Create Lesson (Abolitionist Baseball Cards)

Compare and Contrast

The compare-and-contrast strategy was introduced in Chapter 8. This strategy has been endorsed by researchers as an effective method for students to learn material in any subject (Marzano et al., 2001; Silver et al., 2007). The compare-and-contrast strategy is also perfect for helping students learn both social studies content while working on important literacy skills called for in the Common Core State Standards and the NCSS C3 Framework (National Governors Association Center for Best Practices & Council of Chief State School Officers, 2010).

Using compare and contrast strategies to help build literacy is similar to the other ideas in this chapter. First, you want your students to learn about a particular topic through some sort of medium (e.g., lecture, movie, worksheets, although reading is preferable). Next, students take what they learned, in this case something about two or more individuals, groups, places, or events, and use a graphic organizer to compare and contrast the two. There are many different types of graphic organizers that can be used for comparing and contrasting, including two and three circle Venn diagrams, Frayer models, T-Charts, Y-Charts, concept maps, and comprehension cubes. No matter which instructional tool you use to guide students through comparing and contrasting, be certain to move beyond the graphic organizer and invite students to write about their comparisons in greater detail to share their knowledge.

Below is an example of a three-ring Venn diagram lesson, one of the many ways to compare and contrast (see Figures 11.2 & 11.3). Often teachers find that their students have difficulties working with these diagrams and become confused about where to place the similarities and differences between the three topics being compared. The sample activity offers a solution that will help make the process less confusing. Remember that you are teaching both social studies and literacy. Needed is careful planning that does not overemphasize either content area.

Today you are going to learn about the similarities and differences of the command, market, and traditional economic systems. More importantly, you will write an expository essay comparing and contrasting the three. Using the sources provided, you will need to complete the three-ring Venn diagram. To help you make the Venn diagram easier to complete make the following additions to the three circles:

Place a 1 in the outer part of the command circle. This area is for the difference between the command economy and the other two systems.

Place a 2 in the outer part of the market circle. This area is for the differences between the market economy and the other two systems.

Place a 3 in the outer part of the traditional circle. This area is for the differences between the traditional and the other two systems.

Place a 4 in the middle of the command and the market circles. This area is for the similarities between the command and the market systems.

Place a 5 in the middle of the market and traditional circles. This area is for the similarities between the market and the traditional systems.

Place a 6 in the middle of the traditional and command circles. This area is for the similarities between the traditional and command systems.

Place a 7 in the middle of all three circles. This area is the similarities between all three systems.

FIGURE 11.2. Sample Compare and Contrast Lesson (Economic Systems)

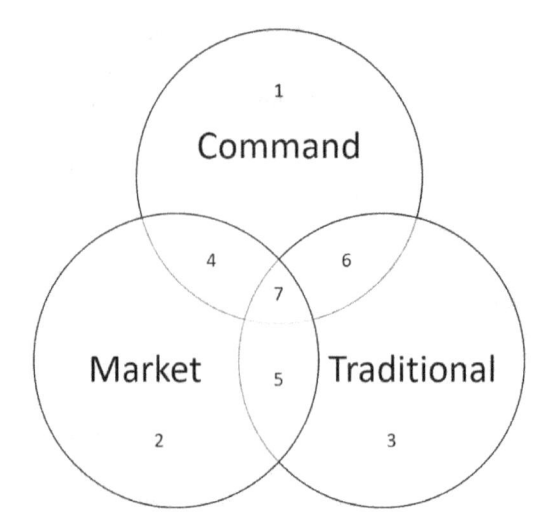

268 • TEACHING MIDDLE LEVEL SOCIAL STUDIES (3RD EDITION)

FIGURE 11.3. Sample Three Ring Venn Diagram—Comparison of Economic Systems

Individual Activity: The Compare and Contrast Strategy

In your reflective journal answer the following questions:

- What do you think are the strengths of the compare and contrast strategy?
- What are some weaknesses?
- What are some ways you can adapt the strategy?
- How would you use it in your classes?

Images from the Past and Present

The rationale for the use of primary images was introduced in Chapter 4, with strategies that could be used in their study. Along with those ideas, a great way to help bring literacy to the social studies classroom is to have students compare and contrast images from the past to those from the present. Providing students opportunities to examine images from the past and compare them with today helps them gain a better understanding and personal connection to history (Boyle et al., 2010). Encouraging them to write about the way's things have changed or stayed the same offers students a better way to make connections to the past than by simply talking about it. Figure 11.4 is an example of a worksheet that can be used to facilitate connections between past and present images of schools. To support their completion of this work, students will need background knowledge on Indian Residential Schools and racially segregated schools prior to the 1954 Brown v Board of Education Supreme Court ruling. You will notice this graphic organizer includes a rationale for each question to facilitate your own understanding of each question. These rationales can be omitted when working with middle

Building Literacy in Middle Level Social Studies • 269

Classrooms: Past and Present • Image 1: Indian Residential Schools in the USA (1870–1973) • Image 2: Racially segregated schools prior to Brown v. Board of Education (1954) • Image 3: Present day classroom (can be an image found online or one of your own classroom)
To facilitate a detailed evaluation of each image: 1. Describe three details you notice in each image
To encourage wonderings and connections with people: 2. What are two questions you have about each image? 3. What do you think the students in each image are thinking about?
To encourage comparison: 4. Name two ways that school/classrooms have remained the same
To encourage contrast: 5. Name two ways schools have changed
To encourage application of knowledge: 6. What is one way you think schools should change in the future?

FIGURE 11.4. Sample Past and Present Images Strategy

level learners. Again, the goals are to learn about the past, make connections to the present, and to improve literacy skills. After completion students should use their responses as an outline for writing about the content learned, ideally to an authentic audience such as a community member.

Individual Activity: Using Images from the Past and Present

In your reflective journal answer the following questions:

- What are strengths of the past and present image strategy?
- What are some weaknesses?
- What are some ways you can adapt the strategy?
- How would you use it in your classes?

Inquiry

The inquiry strategy was also introduced in Chapter 4. A well-developed inquiry-based lesson is the culmination of all of the strategies discussed so far.

Remember, when developing an inquiry-based lesson, make sure to use primary and secondary sources (including the textbook), base the lesson on a problem/sparking question, and include a graphic organizer to help students organize their thoughts as they analyze the sources to answer the questions. An inquiry-based lesson should allow students opportunity to develop their own conclusions based on documented evidence. Students must use the sources as their guide when writing about why they answered the question in the way they chose. For the most part, any writing assignment based on inquiry will be persuasive in nature. Karrie uses an inquiry-based lesson when she introduces the Leo Frank Case to students in her eighth grade Georgia Studies class. She presents students with the crime scene and a brief background about Mary Phagan, the 13-year-old murder victim. She gives students written statements of suspects and people involved in the case. They are required to examine the evidence and complete a homicide report with information about the victim and the crime. Students develop a list of suspects and a justification for why they believe these individuals are suspicious. By giving them the opportunity to examine evidence, Karrie is encouraging students to think critically about the topic rather than just telling them about what happened in the 1913 court case.

Chapter 4 offers examples of inquiry based, problem-solving lessons. The full lesson plan "Do Women Have Equal Rights" is below (Figure 11.5, Table 11.5).

TABLE 11.5. Sample Inquiry Chart (Women's Rights)

Topic	What I Know (List what you already Know.)	What does the textbook reading say?	What does the song say?	What does the fact sheet say?	Summary
Type of source	x				
Who were some of the most important women in the Suffrage Movement?				x	
When did women gain the right to vote?			x	x	
What were some other rights that women did not have before 1920?					
List some positive changes for women since 1920.					
List some inequalities women still face today.			x		
Interesting Facts	x				
New Questions?	x				

x=information not in source.

Building Literacy in Middle Level Social Studies • 271

1. Materials
   - Textbook: Women's Suffrage
   - Handout: Lyrics Let Us All Speak Our Minds Worksheet (Song Optional) https://digital.lib.niu.edu/illinois/gildedage/media
   - Handout: Factsheet on Women's Rights
   - Handout: Women's Suffrage Historical Inquiry Chart - Your Turn Question
2. Essential Question:
   - What was the significance of the Suffrage movement?
3. Activating Strategy:
   - Ask students if they think that women in the United States today have equal rights with men. On the board create a T-chart with the words "Yes" and "No." Ask students to tell you their answers and the reasons why they think women do or do not have equal rights. After completing the chart, have students write down their own opinion and to back it up with the facts listed on the board.
   - Tell students that no matter their answer, women in the United States have made many political, social, and economic gains over the past 90 years, and much of this equality is due to the suffrage movement. Explain to them that today they are going to learn about the women's suffrage movement and some of its leaders, the political, social, and economic changes due to the women's suffrage movement, and how it has affected today's society. Additionally, explain to students that they will have the opportunity to change or defend their answers to the question "Do women have equal rights?" based on the documents that they use today.
4. Instructional Strategy:
   - Have students read their textbook about women's suffrage.
   - Have them fill out column 1 of their historical inquiry chart.
   - Go over the answers to make sure students have the column filled out correctly.
   - Play the song (if possible) "Let Us All Speak Our Minds." Project the lyrics on the screen. Be sure to explain what the song lyrics mean if your students do not understand them.
   - Have students fill out column 2 of their historical inquiry chart.
   - Go over the answers to make sure students have the column filled out correctly.
   - In pairs, have students review the "Factsheet on Women in the United States."
   - Have students fill out column 3 of their historical inquiry chart.
   - Go over the answers to make sure students have the column filled out correctly.
   - X's mean the information is not found in the chart.

(continues)

FIGURE 11.5. Sample Historical Inquiry Lesson Plan: Do Women Have Equal Rights?

---

5. Summarizing Strategy:
   - Project the "Your Turn" question. Have students complete the activity and discuss as a class.
6. Differentiation:
   - Provide students, who will find the task of creating a historical inquiry chart difficult, a partially created chart.
   - Model for students how to fill in the chart.
   - Do one of the columns together as a class.
   - Use read aloud and think aloud strategies.

Your Turn Question:

In 3-5 sentences, write a persuasive newspaper article addressing the following question: "Do women have equal rights today? Why or why not?" Make sure to use examples from your chart to support your opinion.
   - There has never been a female U.S President and only one female Vice President.
   - Of over 3000 counties in the United States, 61 are named in honor of women.
   - In 2021 there are 9 female governors, 24 U.S. Senators, and 118 U.S. Representatives.
   - In 1972, 26% of Americans said they would not vote for a woman for president; in 2006 the number was only 5%
   - In the 1970s, only 10% of doctors were female. In 2019, 36% of doctors were female and 50.5% of medical students were female.
   - In 2019, 56% of college students were women.

FIGURE 11.5. Continued

In addition, the Stanford History Group offers many free inquiry-based U.S. and World history lessons.

This inquiry strategy is strongly aligned with the inquiry arc of the C3 Framework (NCSS, 2013). The Inquiry Arc contains four key dimensions which introduce students to the skills necessary to develop and answer questions and engage in actions that address those questions. Table 11.6 below details each of the four dimensions. Sample worksheets that pair with the inquiry arc along with sample lesson plans which can be searched by both content and grade level can be found online at C3teachers.org/inquiry-design-model.

Individual Activity: Reflecting on the Inquiry Strategy

In your reflective journal answer the following questions:

- What do you think are the strengths of the inquiry/problem solving strategy?
- What are some weaknesses?

TABLE 11.6. NCSS C3 Dimensions

Dimension 1: Developing Questions and Planning Inquiries	Dimension 2: Applying Disciplinary Tools and Concepts	Dimension 3: Evaluating Sources and Using Evidence	Dimension 4: Communicating Conclusions and Taking Informed Action
Developing meaningful questions and planning insightful inquires	Civics	Gathering and Evaluating Resources	Communicating and Critiquing Conclusions
	Economics		
	Geography	Developing Claims and Using Evidence	Taking Informed Action
	History		

- What are some ways you can adapt the strategy?
- How would you use it in your classes?

SUMMARY

This chapter provided a rationale for the integration of literacy and social studies, proclaiming a need for including historically marginalized voices and reviewing resources for finding high quality literature that can be used in social studies. The importance of critical literacy was then discussed as well as how integration supports both overarching literacy and social studies instructional goals. Lastly, this chapter described five additional strategies for building literacy skills during social studies. Although many of these ideas and lessons were introduced earlier in the book, examples and step-by-step lesson plans were provided.

If you have just one take away from this chapter, we hope it is that you will be responsible for not only teaching social studies content but also reading and writing as well. As long as mandates that emphasize literacy skills are enforced, you will be responsible for helping your school and your students meet the reading and writing goals that are required by this legislation. Integrating social studies with literacy is also a chance to expand the social studies curriculum to include historically marginalized voices and support the development of informed and active individuals who can critically read and write about the content they learn in social studies class. The integrated social studies and literacy lessons presented here should help your students learn to love social studies and understand its importance to their lives.

COLLABORATIVE ACTIVITY: REFLECTING ON THE CHAPTER

In a group of three discuss the following questions:

- Why is it important to use social studies courses as a platform for building literacy?
- How does it make you feel that you will not only be expected to teach social studies content but critical literacy also?

- What strategies from the chapter do you think you could incorporate into your classes from day one?
- Which ones do you think will take more time to establish in your classes?
- Are there any strategies that you will be comfortable with using when you begin student teaching? If so which ones?

WEBSITE RESOURCES

- **Blabberize** (https://blabberize.com/) is a free website that allows users to insert an image and use a voice recording to make the image "speak."
- **Dr. Bill McBride** (http://billmcbride.pbworks.com/w/page/14094960/Welcome%20to%20my%20Wiki) is one of the authors of the book *Building Literacy in Social Studies: Strategies for Improving Comprehension and Critical Thinking* on which my Top 10 strategies were based. On his site Dr. McBride provides several resources based on his work.
- **Gilder Lehrman Institute of American History** (http://www.gilderlehrman.org/) "is a nonprofit organization supporting the study and love of American history through a wide range of programs and resources for students, teachers, scholars, and history enthusiasts throughout the nation." Their website offers teachers access to a wide variety of historical documents, curriculum modules, podcasts, online exhibitions, and online journals which provide teachers with lesson plans and ideas.
- **Library of Congress** (http://www.loc.gov/index.html) offers teachers access to a wide variety of primary sources including prints and photographs, historic newspapers, performing arts, sound recordings, films, maps, and manuscripts. Their website offers features such as "Today in History," "Places in the News," and teacher resources.
- **National Archives** (http://www.archives.gov/) offers teaches a wide variety of resources and includes lesson plans and activities, information about using primary sources, and state and regional resources. Opportunities for professional development are presented as well.
- **National History Education Clearinghouse** (http://teachinghistory.org/) offers access to primary and secondary sources to teachers K–12. The website includes a list of "quick links" to help middle grades U.S. history teachers located resources and lesson plans.
- **On the Trail of Tears: History is Boring? Stuff it!** (http://trailofthetrail.blogspot.com/2011/02/history-is-boring-stuff-it.html#!/2011/02/history-is-boring-stuff-it.html) is a blog by Jeff Bishop who serves as the president of the Trail of Tears Association, a group interested in preserving historic Trail of Tears sites. In 2011, Mr. Bishop interviewed two teachers who were using the historic figure statue project in their classes. The teachers, Mike Breedon and Mark Schock, were in one of Scott's workshops where he taught them the activity. The page listed is an interesting read about how

the teachers used the historic figures statue project with their students and how much they enjoyed the assignment.
- **Reading Educator** (http://www.readingeducator.com/) is a group that helps content area teachers use reading "...to pursue and acquire understanding about the world through the study of texts. Their website offers effective metacognitive reading strategies, sample lesson plans implementing reading strategies, video demonstrations of teachers modeling strategies, tools for integrating reading strategies, and specific content area suggestions.
- **Reading Quest** (http://www.readingquest.org) is a website "designed for social studies teachers who wish to more effectively engage their students with the content in their classes." The website offers several resources and strategies for building literacy in social studies.
- **Smithsonian Institution** (http://www.si.edu/) "seeks to bring content experts and educators together to help strengthen American education and enhance our nation's ability to compete globally. The Smithsonian serves as a laboratory to create models and methods of innovative informal education and link them to the formal education system." Their website offers teachers access to lesson plans developed to align with state standards and access to a variety of resources from many museums including the Air and Space, American History, and the Portrait Gallery.
- **Stanford History Education Group** (http://sheg.stanford.edu/?q=node/45) Stanford history Education Group is directed by Sam Wineburg who is one of the most well-known researchers of history education in the country. The group's "Reading Like a Historian" curriculum "engages students in historical inquiry. Each lesson revolves around a central historical question and features sets of primary documents modified for groups of students with diverse reading skills and abilities." Their website offers teachers over 75 free inquiry-based U.S. and World history lesson plans.
- **Voice Thread** (https://voicethread.com/products/k12/) is "a platform where students develop critical thinking, communication, collaboration, and creativity skills."

REFERENCES

Boyle, C., Conklin, B., Dustman, J., & Vest, K. (2010). *Document-based assessment activities.* Shell Education.

Brighton, K. (2007). *Coming of age: The education and development of young adolescent.* National Middle School Association (NMSA).

Brown, A. L., & Au, W. (2014). Race, memory, and master narratives: A critical essay on U.S. curriculum history. *Curriculum Inquiry, 44*(3), 358–389. doi:10.1111/curi.12049.

Calderon, D. (2014). Speaking back to manifest destinies: A land education-based approach to critical curriculum inquiry. *Environmental Education Research, 20*(1), 24–36.

Demoiny, S. B., & Ferraras-Stone, J. (2018). Critical literacy in elementary social studies: Juxtaposing historical master and counter narratives in picture books. *The Social Studies, 109*(2), 64–73.

Gay, G. (2018). *Culturally responsive teaching: Theory, research, and practice.* Teachers College Press.

Journell, W. (2009). An incomplete history: Representation of American Indians in state social studies standards. *Journal of American Indian Education, 48*(2), 18–32.

Keenan, H. B. (2019). Visiting Chutchui: The making of a colonial counter story on an elementary school field trip. *Theory & Research in Social Education, 47,* 52–75.

Ladson-Billings, G. (2003). Lies my teacher still tells. In G. Ladson-Billings (Ed.)., *Critical race theories perspectives on social studies: The profession, policies, and curriculum* (pp. 1–11). Information Age.

Los Angeles Times. (1998). To our readers. https://www.latimes.com/archives/la-xpm-1998-sep-13-mn-22400-story.htmlhttps://www.latimes.com/archives/la-xpm-1998-sep-13-mn-22400-story.html

Loewen, J. W. (2008). *Lies my teacher told me: Everything your American history textbook got wrong.* The New Press.

Marzano, R., Pickering, D., & Pollack, J. (2001). *Classroom instruction that works.* ASCD.

Meller, W. B., Richardson, D., & Hatch, J. A. (2009). Using read-alouds with critical literacy literature in K–3 classrooms. *Young Children, 64*(6), 76–78.

Monforti, J. L., & McGlynn, A. (2010). Aqui estamos? A survey of Latino portrayal in introductory U.S. government and politics textbooks. *Political Science & Politics, 43*(2), 309–316. doi:10.1017/S1049096510000181.

Monte-Sano, C. (2010). Disciplinary literacy in history: An exploration of the historical nature of adolescents' writing. *The Journal of Learning Sciences, 19*(4), 539–568.

McLaughlin, M., & DeVoogd, G. (2004). Critical literacy as comprehension: Expanding reader response. *International Reading Association, 48*(1), 52–62.

National Council for the Social Studies. (2013). *Social studies for the next generation: Purposes, practices, and implications of the College, Career, and Civic Life (C3) Framework for social studies state standards.* NCSS.

National Council of Teachers of English and International Reading Association. (1996). *Standards for the English language arts.* National Council of Teachers of English.

National Council for the Social Studies. (2010). *National curriculum standards for social studies: Executive summary.* https://www.socialstudies.org/standards/execsummary

National Governors Association Center for Best Practices & Council of Chief State School Officers. (2010). *Common core state standards for English language arts and literacy in history/social studies, science, and technical subjects.* Authors.

Ogle, D., Klemp, R., & McBride, B. (2007). *Building literacy in social studies: Strategies for improving comprehension and critical thinking.* ASCD.

Quote Fancy. (n.d.). *Annie Proulx quotes.* https://quotefancy.com/quote/1373917/Annie-Proulx-Writing-comes-from-reading-and-reading-is-the-finest-teacher-of-how-to-write

Sabzalian, L. (2019). *Indigenous children's survivance in public schools (indigenous and decolonizing studies in education).* Routledge Education.

Shear, S. (2015). Cultural genocide masked as education: U.S. history textbooks' coverage of Indigenous education policies. In P. T. Chandler (Ed.), *Doing race in social studies Critical perspectives* (pp. 13–40). Information Age Publishing.

Silver, H. F., Strong, R. W., & Perini, M. J. (2007). *The strategic teacher: Selecting the right research-based strategy for every lesson.* ASCD

Suh, Y., An, S., & Forest, D. (2014). Immigration, imagined communities, and collective memories of Asian American experiences: A content analysis of Asian American experiences in Virginia U.S. history textbooks. *The Journal of Social Studies Research, 39*(1), 39–51. doi:10.1016/j. jssr.2014.05.002.

Winstead, L. (2011). The impact of NCLB and accountability on social studies: Teacher experiences and perceptions about teaching social studies. *The Social Studies, 102*(5), 221–227.

CHAPTER 12

INTEGRATING THE "CORE" SUBJECTS IN MIDDLE LEVEL SOCIAL STUDIES

This is not a question of whether academic standards should be promoted, but how they fit into a broader conception of educational achievement.
—*Ken Robinson (2001, p. 45)*

It is a sound educational principle that students should be introduced to scientific subject-matter and be initiated into its facts and laws through acquaintances with everyday social applications.
—*John Dewey (1938)*

Activity List
- Reflecting on the Chapter.

INTRODUCTION

In addition to a deep ability to identify, analyze, and critique their chosen subject, experts understand how different concepts within their expertise interrelate with concepts outside it. Expert winemakers draw from chemistry, geology, climatology, economics, biology, and history in perfecting their product. Similarly, successful navigators of the "golden" age of exploration considered physics, oceanography, astronomy, physiology, measurement, and psychology to complete their journeys. That social studies teachers—indeed all teachers—understand the relationships between the various subject matters of human development, educational psychology, social and cultural awareness, assessment and measurement, and their subject areas is what makes them successful with students. The work of the teacher blends together and applies a wide variety of concepts from often traditionally "separated" subject areas.

Indeed, we cannot think of an activity or concept that does not employ knowledge, skills, or themes from multiple subjects. As we explore the American Revolution with our students, for example, we may bring in civics concepts such as taxation and protest, health and hygiene concepts when discussing soldier deaths, geography when understanding British blockades, and music and other arts that stirred the hearts of rebels. If working with students on the various regions of the United States in a geography class, students compare economic characteristics, cultural and linguistic differences, histories, and climate. A current events class may explore various political theories, finance concepts such as inflation, globalization, or religion. State or local history classes may use mathematics to better understand demographic changes, delve into how technological innovation has changed urban planning, or community contributions to broader artistic culture. The natures of the specific subjects of history, geography, civics, economics, sociology, and culture inherently employ knowledge, concepts, and skills from a vast variety of other subjects.

The traditional and often-practiced approach to school, however, separates subjects and concepts from one another. Students have, perhaps seven class periods a day in which they explore and experience discrete subject areas. First period is science, second period is English Language Arts, third period is math, and so forth throughout the school day. Physical education, music, art, and social studies, likewise have specific, separate times of study. Students "do" science in science, math in math, and social studies in social studies. Knowledge, concepts, skills, and experiences in these discrete classes are frequently isolated from one another. As a result, students may go through their elementary, middle, and high school educations without the experience in—or realization of—the interrelated nature of these knowledge, concepts, and skills.

Acknowledging the obvious bias, we argue that social studies classes have the potential to be the most integrative, multidisciplinary, and interdisciplinary classes students take. Though we make the philosophical argument that concepts from all classes are inherently integrated with one another, we recognize and appreciate the practical barriers teachers face when encouraging their students to think in integrative, multidisciplinary, and interdisciplinary ways. Scripted curriculums, focus on subject-based standardized assessments, and pressure to "teach the basics" limits teachers in many settings to classroom experiences that isolate subjects and concepts from one another. Depending on your setting, curriculum, and teaching assignment, you may feel strong pressure to stick closely to a traditional subject-approach to teaching. With this in mind, we encourage you to consider ways, formally and informally, to assist your students in seeing how concepts, themes, knowledge, and skills from one classroom setting may be applied in others. Indeed, we encourage you to consider how you may provide classroom experiences to bring your students to "expert" level in understanding the integrated, multidisciplinary, and interdisciplinary natures of learning (Colwell et al., 2020).

MULTIDISCIPLINARY AND INTERDISCIPLINARY APPROACHES

Integration or blending of subjects together is not an either/or proposition. It is not a question of whether subjects, topics, concepts, or activities are integrated, it is a question of; "to what degree are students encouraged to see relationships between learning experiences from their various classes?." Approaching subject integration with this question as its basis encourages teachers to find ways, large and small, to blend their subjects together without the often-intimidating labels, formal processes, or in-depth coordination that is associated with blending subjects together (Colwell et al., 2020; Moser et al., 2019). It has been our experience that taking advantage of frequent, small, and informal subject integration opportunities encourages both teacher and students to begin to see their world as integrated, multidisciplinary, and interdisciplinary.

Viewing subject integration as existing on a spectrum rather than as an "all or nothing" dichotomy alleviates apprehension that often accompanies this topic. Approaching subject integration as a spectrum encourages teachers to take small yet important steps toward this important work. Both ends of this spectrum are highly impractical, but the spectrum approach helps teachers frame to what extent their classrooms encourage application of knowledge, concepts, and skills in various settings. On one extreme is complete subject isolation. In history class, explored are no concepts from science, technology, culture, mathematics, or Language Arts. History is history and that is that. This theoretical class makes no use of speeches, numbers, maps, graphs or charts, artistic works, or economic principles. Absent from this theoretical class is opportunity for deep, meaningful, or relevant student learning. On the other end of the integrative spectrum is a complete absence of references to subjects. This theoretical class does not classify knowledge, skills, or concepts into disciplines, maintaining a universal approach to phenomenon and learning. There is no history class, and indeed there is no school at all because school is everywhere. Though an initially attractive thought to many students, this complete absence of subjects, structures, or disciplines is not easily digestible and does not meet the practical limitations established by state boards of education or local school systems.

Because both ends of the integration spectrum are impossible to implement, we encourage you to look more toward the center when considering how your students might experience the interrelated nature of knowledge, skills, and dispositions. As you read through the following sections, you are encouraged to consider how the different concepts and examples may be specifically employed in your classrooms.

Multidisciplinary Approaches

A multidisciplinary approach to a topic, theme, concept or skill approaches the target from various perspectives that remain distinct from one another. More easily accomplished in most schools because of schedule and mandated curriculums, a multidisciplinary approach encourages students to study topics from various disciplinary perspectives. In studying weather for example, (see Figure 12.1), exploration of the topic occurs from various disciplinary viewpoints that have broad connections to one another. A science class may discuss how topographical factors impact weather patterns while the social studies class applies the concepts learned in science to a map of Africa. A math class, meanwhile, may be calculating relative humidity while a Language Arts class may be working with adjectives that help describe nuances in how people experience weather. Throughout their day, in this case, students are experiencing weather from multiple perspectives while the classes and experiences remain distinct. Further promoting the idea that multidisciplinary units are achievable with some coordination, easily done is the connection of learning standards from various subject areas.

Multidisciplinary approaches take coordination between teachers so there is a coherent and easily identifiable theme, concept, or skill addressed in multiple

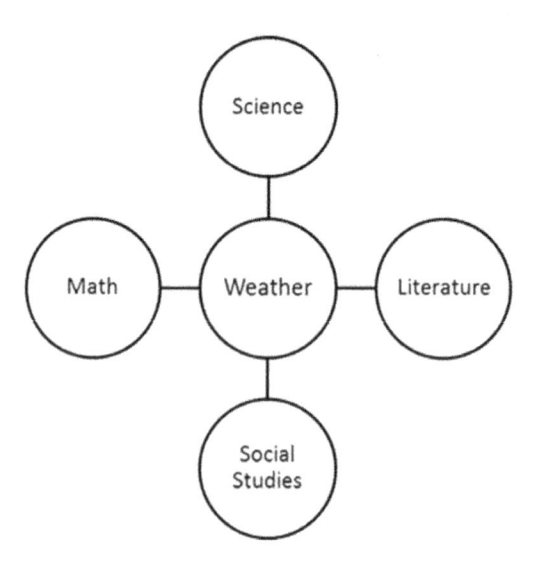

FIGURE 12.1. A Multidisciplinary Approach to Exploring Weather Concepts

classes. Though many students may naturally find these connections, explicit description of the commonality encourages students to see the classes as interrelated. Planning for a multidisciplinary unit requires selecting a specific topic, skill, or concept and coordinating with other teachers to address it from different perspectives. To begin the process—and perhaps to assist in justification to administrators—Moser et al. (2019) recommend team teachers collaboratively analyze discipline-based standards for ways to connect classes through multidisciplinary experiences. Through the process, teachers learn more about one another's curriculums, texts, classroom activities, and assessments. In a multidisciplinary study of poverty, for example, a social studies teacher may learn more about text annotation strategies used in Language Arts as both classes explore *A Christmas Carol* by Charles Dickens. Similarly, a science teacher may work with a math teacher to create an assessment connecting standard of living, disease, poverty, and statistics. In this example, students may study poverty from historical and contemporary perspectives, explore the technology gap that exists in countries with large gaps between the wealthy and the poor, analyze food consumption patterns and healthcare access according to social class, and engage in other activities that approach the many aspects of poverty and wealth distribution.

It is the broad goal of the multidisciplinary approach to encourage students to find connections between subject-area disciplines, texts, and learning approaches through a common theme. More easily employed in most schools than interdisciplinary approaches, formal multidisciplinary units create continuity through students' school days by connecting classes together. Informally, teachers can provide experiences for students where they see how math, science, language arts, technology, fine arts, and social studies blend together to inform the subject of their study.

Interdisciplinary Approaches

Distinct in two ways from multidisciplinary approaches exploring common themes from multiple subject perspectives, interdisciplinary approaches place greater focus on students' exploration of complex or essential questions and effectively blur lines between traditional subject areas (Brown & Knowles, 2014). Broad, complex essential questions lie at the heart of interdisciplinary units. It can be difficult for students and their teachers to conceptualize deeply interdisciplinary experiences because of the conditioned desire to see the world through disciplinary lenses. Most teachers were educated in discipline-based settings where viewing "math as math" and "science as science" was rewarded with high grades. When considering interdisciplinary experiences, we recommend focusing on broad inquiry skills such as critical question asking, seeking and evaluating resources, and effective communication of results. Indeed, employing the inquiry arc of the C3 Framework can be done with any subject area and any essential question of inquiry (NCSS, 2013). Taking emphasis away from "what subject the

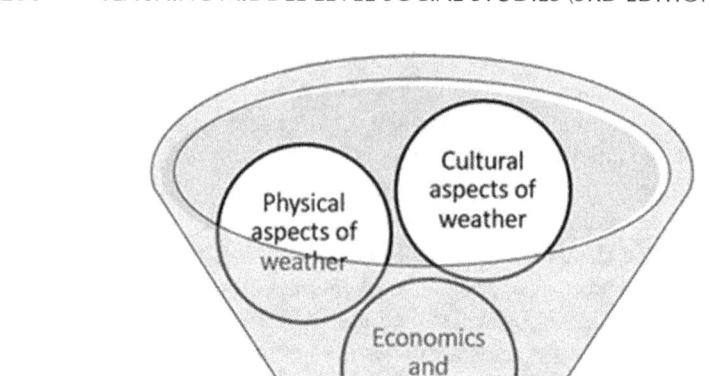

FIGURE 12.2. An Interdisciplinary Approach to Exploring Weather Concepts

question is related to" and placing emphasis on the process of exploring the question helps in viewing inquiry from an interdisciplinary lens.

Figure 12.2 approaches the question, "Why is weather important?" from an interdisciplinary standpoint. Not emphasized are the classes in which students are enrolled, but concepts that cross through science, geography, culture, and history. An added benefit of interdisciplinary work is students' inclination to craft follow-up questions during their inquiry. "How does weather impact culture?," "What happens to the economy if weather becomes more severe?," and "What might life be like if weather was predictable a month ahead of time?" are a few possibilities students may consider in their exploration of daily weather events.

Often crafted by students, essential questions are addressed through learning experiences organized by their teachers. It may be that the questions themselves are unanswerable in absolute ways. The intent of exploring the question is to apply knowledge, concepts, skills, and dispositions in the exploration process to encourage students to see the relevance and beauty of intellectual exploration. It is through the process of exploration that students employ knowledge, concepts, skills, and dispositions often emphasized in traditional disciplinary classroom experiences. Table 12.1 provides a list of exploratory questions posed by 8th graders. These unedited inquiries compel readers away from specific subject areas toward broad concepts. They have the additional benefit of providing a window into the interests and curiosities of young adolescents. In our experience, encouraging middle school students to wonder—and follow up on that wondering—rarely dis-

Integrating the "Core" Subjects in Middle Level Social Studies • **285**

TABLE 12.1. Example Student-Created Interdisciplinary Questions

Why do people taste, dress, and have different likes?
Why do people seem to judge others?
Why do people have to change so much while growing older?
Why do people like different types of clothing in different places?
Why do humans change what they like?
What exactly makes us who we are?
Why is there so much racism in the world?
Why do people make up rules and laws that people have to follow, or they get punished?
Why do people have something to believe in: God or religion?
Why do animals live in the habitats they do?
Why do people get more technologies every year?
What would society be like today if we suddenly didn't have electricity, grocery stores, cares, or cell phones?
Why is the world always fighting?
How does transportation make our community easier? What would we use if we didn't have it?
What makes/who made Paris, France the fashion capital of the world? Why not somewhere in Africa or South America?
Why do some countries have certain sports when others don't?
How does the population of animals affect us? (Like animals going extinct)
Why do we need money?
How do submarines work?
How do other people communicate?
What would happen if the sun went out?
Why can't there be world peace?
Why do political people always argue about the same thing for years?
Why is there war?
What would happen if we had a world drought?
How does temperature change the way people behave?
What was meat packing like in 1900?

appoints. Indeed, many questions of interdisciplinary study crafted by modern middle school students are as old as inquiry itself.

Broad shifts in academic standards away from content knowledge toward skills and processes bolsters employment of interdisciplinary approaches. The C3 Standards (NCSS, 2013), for example, encourage the creation of meaningful, complex questions, exploration of sources of information, argument crafting, communication of results, and action beyond the classroom. This inquiry arc is well-suited for interdisciplinary units that set aside traditional subjects for integrated educational experiences. Similarly, the Next Generation Science Standards, (NGSS), (National Research Council, 2012), encourages learners to view concepts as applicable beyond the science discipline.

Given the practical considerations of time, scheduling, space, and standards applied to students and teachers, Interdisciplinary Units are more difficult to execute than Multidisciplinary Units. Creation and refinement of questions, teacher coordination of experiences, scheduling experiences in ways that move away from traditional class periods, and student demonstration of the results of their exploration all take considerable time, thought, and administrative support. Teachers who look at calendars placed next to required curriculum may be hesitant to engage in the work of interdisciplinary studies. Those teachers—indeed all teachers—are encouraged to consider the joy, student-centered nature, and intellectual benefits interdisciplinary units bring. It has been our experience that even years later, former students recall interdisciplinary work more clearly and more profoundly than other middle school classroom experiences.

BENEFITS OF SUBJECT INTEGRATION

With focus on transfer of knowledge, employment of skill, and applicability of concepts in multiple settings, integrative approaches to social studies are inherently complex. Not to be confused with the "difficultness" of the experience, complexity implies cognitive work beyond rote memorization, summarization, or paraphrasing. Classrooms in which employment of integrative, multidisciplinary, or interdisciplinary approaches occur will have students who are actively engaged in analysis, application, critique, evaluation, and creation of information and concepts (Senn et al., 2019). In settings where authentic multidisciplinary and interdisciplinary work takes place, the common student complaint of "pointless busywork" is less frequent because the work and experience is focused on application beyond school walls. Encouraging students to "think like social scientists," integrative work results in deeper inquiry, reinforcement of knowledge, growth of skill, and encouragement of curiosity that teachers desperately seek, and students desperately need.

The Association of Middle Level Education (formerly the National Middle School Association) supports curriculum that encourages "…students to pursue answers to questions they have about themselves, content, and the world," (NMSA, 2010, p. 22). Complimenting this philosophy, the inquiry arc of the C3 Standards, (NCSS, 2013), inherently encourages integrative work. Though the C3 standards frame disciplines such as economics, geography, civics, and history, the standards in these categories are broad enough to easily cross into other traditional subject areas.

The following sections briefly describe how other disciplines commonly found in middle schools may be integrated into social studies. Though violating the philosophy of genuinely interdisciplinary work, these sections are intended as starting places for your future integrative work.

Integrating the "Core" Subjects in Middle Level Social Studies • **287**

TABLE 12.2. Examples of Multidisciplinary and Interdisciplinary Approaches

Topic	Multidisciplinary Approach	Interdisciplinary Approach
American Revolution	The art of revolution: Annotation of Declaration of Independence Medicine of the war Reading of historical novels Technology of the war	Is violence ever justifiable? Is war worth it? Was life harder in the 1770s? What does it mean to be patriotic?
Ancient Civilizations	Ancient understandings of the world Law and order of the ancient world Oral tradition as primary sources Measurement of the Wonders of the Ancient World Technology of Rome	Has human nature always been the same? Have stories fundamentally changed in 6000 years? Was life simpler in 1000 B.C.E.? What technologies are most fundamental to society?
Civics	Annotation of founding documents and presidential speeches Demographics and voting patterns Technology and democracy	Are local or national governments more effective at governance? Can true representation in government exist? Is mass communication a benefit or a threat to democracy? Where is the balance between individual freedom and responsibility?
Economics	Economic policy and standard of living Percentages Portrayal of various economic classes in literature—stereotypes	Does every person have the right to a basic standard of living? How much sacrifice are you willing to make for a better environment? What is true wealth?
United States/World Geography	Climate and economic activity Geography and cultural norms Regional stories, traditions, and histories Technology, movement, and commerce	Are the regions of the United States more similar or different to one another? Is there one American identity? Which region has it "easiest"? What can people of different places learn from one another?

English Language Arts

Most broadly, concepts and skills addressed within English Language Arts classes—reading, writing, speaking, listening, and viewing—focus on the development of information analysis and effective communication. Considering activities that occur in Language Arts classes such as study of grammar and syntax, figurative language, themes and perspective, speech presentation, and composition, the goals of social studies and the language arts have much in common. Indeed, topics, concepts, and experiences within social studies classes may provide rich places to learn about text comparison and critical analysis in research, key dimensions of the Common Core English Language Arts standards (National Governors Association Center for Best Practices, 2010).

Specifically, the inquiry arc of the C3 Framework (NCSS, 2013) places a strong focus on textual analysis (domain 3) and communication of results (domain 4). Expanding the view of language arts beyond traditional writing, providing experiences in which they grow in their recognition of texts to include visual texts, informational texts, artifacts, sound recordings, and other sources, students can benefit from approaching a topic through various modes of information (Lupo et al., 2020). Applied, geography classes studying sub-Saharan Africa deeply benefit from analysis of themes of oral traditions; ancient history classes' exploration of the effectiveness of early writing techniques such as hieroglyphics and cuneiform provide insights into syntax; civics classes' investigation of free speech issues benefit from discussions of banned books; and economics classes grow in their understanding of inequality through exposure to, and analysis of, underrepresented or marginalized authors.

From creative and emotional standpoints, integrative work between Language Arts and social studies has deep potential. Many social studies classes have for generations studied speeches and letters of peoples of the past. Both fiction and non-fiction works provide case studies in the communication of ideas, feelings, experiences, and perspectives. Common in schools are two-subject integrative experiences in which students read history-based works in Language Arts class while examining specific time periods or cultures in social studies. From the timeless themes of Shakespeare to the raw and relevant emotion of Eminem, integrating Language Arts concepts with social studies experiences benefits students in both areas.

Fine Arts

Easily integrated into social studies classes, fine arts such as music, poetry, visual, and performing arts are modes of creative communication and expression across time, culture, economics, emotion, and geography. With emphasis on creation, annotation, analysis, themes, and exploration of common or unique perspectives, employment of the fine arts is similar to the employment of the language arts in social studies classes. Readers of the National Coalition for Core Arts Standards (National Coalition for Core Arts Standards, 2014) will find familiar themes in both Language Arts standards and the C3 (NCSS, 2013) standards. Specifically, these standards, encourage students through an arc like the inquiry arc of the C3 standards in which students are:

a. Creating—Conceiving and developing new artistic ideas and work.
b. Performing, presenting, producing—
   i. Performing (dance, music, theatre): Realizing artistic ideas and work through interpretation and presentation.

ii. Presenting (visual arts): Interpreting and sharing artistic work.
   iii. Producing (media arts): Realizing and presenting artistic ideas and work.
  c. Responding—Understanding and evaluating how the arts convey meaning
  d. Connecting—Relating artistic ideas and work with personal meaning and eternal context (National Coalition for Core Arts Standards, 2014)

Applied in social studies classes, the blending of the creative and fine arts may reveal: changes in culture due to technology; insights into personal and collective experiences; social injustices and advances; commonalities in the human emotional experience; and critiques of societal improvement, among many other concepts. Broadly, the social studies is the exploration of the human experience. Without meaningful integration of how humans express themselves, this exploration is incomplete.

Mathematics

Systematic, logical processes to create data for interpretation, concepts and skills explored in math are well-applied in social studies classes. Having an undeserved reputation for being irrelevant beyond the classroom, mathematical concepts such as probability, statistics, algebra, and geometry, to name a few, are deeply important to making sense of the concepts explored in social studies. Though common understanding of math classes focuses on specific skills, broad objectives of math have students:

  a. Make sense of problems and persevere in solving them;
  b. Reason abstractly and quantitatively;
  c. Construct viable arguments and critique the reasoning of others;
  d. Model with mathematics;
  e. Use appropriate tools strategically;
  f. Attend to precision;
  g. Look for and make use of structure; and
  h. Look for and express regularity in repeated reasoning (National Governors Association Center for Best Practices & Council of Chief State School Officers, 2010)

Like other subject areas, broad goals of math classes focus on problem analysis, systematic solution finding, and effective communication of reasoning. Applied in social studies classrooms, students analyze changes in variables in courses such as geography, explore the use and misuse of probability in civics classes, compare demographic data in history classes, and seek meaning in inequality in economics courses. Specifically, consider the use and misuse of averages when investigating census data; how statistics are twisted in propaganda documents; how measurement error and standard deviation impact public policy, and how slight changes in variables impact climate or economic well-being.

Honed through math curriculum, concepts and skills see application and impact in social studies classes. As with other disciplines, when students consider sources of data, as encouraged by the C3 standards, (NCSS, 2013), recognizing and understanding the use and misuse of numerical data and logic is vital. To be better consumers of information, students require experiences in which they purposefully and intentionally employ mathematical skill. Social studies classes provide compelling topics and case-studies of how and why it is important to understand and apply mathematical concepts.

Physical Education and Health

It may seem a stretch to integrate physical education and health concepts in the social studies classroom. Upon closer investigation, however, experiences and concepts from health and physical education classes have strong ties to many concepts within social studies. Broadly, it is the goal of physical education classes to increase literacy in movement, health-enhancing physical activity, responsible personal and social behavior, and, "...the value of physical activity for health, enjoyment, challenge, self-expression and/or social interaction." (SHAPE America—Society of Health and Physical Educators, 2013).

From the cultural, economic, and social implications of professional sports and Title IX to the public policy impact of communicable diseases, concepts within health and physical education merge well with social studies topics. Strongly tying physical education and social studies together, spatial awareness and gross and fine motor skills invigorate classrooms and strengthen conceptual understanding in both subject areas. There are countless opportunities to blend physical and spatial opportunities with social studies. For example, you may; employ students to serve as planets in a classroom (or playground) wide model of the solar system in a geography class; encourage creation of interpretive dance to convey struggles of immigrants; or have students create human outlines of historic objects such as Lincoln's home or Washington's Fort Necessity. A key question in integrating physical movement into the social studies classroom is; "How can we bring this concept to life in the physical world?"

Deeply connected to many social studies concepts is health education. Through study of concepts such as disease, lifestyle, substance use and abuse, and human physiology, students are encouraged to see connection between their health and the broader community. Public health policy and civics classes, diet and history, medical technology and warfare, and adolescent development and modern American culture are just a few examples of how health and social studies merge. Exploration of the relationships between COVID-19, economic insecurity, government support of individuals and institutions, and personal freedom vs. personal responsibility demonstrates the impact of health processes, policies upon many concepts studied in social studies classes. Indeed, we challenge you to consider an aspect of health education that cannot be directly connected to history, geography, economics, culture, or civics.

In considering how you might engage students in physical experiences in your social studies classes, we encourage you to deeply consider risks that your students or you may encounter by doing so. A tug-of-war simulation serving as a metaphor for the British versus the Colonists and French, for example, constitutes a safety risk for middle school students. Overenthusiastic students may jerk at the rope, causing falls or other injuries—something we wish to avoid in social studies classes. Indeed, Ben watched with horror as a group of preservice teachers pulled at a rope on the quad. During the execution of this lesson plan demonstration, one of the college juniors slipped and fell right into some mud, ruining her (formerly) bright-white pants. Ben and the preservice teachers were grateful no one was hurt and that we could use this experience as a clear demonstration of the risks of physical feats in the classroom.

Activities "beyond the normal" may also inadvertently expose students to psychological risks. Wright-Maley (2015), for example, describes how a simulation regarding social class inadvertently shifted to an "experience of projected racism" (p. 67). Though integrating physical movement into social studies classes will certainly invigorate your class, the physical layout of the room and the task with which you engage your students requires deep consideration to ensure safety and relevance of the experience. Encouraging students to sit on the floor as if they were in trench warfare, lining them up in rows to simulate the horrors of the experience of being kidnapped by slave traders, and other experiences are deeply inappropriate for any student. In encouraging you to "push the envelope" of social studies pedagogy, we also encourage you to systematically consider every step of your lesson from the student, administrator, and parent perspective. We believe that it is better to ask for permission and guidance than it is to ask for forgiveness. When considering lessons involving movement or scenario, we recommend you discuss your innovative ideas with your building administrator and trusted peer network. You may also invite colleagues to participate!

Science

Fundamentally impacting human activities explored in social studies are concepts that students study in science courses. Life science, earth science, chemistry, biology, among other broad disciplines of study have strong ties to geography, history, economics, civics, and culture. Often, for example, many worlds or US geography courses begin their study by exploring systems and concepts such as climate, seasons, plate tectonics, natural disasters, and natural resources. Deeply infused into history, similarly, are concepts from biology, chemistry, and physics when investigating topics such as the rise of civilization, the industrial revolution and modern medicine, and the cold war. Led to maps of oil deposits, navigable waterways, and arable or non-arable lands, students can easily tie earth science concepts with economic principles. The bonds between science and social studies are plentiful and strong.

Reflecting ties between science and social studies, the Next Generation Science Standards, (NGSS), reference relationships between Earth systems and human activity, Engineering design, biological evolution, and the interactions of variables within ecosystems (NGSS Lead States, 2013). Intentionally and explicitly crafting experiences tying science to social studies encourages students to see interrelatedness between natural and human-created processes and social characteristics of the past, present, and potential future. Found in the study of climate change, a clear and compelling example of the interrelatedness of science and social studies presents itself. Experiences in learning about biological, chemical, and physical processes and their impact on social, economic, historical, and cultural attributes may inspire students to save their own futures. Other important and compelling topics blending science and social studies include: Bioethics and civil liberties; technology and international politics; chemical innovation and environmental studies; agriculture and early society; and space exploration and future societal norms. These few topics are just a sampling of important paths of inquiry for both science and social studies classes.

STEAM

Often nested in engineering, career, technical, or exploratory classes STEAM (Science, Technology, Engineering, Arts, and Math) concepts are inherently interdisciplinary. What we believe is missing from this wonderfully applicable and practical addition to many middle schools are additional emphases on civics, history, culture, and economics. STEAM (or its predecessor STEM, which did not include emphasis on arts), classes engage students with literal bridge building, experience in hydrodynamics, architectural design, pneumatics, medical technologies, and career-based experiences. Often left out of these experiences, however, are connections to concepts such as culture, economics, history, societal norms, social justice, among others.

Collaboration between technology and social studies teachers presents students with opportunities to see the impact of the concepts experienced in STEAM classes. The history and impact of changing architecture (such as indoor plumbing) on societal norms, engineering and civil liberties (video technology, facial recognition, predictive advertisements on social media, and privacy), aerodynamics and conflict, and communication and youth development, (cell phones and social media). As with other subject areas, concepts and experiences from STEAM courses lend themselves well to social studies classes. Both multidisciplinary and interdisciplinary approaches to STEAM concepts assists students in applying them in various geographic, cultural, historical, and economic contexts. Developing inquiry questions, as suggested by Dimension 1 of the C3 framework, (NCSS, 2013), students naturally blend STEAM concepts with concepts nested in the social studies. Given the opportunity in your classroom, the subsequent explorations may yield surprising and profound results.

CONCLUSION

The disciplines within the social studies are inherently multidisciplinary and interdisciplinary. Concepts within geography, history, economics, civics, and culture intermingle to impact and inform human and non-human experiences. Your classroom may be a crucible for blending often-thought-of distinct subjects into meaningful inquiries into society's most complex problems. With a bit of time, thought, creativity, and student input, your social studies class can be a place where concepts from all other classes see relevance. In considering the importance of this work, we turn to the introductory statement of the C3 Standards (NCSS 2013) referenced throughout this book:

> Now more than ever, students need the intellectual power to recognize societal problems; ask good questions and develop robust investigations into them; consider possible solutions and consequences; separate evidence-based claims from parochial opinions; and communicate and act upon what they learn. And most importantly, they must possess the capability and commitment to repeat that process as long as is necessary. Young people need strong tools for, and methods of, clear and disciplined thinking in order to traverse successfully the worlds of college, career, and civic life. (NCSS, 2013, p. 6)

It is through blending and applying language arts, fine arts, mathematics, physical and health education, science, STEAM, and social studies that this work may be better accomplished.

COLLABORATIVE ACTIVITY: REFLECTING ON THE CHAPTER

With a partner discuss the following questions:

- What is the difference between multidisciplinary and interdisciplinary approaches to teaching social studies?
- How does it make you feel that you expected to integrate social studies content with other disciplines also?
- What strategies from the chapter do you think you could incorporate into your classes from day one?
- Which ones do you think will take more time to establish in your classes?
- Are there any strategies that you will be comfortable with using when you begin student teaching? If so which ones?

WEBSITE RESOURCES

- The **American Federation of Teachers** (https://www.aft.org/education/igniting-fire/project-examples-resources-and-websites/interdisciplinary-project) maintains a website of interdisciplinary project ideas.
- The **Association for Supervision and Curriculum Development (ASCD)** (http://www.ascd.org/Default.aspx) is a leading educational or-

ganization promoting interactive, engaging teaching approaches. Exemplifying dedication to innovation, this chapter from an ASCD publication discusses integrated curriculum, provides examples of interdisciplinary and multidisciplinary topics, and described various roles teachers and students play in IDU and MDU work. The chapter can be accessed at http://www.ascd.org/publications/books/103011/chapters/What-Is-Integrated-Curriculum%C2%A2.aspx

- The **Montana Department of Education** (https://mhs.mt.gov/education/Educators/Interdisciplinary-Lesson-Plans) maintains a website with examples of interdisciplinary lesson plan ideas.

REFERENCES

Brown, D. F., & Knowles, T. (2014). *What every middle school teacher should know.* (3rd ed.). Heinemann.

Colwell, J., Hutchinson, A., & Woodward, L. (2020). *Digitally supported disciplinary literacy for diverse K–5 classrooms.* Teachers College Press.

Dewey, J. (1938). *Experience and education.* Macmillan Publishing Company.

Lupo, S. M., Berry, A., Thacker, E., Sawyer, A., & Merritt, J. (2020). Rethinking text sets to support knowledge building and interdisciplinary learning. *The Reading Teacher, 73*(4), 513–524.

Moser, K. M., Ivy, J., & Hopper, P. F. (2019). Rethinking content teaching at the middle level: An interdisciplinary approach. *Middle School Journal, 50*(2), 17–27. DOI: 10.1080/00940771.2019.1576579

National Coalition for Core Arts Standards. (2014). *National core arts standards. Rights Administered by the state Education Agency Directors of Arts Education.* Author.

National Council for the Social Studies (NCSS). (2013). *The college, career, and civic life (C3) framework for social studies state standards: Guidance for enhancing the rigor of K–12 civics, economics, geography, and history.* Author.

National Governors Association Center for Best Practices. (2010). *Common core state standards.* Author.

National Middle School Association. (2010). *This we believe: Keys to educating young adolescents.* Author.

National Research Council. (2012). *A Framework for K–12 science education: Practices, crosscutting concepts, and core ideas.* National Academy Press. https://doi.org/10.17226/13165

NGSS Lead States. (2013). *Next generation science standards: For states, BysStates.* The National Academies Press.

Robinson, K. (2001). Mind the gap: The creative conundrum. *Critical Quarterly, 43*(1), 41–45.

Senn, G., McMurtrie, D., & Coleman, B. (2019). Collaboration in the middle: Teachers in interdisciplinary planning. *Current issues in Middle Level Education, 24*(1), 1–4.

SHAPE America—Society of Health and Physical Educators. (2013) *National standards for K–12 physical education.* Author.

Wright-Maley, C. (2015). Beyond the "Babel problem": Defining simulations for the social studies. *The Journal of Social Studies Research, 39*(2), 63–77. DOI: 10.1016/j.jssr.2014.10.001

CHAPTER 13

USING YOUR SOCIAL STUDIES RESOURCES EFFECTIVELY

Texts in disciplines and subject areas control, to some extent, what can be known and learned
—*Elizabeth Moje (Moje et al., 2011, p. 455)*

...The teaching of history, more than any other discipline, is dominated by textbooks...the books are boring...they leave out anything that might reflect badly upon our national character.
—*James Loewen (1995)*

Activity List
- Resources Examined during Social Studies.
- Recognizing the Limitations of Textbooks.
- Texts and Resources to Expand Beyond the Textbook.
- Effectively Using and Comparing your Resources.

COLLABORATIVE ACTIVITY: RESOURCES EXAMINED DURING SOCIAL STUDIES

In your reflective journal create a list of the variety of resources you have seen used to teach social studies. To the best of your ability, rank these in order from most to least often used. Once you have your list, discuss with a partner the answers to the following questions:

- Which types of resources have you seen most often used? Why do you think that is the case?
- What role have textbooks played during social studies based on your observations and experiences?
- What might be some concerns with relying on the textbook as the only source of information?
- What types of resources tend to be overlooked during social studies that you think might be important to consider?

INTRODUCTION

When many people think of their social studies experiences, they think of textbooks. Research tells us that your recollection is correct because empirical evidence makes clear that, in many classrooms, textbooks are the dominant resource used to teach social studies (e.g., Alridge, 2006; Hawkman et al., 2015). This is despite the fact that researchers and academics spend quite a bit of time discussing the weaknesses of textbooks with their students, often writing scathing critiques about their content biases and over use by educators (e.g., Apple & Christian-Smith, 1991; Fitzgerald, 1979; Loewen, 1995, 2007, 2010; Shaver et al., 1979). There are a variety of reasons why overreliance on the textbook is concerning that will be discussed in this chapter (also see Chapter 11 for some previously discussed concerns), but perhaps the most pressing is that the dominance of textbooks in the classroom leaves little other time to explore additional resources and perspectives. Reading from only one source, whether textbook or otherwise, distorts the very nature of social studies. Recall that the primary purpose of social studies is to "help young people make informed and reasoned decisions for the public good as citizens of a culturally diverse, democratic society in an interdependent world" (NCSS, 2010). Students cannot be expected to learn how to make reasoned decisions and consider differing perspectives if they are exposed to a "single story" (Adichie, 2009). Throughout this chapter, when we refer to "textbooks," we mean both hardcopy and digital. Because there are many similarities in structure, content, writing style, and how teachers and students use both hardcopy and digital textbooks, we use the term interchangeably. Though there are certainly differences, such as availability of additional primary sources, multimedia clips, and integrated web links, using digital textbooks exclusively—as one might do with a hardcopy text—has very similar limitations. Broadly, it is our suggestion to vary the sources and modes of your content, regardless of whether it is on paper or screen.

We are not recommending eliminating the textbook and starting from scratch in your lesson planning. Let us be clear that we are advocating for the critical analysis of textbooks for both the content included and that which has been omitted. Comparing the textbook with other resources can be a powerful learning experience for middle grade students, enabling them to see that histories commonly told in schools are not "fact" but rather tend to reflect the perspectives of those in power and neglect the stories and perspectives of marginalized communities.

This chapter argues that using your social studies resources effectively entails 1) recognizing the limitations of your textbook and 2) expanding beyond the textbook. In other words, teachers in the middle grades can critically evaluate the textbook with all its flaws and conceptualize it as but *one* potential resource in the classroom, not *the* end-all-be-all resource. This expansion beyond the textbook involves gathering a variety of texts and resources with differing perspectives and biases and then teaching students to compare those sources and evaluate their claims based on evidence in order to draw conclusions. It is through careful selection of textual resources with a variety of perspectives and genres that teachers in the middle grades can address key aspects of both the C3 Framework (NCSS, 2013) and the Common Core State Standards for English Language Arts and Literacy in History/Social Studies, Science, and Technical Subjects (NGA & CCSSO, 2010). For example, the CCSS expect seventh graders to be able to analyze an author's point of view; compare and contrast written with audio and visual texts, making note of how the medium affects the message; and notice how differing authors address the same content with different interpretations and evidence (NGA & CCSSO, 2010, Standards RI.7.6, 7, & 9). These skills can be addressed in social studies as students compare texts with different points of view and genres. Similarly, by the end of grade 8, the C3 Framework asks that students be able to evaluate a source's credibility and develop both claims and counterclaims through evaluation of multiple sources (NCSS, 2010, Standards D3.1-4.6-8). Again, these disciplinary skills come through comparison across sources, not through reading a textbook (or any one resource).

This chapter will expand on what you learned in Chapter 11 about the many connections between literacy and social studies and focus on the limitations of textbooks and how to expand your classroom resources used to teach social studies. It includes not only written resources such as newspaper articles and trade books, but also visual (e.g., video, political cartoons, photographs, art) and audio (e.g., podcasts) sources. Perhaps just as importantly, this chapter gives you strategies to make the most of whichever resources you choose to use, emphasizing that no one source will ever be adequate or tell the entire story. Many of these strategies have been introduced earlier in the book at various levels of detail and will be mentioned as a reminder. However, there will be a few strategies not yet examined before that can be considered additions to your "teaching toolkit."

RECOGNIZING SOME OF THE LIMITATIONS OF TEXTBOOKS

Many textbook analyses focus on the textbook portrayals of historic events or eras (Roberts, 2014). Almost all these studies are qualitative studies where authors examine a specific number of textbooks, code their data, and then present their findings. In the end, most of the researchers strongly critique textbooks for not portraying the event or era in what they deem is a correct fashion (e.g., Armitage, 2001; Lindaman & Ward, 2004; Von Borries, 2003; Wasburn, 1997), as well as for their selection of the images contained within (Roberts, 2014). Before discussing the most prominent critiques in greater depth, a critical analysis of the textbook industry itself may help explain some of the consistent weaknesses of textbooks.

The Textbook Industry

Most critics agree that state adoption boards, textbook publishers, special interest groups, and textbook authors all have some responsibility for producing biased, boring, and inaccurate textbooks. According to critics, all these groups have selfish and myopic agendas that affect the historical, economic, political, and social understanding of America's youth (Roberts, 2009). State adoption boards, for example, are often used as censors, especially at the state level, who insist that textbooks avoid topics and treatments that might offend some parents and other special interest groups (Apple, 2001; Keith, 1991; Loewen, 1995). Loewen (1995) explains that states with adoption committees pressure publishers overtly to espouse certain points of view (p. 280). Apple (2001) mentions that "...the writing, editing, promotion, and general orientation strategy of such production is quite often aimed toward guaranteeing a place on state approved material" (p. 33). Both Loewen (1995) and FitzGerald (1979) illustrate this with the well-known example that "for years any textbook sold in Dixie had to call the Civil War 'the War Between the States'" (Loewen, 1995, p. 280). This state-backed bias continues today; for example, in the state of Texas, "textbooks shall not contain material which serves to undermine authority" (Apple, 2001, p. 55). States without adoption committees often buy these same books, so the views of one state can influence many others (Loewen, 1995). This is the reason the Texas curriculum changes in 2010 made national headlines (see Chapter 2).

Critics also accuse textbook publishers of the many weaknesses found in textbooks (Apple, 2001; Apple & Christian-Smith, 1991; FitzGerald, 1979; Loewen, 1995, p. 281). One reason for this is that the publishing industry is largely controlled by a handful of players; in 2001, the four largest textbook companies controlled 32% of the market, while the top eight control 53% (Apple, 2001, p. 29). This causes textbook publishing, for all intents and purposes, to be a "copy-cat" industry (Loewen, 1995, p. 281). That is to say, due to the large market share of the major textbook companies, every other publisher tries to emulate the success of the largest selling textbook in the subject area. States with large populations also wield significant control given the substantial number of texts they purchase each year; districts in smaller states often end up purchasing textbooks written to meet the standards of big states like Texas and California (Walker, 2016). Loewen (1995) contends that in the subject of history, the largest selling textbooks tend to be boring and biased, which results in most history textbooks following suit. Apple (2001) adds an additional insight into the problems of the textbook publishing industry, explaining that many textbook editors are male who may be unaware of patriarchal tendencies or worldviews (p. 30). Special interest groups also play a role in what textbook publishers include and omit from their textbooks (Roberts, 2009). Textbooks publishers seek to make a profit and a large textbook publisher will typically make millions of dollars in sales (Apple, 2001; Apple & Christian-Smith, 1991). Textbook publishers understand what types of textbooks will sell and realize that if they stray too far from the beaten path, they may become the target of special interest groups. If this happens, they are less likely to be selected by state adoption boards.

Similarly, to textbook publishers, textbook authors themselves are also partly to blame for the quality (or lack thereof) of their textbooks. The same market concerns that drive publishers also inform authors; many textbook authors want to write textbooks that sell, and, if royalties are involved, sell a lot (Unger, 1983). Loewen (1995) quotes one textbook author as saying he wrote texts that are "a McDonald's version of history—if it has any flavor, people will not buy it." (p. 284). And due to the large amount of power held by the textbook adoption committees and publishing houses, many textbook authors have a relatively limited amount of freedom over their work. Many others have little knowledge of the textbook adoption process and tend to rely heavily on publishers' input to guide their writing. In addition, Loewen (1995) explains that textbook authors tend to write biased textbooks in part because "the enterprise of writing a high school American history textbook converts historians into patriots" (p. 285). No matter how critical textbook authors are in their writing for college-aged students and adults, they want their secondary school textbooks to promote citizenship, and help students take pride in their country (p. 285) or in Scott's state history textbook, pride of their state (Roberts, 2013). Some authors simply do not think that younger students will be able to understand or should not have to deal with critical issues (Loewen, 2007).

Eurocentric and Xenophobic Views

Many researchers attack American history textbooks for being Euro and Anglo-centric, xenophobic, racist, and of the settler colonial mentality (e.g., Axtell, 1987; Harrison, 2002; Loewen, 1995; Lucy et al., 2020; Salvucci, 1991). As discussed in Chapter 11, social studies textbooks tend to omit perspectives of historically marginalized groups altogether, instead adopting a Eurocentric stance that paints a one-sided and sanitized version of the past (e.g., Calderon, 2014; Lucy et al., 2020; Shear, 2015). For example, Christopher Columbus is typically presented in textbooks as a famous explorer who set the stage for the establishment of the United States, yet many Indigenous peoples of North America consider him to be an invader of their lands and established nations. Dunbar-Ortiz (2016) explains that this myth of discovery is probably the most important myth to deal with because it goes to the core of the contradiction between the national narrative, the United States origin story of a democratic republic being born out of opposition to empire and starting something new in the world, [and that] within 20 years of 25 years of independence the United States Supreme Court was invoking the doctrine of discovery as law.

A settler/colonialist mentality pervades textbooks beyond the "discovery" myth, including such topics as the Lewis and Clark Expedition and the expansion of the United States into Indigenous nations' lands (Schmitke et al., 2020). In a critique of widely adopted U.S. history textbooks, Stanton (2014) concluded that textbooks exclude the historical agency of Indigenous peoples, instead confining "Native experiences to interactions with Whites" (p. 658). She goes on to explain that textbooks tend to overemphasize acts of violence and lawlessness by Indigenous peoples and thereby position the actions of non-Native individuals as somehow justified, even if atrocious (Stanton, 2014). Learning standards themselves are typically positioned within a settler colonial mentality, further complicating the use of textbooks as a sole source of information given that they are often chosen for their alignment to state standards. Take, for instance, the work of Shear et al. (2015) who analyzed U.S. History curriculum standards for all 50 states and the District of Columbia. The researchers concluded that the standards overwhelmingly position Indigenous Peoples in a pre-1900s context, directing students to "see Indigenous Peoples as a long since forgotten episode in the country's development" (p. 89). As Dunbar-Ortiz and Gilio-Whitaker (2016) explain, this implies that Native people exist purely as historical figures whose narrative somehow ended long ago.

Heroification

Textbooks often employ heroification of the historical figures they choose to include, essentially making flesh and blood historical figures into almost mythical heroes (e.g., Alridge, 2006; Loewen, 1995; Shimony, 2003). This is a problem given that heroification, and to some degree vilification, of historic figures in textbooks is often used to illustrate character traits that the authors, adoption committees, and publishers (and in some cases state and national governments) would like for student readers to emulate or disdain (e.g., Alridge, 2006; Gilbert, 2003; Harrison, 2002; Loewen, 1995). In this way, heroification causes those involved in producing textbooks (authors and publishers) to become extremely selective in choosing the historical figures that they select for their books (e.g., FitzGerald, 1979; Loewen, 1995). Once these figures are chosen, the facts are selectively included or omitted, and, in some cases, "facts" are completely fabricated (Alridge, 2006; Loewen, 1995). For example, Loewen (1995) claims that when students are taught about Helen Keller, they only learn about Keller's early life as the girl who conquered the challenges of being both deaf and blind. What textbooks do not discuss is that Keller became a radical socialist and supported many causes and organizations such as the NAACP, Women's Suffrage, and even the creation of the Soviet Union (pp. 21–22). According to Loewen (1995), this information diminishes the actual lessons that Keller wanted us to learn about her life and her struggle against the forces she felt led to oppression for many Americans (p. 20).

Bland and Boring

Furthermore, textbooks are often described as dense, difficult to read, and downright boring for students, taking on the voice of an omniscient narrator sharing a long list of dates and "facts" to be recalled with little bearing on the present (Loewen, 1995). Instead of seeing how the past can illuminate the present (and vice versa), students come to think of social studies itself as irrelevant to their lives (Loewen, 1995). Even the images within textbooks have been criticized (Roberts, 2009). For example, Masur (1998) argues that the images in textbooks provide students with a superficial understanding of the place and meaning of images in American history (p. 1409). These images found in elementary and secondary school textbooks are also regularly criticized for being much less controversial than those found in college textbooks or trade books (FitzGerald, 1979; Loewen, 1995; Masur, 1998). Critics contend that these "fluff" images dilute some of the purposes of teaching history.

For instance, Loewen (2007) uses five of the most famous images from the Vietnam War to illustrate the lack of controversial images in textbooks. He reported that in the textbooks he examined, many of the most well-known images from the war were not found. In fact, there were no pictures of any of the violence or atrocities that occurred during the war. To illustrate this point, Ben took his US History students one step further and asked them to find a picture of "a person who is dead in the picture." Throughout the entirety of the American history his students are currently assigned, only a single drawing depicting the explosion of the USS Maine has, at a distance, individuals who are deceased.

COLLABORATIVE ACTIVITY: RECOGNIZING THE LIMITATIONS OF TEXTBOOKS

In your reflective journal, independently answer the following questions:

- What do you remember about your social studies textbook from when you were in middle grades given what you've just read?
- Whose viewpoints tended to be expressed?
- Whose voices were missing, silenced, or discounted?
- Table 13.1 shares multiple articles about how textbooks have portrayed a wide variety of social studies topics in the past. Form a group of 3–4 classmates and assign each group member one article of interest to explore. A web link is provided for articles that are accessible to the public; for other articles you should be able to use your access through your college or university to obtain articles via providers such as JSTOR or EBSCO. Read

TABLE 13.1. Textbook Analysis Articles

Author	Title	Year	Journal	Location/Web Link
D.P. Alridge	The limits of master narratives in history books: An analysis of representations of Martin Luther King, Jr.	2006	Teachers College Record	ERIC www.eric.ed.gov/ERICWebPortal/recordDetail?accno=EJ733292
P. Boyer	In search of the fourth "R:" The treatment of religions in American history textbooks and survey courses.	1996	The History Teacher	JSTOR http://www.jstor.org/stable/494740?seq=1 - page_scan_tab_contents
J. Bickford III, & T. Byas	Martin Luther King's historical representation within primary, intermediate, and middle level books.	2019	The History Teacher	The History Teacher http://www.societyforhistoryeducation.org/A19Preview.html
C. H. Bohan, L. Y. Bradshaw, & W. H. Morris, Jr.	The mint julep consensus: An analysis of later 19th century Southern and Northern textbooks and their impact on the history curriculum.	2020	The Journal of Social Studies Research	Science Direct https://www.sciencedirect.com/science/article/abs/pii/S0885985X18302365?via%3Dihub
T. Cargill, & T. Mayer	The Great Depression and history textbooks.	1998	The History Teacher	JSTOR https://www.jstor.org/stable/494309?seq=1
A.J. Eksterowicz & R. P. Watson	Treatment of First Ladies in American government and presidency textbooks.	2000	PS: Political Science and Politics	JSTOR https://www.jstor.org/stable/420863?seq=1
D. Gilbert	Emiliano Zapata: Textbook hero.	2003	Mexican Studies	JSTOR https://www.jstor.org/stable/10.1525/msem.2003.19.1.127
V. Gosse	Consensus and contradiction in the textbook treatments of the Sixties.	1995	The Journal of American History	JSTOR https://www.jstor.org/stable/2082198?seq=1
E. Jennings	"Reinventing Jeanne:" The iconology of Joan of Arc in Vichy schoolbooks, 1940–1944	1994	Journal of Contemporary History	JSTOR https://www.jstor.org/stable/260683?seq=1
L.P. Masur	"Pictures have now become a necessity:" The use of images in American history textbooks.	1998	Journal of American History	JSTOR https://www.jstor.org/stable/2568088?seq=1
M. Pearcy	We are not enemies: An analysis of textbook depictions of Fort Sumter and the beginning of the Civil War.	2019	The History Teacher	The History Teacher http://www.societyforhistoryeducation.org/pdfs/A19_Pearcy.pdf

TABLE 13.1. Continued

Author	Title	Year	Journal	Location/Web Link
A. Pellegrino, L. Mann, & W. B. Russell	To lift as we climb: A textbook analysis of the segregated school experience.	2013	*The High School Journal*	ERIC https://eric.ed.gov/?id=EJ1014006
S.L. Roberts	A Review of Social Studies Textbook Content Analyses Since 2002.	2014	*Social Studies Research and Practice*	SSRP http://www.socstrpr.org/wp-content/uploads/2015/01/MS-06594Roberts.pdf
J. M. Sanchez	Old habits die hard: The textbook presidency is alive and well.	1996	*P.S. Political Science and Politics*	JSTOR https://www.jstor.org/stable/420196?seq=1
T. T. Shimony	The Pantheon of national hero prototypes in educational texts: Understanding curriculum as narrative of national heroism.	2003	*Jewish History*	JSTOR https://www.jstor.org/stable/20101507?seq=1
S. M. Stern	The struggle to teach the whole story: Calvin Coolidge and American history education	1996	*New England Journal of History*	ERIC https://eric.ed.gov/?q=presidents&ff1=subUnited+States+History&ff2=souNew+England+Journal+of+History&id=EJ569365
Y. Suh, S. An, & D. Forest	Immigration, imagined communities, and collective memories of Asian American experiences: A content analysis of Asian American experiences in Virginia U.S. history textbooks.	2015	*The Journal of Social Studies Research*	Science Direct https://www.sciencedirect.com/science/article/abs/pii/S0885985X14000382
B. Von Borries	The Third Reich in German history textbooks since 1945.	2001	*Journal of Contemporary History*	JSTOR https://www.jstor.org/stable/3180696?seq=1
S. J. Walker	The origins of the Cold War in United States textbooks.	1995	*Journal of American History*	JSTOR https://www.jstor.org/stable/2081654?seq=1
L. H. Wasburn	Accounts of slavery: An analysis of United States history textbooks from 1900 to 1992.	1997	*Theory and Research in Social Education*	Taylor and Francis https://www.tandfonline.com/doi/abs/10.1080/00933104.1997.10505824

through the article and answer the following questions in your reflective journal. Discuss your findings with your group.
  - Do you agree with the author's perspective about the textbook portrayal of the topic?
  - Do you think the author's own biases about the topic are apparent?
- How would you use what you learned in lesson planning for your middle level social studies classes?
- Examine a middle level textbook about the same topic. Are the textbook analysis author's opinions about the portrayal of the topic apparent in the textbook that you are examining? Provide specific examples.

RESOURCES TO EXPAND BEYOND THE TEXTBOOK

Now that you are better aware of some of the limitations of your textbook, you are ready to expand beyond that single story. Of course, reliance on any one source limits students' understanding of historical inquiry (e.g., Alridge, 2006; Loewen, 1995); expanding your resources beyond the textbook and helping students learn to critically examine and compare selected texts is essential to developing students' disciplinary literacy and ability to make informed decisions as citizens of our nation and world. As educators, it is essential to deepen your own content knowledge so that each time you teach you know what has been omitted from or romanticized in the textbook and can decide how best to incorporate differing perspectives to your students through various written, visual and audio resources. The key is that as you add these resources you do so purposefully in a manner that includes and honors all voices.

Once you have identified gaps and misrepresentations in the textbook for any new aspect of your social studies curriculum, you can then begin to strategically identify and gather a wide range of written, visual, and audio resources (both primary and secondary sources) for students to examine in whole group, small groups, and independently with a critical literacy stance. This implies you will need to explicitly teach your students how to evaluate and document the claims and biases of each source, including the textbook, using evidence from the text, then comparing the perspectives of these sources as called for in the C3 Framework (NCSS, 2013).

Written Resources

There are a variety of written sources teachers of the middle grades can use to expand beyond the single story presented in your textbook. One of Steph's personal favorites are trade books, both narrative and informational. Trade books offer many benefits, such as allowing teachers to differentiate the challenge of reading materials for students and thereby provide access to new content that was less accessible in the textbook for students reading below grade level. Careful selection of trade books that confront omissions or biases in the textbook also provide an opportunity for students to ask their questions to explore via inquiry projects, such as why particular viewpoints were omitted from the textbook altogether and what ramifications might that have on our understanding of historical events in relation to today. For example, Brugar and Clabough (2017) describe classroom activities for inquiry with middle school students beginning with a reading of the thought-provoking book, *Fighting for Justice: Fred Korematsu Speaks Up* by Laura Atkins and Stan Yogi. In this text, a variety of primary source materials are included, such as personal letters, journal entries, poems, and government documents. The researchers explain how this written resource is ripe for inquiry using the C3 Framework (NCSS, 2013) because the varied sources within well support the asking of compelling questions as well as comparison of sources (Brugar & Clabough, 2017).

With trade books, teachers can intentionally create text sets that explore perspectives of diverse groups and traditionally marginalized communities consistently not represented in textbooks. Teachers can then help students compare those text sets and attempt to explain and decipher the reason behind any differences in sources (Ogle et al., 2007). For example, Tschida and Brown Buchanan (2017) gathered a set of texts that prompt conversations about family diversity and confront the "single story" (Adichie, 2009) of families being defined as heteronormative nuclear units. Similarly, Libresco et al. (2011) created a text set on immigration to challenge the idea that there is *one* immigration experience across groups, families, and time. And in a recently published article, Demoiny and Ferreras-Stone (2020) share text sets on key social studies content areas that highlight the diversity of experiences of Latinx peoples in the United States, another perspective not well represented in textbooks or even in children's literature in general (Cooperative Children's Book Center, 2019).

Chapter 11 included a table with a variety of resources for accessing trade books you can then compare to the textbook, such as the NCSS Notable Trade Books for Young People annual list. You should also stay on top of new trade books by subscribing to magazines and journals that regularly review new material, such as *Social Studies Research and Practice*, *Social Education*, and *Middle Level Learning*. Your school and community librarians are also knowledgeable about published trade books on various topics as well as any texts coming out soon; beginning conversations with these experts will likely enable you to locate many texts you were not aware of. Just as with any other resource you use in your classroom, of course, be wary that tradebooks often present historically inaccurate or biased representations. For example, in a review of tradebooks written about Eleanor Roosevelt, Bickford and Badal (2016) found that a majority of the tradebooks examined for use in the middle grades either minimized or omitted key information regarding Roosevelt's life, including her family wealth, diverse initiatives, and encountering of reactionary resistance.

Internet sources and news sites offer still another resource often untapped in the social studies classroom. Perhaps even more so than published materials, teachers should help students see that online information reflects the biases and perspectives of those who created it. In their article *Misinformation in the Information Age: What Teachers Can Do to Support Students*, Hodgin and Kahne (2018) make the plea for social studies educators to attend to civic media literacy in their classrooms, noting the sheer number of youth and adults who struggle to ascertain the accuracy of information found online.

Visual Resources

Visual texts and resources, such as photographs and video, have long been successfully used in social studies lessons as a possible resource to compare with the textbook and critically examine such concepts as bias and perspective. Heafner and Massey (2016) encourage educators to consider beginning new inquiries by showing a collection of images and leading students through what they refer to as a Visual Inventory. As one example, the researchers describe one such Visual Inventory used to compare images of Phinneas Gage, asking students, "Do these images show the same person or different people? What is your evidence that supports your answer?" (p. 334). Then, students are asked to draw comparisons and note differences between the images, leading them finally to formulate their own wonderings to explore via additional written resources. Similarly, although aimed at elementary teachers, Barton (2001) encourages educators to support students in their analysis of authentic photographs in order to better understand how readers of images attempt to place photos into a larger historical context. As with written text sets, Barton (2001) notes that using sets of photographs can support essential historical inquiry skills.

Much like a Language Arts teacher might allow students to watch a video adaptation of a piece of literature recently explored in class, social studies educators can add in videos as motivating and engaging resources to examine topics such as immigration or other important and sometimes neglected matters and then compare those representations with textbook portrayals of events and people. Hilburn and Brown Buchanan (2016) clarify that it is not necessary to view an entire documentary or film in its entirety. Rather, the authors explain that "viewing specific 10–15-minute excerpts can be very engaging and as meaningful (for your pedagogical purposes), while allowing you to devote most of the class time to analyzing a film clip's content with your students" (p. 3). Hilburn and Brown Buchanan (2016) recommend multiple strategies to consider when using film as a resource in the classroom, including what they refer to as backchanneling in which the class watches selections of a film and simultaneously responds in writing to particular teacher questions or free response. Only after the entire clip has been shared are students invited to engage in small and whole-group discussions, thereby providing students critical thinking time to consider the film they're "reading." Of course, just as was the case with the textbook, it's important to note that visual resources mirror the cultural and political context in which they were created. As Stoddard (2009) explains, "teachers need to assume as a rule, however, that films are not objective or value "neutral" and will not serve as a comprehensive history for a deliberative activity" (p. 429). As discussed in prior chapters, Roberts and Elfer (2018, 2021) developed the *History or Hollywood?* strategy to assist teachers use movies as one of many sources to help students to evaluate and better understand historical topics.

Another potential visual resource to consider when teaching students how to critically consume images comes through photo blogging. According to Barrow (2019), photo blogging involves showcasing photos and then telling the stories behind those photos. Students can both critically consume and construct their own photo blogs, such as the middle grades history students who created their own photo blogs called the Humans of the Civil War (Barrow et al., 2017). Barrow (2019) explains that photo blogs offer a unique entry point into teaching students about perspectives in present-day media given their active engagement with social media as consumers and producers. She provides a sample lesson plan aligned to the C3 Framework (NCSS, 2013) complete with compelling and supporting questions, such as "How do images shape our understanding of events, people, and the world around us?" and "how does a photograph reflect larger political, economic, and cultural change?" (Barrow, 2019, p. 111).

Audio Resources

There are a variety of audio resources available to teachers to explore, such as historical radio broadcasts and interviews included in the StoryCorps' archive Podcasts, audio files available on the internet, are a personal favorite of Jessica. Much like a television series, podcasts often have series and episodes. Many podcasts that cover social studies content are available for free. Table 13.2 outlines some free podcasts that discuss important social studies content.

Podcasts such as these can be used to strengthen your own pedagogy and deepen your content knowledge. For example, you might consider listening to *Visions of Education* to listen to new social studies frameworks or gain ready to use ideas such as social studies text sets which can be used in your classroom with your students. As another example, you might choose to listen to *Stuff You Missed In History Class* to hear perspectives which were not included in your own social studies education and are likely omitted from today's textbooks as well. One unique advantage that podcasts have is that you can listen to them while you exercise (or multitask in some other way), thus allowing you to find the time to deepen your content knowledge. When podcasts have been used in conjunction with college courses researchers found that students describe them to be both a source of enjoyment and useful educational tool (Hill et al., 2012; Merhi, 2015; Shim, et al., 2007; Zacharis, 2012). In fact, some of Jessica's college students have enjoyed their assigned podcasts so much they have recommended the podcast to family and friends.

TABLE 13.2. Audio Resources for Social Studies

Podcast Series Name	Description	Website
All My Relations	This podcast was created by Matika Wilbur Swinomish and Tulalip Nation) and Adriane Keene (Cherokee Nation). Here they discuss important indigenous perspectives for current and past events.	https://www.allmyrelationspodcast.com/who-we-are
At Liberty	The ACLU puts together a weekly podcast to explore the civil rights issues from both the past and present day. This is a great way for students to make connections between historical and current events.	https://www.aclu.org/podcast/podcast-at-liberty
Back Story	This podcast uses current events in America to take a deep dive into our past	https://www.backstoryradio.org/
Latino USA	Their website details that this podcast creates content "empowering people to navigate the complexities of an increasingly diverse and connected world."	https://www.latinousa.org/about/
Queer America	This podcast series is available through the Teaching Tolerance webpage. Their website details that "without LGTBQ history, there is no American History."	https://www.tolerance.org/podcasts/queer-america
Stuff You Missed In History Class	As the title suggests this podcast discusses important topics that may not have been covered in history class. Each podcasts dives into a particular topic.	https://www.iheart.com/podcast/stuff-you-missed-in-history-cl-21124503/
Teaching Hard History	This podcast series is available through the Teaching Tolerance webpage and discusses the importance and intricacies of teaching slavery.	https://www.tolerance.org/podcasts/teaching-hard-history/american-slavery
Visions of Education	Authors of recent articles focusing on Social Studies education or interviewed in this podcast series. Social Studies educators can gain insights on new frameworks as well as classroom ready ideas.	https://visionsofed.com/podcast/

When teaching about the Georgia Standard of Excellence, "Analyze how rights were denied to African Americans or Blacks through disenfranchisement." (Georgia Department of Education, 2016, p. 28), Karrie uses the podcast, "Buried Truths," with her 8th grade Georgia Studies classes. The podcast discusses true stories of racial inequities in Georgia. In season one, host Hank Klibanoff discusses voting rights and disenfranchisement in the case of a young black man, Isaiah Nixon, who was killed by klansmen in 1948. He was killed because he legally cast his vote in the 1948 Democratic Primaries in Georgia. The students become really engaged in the topic when they are listening to a true story. Using the podcast, which includes archival audio, helps the students connect the standard to real people and events. Students explore the pain of Isaiah Nixon's family and the unjust nature of disenfranchisement during the New South Era of Georgia's history.

Podcasts, like every other source, should be checked for accuracy. While investigating its accuracy you should also consider how the author of the podcasts gained knowledge about the event. For example, did they personally experience it? Or, did a family member experience it? If the answer to either of these questions is yes, it's likely the podcast brings historical events to life in a way that textbooks simply cannot. Hearing the podcast authors describe an event will help students make connections with events from the past and understand that real people were impacted by the events they are learning about. For this reason, identifying clips ahead of time which can be shared with the class is often helpful.

Individual Activity: Texts and Resources to Expand Beyond the Textbook

Reflect on the numerous resources and texts discussed in this text. In your reflective journal, answer the following questions:

- Which resources have you observed used in classrooms, and what was your experience with those resources?
- Are there any resources that you have not considered as potential sources of information that you plan to use in your future classroom? Which ones and why?
- What remaining questions do you have about expanding beyond the textbook with primary and secondary sources?

EFFECTIVELY USING AND COMPARING YOUR RESOURCES

As stated earlier, any effective social studies unit will employ a variety of written, visual, and when possible, audio resources for students to examine and compare to the textbook. It is up to the classroom teacher to model and guide students in analyzing those resources for potential bias and claims and evaluating said claims based on evidence. Perhaps the most challenging component comes when students are faced with the daunting task of comparing sources and drawing definitive conclusion as to what really happened. As VanSledright and Frankes (2000) explain, students need support regarding evaluating the validity and reliability of evidence as related to authors' claims coupled with what to do when sources present conflicting data.

Think-Alouds

One instructional strategy to model the thinking important in resource comparison involves using think-alouds. According to Strachan and Whitlock (2015), educators can lay the groundwork for comparing multiple sources by modeling their own thinking about how they assess potential bias and missing perspectives during interactive read-alouds, as well as how they determine the extent to which an author supports their claims with appropriate evidence. Burstein and Hutton (2005) hint at the benefits of think-alouds in their encouragement to compare multicultural children's literature with informational text types, claiming that it is modeling and comparing differing perspectives that enable students to take up this critical thinking practice. As part of larger inquiry units, Heafner and Massey (2016) encourage teachers to think aloud as they read small chunks of text for students, later giving additional small chunks to partners, small groups, and eventually individual students when they are ready.

To be clear, it is not simply the reading aloud of differing sources, but the thinking aloud and questioning by the teacher that offers a model for middle-grade students to emulate. In addition to the critical literacy questions encouraged in chapter 11, teachers might stop during their reading, listening to, or viewing of any resource and ask questions such as, "What is the author claiming here? What evidence are they using to support that claim? Are there any viewpoints not included here? Am I convinced of their claims, or do I need additional information? What questions do I now have?" By stopping to model the types of questions and thinking critical consumers engage in, educators allow students to see the complex nature of critically examining and comparing resources. This type of modeling will be especially helpful for students as they learn how to fact check information that is readily available on the internet and learn to define what "fake news" entails and what it does not (Kassinger & Kenneth, 2018). Numerous resources are available to support you in knowing which habits of mind are important to model through think-alouds, including questions to ask, frameworks for fact-checking, or steps to follow when examining the credibility and reliability of sources (see Manfra & Holmes, 2018 for a list of resources). Plus, by helping students draw connections to their present-day experiences, educators encourage students to see the importance of social studies in their day-to-day lives.

Karrie often connects the "fake news" media of today to her lessons in Georgia Studies. When teaching about the 1906 Atlanta Riot and the Leo Frank Case of 1913, it is important for students to understand how the media played into the events in the past. Students can connect this to their experiences today. It helps them understand the importance of thinking critically and examining sources for accuracy and bias.

Inquiry Circles

Chapter 11 explored the strategy of inquiry-based projects, but they are so powerful it bears repeating. Any inquiry-based lesson will include some driving question or problem to explore through use of a variety of primary and secondary sources (including the textbook). In inquiry circles, students work in small groups to pursue questions and curiosities of their own choosing related to the standards through examination of a collection of resources (Harvey & Daniels, 2009). A key aspect of inquiry circles is that activities move beyond simple fact-finding or completion of graphic organizers. Instead, students work to collaboratively build their own knowledge by synthesizing ideas from various sources and then actively share that knowledge with others, such as those in the school or broader community (Harvey & Daniels, 2009). Recall the example from Heafner and Massey (2016) regarding the examination of Phineas Gage. Through the sharing of thought-provoking images and short selections of text, students were then able to compile their own list of questions to collaboratively explore with collections of text the students had located on their own (after some teaching on how to do this). This type of student-led work supports not only disciplinary literacy and concept development, but also motivation.

Book Reviews

It has already been suggested, after critical analysis of any resource, that if students believe their textbook or other resource provides an inaccurate or biased depiction of a social studies topic, they should be encouraged to assert and document their criticisms and then to write the author and publisher of the offending text, asking for corrections or at least a rationale behind what they wrote (Bain, 2006; Loewen, 2007). Students can also post public "book reviews" online, sharing their concerns about the resource with future students and readers much as any concerned citizen might do. Steph worked with one group of fifth graders who even shared their written concerns about their textbook to the local school board. Although your students may receive little more than a polite acknowledgement, if anything, this exercise will most certainly offer your students a sense of empowerment as they had the chance to speak their mind (Loewen, 2007). In addition, taking an active role in their schooling is one of the key components in the purposes of social studies education: developing informed and active citizens. It also directly supports Dimension 4 of the C3 Framework: Communicating Conclusions and Taking Informed Action (NCSS, 2013).

Comparing Textbooks

An often-overlooked strategy involves the use of comparing older textbooks to newer ones (Loewen, 2010; Roberts, 2011). This strategy allows students to see that, even with the same publisher, new research and discoveries, along with shifts in society's ideals, values, and beliefs change the presentation of history from one generation to the next (Loewen, 2007). Simply comparing the view of a 1960s textbook on civil rights to one from the present will provide your students with a shocking and unforgettable view of how mainstream perspectives change over time (Loewen, 2007, 2010). Adding in present day trade books or podcasts can highlight how some perspectives continue to be avoided or neglected (e.g., institutional racism).

A similar approach is to have students compare two or more recent textbooks to one another. This is especially effective in state history where students have the opportunity to examine these texts for possible regional biases. In Scott's 8th grade social studies courses, when studying the presidency of Jimmy Carter, he often had his students examine Carter's portrayal in their Georgia studies textbook, a national middle school text, a South Carolina history textbook, and a documentary. Students used a chart to compare the similarities and differences between the sources and answered questions such as "Based on your findings, which sources do you feel are the most accurate about Carter's presidency? Why?" and "Based on your findings, which sources do you think are the least accurate? Why?" (Roberts, 2009, p. 233). Ben's students find varying details surrounding Christopher Columbus' landing in the Caribbean. While some textbooks discuss atrocities committed by the new arrivals, others portray them as benevolent ambassadors, bearing gifts of technology and culture. Shown in figure 13.1 are textbooks and questions Ben has his students use when doing their textbook analysis of the Christopher Columbus story.

In addition to the above strategies, there is a wide variety of strategies for using of multiple sources to teach new concepts. See Figure 13.2 for a review.

Shown below are different history texts and pages on which you can find information about the arrival to America by Europeans. Take some time with your group members to look over the different secondary sources, focusing on the questions below.

A. *America: History of Our Nation*, 2007, pp. 36–41
B. *American History*, 1982, pp. 11, 19–23
C. *American Nation*, 1998, pp. 67–70
D. *Challenge of Freedom*, 1990, pp. 37–40
E. *The History of the American People*, 1920, pp. 23–26

1. Describe some differences/similarities in the way Indigenous Peoples are presented in the different texts. (Be sure to identify which texts you are talking about)
2. Describe some of the differences/similarities Christopher Columbus is talked about in the different texts.
3. Describe some of the differences/similarities the Vikings are presented in the different texts.
4. Who discovered America, according to two or three of the different texts?
5. Why do you suppose there are differences between the texts? Shouldn't this all have been figured out by now?
6. Which of the texts do you trust the most? Which the least? What is your evidence?

FIGURE 13.1. Different Views of the Arrival of the Europeans

1. Advanced Graphic Organizers
2. Cause and Effect Analysis
3. Circle of Knowledge
4. Compare and Contrast
5. Concept Definition Maps
6. Comprehension Cubes
7. Create/Hands-on Projects
8. Frayer Models
9. Inquiry Based Projects
10. Jigsaw
11. K W L Charts
12. Learning Logs
13. 13 Predicting ABC Charts
14. Primary Source Analysis
15. Project Research
16. T-Charts
17. Think-Pair-Share
18. Timeline Development
19. Venn Diagrams
20. Web-based/cloud-based Projects

FIGURE 13.2. 20 Strategies for Incorporating Multiple Resources (In Alphabetical Order)

Individual Activity: Effectively Using and Comparing your Resources

Go back through the strategies and methods offered in the text. In your reflective journal answer the following questions:

- Which strategies seem most conducive to evaluating and drawing comparisons between the textbook and other resources? Why?
- What do you think are some strategies you might use when incorporating multiple resources into your lessons?
- Are there examples of strategies that you do not think appropriate for middle level learners? Why?

SUMMARY

This chapter examined a large body of literature critical of textbooks and their use, arguing instead that middle grades educators identify the limitations of their own textbook and then expand upon the "single story" within through the strategic use of written, visual, and audio resources. A critical component of building a collection of resources involves including perspectives of those from typically marginalized communities, both past and present. This chapter also included strategies to support students learning how to use and compare resources, including think-alouds, inquiry circles, and book reviews. The next chapter will discuss the recent past and new directions of social studies education.

Individual Activity: Reflecting on the Chapter

Create a lesson plan based on what you have learned about using your social studies resources more effectively. Use the following questions as a guide for creating the lesson:

- How will you make sure that perspectives omitted from your textbook are included?
- What are some strategies for incorporating multiple resources into your middle level social studies classes?

WEBSITE RESOURCES

- **All My Relations** (https://www.allmyrelationspodcast.com/) is a podcast that examines present day issues of Indigenous peoples with the hope of highlighting Indigenous voices in mainstream media.
- **At Liberty** (https://www.aclu.org/podcast/podcast-at-liberty) is a weekly podcast produced by the ACLU. It examines current issues related to civil rights and civil liberties issues.
- **BackStory** (https://www.backstoryradio.org) was a weekly podcast connecting current events with a thorough review of the past. The podcast ended in June 2020 but all previous episodes are still available for review.
- **Education Resources Information Center (ERIC)** (http://www.eric.ed.gov/) "provides access to more than 1.4 million bibliographical records of journal articles and other education-related materials." You should have access to the collection through your college or university's library.
- **JSTOR** (http://www.jstor.org/) is a non-profit service that helps researchers and students find digital copies of over 1000 academic journals. You should have access to the collection through your college or university's library.
- **Latino USA (https://www.latinousa.org/)** is a news and cultural public radio program produced by the Futuro Media Group. According to their website, Futuro Media Group is "committed to telling stories often overlooked by mainstream media by expanding narratives as we report on issues where we see a lack of racial equity."
- **The National Council for the Social Studies Notable Social Studies Tradebooks for Young People** (https://www.socialstudies.org/publications/notables) is an annual list of high quality tradebooks written for students grades K–8 on a variety of topics and content areas.

- **StoryCorps Archive** (https://storycorps.org/discover/archive/) features a significant digital collection of human voices and conversations. The complete collection is housed at the American Folklife Center at the Library of Congress in Washington, D.C.
- **Stuff You Missed in History Class** (https://www.iheart.com/podcast/stuff-you-missed-in-history-cl-21124503/) is a podcast produced by iHeart Radio examining a wide range of topics often overlooked in classrooms.
- **Teaching Tolerance** (https://www.tolerance.org/) offers free educational resources for K–12 teachers focused on social justice and anti-bias.
- **Visions of Education** (https://visionsofed.com/podcast/) is a weekly podcast produced by Dan Krutka and Michael Milton focused on topics related to social studies, social media, and social justice within education.

REFERENCES

Adichie, C. N. (Speaker). TED Conferences LLC. (Producer). (2009, July). *The danger of a single story*. http://www.ted.com/talks/chimamanda_adichie_the_danger_of_a_single_story

Alridge, D. P. (2006). The limits of master narratives in history textbooks: An analysis of representations of Martin Luther King, Jr. *Teacher's College Record, 108*(4), 662–686.

Apple, M. W. (2001). *Educating the "right" way: Markets, standards, God, and inequality.* RoutledgeFalmer.

Apple, M. W., & Christian-Smith, L. K. (1991). *The politics of the textbook.* RoutlageFalmer

Armitage, S. H. (2001). From the inside out: Rewriting regional history. *Frontiers, 22*(3), 32–47

Axtell, J. (1987). Europeans, Indians, and the age of discovery in American history textbooks. *The American History Review, 92*(3), 621–632.

Bain, R. B. (2006). Rounding up the usual suspects: Facing the authority hidden in the history classroom. *Teachers College Record, 108*(10), 2080–2214.

Barrow, E. C. (2019). Every picture tells a story: Teaching the past with photoblogs. *Social Education, 83*(2), 108–112.

Barrow, E., Anderson, J., & Horner, M. (2017). The role of photoblogs in social studies classroom: Learning about the people of the Civil War. *Contemporary Issues in Technology and Teacher Education, 17*(4), 504–521.

Barton, K. C. (2001). A picture's worth: Analyzing historical photographs in the elementary grades. *Social Education, 65*(5), 278–283.

Bickford, J. H., & Badal, T. A. (2016). Trade books' historical representation of Eleanor Roosevelt, first lady of the world. *Social Studies Research and Practice, 11*(3), 1–18.

Brugar, K., & Clabough, J. (2017). Fred Korematsu speaks up: Using nonfiction with the inquiry arc of the C3 framework. *Middle Level Learning, 60*, 2–6.

Burstein, J. H., & Hutton, L. (2005). Planning and teaching with multiple perspectives. *Social Studies and the Young Learner, 18*(1), 15–17.

Calderon, D. (2014). Speaking back to manifest destinies: A land education-based approach to critical curriculum inquiry. *Environmental Education Research, 20*(1), 24–36.

Cooperative Children's Book Center. (2019). *Publishing statistics on children's/YA books about people of color and First/Native nations and by people of color and First/Native nations authors and illustrators.* https://ccbc.education.wisc.edu/books/pcstats.asp

Demoiny, S. B., & Ferreras-Stone, J., (2020). We are history too: Using text sets to honor Latinx stories in social studies and ELA integrated instruction. *The Councilor: A Journal of the Social Studies, 81*(1), 1–21.

Dunbar-Ortiz, R. (October, 2016). Columbus Day, Indigenous Peoples Day and the problem with 'discovery'. *Time Magazine.* https://time.com/4523330/columbus-day-indigenous-peoples-day-history/

Dunbar-Ortiz, R., & Gilio-Whitaker, D. (2016). *"All the real Indians died off": And 20 other myths about Native Americans.* Beacon Press.

FitzGerald, F. (1979). *America revised* (p. 10). Little, Brown and Company.

Georgia Department of Education. (2016). *Social studies standards of excellence, grade 6–grade 8.* Author. https://www.georgiastandards.org/Georgia-Standards/Documents/Social-Studies-6-8-Georgia-Standards.pdf

Gilbert, D. (2003). Emiliano Zapata: Textbook hero. *Mexican Studies, 19*(1), 127–159.

Harrison, C. (2002). Teaching the French Revolution: Lessons and imagery from nineteenth and twentieth century textbooks. *The History Teacher, 35*(2), 137–162.

Harvey, S., & Daniels, H. (2009). *Comprehension & collaboration: Inquiry circles in action.* Heinemann.

Hawkman, A. M., Castro, A. J., Bennett, L. B., & Barrow, L. H. (2015). Where is the content?: Elementary social studies in preservice field experiences. *The Journal of Social Studies Research, 39*(4), 197–206.

Heafner, T. L., & Massey, D. D. (2016). Initiating C3 inquiry: Using texts and curiosity to inspire readers. *Social Education, 80*(6), 333–342.

Hilburn, J., & Brown Buchanan, L. (2016). Immigration today: Three strategies for teaching with film. *Middle Level Learning, 55,* 2–11.

Hill, J., Nelson, A., France, D., & Woodland, W. (2012). Integrating podcast technology effectively into student learning. *A Journal of Geography in Higher Education, 36*(3), 437–454

Hodgin, E., & Kahne, J. (2018). Misinformation in the information age: What teachers can do to support students. *Social Education, 82*(4), 208–211.

Kassinger, A., & Kenneth, K. (2018). Facing fake news: Five challenges and first amendment solutions. *Social Education, 82*(4), 235–237.

Keith, S. (1991). The determinants of textbook context. Altbach, P.G.(Ed.), *Textbooks in American society* (pp. 43–60). State University of New York Press.

Libresco, A. S., Balantic, J., & Kipling, J. C. (2011). Uncovering immigrants' stories: It all begins with picture books. *Social Studies and the Young Learner, 23*(4), P1–P4.

Lindaman, D., & Ward, K. (2004). *History lessons: How textbooks from around the world portray U.S. history.* The New Press.

Loewen, J. W. (1995). *Lies my teacher told me: Everything your American history textbook got wrong.* The New Press.

Loewen, J. W. (2007). *Lies my teacher told me: Everything your American history textbook got wrong* (Completely revised and updated edition). Simon & Schuster.

Loewen, J. W. (2010). *Teaching what really happened: How to avoid the tyranny of textbooks and get students excited about doing history.* Teachers College Press.

Lucy, L., Demszky, D., Bromley, P., & Jurafsky, D. (2020). Content analysis of textbooks via natural language processing: Findings on gender, race, and ethnicity in Texas U.S. history textbooks. *AERA Open, 6*(3), 1–27. Doi: 10.1177/2332858420940312

Manfra, M. M., & Holmes, C. (2018). Media literacy and fake news in the social studies. *Social Education, 82*(2), 91–95.

Masur, L. P. (1998). "Pictures have now become a necessity:" The use of images in American history textbooks. *Journal of American History, 84*(4), 1409–1424.

Merhi, M. I. (2015). Factors influencing higher education students to adopt podcast: An empirical study. *Computers & Education, 83*, 32–43.

Moje, E. B., Stockdill, D., Kim, K., & Kim, H. (2011). The role of text in disciplinary learning. In M. L. Kamil, P. D. Pearson, E. B. Moje, & P. Afflerbach (Eds.), *Handbook of reading research* (Vol. IV, pp. 453–486). Routledge.

National Council for the Social Studies. (2010). *National curriculum standards for social studies: Executive summary*. https://www.socialstudies.org/standards/execsummary

National Council for the Social Studies (NCSS). (2013). *The college, career, and civic life C3 Framework for social studies standards: Guidance for enhancing the rigor of K–12 civics, economics, geography, and history.* NCSS

Ogle, D., Klemp, R., & McBride, B. (2007). *Building literacy in social studies: Strategies for improving comprehension and critical thinking*. Association for Supervision and Curriculum Development.

Roberts, S. L. (2009). *The textbook presidency theory and its relationship to the portrayals of 20th and 21st century presidents found in the middle level state history textbook of Arkansas, California, Connecticut, Georgia, Illinois, Iowa, Massachusetts, Missouri, Nebraska, New York, Ohio, Texas, Vermont, and Virginia* (Doctoral Dissertation, University of Georgia, 2009).

Roberts, S. L. (2011). Did Georgia (eventually) like Ike? Perceptions of 20th and 21st century presidents in Georgia history textbooks: 1951–2005. *Georgia Social Studies Journal, 1*(1),1–18.

Roberts, S. L. (2013). "Georgia on my mind:" Writing the "new" state history textbook in the post-Loewen world. *The History Teacher, 46*(1), 41–61.

Roberts, S. L. (2014). A review of social studies textbook content analyses since 2002. *Social Studies Research and Practice, 9*(3), 51–65.

Roberts, S. L., & Elfer, C. J. (Eds.). (2018). *Hollywood or history? An inquiry-based strategy for using film to teach United States history*. Information Age Publishing.

Roberts, S. L., & Elfer, C. J. (Eds.). (2021). *Hollywood or history? An inquiry-based strategy for using film to teach World history*. Information Age Publishing.

Salvucci, L. K. (1991). Mexico, Mexicans, and Mexican Americans in secondary-school United States history textbooks. *The History Teacher, 24*(2), 203–222.

Schmitke, A., Sabzalian, L., & Edmundson, J. (2020). *Teaching critically about Lewis and Clark: Challenging dominant narratives in K–12 curriculum.* Teachers College Press.

Shaver, J. P., Davis, O. L., & Helburn, S. W. (1979). The status of social studies education: Impressions from three NSF studies. *Social Education, 43*(2), 150–153.

Shear, S. (2015). Cultural genocide masked as education: U.S. history textbooks' coverage of Indigenous education policies. In P. T. Chandler (ed.), Doing race in social studies: Critical perspectives (pp. 13–40). Information Age Publishing.

Shear, S. B., Knowles, R. T., Soden, G. J., & Castro, A. J. (2015). Manifesting destiny: Re/presentations of Indigenous Peoples in K–12 U.S. history standards. *Theory & Research in Social Education, 43*(1), 68–101.

Shim, J. P., Shropshire, J., Park, S., & Harris, H. (2007). Podcasting for e-learning, communication, and delivery. *Industrial Management and Data Systems, 107*(4), 587–600.

Shimony, T. T. (2003). The pantheon of national hero prototypes in educational texts understanding curriculum as narrative of national heroism. *Jewish History, 17*(3), 309–332.

Stanton, C. R. (2014). The curricular Indian agent: Discursive colonization and indigenous (dys)agency in U.S. history textbooks. *Curriculum Inquiry, 44*(5), 649–676.

Stoddard, J. D. (2009). The ideological implications of using "educational" film to teach controversial events. *Curriculum Inquiry, 39*(3), 407–433.

Strachan, S. L., & Whitlock, A. M. (2015). Five ways that read alouds can help K–8 teachers address the college, career, and civic life (C3) framework. *Oregon Journal of the Social Studies, 3*(2), 52–57.

Tschida, C. M., & Brown Buchanan, L. (2017). Tackling controversial topics: Developing thematic text sets for elementary social studies. *Social Studies Research and Practice, 10*(3), 40–56.

Unger, I. (1983). The adventures (and misadventures) of a textbook author. *The History Teacher, 16*(2), 201–207.

VanSledright, B. A., & Frankes, L. (2000). Concept-and strategic-knowledge development in historical study: A comparative exploration in two fourth-grade classrooms. *Cognition and Instruction, 18*(2), 239–283.

Von Borries, B. (2003). The Third Reich in German history textbooks since 1945. *Journal of Contemporary History, 38*(1), 45–62.

Walker, T. (2016). Educators call attention to racist stereotypes in textbooks, impact on students. *NEA Today.* https://www.nea.org/advocating-for-change/new-from-nea/educators-call-attention-racist-stereotypes-textbooks-impact

Wasburn, L. H. (1997). Accounts of slavery: An analysis of United States history textbooks from 1900 to 1992. *Theory and Research in Social Education, 25*(4), 470–491.

Zacharis, N. Z. (2012). Predicting college students' acceptance of podcasting as a learning tool. *Interactive Technology and Smart Education, 9*(3), 171–183.

CHAPTER 14

THE RECENT PAST AND NEW DIRECTIONS IN SOCIAL STUDIES

Only a teacher? Thank God I have a calling to the greatest profession of all! I must be vigilant every day lest I lose one fragile opportunity to improve tomorrow.
—*Ivan Welton Fitzwater (Hodges, 2012)*

Any teacher that can be replaced by a computer should be.
—*David Thornburg paraphrasing Arthur C. Clarke (Masters, 2019)*

Activity List
- Social Studies: Where has it been? Where is it going?
- Impact of The No Child Left Behind Act.
- The Common Core Standards.
- Recent Societal Controversies.
- Technology and Social Studies.
- Reflecting on the Chapter.

COLLABORATIVE ACTIVITY: SOCIAL STUDIES: WHERE HAS IT BEEN? WHERE IS IT GOING?

Work with a partner to answer the following questions:

- How do you think social studies has been affected, both positively and negatively, by recent historical events, social movements, and controversies?
- Describe the role of social studies teachers in interpreting current events with their students.
- How do you think technology and the concept of remote learning will affect social studies teaching and learning over the next 10 to 20 years?

INTRODUCTION

Since the publication of the 2nd edition of this text in 2015, we have seen dramatic events that have profoundly impacted all teaching and learning. Turbulent political rhetoric, contested election processes, murders of many innocent citizens, armed rebellion, and COVID-19, to name a few. Because it is the nature of our subject to explore history, economics, government, culture, and other topics, the work of social studies teachers has changed dramatically and has never been more important as we face these events and issues head on within our profession and inside our classrooms.

In our time as social studies educators, we have witnessed great changes, both positive and negative, in teaching the subject. While we are not old enough to claim that we had to "walk uphill both ways" to teach, we can relate to you the changes we have been a part of over the past several years. For example, while we have never solely used a chalkboard and had computers in our classrooms from day one, we have seen the advent of smart boards, projectors, Google docs and other cloud-based collaborative systems, and remote learning. We remember the outrage of our colleagues when they were told that they were going to have to use email and again when parents were told they would have access to their children's grades on the teachers' online gradebooks. We have seen teachers gain access to laptops and wireless Internet and the emergence of thousands of web-based teacher blogs, providing access to free lesson plans and resources. Since the turn of the century, a large number of sites have been created for teachers to share lesson plans and ideas with one another. The explosion of access to information has also impacted our work. Important academic articles are no longer relegated to dusty library shelves as they are now easily found on the Internet to be reflected on and discussed by both practitioners and academics. We can with confidence say we have seen the transition, both chronologically and societally, from one century to the next.

The school years of 2019–2020 and 2020–2021 have seen the most abrupt and disruptive change in American educational history. Immediately forced to "go remote" for months—and for many schools, entire academic years—teachers, students, and their parents have had to negotiate a previously inconceivable learning landscape. Remote check-ins, Zoom and Google Meets security, and the tragedy of unacceptable learning environments and denied educational opportunities have become main concerns for teachers and parents during the pandemic shutdowns and remote learning. More broadly, students, parents, and teachers struggled to find a work/life balance in light of 24-hour access to their learning environments and the demands of a fundamental shift in the learning landscape (Smith & Falbe, 2020). Teachers, have, by and large worked to meet the challenge. Though blended and remote learning environments cannot replicate face-to-face experiences, social studies teachers—like so many others—have embraced the circumstances and worked to provide the best education they can. Encouraging students to analyze social media sources, exploration of home environments for social studies concepts, maintaining collaboration through cloud-based discussions, and vibrant, deeply engaging discussions via Zoom and Google Meets among other platforms, teachers have demonstrated their innovativeness, creativity, and dedication to their students.

Adding to the challenge and the opportunity for social studies teachers has been the increasing politicization of curriculum, teaching, and the learning process itself. Though we assert that curriculum, teachers, and the learning process have never been politically neutral, the following events represent a few of the highly politicized events making their way into social studies classrooms since the 2nd Edition of this text: the 2016 election of Donald Trump; decisions of the Trump administration regarding immigration and climate change; the Black Lives Matter Movement; the National Anthem controversy; the maintenance or removal of Confederate statutes, memorials, building and street names; the 2020 election and subsequent, unfounded claims of fraud; the January 6, 2021 Capitol insurrection; the impeachments and Senate trials of Donald Trump; personal choice and mask-wearing during the COVID-19 pandemic; the 1619 Project and the 1776 Commission; and others. With ever-increasing scrutiny of curriculum, teacher interpretation of that curriculum, and the societal debate regarding the role of controversy in the classroom, it has never been a more challenging, thought-provoking, interesting, or important time to do the work of social studies teaching and learning.

Despite the challenges, we are optimistic and look forward to seeing what the future has in store for social studies education. Since the publication of the second edition of the book, many states have increased civics and history requirements, have worked to make curriculum more inclusive of marginalized voices, and provided technology infrastructure to students and teachers. We have no doubt that social studies teachers will continue to be innovative, resilient, collaborative, and thoughtful in their approach to the ever-changing social and economic landscape.

This chapter will address three recent trends in social studies teaching and learning. We first offer an examination of the successes and failures of recent federal education policies and their effects on the social studies. We then explore past and current controversies representing the ongoing and increasing politicization of social studies teaching and learning. We conclude with insights into the continually changing relationship between technology and social studies teaching and learning.

FEDERAL EDUCATION POLICIES, CHANGING STANDARDS, AND THE SOCIAL STUDIES

To understand the current nesting of social studies within the larger educational landscape, it is necessary to look back at the past two decades of federal education policy and changes in social studies learning standards. While these federal initiatives are no longer the laws of the land, they continue to influence educational policy and practice. From an ongoing focus on test-score data to determine teacher and school effectiveness to the continued marginalization of social studies, science, and the arts in lieu of reading, writing, and math, the impacts of several federal initiatives reverberate through the educational landscape. In this section, we discuss the No Child Left Behind Act of 2002, The Race to the Top Initiative, starting in 2009, and the Common Core Standards initiative of 2010.

The No Child Left Behind Act

The No Child Left Behind Act (NCLB) was signed into law in 2002 after being approved by an overwhelming majority in both the House of Representatives and the Senate. The act required that any school receiving federal funding had to administer a statewide-standardized test in reading and math. Schools were required to demonstrate Adequate Yearly Progress (AYP) each year (U.S. Department of Education, 2010). Under the law, all schools were to have 100% of their students on grade level reading and mathematics, as measured by the tests, by 2014 which included most ELL and special education students (Hefling & Feller, 2012).

Schools that did not meet these standards faced increasing penalties. Those that did not meet AYP for two consecutive years were publicly labeled as "needs improvement schools" and were required to develop a two-year action plan. The school's students also had the option to transfer to better performing schools in the district. In the third year of needing improvement, schools were required to offer free tutoring and other support to their students. In the fourth year, various penalties could be given to the schools such as firing staff members, changing the curriculum, and/or extending the school day. If a school did not meet AYP for five years in a row, the school was subject to complete restructuring. Finally, if a school failed for six years it was subject to closure, becoming a charter or private school, or being directly operated by the state board of education.

Successes of No Child Left Behind

Though there were numerous criticisms of the NCLB Act that we will examine, the program had some strong points and successes. The most striking was that the federal government formally acknowledged the achievement gap in schools based on factors such as race and poverty. The NCLB Act sought to help at-risk students perform at a higher level and offered concrete goals and mandates for doing so. Under the act, teachers and administrators were required to develop data and researched based teaching strategies to help their students achieve at a higher level. Though often accused of making teachers teach to the test (Adler-Greene, 2019), NCLB helped schools examine and train teachers to understand and incorporate lessons based on learning styles, multiple intelligences, and differentiated instruction. It also held teachers accountable and helped them understand that they could not afford to "write off" any child. Therefore, partly due to NCLB, students' test scores in reading and mathematics showed improvement since its inception. Despite efforts to close the achievement gap, it remains (Vasquez-Heilig et al., 2018).

Failures of No Child Left Behind

Though showing some successes, the failures of the NCLB Act were numerous (see Figure 14.1). The act has been attacked and criticized by numerous individuals and groups from all points on the political spectrum (Hefling & Feller, 2012).

Figure 14.1 offers just a sample of the many complaints that have been leveled at NCLB and the damaging effects it had on America's public schools. However, one of the subjects that appeared to lose the most from the NCLB Act was social studies.

Impact of NCLB on Middle Level Social Studies Education

Though no longer in effect, the influence of No Child Left Behind on middle level social studies education continues to be considerable. As mentioned previously, the amount of time social studies is taught in elementary school is minimal when compared to that of reading and mathematics (Heafner, 2018; McMahon

---

- The federal government had no constitutional right to enact such laws.
- The act caused teachers to focus too much on standards and teaching to the test.
- The consequences of not making AYP were too punitive in nature.
- The federal government did not offer enough funding to meet the goals of the program.
- The standardized tests used to measure performance were not reliable, valid, or fair.
- Students viewed as having no chance at passing were looked over in lieu of students on the border of pass/failure.
- The act caused teachers and administrators to cheat on tests.
- The act caused an increase in segregated schools as whites and richer students took advantage of moving away from failing schools.
- The funding for gifted students was limited as states moved funding from gifted programs to meet other demands.

FIGURE 14.1. Critiques of the No Child Left Behind Act -The goals of the program were unrealistic.

Whitlock & Brugar, 2019). In some states social studies has been left out entirely or rarely taught at the lower grade levels (Bailey et al., 2006; Fitchett & Heafner, 2010; Heafner, 2018; VanFossen, 2005).

Given the limited attention to social studies in elementary school, it is not surprising that middle school teachers often complain about incoming students' lack of knowledge and skills— twin realities that make their jobs more difficult. Middle school teachers also find their subject and jobs devalued. Due to budget cuts, many middle schools are requiring that their social studies teachers be certified in other subjects, especially in Language Arts and mathematics. This requirement can communicate that social studies is not important. NCLB can be linked to this, as social studies was not part of the Federal law that required AYP (van Hover et al., 2010; Willis, 2007). Another negative element is that students were not gaining an appreciation of the subject because sometimes a school's least experienced teachers were being required to teach social studies. School administrators knew that those teachers' students' test scores did not matter and did not count against them (Bailey et al., 2006).

In many cases, though their subjects did not count toward AYP, social studies teachers still found their job performance being judged based on student test scores, as many states required a standardized social studies test. Social studies teachers faced giving these state mandated standardized tests to students who knew that the subject did not count for promotion and therefore had little incentive to do well. These tests were also often given on the last day of the testing week, when students were burnt-out on testing. This caused middle level social studies teachers to seek jobs at the high school level where in most states, U.S. history, world history, and economics counted—and continues to count— toward graduation and are still viewed as important. Those that stay at the middle school level now wish that their subject area's test would count for students' promotion (van Hover et al., 2010; Willis, 2007).

NCLB did not have the support needed to gain reauthorization in 2007. After five years of controversy and with the clear understanding that 100% success on standardized tests was not attainable, the Obama administration granted waivers to schools that did not achieve the ever-increasing standards of NCLB. It was not until 2014 that the Every Student Succeeds Act (2015) (ESSA)—the successor of NCLB— the was enacted. Maintaining testing requirements but passing along accountability authority to states, ESSA worked to address the biggest criticisms of NCLB—100% account rates and heavy-handed punitive measures of the federal government.

COLLABORATIVE ACTIVITY: IMPACT OF THE NO CHILD LEFT BEHIND ACT

Answer the following questions in your reflective journal and share your answers with a partner:

- Describe the biggest positive impacts of NCLB regarding social studies teaching and learning.
- Describe the biggest negative impacts of NCLB regarding social studies teaching and learning.
- Given ongoing emphasis on reading, writing, and math, how can social studies be best integrated into the daily experiences of elementary school students?

Race to the Top

Not directly replacing No Child Left Behind but deeply influencing teaching and learning, the 2009 Race to the Top initiative was a funding competition sponsored by the U.S. Department of Education. Race to the Top was designed to change the policies of state and local school districts throughout the nation while maintaining many aspects of NCLB. With Race to the Top, states competed for a portion of a 4.35-billion-dollar prize (U.S. Department of Education, 2012). By 2011, 12 states had been awarded prize money ranging from $75 million (Rhode Island) to $700 million (Florida and New York) (U.S. Department of Education, 2011). In order to win these monetary awards, states were required to demonstrate a commitment to education and make, in some cases, sweeping changes to their education systems. Some of these included providing support to teachers and principals, turning around the lowest achieving schools, and developing and implementing common, high-quality assessments (U.S. Department of Education, 2012).

Like NCLB, the Race to the Top program had many critics. While the money the program provided to school districts was important, when analyzed, the actual amount each state received was relatively small. Many critics argued that the cost of the changes that the school districts had to make in order to meet the requirements of Race to the Top, such as new teacher evaluation systems and opening charter or other innovative schools, used the bulk of the funds provided.

There were other critiques as well. For instance, many conservatives argued that the federal government should not be involved in local and state schools, though this program was a contest and not a mandate like NCLB. Teacher and educational groups claimed that the performance-based pay that the program required was unfair as many states were threatening to not pay teachers for advanced degrees or years taught. In addition to the already problematic concept of not paying teachers for longevity and degrees, there was concern about how schools, which were in dire financial straits due to the Great Recession of 2007/2008, would be able to afford to pay teachers more for positive performance (which was one of the promises of the program). Some argued the focus on standardized testing on which the program was based was no different than the over-reliance on standardized tests used in the NCLB Act that had already been proven to be ineffective. Finally, some states, opted to remove themselves from the competition due to objections over the Common Core Curriculum, which Race to the Top encouraged, but did not mandate.

Effects of Race to the Top on Social Studies Education

Race to the Top had two main impacts on the teaching and learning of social studies. The first was the implementation in many states of the Common Core standards (National Governors Association Center for Best Practices, 2010). The second was the requirement that states allow the use of value-added measurements in teacher evaluations. Each of these requirements continue to impact social studies teachers.

The Race to the Top emphasis on states' implementation of the Common Core standards maintained deep focus on reading, writing, and math at the cost of science, social studies, and the fine arts. With limited resources and time, school districts spent valuable funds and professional development opportunities on a small set of skills. Though we certainly agree reading, writing, and math are fundamental to students' short- and long-term success, education policy must also recognize and value their responsibility in educating students in citizenship, civics, and the social sciences broadly. Indeed, though the Common Core standards address historical thinking and source analysis, much professional development, student testing, and teacher evaluation does not.

Another aspect of the Race to the Top initiative was the focus on "value-added" measurements as a tool for teacher evaluation. This method, which attempts to measure the "contribution" of a teacher's activities to student growth takes test scores from previous years and compares them to current years in an effort to show any positive or negative impacts a teacher has on student performance (Chetty et al., 2014). Additionally, value-added approaches may use a pre-test/post-test approach where students are tested early in a year or unit of study, the teacher executes lesson plans with the students, and then students are given a post-test. The difference in scores is then used as an indication of the impact of the teacher upon student learning. These types of teacher evaluation tools are still in place today and often involve a very complicated formula to determine a teacher's success in the classroom. As a current classroom teacher, Karrie is still evaluated based on student growth as measured by standardized tests from one year to the next.

It is argued that many factors impact a students' performance on tests and that to use them to evaluate teachers ignores important variables outside a teacher's influence. Additionally, the use of tests takes focus off important skills such as advocacy, creation, empathy, and dialogue; skills vital to the social studies experience. In working to grow test scores as much as possible, teachers are pressured or put pressure on themselves to narrow their curriculum and focus only on concepts or content addressed by these tests. The result is often a minimization of deep, meaningful social studies experiences as teachers work to grow students' test-taking skill. Though we believe tests are important forms of assessment, much of the vital work of social studies teachers is not realized for decades, as student-citizens engage with their communities throughout their lives.

Class Activity: Race to the Top

With your classmates:

- Discuss what role federal and state governments should have in determining what defines a successful school.
- Discuss the positive and negative aspects of using student test scores for teachers' evaluations.
- If you were to create an assessment to measure a students' success in social studies, what concepts would that test address?

The Common Core Standards

To gain a better chance of securing Race to the Top funds, states were encouraged to adopt the Common Core Standards. As of February 2021, 41 states and the District of Columbia have adopted Common Core standards in mathematics and language arts in some form (i.e., writing, speaking and listening, reading) (Association for Supervision and Curriculum Development, 2021; Common Core State Standards Initiative, 2011). While there are currently no official social studies content standards in the Common Core framework, standards exist for the analysis of informational texts found in social studies and science disciplines. Blended with standards for language arts classes, social studies documents will be used for analysis on the language arts common core examinations. Additionally, the C3 standards are connected to and reference the Common Core Standards (National Council for the Social Studies, 2013). Proponents laud the initiative for its focus on skills to help prepare students for college and career, and the move away from multiple choice standardized assessments. Critics fear that the Common Core standards weaken their own state standards. Additionally, critics argue that you cannot make one size fits all national standards, and that it is too difficult for some poorer districts and states to grade non-multiple choice, open-ended exams (Voice of America, 2011a,b). States that employ the Common Core standards continue to see opposition to their use and to the associated standardized testing, generally because they are viewed as an overreach of the federal government.

Effects of the Common Core Curriculum on Social Studies Instruction

The Common Core standards have had a profound impact on middle grades social studies teaching. For one, language arts teachers collaborate with social studies teachers regarding social studies content knowledge and the analysis of primary and secondary source documents their students are required to analyze (see Figure 14.2). More importantly, due to the fact that the tests are more document-

- "Letter on Thomas Jefferson" by John Adams (1776)
- "Narrative of the Life of Frederick Douglass, an American Slave" by Frederick Douglass (1845)
- "Blood, Toil, Tears, and Sweat: Address to parliament on May 13th, 1940" by Winston Churchill (1940)
- "Harriet Tubman: Conductor on the Underground Railroad" by Ann Petry (1955)
- "Travels with Charley: In Search of America" by John Steinbeck (1962)

FIGURE 14.2. Sample Common Core Informational Texts (Literary Nonfiction: Grades 6–8) Source: Common Core State Standards for English Language Arts & Literacy in History, Social Studies, Science, and Technical Subjects

Key Ideas and Details

1. Cite specific textual evidence to support analysis of primary and secondary sources.
2. Determine the central ideas or information of a primary or secondary source; provide an accurate summary of the source distinct from prior knowledge or opinions.
3. Identify key steps in a text's description of a process related to history/social studies (e.g., how a bill becomes a law, how interest rates are raised or lowered).
   a. Craft and Structure
4. Determine the meaning of words and praises as they are used in a text, including vocabulary specific to domains related to history/social studies.
5. Describe how a text presents information (e.g., sequentially, comparatively, casually).
6. Identify aspects of a text that reveal an author's point of view or purpose (e.g., loaded language, inclusion or avoidance of particular facts).
   a. Integration of Knowledge and Ideas
7. Integrate visual information (e.g., in charts, graphs, photographs, videos, or maps) with other information in print and digital texts.
8. Distinguish among fact, opinion, and reasoned judgment in a text.
9. Analyze the relationship between a primary and secondary source on the same topic.
   a. Range of Reading and Level of Text Complexity
10. By the end of grade 8, read and comprehend history/social studies texts in the grades 6–8 text complexity band independently and proficiently.

FIGURE 14.3. Common Core Reading Standards for History/Social Studies Grades 6–8. Source: Common Core State Standards for English Language Arts & Literacy in History, Social Studies, Science, and Technical Subjects

based and less multiple-choice questions, it is up to you as social studies expert to employ strategies to help students prepare for these exams including primary source analysis, historical inquiry, jigsaws, and the Circle of Knowledge (see Figures 14.3 and 14.4) as opposed to traditional lecture and note taking (Common Core State Standards Initiative, 2011).

Though the current educational landscape continues to marginalize the social studies, that there is focus on analysis and evaluation of primary and secondary sources gives you unique influence on a students' learning experience. Your

---

Text Types and Purposes
1. Write arguments focused on discipline-specific continent
   a. Introduce claim(s) about a topic or issue, acknowledge and distinguish the claim(s) from alternate or opposing claims and organize the reasons and evidence logically.
   b. Support claim(s) with logical reasoning and relevant, accurate data and evidence that demonstrate an understanding of the topic or text, using credible sources.
   c. Use words, phrases, and clauses to create cohesion and clarify the relationships among claim(s), counterclaims, reasons, and evidence.
   d. Establish and maintain a formal style.
   e. Provide a concluding statement or section that follows from and supports the argument presented.
2. Write informative/explanatory texts, including the narration of historical events...
   a. Introduce a topic clearly, previewing what is to follow; organize ideas, concepts, and information into broader categories as appropriate to achieving purpose; including formatting (e.g., headings), graphics (e.g., charts, tables), and multimedia when useful to aiding comprehension.
   b. Develop the topic with relevant, well-chosen facts, definitions, concrete details, quotations, or other information and examples.
   c. Use appropriate and varied transitions to create cohesion and clarify the relationships among ideas and concepts.
   d. Use precise language and domain-specific vocabulary to inform about or explain the topic.
   e. Establish and maintain a formal style and objective tone.
   f. Provide a concluding statement or section that follows from and supports the information or explanation presented. (continues)

FIGURE 14.4. Common Core Writing Standards for History/Social Studies Grades 6–8. Source: Common Core State Standards for English Language Arts & Literacy in History, Social Studies, Science, and Technical Subjects http://www.corestandards.org/the-standards

> 3. In history/social studies students must be able to incorporate narrative accounts into their analyses of individual or events of historical importance.
>
> **Production and Distribution of Writing**
> 4. Produce clear and coherent writing in which the development, organization, and style are appropriate to task, purpose, and audience.
> 5. With some guidance and support from peers and adults, develop and strengthen writing as needed by planning, revising, editing, rewriting, or trying a new approach, focusing on how well purpose and audience have been addressed.
> 6. Use technology, including the Internet, to produce and publish writing and present the relationships between information and ideas clearly and efficiently.
>
> **Research to Build and Present Knowledge**
> 7. Conduct short research projects to answer a question (including a self-generated question), drawing on several sources and generating additional related focused questions that allow for multiple avenues or exploration.
> 8. Gather relevant information from multiple print and digital sources, using search terms effectively, assess the credibility and accuracy of each source; and quote or paraphrase the data and conclusions of others while avoiding plagiarism and following a standard format for citation.
> 9. Draw evidence from informational texts to support analysis, reflection, and research.
>
> **Range of Writing**
> 10. Write routinely over extended time frames (time for reflection and revision) and shorter time frames (a single sitting or day or two) for a range of discipline-specific tasks, purposes, and audiences.

FIGURE 14.4. Continued

knowledge of important primary source documents and how to analyze them make you an invaluable member of your school. Additionally, if you make routine use of the social studies strategies offered throughout the book, your classes will be viewed as assets to the middle school curriculum, not as a subject that does not matter. We look forward to social studies programs based on inquiry and the incorporation of life skills as opposed to rote memorization and recall. More recent federal policy under the "Every Student Succeeds Act" continues to maintain focus on testing of literacy and math skills (Every Student Succeeds Act, 2015). Despite the ongoing focus on testing and a narrow—but important—set of skills, we are optimistic that the value of concepts within the social studies will be rediscovered through federal legislation and acted upon with increased resources at the federal, state, and local levels.

COLLABORATIVE ACTIVITY: THE COMMON CORE STANDARDS

In your reflective journal answer the following questions and then discuss your answers with a classmate:

- Examine Figure 14.2 and locate some of the documents listed. Do you think that these are age-appropriate materials for middle level students? Why or Why not?
- Examine Figures 14.3 and 14.4 What do you like about these standards? What do you think are some of their weaknesses? What strategies will you use to incorporate these standards into your social studies lessons?
- While the Common Core Curriculum standards may bring positive effects for social studies educators, there may not be common standards for social studies content. Why do you think this may be the case?
- Would you want common content standards for social studies? Why or Why not?

CONTROVERSIES IMPACTING SOCIAL STUDIES TEACHING AND LEARNING

Due to its very nature, social studies is probably the most controversial subject in schools (Loewen, 1995). Though the theory of evolution is a lynchpin for debate in science courses and the use of classic books in English classes such as *Huckleberry Finn* and *The Catcher in the Rye* can prove controversial, social studies, with its focus on social and political issues, has the potential to create a nationwide controversy. Many of us have been warned to never talk about race, religion or politics in a formal gathering, yet as middle level social studies teachers we discuss these topics with our 10- to 14-year-old students every day. Ben often reminded his students that they could not effectively discuss the history of the United States without discussing topics of religion or politics. As the periodic table is fundamental to the understanding of chemistry, beliefs and interactions of individuals and groups are fundamental to the understanding of their societies (Gunn et al., 2020). Recent debates directly impacting social studies teachers and their students include: what—and whose—history should be taught in schools; what topics should be avoided; whether teachers should discuss their bias; and how patriotism should be demonstrated. As we wade through these complex issues, we strongly encourage you as emerging and ongoing social studies professionals to engage in dialogue with administrators and trusted peers regarding the best approaches for your students.

Because social studies is by its nature controversial, it is important to embrace dialogue regarding controversy in our field. As a social studies teacher you may find yourself in the center of a controversy at the local, state, or even national level. You will be recognized in your school and in your community as an expert in controversy and politics and may be questioned by well or ill meaning individuals of your personal opinions on controversial subjects. With these ideas in mind, let us consider social studies controversies that have made national headlines. Though you may not be directly involved in events regarding these controversies, your students will surely ask you about them. It is thus important for you to know what they are, what caused them, and decide what you can learn from them to help you prepare to engage with your students about them.

Texas Curriculum Controversy

Serving as a case study of a broader, ongoing societal debate about who selects social studies curriculum, we return to the Texas curriculum controversy discussed in Chapter 2. In sum, this controversy had nothing to do with the actions of an individual teacher but stemmed from a debate between a review board dominated by conservative-minded individuals and the beliefs of professional historians, social scientists, and special interest groups from all sides of the political spectrum. The debate drew national headlines because textbooks written for the large state of Texas are often sold to smaller states that may not have textbook adoption boards. Many were concerned that the conservative viewpoints of Texas would dominate the national memory of all Americans (see Figure 2.2).

As a social studies teacher there are several things to learn from this controversy. For one, you should not be a passive bystander when it comes to the development of the standards of your state. For the most part, state adoption committees for standards and textbooks hold meetings and conduct formal reviews that are open to the public. Going beyond the textbook, there is growing recognition that supplementary materials used in the classroom are also open to scrutiny. Ben has been asked about primary sources such as letters and photographs he uses in his classroom. As a social studies teacher you should attend, take part, and voice your opinion on all materials you are required or choose to use. No matter your political views, your opinion counts when it comes to what students in your state will learn for many years into the future.

Additionally, this controversy should demonstrate to you the power and importance that history/social studies has on the community. It also should show that the number of people, places, and events that can be taught is finite and for every person that is added to the list of historical figures in state standards, there are those who are left out. While we are proponents of using the standards as a guide for instruction, this is not to say that you cannot add other individuals, groups, and events in your classes (Roberts et al., 2020). For example, if your state removed Thomas Jefferson from their standards due to his beliefs about the separation of church and state, but you think he is important for your students to learn about, you can add him to the list of founders and have your students compare and contrast his views to the others.

Finally, this episode should illustrate that no matter what you teach, or how you teach it, you may offend someone. When teaching controversial issues in social studies it is important that you have a solid rationale concerning why you taught a subject the way you did. While it is okay to play devil's advocate in a debate to help students see an issue from all sides, you are better off letting your students determine and debate their own views and not overtly forcing your beliefs upon them. To work to solve potential problems before they happen, Ben discusses this concept frequently with his 8th grade students to ensure they understand his role in their discourse.

The 1619 Project, the 1776 Commission, and "Whose History" Gets Taught

Also reflecting the politicized nature of curriculum selection and interpretation are the recent 1619 Project and the 1776 Commission Reports. (1619 Project, 2019; Exec. Order No. 13958, 2020). Critically viewing the "traditional" narrative of the founding of the United States, the 1619 Project encourages students to explore marginalized narratives and to critique the decisions and non-actions of George Washington, Thomas Jefferson, and other political and economic leaders of early American history. An introductory statement of the 1619 Project (2019) frames the founding of the United States differently than generations of students were taught:

> What if, however, we were to tell you that this fact, which is taught in our schools and unanimously celebrated every Fourth of July, is wrong, and that the country's true birth date, the moment that its defining contradictions first came into the world, was in late August of 1619? Though the exact date has been lost to history (it has come to be observed on Aug. 20), that was when a ship arrived at Point Comfort in the British colony of Virginia, bearing a cargo of 20 to 30 enslaved Africans. Their arrival inaugurated a barbaric system of chattel slavery that would last for the next 250 years. This is sometimes referred to as the country's original sin, but it is more than that: It is the country's very origin. (p. 4)

Critics of the 1619 Project argue this curriculum works to indoctrinate students against the narrative that the United States was founded as a free country with equal opportunity for all. To counter this curriculum, the 1776 Commission report states curriculums such as the 1619 Project: "…shames Americans by highlighting only the sins of their ancestors and teaches claims of systemic racism that can only be eliminated by more discrimination, is an ideology intended to manipulate opinions more than educate minds" (The President's Advisory 1776 Commission, 2021, p. 18).

These conflicting interpretations of events of early American history reflect not only the truth that interpretation is a major element of historical and social studies exploration, but also of the fact that passions, special interests, and politics play a role in what takes place in social studies classrooms. As social studies professionals, it is our obligation to our students and to our profession to engage in dialogue, constructively critique, evaluate, and thoughtfully consider the curriculums we have available to us. Essentially, if we expect our students to grow into adults who can debate and dialogue civically, peacefully, and productively, they need practice doing so. Indeed, we recommend, if appropriate for your setting, you place comments from both the 1619 Project and the 1776 Report next to each other for students to analyze as examples of history interpretation.

Black Lives Matter, Riots vs. Protests, and Culture Wars

Since the publication of the second edition of this text in 2015, America has seen deep divisions and social injustice come into the open in ways not seen since the late 1960s. A variety of events and trends have melded together to create a societal environment of upheaval, political action, and violence. The Black Lives Matter Movement, disagreement on what constitutes a protest vs. riot, and broad culture wars are part of our societal landscape and, resultantly, impact what takes place in our social studies classrooms.

Though there is a tragic, centuries-long history of murders of innocent Black people, the murders of Breonna Taylor, George Floyd, and many others served as catalysts for mass protests for change across the United States. The Black Lives Matter movement, which challenges society and government to consider and change systemically racist policies and processes, saw demonstrations in hundreds of cities. At the same time, looters and rioters—unassociated with the BLM movement—engaged in property destruction and other crimes in many places. Influenced by media outlets, Americans interpreted these events differently, depending deeply on political affiliation and favored media sources. The result was—and is—ongoing debate as to the goals of the BLM movement and what constitutes lawful protest or unlawful rioting. This debate has spilled into social studies classrooms across the country as teachers work to examine these events with their students.

More broadly, conflicts in the political and social arenas impact the teaching and learning of social studies. The rights of LGBTQ+ citizens, inclusion of indigenous nations' history narratives in social studies, climate change policy, immigration policy, religious tolerance, and the grappling of systemic racism are part of societal dialogue, debate, disagreement, and conflict. Students come to their social studies classes having witnessed events, read social media, and talked with parents, friends, and others regarding these concepts. As social studies professionals, it is our duty to empathize with all students, embrace multiple perspectives, and engage in productive dialogue regarding these important topics.

The National Anthem, the Pledge of Allegiance, and Patriotism

During a professional football game in 2016, player Colin Kaepernick knelt during the performance of the Star-Spangled Banner. Protesting police brutality and racism, Kaepernick's action spurred societal debate as to the nature and role of patriotism, patriotic display, and patriotic participation. Central to this debate is the question; "What is and what is not a patriotic act?." As with other concepts, this debate quickly turned its attention to what takes place in schools.

Patriotic education, display, and ceremony have long histories in American schools (Martin, 2012; Mirga, 1998; Mowry, 1888; Wellenreiter, 2020). Recitation of the Pledge of Allegiance, mandated curriculums requiring the teaching of patriotism, and the role of teachers in patriotic education have become impassioned discussion points both inside and outside school systems. Reflecting the imbedded nature of "love of country" in schools, a state statute from Nebraska requires a pledge be taken by teachers:

> All persons engaged in teaching in the public schools of the State of Nebraska and all other employees paid from public school funds, shall sign the following pledge:
> I, ..., do believe in the United States of America as a government of the people, by the people, for the people; whose just powers are derived from the consent of the governed; a democracy in a republic; an indissoluble nation of many sovereign states; a perfect union, one and inseparable; established upon those principles of freedom, equality, justice and humanity for which American patriots sacrificed their lives and fortunes.
> I acknowledge it to be my duty to inculcate in the hearts and minds of all pupils in my care, so far as it is in my power to do, (1) an understanding of the United States Constitution and of the Constitution of Nebraska, (2) a knowledge of the history of the nation and of the sacrifices that have been made in order that it might achieve its present greatness, (3) a love and devotion to the policies and institutions that have made America the finest country in the world in which to live, and (4) opposition to all organizations and activities that would destroy our present form of government. (Nebraska: 79–8, 108. Teachers and employees; pledge; form)

Deeply intertwined with the teaching of US History, the concept and practice of patriotism is an important concept for social studies teachers to examine. Patriotism is often thought of in two widely different ways. *Authoritarian patriotism* is generally described as blind allegiance to specific individuals, groups, or social and government structures while *democratic patriotism* is viewed as a love of country demonstrated through critique, political action, and social change (Altıkulaç, 2016; Becker, 2018; Busey & Walker, 2017; Schatz et al., 1999; Staub, 1997; Westheimer, 2014). The root difference between these two forms of patriotism lies in what an individual chooses to challenge. In Authoritarian patriotism, an individual challenges threats from the outside, while in democratic patriotism, individuals challenge concepts from within. Authoritarian patriotism relies on obedience, conformity, non-questioning loyalty, and deep personal sacrifice. Democratic patriotism relies on constructive critique, dialogue, civic action, and social justice.

When woven with US History, it becomes easy to see how either authoritarian patriotism or democratic patriotism might be emphasized. A US history full of nothing but heroic deeds, untouchable, infallible leaders, and narratives without discussing a country's flaws encourages students to view their country as perfect and without need for improvement. A US history that challenges narratives, describes past and ongoing struggles, and demonstrates complicated leaders emphasizes the need for ongoing critique and civic action. It is often said that an individual can tell the type of government a country has based on the way its history is taught. Authoritarian regimes push the former, while democratic, open societies explore the latter.

Most schools engage in patriotic practice. From recitation of the Pledge of Allegiance to public presentations for veterans, patriotism is deeply embedded in school culture beyond the social studies classrooms. Reflecting Colin Kaepernick's protest, many students have chosen to kneel or not participate in the playing of the Star-Spangled Banner or the Pledge of Allegiance. Understanding and defending a students' right to refuse to participate—for any reason— it is the obligation of social studies teachers to protect students' free speech (Wellenreiter, 2020). Broadly, it is the responsibility of social studies teachers to explore with their students the nature of patriotism, how it is demonstrated, different ways patriotism may be demonstrated, the limits of patriotism, and, ultimately, an individual's right to determine what displays and actions are patriotic.

COLLABORATIVE ACTIVITY: RECENT SOCIETAL CONTROVERSIES

In your reflective journal answer the following questions and then discuss your answers with a classmate:

- Select two of the events or controversies above. Describe how you would discuss them with your students.
- Which of the controversies or topics above might you be most uncomfortable discussing with students? Describe what you might do to lessen this uncomfortableness.
- How do you define "patriotism"? What might your definition say about how you engage with patriotic displays in your school, such as the Pledge of Allegiance or Veteran's Day ceremonies.

TECHNOLOGY AND SOCIAL STUDIES

The worldwide COVID-19 pandemic fundamentally changed the education landscape. With less than 24 hours-notice in many cases, millions of students and hundreds of thousands of teachers were forced to shift from in-person class experienced by generations of students to the mostly unknown realm of online or remote learning (Heckart et al., 2020). Teaching methods, classroom management, student communication and collaboration, curriculum, and all that students, parents, and teachers knew about the school experience were paused while the great remote experiment of 2020 and 2021 took place. The early days of the remote experience saw overwhelmed teachers struggling to identify teaching platforms and activities, confused students and parents who worked to negotiate dozens of emails from school each day, and a society that wondered how long this experiment could be sustained.

As the pandemic wore on, patterns of engagement were established, online classroom norms emerged, and a sense of "we're in this for the long haul" became the challenge of teachers, students, and parents. Chaotic home learning environments, lack of technology access, ever-changing schedules and learning circumstances, and increasing disengagement eroded many students' learning year, putting them at greater risk of academic and financial struggles for the rest of their lives. As of the writing of this chapter in early 2021, millions of students have returned to schools with temperature checks, social distancing, and face masks. Millions more remain in remote and online learning situations as their communities struggle to determine whether it is safe enough for students and teachers to return. It is too early for us to tell how the COVID-19 pandemic will end and what implications it will have for students, families, and teachers. We are certain that there has been a newfound understanding of the importance of personal interaction and deep educational experience. Similarly, we are certain that teachers will be more confident in their exploration of ever-emerging technological approaches to education. With all the tragedies of the COVID-19 pandemic, with the hundreds of thousands of lives lost, we are certain that the remote learning experiences forced upon society by COVID-19 will be used to advance the field of education.

Described below are three emerging challenges teachers and students have faced during the remote learning experiment. We weave these challenges together with considerations for your use of technology during both face-to-face teaching and online/remote teaching environments. Rather than place deep emphasis on specific programs, platforms, or websites, we ask you to consider broad concepts regarding technology integration into your classroom (We do, however, present recent websites and platforms in Figure 14.5). It is our hope that you can experience with your students the best of in-person learning and the opportunities presented by remote/online learning.

Online Curriculum, Activities, and Assessments

Well before the COVID-19 pandemic, teachers often struggled to identify high-quality digital curriculum, class activities, and assessments. Accurate and bona fide websites for information, access to needed materials for online class activities, and high-quality, adaptable assessments were difficult to obtain. Teachers often went to their preferred search engine and tried to sift through the millions of websites that they invariably encountered. Once located, high quality, expert-refereed websites such as the ones maintained by the Library of Congress, the National Archives, and professional organizations served as important venues of resources. Similarly, universities, professional organizations, and non-profits

Tool	Website	Description
Blooket	https://www.blooket.com/	Blooket is an interactive game style review platform that allows teachers to create lessons and review games for students. There are multiple game modes including races, battle royale, factory builds, and more. Blooket is different from many of the other review games because it allows students to select a Blook and use their personalized account to collect game tokens and track their own learning statistics. They can even see how they measure up against other Blooks across the world.
Gimkit	https://www.gimkit.com/	Gimkit is a gameshow style platform. It can be used to introduce new topics and vocabulary or as an interactive review. Students answer teacher designated questions using a digital device. The program offers many engaging modes of play such as, the floor is lava, humans vs. zombies, boss battle, super rich, and more. Gimkit can be used with live instruction or as an individual assignment. Karrie uses Gimkit to help students review content before a quiz or test. The students beg to play and get visibly upset if she doesn't plan a Gimkit review. Their favorite mode of play is "Trust No One." This is similar to the popular app, "Among Us." Students get very competitive and have a lot of fun while reviewing content.
Jamboard	https://jamboard.google.com/	Like Kami, Jamboard is a Google Chrome extension. It is an interactive digital whiteboard that updates in real time.
Kahoot	https://kahoot.com/	Similar to Gimkit, Kahoot is a game-based learning tool that creates interactive trivia style games for students to learn and review. The program offers two styles of play, live or independent. Teachers can choose from ready-made games or create their own based on the material they wish to cover. Students compete to answer the most questions correctly and to be the fastest respondent.
Kami	https://www.kamiapp.com/	Kami is a Google Chrome extension that allows teachers to make any document interactive. Using the extension, students can write, type, annotate, and draw on any document, even pdfs, within their browser.
Menti Meter	https://www.mentimeter.com/	Mentimeter is a program that allows teachers to create interactive polls and questions within their presentations. The software utilizes popular gifs and memes to make the polls relevant and timely.

Nearpod	https://nearpod.com/	Nearpod is a platform designed to help make any lesson interactive and engaging for students. Teachers create presentations on any topic or subject. Different student tasks can be embedded throughout the presentation to keep students engaged. Tasks include quizzes, videos, draw-it slides, polls, and so much more. In addition, Nearpod works with Google as an add-on. This means teachers can use previously created Google Slide Presentations and make them interactive. Students can follow along live on their device or complete Nearpod lessons independently.
Padlet	https://padlet.com	Padlet is a digital bulletin board. The program allows teachers to create questions, surveys, etc. and place them on a board that students can access from their own device. Students may add comments to the board that appear as sticky notes for others to see. Padlet is great as a quick ticket out the door or formative check. It gives students the ability to participate without having to raise their hand or speak in front of others.
Peardeck	https://www.peardeck.com/	Similar to Nearpod, Peardeck is an interactive slide presentation tool that allows students to participate in presentations by answering questions on their own device. Teachers can create presentations that they want to use with their students and insert different types of questions and activities to help increase engagement within the classroom.
Quizizz	https://quizizz.com/	Lie Kahoot, Quizizz is a trivia style game. With the program, teachers can create multiple choice style assessments that students complete online using a code that is provided when teachers assign the Quizizz. Teachers get a report of how students did on each question. Karrie uses Quizizz for the students to preview new content or as a quick formative assessment to see how students are understanding the material they have been presented. She also uses the program as a tool for students to review independently or at home before a summative assessment.

FIGURE 14.5. Digital Educational Tools

have grown in their sophistication and flexibility with online lesson plans, virtual learning experiences, and assessments.

In determining the usefulness and appropriateness of specific online resources, from Digital Textbook pages to Wikipedia entries to websites selling teacher-created lesson plans and activities, we ask you to consider the following questions:

- Is the website hosted by an identified institution or organization?
- Is there contact information for the host or the individual(s) responsible for the content?
- Is the content biased in its presentation?
- Is appropriate source citation included both in the text and as a separate reference section?
- Is the content age and developmentally appropriate for your students?
- Does the content align well with your state, district, school, or individual learning standards and specific learning objectives?
- Does the content work to advance the knowledge and experience of your students?
- Are the assessments reasonable and well-aligned to the other experiences of your students?
- Are the content, activities, and assessments inclusive to all students?

While there is no complete formula for determining the appropriateness of specific online resources, these questions provide a starting point for determining the appropriateness and educational value of online resources. Additionally, supportive administrators and trusted peers can be used as sounding boards when considering whether to use a specific online resource, lesson plan, or assessment.

Online Classroom Management

Another aspect of the integration of technology and the classroom that presents both challenges and opportunities is the employment of online classroom management strategies. The online venue is fundamentally different than in-person classrooms for two main reasons. First, participants in online learning venues have limited access to the non-verbal forms of communication so important to overall communication. Nuanced facial expressions, sitting position and "here and now" aspects of communication such as movement, shared environmental experience, and non-verbal communication between students are limited or absent in online settings. Justified by right to privacy, embarrassment, or practical considerations such as noise in their environments, many students choose to shut off their cameras and microphones, closing out any indication as to their engagement—or even presence—in the class.

Working to maintain deep, meaningful engagement, teachers in remote settings diversify their classes through periodic "check-in questions," small group discussions in breakout rooms, and enthusiastic use of chat features. Requiring students to engage through these venues works to ensure they are interacting with the course concepts and the class itself.

Whether remote or face-to-face, the ongoing and varied use of check-ins and student-centered discussions works to address many concerns teachers have regarding student interactions with one another online. Additionally, requiring students to use their real names, disabling anonymous posting, and having focused and clear learning objectives work to maintain student focus and overall classroom management. We encourage you to be transparent with your students, communicating with them regarding your expectations for online interaction and engaging them in conversation about your standards of behavior. Acknowledging some need for turning off cameras, detailing the multiple reasons for the periodic check-ins (both as assessment and accountability for attention), and dialoging the challenges of anonymous posting, having honest discussions with students about classroom management goes a long way in growing class climate. Broadly, we argue that mutual trust, unambiguous discussions about procedures, and rationales for rules are important regardless of remote or face-to-face learning environments.

Student Collaboration

A fundamental joy of teaching social studies at the middle school level is watching students engage with one another. With a multitude of websites and programs that provide venues for student engagement, we encourage you to consider some broad questions when deciding which platform works best:

- Does the website/platform require student registration? If so, does it require unreasonable student data such as date of birth or other personal information beyond school-issued email addresses?
- Does the website allow for restricted access to only individuals associated with your classroom such as parents and paraprofessionals?
- Does the website/platform allow for disabling anonymous commenting and editing?
- Does the website/platform meet your specific learning objectives?
- Does the website/platform allow for both lower- and higher order thinking and communication skills?
- Does the website/platform allow teachers and others to view editing history of collaborative documents?
- Does the website/platform allow for documents or file folders to be private between individual students and teachers?

As with the landscape of digital curricular materials, primary and secondary sources, and assessments, the world of online and cloud-based student collaboration is in constant development. In assessing whether a specific platform for student collaboration is appropriate for your students, we ask you to consider student safety and privacy, the ability for the teacher to wholly observe student interaction, whether the platform allows users to see changes and contributions in editing and whether the platform works to enhance student collaboration generally.

Broadly, when considering ways to integrate technology into your classroom, whether with curriculum opportunities, assessments, student interaction, or student creativity, student safety and privacy are of utmost concern. Accuracy of information, quality of assessments, and focus on both lower and higher order skills are also important considerations. As you decide which websites, programs, apps, and meeting rooms best suit your students' needs, we encourage you to keep one eye toward innovations coming from colleagues and the broad world of education. If we have learned anything about technology integration in middle school classrooms, it is that the only constant is change.

COLLABORATIVE ACTIVITY: TECHNOLOGY AND SOCIAL STUDIES

In your reflective journal answer the following questions and then discuss your answers with a classmate:

- Describe what platforms, websites, and apps you have used as a student. What worked well? What did not?
- What questions might you ask of a website, app, or platform before using it with your students?
- Describe the differences between communicating in person and communicating online. What are advantages and disadvantages of each?
- What, in your opinion, might the next big advance in educational technology be?

SUMMARY

The recent past has demonstrated the vital importance of deep, meaningful social studies experiences for our students. Understanding of multiple history narratives, viewing past and current events from multiple perspectives, effective and thorough analysis of information, and civic—and civil—dialogue regarding society's challenges and opportunities are reflected in the class activities we design for students. Indeed, we believe there is no more important, exciting, or challenging time to be a middle school social studies teacher. Added to these challenges and opportunities are ever-emerging technologies that also influence the work we do. As you step into the ever-changing education landscape, we encourage you to continue to dialogue with colleagues, read widely and deeply about trends in social studies and educational technologies, and directly discuss with your students current events, societal debates, and controversies they observe in their lives outside of school.

COLLABORATIVE ACTIVITY: REFLECTING ON THE CHAPTER

After reading the chapter, reflect on the events of social studies' recent past and future. Then answer the following questions and discuss with a classmate:

- What most excites you about becoming a middle grades social studies teacher?
- What most concerns you about teaching social studies?
- How might you best handle the challenges and possibilities that lie ahead in the future?

WEBSITE RESOURCES

- **Common Core State Standards Initiative** (http://www.corestandards.org/) offers information about the Common Core Standards, which states have adopted them, and how they are going to affect teacher instruction. The website describes the standards in detail and offers a page devoted to dispelling myths about the standards.
- **Common Sense Media (https://www.commonsensemedia.org/)** Provide resources, reviews of educational technology tools, and is dedicated to advocating for safe, reasonable technology use inside and outside the classroom. Of particular note is the App review feature which provides privacy ratings.
- **Florida Center for Instructional Technology** (http://fcit.usf.edu/) is affiliated with the University of South Florida and the Florida Department of Education. The website offers over 95,000 "digital assets" including clip art, images, and resources. One of the most impressive pages on the site is their technology image matrix (https://fcit.usf.edu/matrix/matrix/that offers teachers both a written matrix as well as video clips of classroom teachers demonstrating how to incorporate technology, at various levels, into their social studies classes along with full lesson plans based on the videos.
- **International Society for Technology in Education** (https://www.iste.org/about/about-iste) "inspires the creation of solutions and connections that improve opportunities for all learners by delivering: practical guidance, evidence-based professional learning, virtual networks, thought-provoking events and the ISTE Standards."
- **Netiquette** (http://www.networketiquette.net/) is a website that offers tips about appropriate behaviors and practices on the Internet. The tips from this website can be given to students as a guide to set norms for appropriate Internet use.
- **Stanford History Education Group** (https://cor.stanford.edu/) Civic Online Reasoning "the COR curriculum provides free lessons and assess-

ments that help you teach students to evaluate online information that affects them, their communities, and the world."
- **The U.S. Department of Education** (http://www2.ed.gov/) website offers information about any federal education program including No Child Left Behind, Race to the Top, and the Every Student Succeeds Act.

REFERENCES

The 1619 Project. (2019). *The 1619 Project.* https://www.nytimes.com/interactive/2019/08/14/magazine/1619-america-slavery.html

Adler-Greene, L. (2019). Every Student Succeeds Act: Are schools making sure every student succeeds? *Touro Law Review, 35*(1), 11–23.

Altıkulaç, A. (2016). Patriotism and global citizenship as values: A research on social studies teacher candidates. *Journal of Education and Practice, 7*(36), 26–33.

Association for Supervision and Curriculum Development. (2021, February 10). *Common core standards adoption by state.* http://www.ascd.org/common-core-state-standards/common-core-state-standards-adoption-map.aspx.

Bailey, G., Shaw Jr., E. L., & Hollifield, D. (2006). The devaluation of social studies in the elementary grades. *Journal of Social Studies Research, 30*(2), 18–29.

Becker, M. N. (2018). Loving America with open eyes: A student-driven study of US rights in the age of Trump. In *Am I patriotic? Learning and teaching complexities of patriotism here and now.* Bank Street Occasional Paper Series No. 40. Bank Street College of Education.

Busey, C. L., & Walker, I. (2017). A dream and a bus: Black critical patriotism in elementary social studies standards. *Theory and Research in Social Education, 45*(4), 456–488.

Chetty, R., Firedman, J. N., & Rockoff, J. E. (2014). Measuring the impacts of teachers II: Teacher value-added and student outcomes in adulthood. *American Economic Review, 104*(9), 2633–2679.

Common Core State Standards Initiative. (2011). *Common Standards.* http://www.corestandards.org/

Every Student Succeeds Act, 20 U.S.C §6301 (2015). https//www.congress.gov/114/plaws/pub95/PLAW-114publ95.pdf

Exec. Order No. 13958, 85 FR 70951, (November 2, 2020).

Fitchett, P. G., & Heafner, T. L. (2010). A national perspective on the effects of high-stakes testing and standardization on elementary social studies marginalization. *Theory and Research in Social Education, 38*(1), 114–130.

Gunn, A. A., Bennett, S. V., & van Beynen, K. (2020). Multicultural literature in K–6 classrooms. *Social Studies and the Young Learner, 33*(1), 10–16.

Heafner, T. L. (2018). More social studies? Examining instructional policies of time and testing in elementary school. *Journal of Social Studies Research, 42*(3), 229–237. https://doi-org.libproxy.lib.ilstu.edu/10.1016/j.jssr.2017.08.004

Heckart, K., Reiter, J., Ingold, J., Seitz, Z., Francis, A., & Hitchcock, C. (2020). Teaching remotely during the Coronavirus pandemic. *Social Education, 84*(3), 146–151.

Hefling, K., & Feller, B. (2012). *No child left behind: 10 states receive waiver from education law's sweeping requirements.* http://www.huffingtonpost.com/2012/02/09/no-child-left-behind-waivers_n_1264872.html

Hodges. D. (Ed.). (2012). *The little red book of teacher's wisdom.* Skyhorse.
Loewen, J. W. (1995). *Lies my teacher told me: Everything your American history textbook got wrong.* The New Press.
Masters, K. (2019). Artificial intelligence in medical education. *Medical Teacher, 41*(9), 976–980.
Martin, L. A. (2012). Blind patriotism or active citizenship? How do students interpret the Pledge of Allegiance? *Action in Teacher Education, 34*, 55–64.
McMahon Whitlock, A., & Brugar, K.A., (2019). Teaching elementary social studies during snack time and other unstructures spaces. *Journal of Social Studies Research, 43*(3), 229–239.
Mirga, T. (1988). Conflicts over pledge: A long, tense history. *Education Week, 8*(1), 21.
Mowry, W. A. (1888). The promotion of patriotism. *Education, 9*(3), 197–200.
National Council for the Social Studies. (2013). *The college, career, and civil life (C3) Framework for social studies state standards: Guidance for enhancing the rigor of K–12 civics, economics, geography, and history.* NCSS.
National Governors Association Center for Best Practices. (2010). *Common core state standards.* Author.
Nebraska Administrative Code, Title 92, Ch. 10 § 003.12
The President's Advisory 1776 Commission (2021). *The 1776 Report.* Author.
Roberts, S. L., Butler, B. M., Elfer, C. J., Kendrick, D. T., & Widdall, V. (2020). "Isn't it peachy:" The successes and pitfalls of teaching complicated topics in eighth grade Georgia studies. In T. Flint & N. Keefer (Eds.). *Critical perspectives on teaching in the southern United States* (pp. 143–160). Lexington Books.
Schatz, R. T., Staub, E., & Lavine, H. (1999). On the varieties of national attachment: Blind versus constructive patriotism. *Political Psychology, 20*(1), 151–174.
Smith, K. W., & Falbe, K. N. (2020). In a spirit of curiosity, concern, collaboration, and humility. Considering the work of middle grades education in the context of a pandemic. *Middle Grades Review, 6*(2), Article 3.
Staub, E. (1997). Blind versus constructive patriotism: Moving from embeddedness in the group to critical loyalty and action. In D. Bar-Tal & E. Staub (Eds.), *Patriotism in the lives of individuals and nations* (pp. 1–19). Nelson Hall.
U.S. Department of Education. (2009). *No Child Left Behind is working.* http://www2.ed.gov/nclb/overview/importance/nclbworking.html
U.S. Department of Education. (2010). *Elementary and secondary education.* http://www2.ed.gov/policy/elsec/leg/esea02/index.html
U.S. Department of Education. (2011). *Race to the Top fund: Awards.* http://www2.ed.gov/programs/racetothetop/awards.html
U.S. Department of Education. (2012). *Race to the Top fund.* http://www2.ed.gov/programs/racetothetop/index.html
VanFossen, P. J. (2005). "Reading and Math take so much of the time...:" An overview of social studies instruction in elementary classrooms in Indiana. *Theory and Research in Social Education, 33*(3), 376–403.
van Hover, S., Hicks, D., Stoddard, J., & Lisanti, M. (2010). From a roar to a murmur: Virginia's history and social science standards, 1995–2009. *Theory and Research in Social Education, 38*(1), 80–113.

Vasquez-Heilig, J., Jameson Brewer, T., & Ojeda Pedraza, J. (2018). Examining the myth of accountability, high-stakes testing, and the achievement gap. *Journal of Family Strengths, 18*(1), 1–14.

Voice of America. (2011a). *No national standards: Strengths or weaknesses for schools in the U.S.*. http://www.voanews.com/learningenglish/home/education/No-National-Standards-A-Strength-or-Weakness-of-U.S.-Schools-123948044.html

Voice of America. (2011b.) *Should all U.S. students learn the same thing?* http://www.voanews.com/learningenglish/home/education/Should-All-Students-in-U.S.-Learn-the-Same-Things-123503384.html

Wellenreiter, B. R. (2020). When students refuse to recite the Pledge of Allegiance: Preservice teachers' responses. *Clearing House, 93*(1), 19–26.

Westheimer, J. (2014). Teaching students to think about patriotism. In E. W. Ross (Ed.), *The social studies curriculum: Purposes, problems, and possibilities* (4th ed., pp. 127–137). State University of New York Press.

Willis, J. S. (2007). Putting the squeeze on social studies: Managing teaching dilemmas in subject areas excelled from state testing. *Teachers College Record, 109*(8), 1980–2046.

CHAPTER 15

BECOMING A SOCIAL STUDIES PROFESSIONAL

One of the differences between the natural and social sciences is that in the natural sciences, each succeeding generation stands on the shoulders of those that have gone before, while in the social sciences, each generation steps on the faces of its predecessors.
—*David Zeaman (1959)*

What we need is for more people to specialize in the impossible.
—*Theodore Roethke (Crow, 2008)*

Activity List
- Reflecting on the Chapter

INTRODUCTION

Whether you approach this text as an undergraduate preservice teacher seeking initial teaching licensure, as an advanced degree seeking professional looking to enter in the world of teaching, or an experienced teacher wanting additional endorsement areas, your development as a middle level social studies professional will continue to unfold. Your identity deepens with each new student, lesson, professional development opportunity, and collegial interaction. It is our hope that you spend a career as a social studies professional, continually refining your craft, influenced by changing academic standards, best-educational practices, societal norms, and your own experiences. We believe the adage, "You never teach the same lesson twice" is true and it is our hope that you continually grow as a classroom professional, expert in the discipline, and, most of all, as an advocate for strong social studies experiences for students.

The purpose of this chapter is to explore the broad developmental stages social studies professionals may expect to go through during their career. Though the stages shown are general and the paths each of us take are unique, most teachers in most settings can expect to transition through these stages during their career. Certainly, specific variables may impact the length of time for each stage, but it has been our experience that viewing a teaching career through this framework can be helpful in reflection upon growth as a professional.

The chapter then discusses professional development opportunities social studies teachers may use to refine their practices and grow in knowledge and skill. Also explored are the concepts of; seeking advanced degrees, attaining additional certifications, attending and presenting at social studies conferences, and broad advocacy activities for the social studies. We believe that all we do as social studies teachers, from the first lesson to the retirement party, reflect who we are as professionals and reflect the discipline's identity broadly. We take as inspiration the clerk from Geoffrey Chaucer's *The Canterbury Tales,* replacing "he" with "we":

> He took utmost care and heed for his study.
> Not one word spoke he more than was necessary;
> And that was said with due formality and dignity
> And short and lively, and full of high morality.
> Filled with moral virtue was his speech;
> And gladly would he learn and gladly teach.
> (Poulton, 2005)

Developmental Trajectory Though Your Career

Development as a middle level social studies teacher is as unique as the individual. Personal backgrounds, initial professional preparation, school and classroom contexts, and individual personalities all deeply influence how an individual grows as a professional. Though all social studies professionals have different interests, strengths, weaknesses, struggles, and successes, there are four broad stages through which they can expect to travel; Survival, Consolidation, Renewal, and Maturity (Katz, 1972).

We place specific focus on the first two stages, survival and consolidation, because these two stages are the ones where teachers are most likely to leave the profession (Sutcher et al., 2016). Dismayed, we worry about the teacher attrition rates in the United States. Caused by factors such as pay, job satisfaction, retirement, and morale among others, attrition—teachers leaving the profession— is a growing concern across the country (Sutcher et al., 2016). Though there are many reasons teachers leave the profession, it is our hope that deep, meaningful engagement in professional growth throughout your career can serve as reinforcement for remaining in the learning and teaching field. We believe continued professional development can help prevent teachers from leaving the profession. As you progress through this chapter, consider how in each stage your work can continue to be vibrant, fresh, and most impactful upon students. Surely not every day will be your best day, but with strong professional and personal support, your career can be a deeply positive one.

Survival

Being a first-year social studies teacher is difficult. All the authors have stories of survival in their first years that they look back upon with an interesting mix of dread and nostalgia. From the first days of excitement through the weariness of the middle of the first school year, we all describe our first years as one of "just making it through."

Though provided with useful teaching tools and ideas by your professors, cooperating teachers, and this book, once you enter the classroom all the strategies and methods you learned will be temporarily erased from your mind as you work to bridge the divide between theory and practice. Instead of thinking about using inquiry-based activities and interactive, relevant, and interesting technology resources, you may be more worried about learning your content, effective classroom management, how to take attendance, and what to do when the copier jams. As you become more comfortable in your role as social studies educator, however, you will start thinking beyond the day to day and toward your broader growth as a social studies professional. The first stage, survival, is where the teacher places almost exclusive attention on their own ability to make it through the day, week, month, and year. As you grow in your experience, efficiency, and effectiveness both in the classroom with students and after hours with lesson planning and assessment, you will grow in your confidence and teaching will become easier. As noted above, many teachers leave the profession during this stage before they have an opportunity to harvest the fruit of their experiences. As teachers progress from the survival stage to the consolidation stage, they find that the career becomes far more manageable.

Essential to early-career success is the location and utilization of effective, positive mentor relationships and initial support from schools (Kelly et al., 2018; Warsame & Valles, 2018). Effective mentors; introduce the new teacher to people and places; help the new teacher organize the classroom; create a classroom management plan with the new teacher; plan the first day's activities; make resources available; invite the new teacher to observe in their classroom; observe the new teacher; share best practices in teaching; provide ideas for working with parents;

invite the new teacher into a professional group; model positive time and stress management; and encourage the new teacher in other ways (Clement, 2019). Many school districts, recognizing the importance of mentorship, provide new teachers with formal mentors to assist with these responsibilities. Formal mentors are highly experienced teachers identified for their excellence, who agree to help their colleagues learn the profession in their specific school contexts. Often, these relationships last one or two school years. Informal mentors are individuals who naturally grow professionally close to newer teachers. Blending the concepts of trusted colleagues and friends, informal mentors often provide years-long guidance through ethical questions, life/work balance issues, and overall professional development. It has been the authors' experiences that both formal and informal mentors are crucial to overall professional development. Indeed, mentors often become lifelong friends and confidants. Some of Karrie's closest friends both inside and outside of the classroom were either her mentors or mentees. Karrie has developed such close relationships with some of these individuals that their families now vacation together in the summer. The mentor/mentee relationship offers a unique opportunity to bond with another person over shared experiences.

Consolidation

Once a teacher settles into the profession, between years two and four, they enter a distinct new phase described by Katz (1972) as the consolidation stage. In this stage, teachers' thoughts and actions become less oriented on their own survival toward the needs of their students. Moving from day-to-day survival, teachers in this stage, with their increased efficiency and effectiveness, think and act more deeply regarding their students. Essentially, teachers' time and effort become more about their students than it does themselves. We certainly do not mean to imply that teachers in the survival mode place sole focus on themselves. We are suggesting the time, thought, effort, and emotion that go into beginning the teaching career take a significant amount of self-focus later placed on students as a teacher grows in skill. Stroot et al., (1998) frame this shift from teacher-centered to student-centered by describing questions teachers begin to ask themselves in the consolidation stage:

Teachers in the consolidation stage ask questions like; "How can I help a child who does not seem to be learning?" or "How can I deal with a child with a specific discipline problem?," or "How can I change my lessons to meet needs of low ability/high achieving students?" (Stroot et al., 1998, p. 4)

It is within this stage that teachers often state; "Because of what I learned, I deeply revised my lesson plans, classroom management approaches, and assessment strategies." This statement reflects vast growth experienced by teachers in their first years. Similar to the large growth spurts in small time frames experienced when we are young, development in the survival and consolidation stages is fast, comprehensive, and very consuming. It is, perhaps because of the deeply transformative nature of these two stages that early-career teachers leave the profession, assuming the pressures will remain throughout the career. It has been the authors' experiences that the first five years of teaching are the most difficult. Though not accurately described as "easy," once a teacher reaches approximately five-seven years of their career, it does become easier.

Renewal

Observers may marvel at the gracefulness, apparent ease, and flexibility with which veteran teachers perform their craft. Constructed with efficiency, innovation, and with understanding of how students will probably respond, lesson planning often takes less time for teachers in the renewal stage. Assessments and classroom management strategies are well-refined for increased effectiveness and deeper student learning. Between years five and 15, teachers have enough experience to often accurately predict how students will respond before they themselves do. It is within the renewal stage that teachers describe more confidence and more job satisfaction than in previous stages.

With deeper experience, teachers in the renewal stage experiment with new teaching approaches, classroom management strategies, and assessment techniques. They often do this not because what they are using does not work, but because they want to improve upon and refresh their techniques. Teachers in this stage become more active beyond their classroom in many ways. Seeking advanced degrees and certifications, engaging on school curriculum, calendar, and school improvement committees, and increased activity in professional development organizations are just a few ways teachers in the middle of their careers work to remain refreshed. As described earlier, it is often teachers in this stage who are identified for their excellence, flexibility, and professionalism and asked to serve as formal mentors to early-career teachers. Often solidified during this stage of their careers are the professional identities and reputations of teachers. It is because of this that growth in ethical and philosophical practices, continued professional development, and open-mindedness are essential. Rather than being completely content with well-tested approaches, we recommend teachers in this stage work to continually invigorate their own practices through innovation.

Maturity

Often described as "Elder statespersons" of their professions, teachers with deep maturity in their practices and profession have broad, positive impacts on their classrooms, schools, and the larger social studies and educational communities. Rather than the often-negative descriptions of "out of touch," "outdated" and "ready to retire," true elder statespersons of the profession are trusted, insightful, forward-looking, and willing to give back to their profession. Advocates for students, less-experienced colleagues, and education generally, deeply mature teachers, often with 20 or more years of experience, have profound impacts on their local and broad educational communities. Teachers who are deeply mature remain innovative and fresh in their classroom and school approaches. Recognizing that teachers never really perfect their practices, mature teachers continue professional development through conference activities, reading, and perhaps their own research and writing. Serving on school, district, state, and national boards and committees, deeply mature teachers give back to the profession while increasing the scope of their own professional influence. They may teach college courses, serve as cooperating teachers for preservice teachers, or engage the profession in a variety of other ways such as advocating for student-centered policies at state and national levels.

Teachers with more than 15 years of experience face risk of "burnout," or disengagement and disillusionment with the profession. Burnt out teachers are often highly negative, resistant to innovation, and do not seek to improve upon their practices. We believe a key difference between elder statespersons discussed and burnt out teachers is a broad willingness to continue to grow as a professional. Through continued education, professional development opportunities, and willingness to adapt to new teaching environments, teachers can avoid burnout. It is our hope that all social studies teachers eventually become elder statespersons for their students and their profession. Indeed, it is our belief that burnt out teachers who do not desire to change serve their students and the profession best by leaving both.

ACADEMIC STUDY BEYOND THE BACHELOR'S DEGREE

Bachelor (baccalaureate) degree programs, (Bachelor of Science, (B.S.), Bachelor of Arts, (B.A.), Bachelor of Education (B.Ed)), are just the first step in a teacher's professional development. Generally, a requirement for entry into a teaching position in public schools, the "Bachelor's degree" provides the early-career teacher with the essential skills and experiences needed to be successful in the first years of teaching. However, there is more to the educational story. Graduate work in the form of Master, Specialist, and Doctorate degrees further the knowledge base, skill, and experience of teachers who seek them.

Each level of graduate work presents its own benefits and challenges. Many graduate programs in the education field require enrollees to have at least two years of teaching experience to reflect both the time and thought their programs consume, as well as the time, effort, and thought that must go into the survival mode of a teacher's career. It is the authors' broad recommendation that at least two years of classroom experience sufficiently prepares teachers to engage in graduate work. These two years provide essential experiences on which graduate students can rely when engaging in advanced education theory and practice.

Master's Degrees

A Master's Degree, (often just called a "Master's), provides individuals with skills and background beyond the initial bachelor's degree. Master's degrees are generally required for; principals, assistant principals, deans, curriculum coordinators, educational technology coordinators, special education coordinators, school counselors, school psychologists, and other professional service providers.

In Master's programs, graduate students further refine their knowledge of their chosen subject and focus on advanced strategies, often with a professional problem-solving focus. Many Master's programs require internships or job shadowing to further grow a candidate's skill and experience. Common Master's programs in education include study in; educational administration, school counseling, teaching, technology, literacy, and special education.

Understanding that many of their students are part- or full-time educators, Master's degree programs offer evening, weekend, and summer courses. Online programs are becoming increasingly popular because of their flexibility and convenience. Master's programs may last between two and five years, depending on program requirements, course scheduling, and intensity. A common approach is to take up to two courses per semester and perhaps three in summer.

The most important consideration in selecting a Master's program entails understanding your professional goals. Do you wish to further refine your teaching? Are you interested in becoming a principal or dean? Is educational technology integration a deep interest of yours? Because you will be spending significant time and thought—and perhaps money—on a Master's program, it is important to assess your interests and professional goals. Though you may not know precisely where you may be in the future, it is important to have at least a broad understanding of where you see yourself. Further, discussing your options with family, friends, and colleagues can give you meaningful insights into which type of program might work best for you. There are several other factors to consider when deciding to pursue an advanced degree. These include cost, convenience, the type of program (face-to-face, hybrid, or fully online), the potential pay increase, the school's reputation, and, more importantly, if you are willing to work hard and gain all you can from the program to help you become a better teacher. It is also vital to ensure the institution and program are accredited by an oversight organization. Accredited programs are legitimate programs that offer valuable degrees recognized in the field. Non-accredited programs—often called "diploma mills" are predatory, close without warning, and have little or no value in the education field. Your first question about a program in which you are interested should be whether or not it is accredited. The Council for Higher Education Accreditation, (CHEA) maintains a website that provides accreditation information. In addition, most states have a professional licensing commission for teachers that must approve the course before an advanced degree can be added onto a teaching certificate. For instance, in Georgia, The Professional Standards Commission, or PSC, requires teachers register for advanced degrees prior to beginning a program.

Recognizing the value to their students, many school districts and states provide compensation to teachers enrolled in Master's programs. Assisting with tuition and/or increases in salary, many school districts and states make seeking a Master's degree more attractive for teachers. Though many believe teachers should receive additional compensation for earning advanced degrees due to the hard work, loss of personal time, and cost of a program, you should not pursue an advanced degree for the sole purpose of gaining a salary increase. If this is your only motivation, then you will not be gaining all you can from these programs, as students who are in this position may simply count down the days until graduation and have a difficult time staying motivated to learn and benefit from their courses. More importantly, Chang et al. (2020) suggest those who earn Master's degrees solely for monetary purposes do not become better teachers:

> ...[teachers] who earned the degree *solely* to get an upgrade did not become better teachers as a result, nor did their students' outcomes improve....On the other hand, teachers who were motivated, at least in part, by the desire to better serve their students and earned degrees in content-area teaching were said to alter their practices and find innovative ways to promote learning, understanding, and growth in their students. (Chang et al., 2020, p. 83)

It can also be argued that an administrator may choose to hire a teacher new to the profession who does not have a master's degree over one that does, believing that the potential performance difference would be negligible. For the most part, administrators (who usually have advanced degrees themselves) see the benefits of both experience and advanced degrees. If you have proven that you are a good teacher over a few years and choose to improve your practice by earning an advanced degree, we would argue that the vast majority of principals would support you in your decision. Remember that for now, many schools list the data showing the percentages of the teachers in the school with advanced degrees, and in the public's mind, having more teachers with advanced degrees makes a school better.

Specialist or Doctoral Degrees

Upon completion of Master's degrees, individuals are eligible for entry into specialist or doctoral programs. Specialist Degree (Specialist of Education, Ed.S) or Doctoral degree programs, (Doctor of Philosophy, Ph.D., and Doctor of Education Ed.D), prepare enrollees for advanced study, research work, and organizational leadership, depending on the program. Many states require superintendents have, or be close to obtaining, a doctorate degree. Specialist and Doctoral programs, much like Master's programs, often have evening, weekend, and summer coursework and are often offered online. Most specialist or doctoral students take between four and six years to complete program requirements. A major element to many of these programs is the thesis or doctoral dissertation. Either research- or practice-based investigations, dissertations may take from between 18 months-three years, depending on the focus of the work.

As with Master's program work, individuals interested in specialist or doctoral work are advised to clearly articulate their professional goals, (Do you wish to be a superintendent? Do you see yourself as a director of special education? Is the idea of being a university professor attractive? Do you wish to remain in the K–12 classroom as an elder statesperson?), deeply investigate programs, and talk with family, friends, and colleagues.

National Board Certification

The National Board for Professional Teaching Standards (NBPTS) is a national organization that works to; "…advance the quality of teaching and learning through a voluntary advanced certification." This organization provides a reflective framework and process by which teachers can become "Nationally Board Certified." Through rigorous tests, video recording, and reflection, teachers who become nationally board certified demonstrate deep knowledge of students, content, and pedagogy. Many states and school districts offer compensation for becoming nationally board certified and may also pay for at least a portion of the certification process.

PROFESSIONAL ORGANIZATIONS

While earning an advanced degree or national board certification are considerations as you get further into the profession, an immediate step you can take in becoming a social studies professional is to join your state's social studies council. As a middle level social studies teacher you will more than likely be teaching an integrated social studies course that focuses on history, geography, economics, and government. Due to the interdisciplinary nature of middle level social studies courses we would also recommend joining the National Council for the Social Studies. These groups focus on lessons and resources for an integrated approach to teaching the subject. If you have a deep interest in one discipline, there are state and national organizations for each discipline in the social sciences, as well as societies (usually historical) that offer resources and lesson plans to teachers. It does not matter which professional organization(s) you join, so long as you join one. Being a member of an organization offers several benefits, including receiving professional literature to keep you abreast of all that is going on in the field, resources and lesson plans, invitations to attend professional conferences with experts in the field, and the ability to get to know people that have the same interest and passion for the subject.

Membership

Membership in professional organizations provide you with a wide variety of benefits. Reduced registration costs for conferences, practitioner and research publication access, summer seminars and other professional development opportunities, and professional networking are often benefits for members. Reduced membership costs for early career teachers or multiyear memberships may be available to assist in budgeting. Broadly, membership adds your name to the field of professionals interested in advocating for students and for social studies.

Conferences and Conference Presentations

After joining a social studies organization, you will receive information about its conference activities. In developing as a social studies professional, we highly recommend that you plan to attend conferences, as the information and lesson ideas you will gain is invaluable. Though tight school budgets can often make it difficult for administrators to agree to send you to a conference, providing a solid rationale, describing specific intended outcomes, and reporting back on your learning to your colleagues work to justify the expense of registration, travel, lodging (if needed), and substitute teachers. It has been our experience that teachers who go to conferences that engage in sessions, network, and report back to their administration are often given more leeway when deciding which future conferences to attend.

Conference attendance also provides you with professional networking opportunities as you meet and work with people from around your state, region, and throughout the nation. With the help of technology and social media specifically, conference networking can serve as a first step into a vibrant professional community that may have thousands of members. From lesson planning to integration of new standards to broad advocacy for the profession, networking with other professionals is a wonderful way to remain vibrant and fresh in a profession often described as lonesome. It has been our experience that conference attendance can be energizing and refreshing. After attending great presentations, meeting leaders in the field, and mingling with individuals who are just as passionate about social studies as you are, you may find that a day away from school, learning about the latest and greatest in social studies is just the thing you need professionally and personally.

After attending a conference or two, you may want to consider presenting. As a social studies professional, you have probably created great lessons that you would be willing to share with your peers. The outstanding lessons that you present at a conference have the possibility of positively affecting thousands of students you may never meet. We often hear from professionals who believe they are not qualified to present at conferences. Getting away from the feeling of inadequacy and appreciating the fact that you are a unique and competent professional will assist you in "breaking into" the presentation arena. State social studies organizations are warm and welcoming to "new blood" in their presentation lineups. National conferences, likewise, are great places to "break in" to the larger field. In fact, if you attend the National Council for the Social Studies annual conference, you might just see one of the authors of this textbook cheering you on at your session!

Presenting at a conference is a straightforward process. First, you will need to find out when the local, state, or national organization is accepting proposals. You will craft a proposal with a title, a brief (often 30 words or less) summary—called an abstract—that will go in the conference program, a list of objectives for your session, and a brief description of what your session entails. Often submitted online, most proposals are due months before the conference. Once sent, volunteers review your proposal and decide if it should be part of that year's program. In some cases, organizations like NCSS have poster presentations for presentations they like but feel would not draw enough of a crowd as an independent full hour session. The selection of your proposal as a workshop, one-hour session, or a poster presentation is a privilege as you have the opportunity to present teachers with ideas that can help them in their social studies classroom.

If denied, your proposal may get feedback. Reasons may include; lack of clarity in the abstract, a session that is too specific to be interesting to a wide variety of teachers, a session that promotes commercial products such as books or curriculums, or lack of detail in the description. Additionally, rejection of your proposal may occur if it is similar to other proposed offerings. Rejected proposals may not fit well into the schedule or may not align to the conference theme. If your proposal receives a rejection do not give up. We have stories of proposals rejected, then accepted in following years by the same conference. Rejected proposals are not reflections of individuals proposing, but are composed of many factors, some beyond the control of the proposer. As reviewers and conference planners, we have rejected fine proposals for reasons of scheduling, logistics, and physical space limitations.

Executive Boards

Leadership of the professional organization in which you enroll is going to notice your initial membership and conference attendance. After several years of steadfast membership, conference attendance, and conference presentation, the organization's leadership is likely to identify you as a trustworthy, proactive member of the community. Do not be surprised if you are invited—or encouraged to run—for the organization's leadership roles. Conference planning committees, conference program review teams, organization policy and advocacy committees, and regional representative positions are common in state and national organizations. Engaging in these roles truly places individuals at the forefront of social studies advocacy. If "those who show up make the decisions," you can become a decision-maker by putting time and effort into your state and national social studies organizations. You may find participation on executive boards opens opportunities you may have previously viewed as unobtainable. Indeed, many of the authors of this text became familiar with one another through participation on executive boards of their state and national social studies organizations.

National Social Studies Organizations

The primary organization for social studies education is the National Council for Social Studies (NCSS). In addition, there are many content specific national organizations. If you had to choose only one to join, we believe the most important for a middle level social studies educator would be NCSS. With that said, the other organizations offer important content information, lesson plans and resources, as well as workshops and conferences. Table 15.1 provides a list of these organizations along with their websites.

TABLE 15.1. National Social Studies Related Professional Organizations

Organization	Website
Council for Economic Education	http://www.councilforecned.org/
National Council for Geographic Education	https://ncge.org/
National Council for History Education	http://www.nche.net/
National Council for the Social Studies	http://www.socialstudies.org/

State Social Studies Organizations

There are many state and regional social studies organizations that are affiliated with NCSS. Below is a list of these organizations, along with their websites. Most offer student membership discounts and we recommend that you join the one for your state if you have not done so already. These organizations have state-specific resources to assist you in meeting state standards and mandates, often provide innovative, state-specific conference presentations (particularly in state history and geography). They also provide wonderful networking opportunities convenient in geography and financial resources. Long-term engagement at state levels can even increase your influence on state policies and practices as state boards of education often turn to professional organizations when they wish to update learning standards. Table 15.2 provides a list of these organizations along with their websites.

TABLE 15.2. List of Local, State, and Regional Social Studies Councils

State	Organization	Website (if available)
AL	Social Studies Council for Alabama	https://www.alcss.org/
AK	Alaska Council for the Social Studies	https://www.akcss.org/
AZ	Arizona Council for the Social Studies	http://www.azsocialstudies.org
AR	Arkansas Council for the Social Studies	http://arkansascouncilforthesocialstudies.wildapricot.org/
CA	California Council for the Social Studies	https://www.ccss.org/
CA	Southern California Social Science Association	http://www.socalsocialscience.org/
CO	Colorado Council for the Social Studies	http://cosocialstudies.org/
CT	Connecticut Council for the Social Studies	http://www.ctsocialstudies.org/
DE	Social Studies Coalition of Delaware	http://www.sscde.org/
FL	Florida Council for the Social Studies	http://www.fcss.org/
GA	Georgia Council for the Social Studies	http://www.gcss.net/
ID	Idaho Council for the Social Studies	
IL, IN, OH, MI, MN, WI	Great Lakes Regional Council for the Social Studies	

TABLE 15.2. Continued

State	Organization	Website (if available)
IL	Illinois Council for the Social Studies	http://www.illinoiscss.org/
IN	Indiana Council for the Social Studies	http://indianasocialstudies.com/
IA	Iowa Council for the Social Studies	https://iowasocialstudies.org/
KS	Kansas Council for the Social Studies	https://www.kansascouncilss.org/
KY	Kentucky Council for the Social Studies	http://www.kysscouncil.org/
LA	Louisiana Council for the Social Studies	https://sites.google.com/ebrschools.org/lcss2018/home
ME	Maine Council for the Social Studies	http://www.mainecouncilsocialstudies.org/
MD	Maryland Council for the Social Studies	http://www.mdcss.org/
MA	Massachusetts Council for the Social Studies	http://www.masscouncil.org/
MI	Michigan Council for the Social Studies	http://www.mcssmi.org/
MN	Minnesota Council for the Social Studies	http://www.mcss.org
MS	Mississippi Council for the Social Studies	http://www.mcss.org.msstate.edu/
MO	Missouri Council for the Social Studies	http://www.mosocialstudies.com/
MT	Montana Council for the Social Studies	
NE	Nebraska Council for the Social Studies	http://www.nebraskasocialstudiescouncil.org/
NA	Northern Nevada Council for the Social Studies	http://www.nvsocialstudies.org/
NV	Southern Nevada Council for the Social Studies	http://sncss.weebly.com/
NH	New Hampshire Council for the Social Studies	http://www.nhcss.org/
NJ	New Jersey Council for the Social Studies	http://www.njcss.org/
NM	New Mexico Council for the Social Studies	http://www.nmcss.org/
NY	New York State Council for the Social Studies	https://nyscss.wildapricot.org/
NY	Capital District Council for the Social Studies	http://www.cdcss.wildapricot.org/
NY	Central New York Council for the Social Studies	http://www.cnycss.memberlodge.com/
NY	Long Island Council for the Social Studies	http://www.licss.net/
NY	Westchester-Lower Hudson Council for the Social Studies	http://www.wlhcss.info/
NC	North Carolina Council for the Social Studies	http://ncsocialstudies.org/
OH	Ohio Council for the Social Studies	https://ocss.org/
OK	Oklahoma Council for the Social Studies	http://www.okcss.org/
OR	Oregon Council for the Social Studies	http://www.oregonsocialstudies.org/
PA	Pennsylvania Council for the Social Studies	http://pcssonline.org/
PA, NJ, DE, MD, and DC	Middle States Regional Council for the Social Studies	http://www.midstatescouncil.org/
RI	Rhode Island Council for the Social Studies	https://www.risocialstudies.org/

(continues)

TABLE 15.2. Continued

State	Organization	Website (if available)
SC	South Carolina Council for the Social Studies	http://www.sccss.org/
SD	The Great Plains Social Studies Council	https://greatplainssocialstudies.weebly.com/
TN	Tennessee Council for the Social Studies	http://www.tncss.org/
TX	Texas Council for the Social Studies	https://www.txcss.net/
UT	Utah Council for the Social Studies	http://utahcouncilsocialstudies.weebly.com/
VA	Virginia Council for the Social Studies	http://www.vcss.org/
WA	Washington Council for the Social Studies	http://www.wscss.org/
WV	West Virginia Council for the Social Studies	http://wvcss.edublogs.org
WI	Wisconsin Council for the Social Studies	http://www.wcss-wi.org/

INTERNAL ADVOCACY

Participating in Textbook and Curriculum Committees

As a social studies teacher you may have the opportunity to participate in textbook and curriculum committees for your district and state. We believe serving on these committees is important for several reasons. For one, you will become a content expert on the topic that you teach, especially if you teach the same subject for several years. As these committees are open to the public, your expert opinion should be heard during meetings. As shown by controversies regarding mandatory curriculum in Texas and state history textbook controversies in Virginia, it is vital for those involved in teaching the subject to have their voices and experiences heard. Otherwise those who do not have a background in education will make decisions for both you and your students.

Serving as a Role Model at Your School

As the recognized social studies expert in your school, it is up to you to serve as a role model for those in your local environments. Since most middle level teachers work on a team, you can start small by being a team leader or taking on responsibilities such as contacting parent volunteers. In turn, coming to work every day with a positive attitude and a willingness to share and collaborate with other teachers at your school also makes you a role model. Your administrators, your colleagues, and most importantly, your students will see how you approach your subject and your profession. For example, Karrie served as the Curriculum Teacher Leader for her school. Through this position, she attended professional development and conferences, led teacher professional learning, modeled lessons for other teachers, and organized school wide events such as the annual Veteran's Day program and a Black History Month interactive museum.

Another example of being a role model can be working with older teachers who may be showing signs of burnout. Such teachers may sincerely appreciate having the opportunity to hear about your creative teaching ideas and ways to make their classes not only interesting for them but for their students. As a new teacher, there is nothing wrong with sharing your ideas, activities, and lesson plans. In fact, you will be surprised at how many veteran teachers will ask you directly if you could offer them some ideas about teaching social studies. Even without saying a thing, displaying student work in the hallway that shows the effectiveness of strategies that you have learned in your classes and from this book, will have both new and veteran teachers asking you how you conducted the lesson and if you would be willing to share the material with them.

EXTERNAL ADVOCACY

It should come as no surprise that your local community may identify you as an expert in social studies. From social media to local presentations at libraries and civic organizations, your professional communication can help advance civic dialogue and appreciation for the wonderfully complex world of social studies. How you communicate and engage in local, state, and national communities says much about you as a professional and as a person. We encourage you to consider all settings as opportunities to inform the public regarding social studies concepts.

Keeping up-to-date with state legislation regarding social studies and topics that may impact social studies is essential to proactively advocating for your profession. Contacting legislators, letters to editors of local news outlets, and attendance at civic events demonstrates your commitment to your students and your chosen subject.

SUMMARY

In this chapter we discussed ways that you can advance from being a social studies teacher to becoming a social studies professional. Some of these steps will present themselves after you have taught for a year or two. Others, such as joining a national and state social studies organization and volunteering both in your community and for the field, can start today. You are the future of social studies education. It is up to you to continue to stand up for its importance and take an active role in ensuring that the subject and all that goes along with it continue over the next several decades.

COLLABORATIVE ACTIVITY: REFLECTING ON THE CHAPTER

After reading the chapter, reflect on what it takes to be a social studies professional. Then answer the following questions and discuss with a classmate:

- What is the difference between a social studies teacher and a social studies professional?

- What are some things you can start doing now to become a social studies professional?
- Review the website of your state social studies council. What are some of the benefits of being a member of this group?

WEB RESOURCES

- **Council for Higher Education** (https://www.chea.org/search-programs) this organization offers prospective graduate students to "search over 44,000 accredited programs by type or accrediting organization."
- **National Board for Professional Teaching Standards** (https://www.nbpts.org/vision/) is a national organization that works to; "…advance the quality of teaching and learning through a voluntary advanced certification."

REFERENCES

Chang, M-L., Abellán, I. M., Wright, J, Kim, J., & Gaines, R. E. (2020). Do advanced degrees matter? A multiphase mixed-methods study to examine teachers' obtainment of advanced degrees and the impact on student and school growth. *Georgia Educational Researcher, 17(1)*, 61–89. DOI: 10.20429/ger.2020.170105

Clement, M. (2019). A dozen things effective teacher mentors do. *Delta Kappa Gamma Bulletin, 85(4)*, 27–29.

Crow, T. (2008). Let's make it our job to find solutions. *The Learning Professional, 29*(1), 4.

Katz, L. G. (1972). *Developmental stages of preschool teachers.* Educational Resources Information Center Clearinghouse on Early Childhood Education.

Kelly, N., Sim, C., & Ireland, M. (2018). Slipping through the cracks: Teachers who miss out on early career support. *Asia-Pacific Journal of Teacher Education, 46(3)*, 292–316. https://doi.org/10.1080/1359866X.2018.1441366

Poulton, M. (2005). *The Canterbury Tales: Geoffrey Chaucer; An adaptation in two parts by Mike Poulton.* Nick Hern Books in association with the Royal Shakespeare Company.

Stroot, S., Keil, V., Stedman, P., Lohr, L., Faust, R., & Schincariol-Randall, L. (1998). *Peer Assistance and Review Guidebook.* Ohio Department of Education.

Sutcher, L., Darling-Hammond, L., & Carver-Thomas, D. (2016). *A coming crisis in teaching? Teacher supply, demand, and shortages in the U.S.* Learning Policy Institute.

Warsame, K., & Valles, J. (2018). An analysis of effective support structures for novice teachers. *Journal of Teacher Education and Educators, 7*(1), 17–42.

Zeaman, D. (1959). *Skinner's theory of teaching machines. Automatic teaching: The state of the art* (pp. 167–176).

CHAPTER 16

CONCLUDING REMARKS

As we come to the end of the third edition of the book, we confess that writing this was not an easy task. What kept us going was believing that we would help to develop great middle level social studies teachers by sharing the knowledge we accumulated in our careers. In some cases, this book is much like others on the market. Most books help you learn what social studies is, how to create engaging and important social studies lessons, and how to cope with the influence of federal mandates, state and national standards, and high-stakes testing. This book, however, provided unique information about how to teach state history courses, critically important information about how to build literacy skills, Additionally, we believe it is okay to occasionally use your social studies textbook and to lecture, provided in-depth information about how to teach using standards-based practices, and more importantly, it explained your unique role as a ***middle grades*** social studies teacher.

Through this text we hoped to provide you with a book that was easy to read and one that offered you many of the most important things to know about teaching a specific grade level band: middle level social studies. We worked to provide you with direction toward the most accurate social studies information and the best strategies we have found and used in our roles as middle level teachers, college professors, and professional developers. Of course, as we conclude, we feel that we must have missed something or should have given you just one more article, website, strategy, or lesson idea. Still, we could not conclude this book without leaving you with a summary of what we hope were the most important themes, and to offer you a few more pointers about how to teach social studies to 4th–8th graders. You will find these ideas and suggestions below.

MIDDLE LEVEL STUDENTS CAN DO THIS

The most important idea that you should have learned from this book is that middle level students are just as capable as high school students in learning from hands-on, progressive, and complex activities. Contrary to popular views, it is our experiences that middle grades students are deep thinkers, energetic learners, and as worthy of our attention and our efforts as any other age group. The strategies, methods, and lessons that we have shared in this book are all research based or ones that we have used that were successful in our own middle level social studies classes. Bluntly, we learn time and again to not underestimate the ability, skill, articulation, and passion of young adolescents. While some of the lessons such as inquiry may seem daunting, they can be completed by any middle level students no matter their ability levels. You should attempt to use these ideas from the first day you teach (yes, this means student teaching). While you will adapt some of these approaches to meet the needs of your students, these lessons will help with their literacy skills, help students learn to love social studies, and help them understand the subject's importance to their lives, all while having fun in your classes.

PEDAGOGY AND CONTENT KNOWLEDGE ARE EQUALLY IMPORTANT

As Conklin (2010, 2012) and Conklin and Daigle (2012) point out, there is a key difference between the training received by middle and secondary level social studies teachers. Her work shows these teachers have different ideas about how to teach middle school students. For instance, secondary level trained teachers who find themselves at the middle level tend to have great content knowledge about a specific subject but teach their students with traditional techniques such as lectures and worksheets, believing that these students cannot handle more complex lessons. On the other hand, elementary and middle level trained teachers tend to come to the middle level classroom armed with the proper pedagogy for teaching 10–15-year-olds, but often lack the content knowledge needed to teach the subject effectively. It is our hope that through continued professional development, you will work on whichever you believe to be your weakness. Being equipped with both the pedagogy and content knowledge is imperative when teaching at the middle level. Our students need teachers who know what they are teaching about, while using methods that provide students with opportunities to become independent learners.

In Scott's personal experience, for example, he severely lacked both content knowledge and skill in using progressive methods when he started teaching three years after graduating from college. While Scott found himself learning the Georgia studies content knowledge on his own in addition to gaining the best practices for teaching middle level students through trial and error, there are many resources you can use to gain immediate knowledge of both. National and state level organizations offer great learning opportunities and resources. The Internet provides you with thousands of websites that can help as well. In addition, take the initiative and use other resources to help you become a better teacher. Use your planning time to observe some of the more respected teachers in your school (those who teach your grade level and subject area as well as those that do not).

Your college courses cannot teach you everything you need to know to be an effective teacher because the context in which you teach informs how you interact with your students. Karrie remembers feeling woefully unprepared as a first-year teacher. She learned more during her first year in the classroom than she did in all of her years as an undergraduate education major. Student histories and cultures, school policy and procedure, state standards and mandates, among other historical and cultural contexts deeply inform classroom teaching. It will take an individual effort by you to effectively apply your knowledge in your unique environment. While it is a lot of hard work, your students deserve the best social studies teacher possible.

USE MODERATION AND VARIETY

Contrary to what you may have heard or read in your classes, occasionally using the textbook to teach social studies is perfectly okay. So are using worksheets, lectures, and movies. You should also use inquiry-based lessons, K-W-L charts, Venn Diagrams, and all manner of traditional and progressive approaches to teach social studies. The keys to teaching are simple: use moderation and adjust to the needs of your students. The hard part is figuring out what moderation and adjustment look like. One way to help is to use a variety of strategies and approaches to teaching social studies. Keep your students guessing about what is coming next and always find ways to differentiate your instruction. Every lesson can be scaffolded to meet the ability levels of all learners in your classroom.

TIP OF THE ICEBERG

We have provided you with several strategies and lesson ideas throughout the book. However, these are just the tip of the iceberg. Most of the websites we have listed have thousands of lesson plans that you can adapt and use in your classes. In turn, many of the references for each chapter often provide the most recent and important research, along with practical ideas that you can use to become a better social studies teacher or strategies that have been proven to be effective with students. We encourage you to go back and examine the websites and references and start building your own library for each. You will certainly find that adding your own flavor to the approaches and lessons will make them more meaningful for your students.

THE EXCITING FUTURE OF SOCIAL STUDIES

Fundamental changes to the federal initiatives, wide employment of the C3 Framework, and ongoing controversies surrounding Common Core and the politicized nature of curriculum attest to the maelstrom that is current education policy. Daily, it seems, there are suggestions for fundamental changes to how classrooms, learning, and professionalism are to look. No sooner does a teacher gain competence in a standard or approach than politicians or citizen groups criticize it as being inadequate or damaging. We can only hope that due to advocacy of social studies teachers, researchers, and organizations, along with politicians recognizing their own mistakes, the climate will settle into effective approaches and professionalism in the future.

It appears that this renewal has started happening as we have been writing this book. As a social studies teacher, you will more than likely be asked to take the lead in developing lessons that will aid your school in excelling on these tests. We truly believe that both these events will bring social studies back into the forefront of public education.

We are also excited about the improvements in technology and the vast array of Internet resources that are being developed daily. Unlike technological changes in the past, these websites allow students to be both consumers and producers of information. If properly used, cloud-based schools of today and tomorrow will aid in the understanding of social studies topics and help us meet many of the goals of social studies education.

BECOMING A SOCIAL STUDIES PROFESSIONAL

There is an important difference between being a social studies teacher and being a social studies professional. A social studies teacher simply goes to class every day, teaches students for seven hours, and then goes home. A social studies professional, on the other hand, strives to improve his or her content knowledge and pedagogy every day. They do this by earning advanced degrees, by watching the best teachers in their schools, joining professional organizations, attending conferences, and staying abreast of new social studies research and practices that are being released every day. As a college student and student teacher you can begin this journey by joining a professional organization, selecting and reading research about social studies topics you are interested in, observing the strengths and weaknesses of your host teacher, using a balance of traditional and progressive practices when you teach, and volunteering in your school and community for social studies-oriented events.

101 RESOURCES

Throughout the book we have introduced you to strategies and methods that can help as you begin your lesson planning. In Appendix A you will discover a blank lesson plan template you can use as a guide in creating your own social studies lesson for your classes, student teaching (and if you keep the book, your first classroom). In Appendix B, you will find a completed lesson plan based on the template for 8th grade American history students. This lesson plan is based on Roberts and Elfer's (2018, 2021) *Hollywood or History?* strategy and was presented at the 2019 National Council for History Education Conference. This lesson plan can also be adapted for 4th and 5th grade United States history classes. In Appendix C-F you will find tables highlighting 25 lesson plans, resources, and practitioner (teacher) focused articles for each of the four primary disciplines of social studies (economics, geography, government and history). These lesson plans and articles were found on well-respected websites as well as journals such as *The History Teacher, Middle Level Learning, Social Education, The Social Studies, Social Studies Research and Practice* and *Social Studies and the Young Learner.* Some of these articles are accessible to the public, but some are not. If you are still a college/university student, you should be able to locate many of these articles through your library or by joining the National Council for the Social Studies.

CONTACT US

We are and will always be teachers and teacher educators first and writers/researchers second. While we enjoy writing about the subject we love, our top priority is supporting teachers, both pre-service and those already in the classroom. With that said, please feel free to contact us if you have any questions or comments about this book. It would be great to hear from you. Like all textbook writers we have striven to make this book so good that there will be future editions for many years to come. Any feedback that you can provide will help us make future editions better. If you would like to contact us for any reason the best way is to email us directly.

- Scott L. Roberts, Ph.D.: sroberts16@hotmail.com or rober4s@cmich.edu
- Benjamin R. Wellenreiter, Ed.D.: brwelle@ilstu.edu or bwellenreiter@gmail.com
- Jessica Ferreras-Stone, Ph.D.: Jessica.Stone@wwu.edu
- Stephanie L. Strachan, Ph.D.: strachs@wwu.edu
- Karrie L. Palmer, Ed. S.: karriepalmer1977@gmail.com or palmer.karrie@mail.fcboe.org

We wish you the best as you begin your career as a middle grades social studies educator. Though there are many challenges that lie ahead, we know you will rise to meet them.

REFERENCES

Conklin, H. G. (2010). Preparing for the educational black hole? Teachers' learning into two pathways into middle school social studies teaching. *Theory and Research in Social Education, 38*(1), 48–79.

Conklin, H. G. (2012). Company men: Tracing learning from divergent teacher education pathways into practice in middle grades classrooms. *Journal of Teacher Education, 63*(3), 171–184.

Conklin, H. G., & Daigle, E. (2012). Toolboxes for teaching in the middle grades: Opportunities to learn in two preparation pathways. *Theory & Research in Social Education, 40*(2), 164–191.

Roberts, S. L., & Elfer, C. J. (Eds.) (2018). *Hollywood or history? An inquiry-based strategy for using film to teach United States history.* Information Age Publishing.

Roberts, S. L., & Elfer, C. J. (Eds.). (2021). *Hollywood or history? An inquiry-based strategy for using film to teach world history.* Information Age Publishing.

APPENDICES

TEACHING MIDDLE LEVEL SOCIAL STUDIES: A PRACTICAL GUIDE FOR 4TH–8TH GRADES

APPENDIX A

LESSON PLAN TEMPLATE

Lesson Name			
Grade	Subject		Topic
Estimated Time Needed for Lesson:			
State and Common Core Standard	Description		
Standard Number	Detailed description of each standard you are discussing.		
Common Core			

Teaching Middle Level Social Studies: A Practical Guide for 4th–8th Grade (3rd Edition),
pages 371–374.
Copyright © 2022 by Information Age Publishing
www.infoagepub.com
All rights of reproduction in any form reserved.

NCSS C3 Framework	Description
Dimension	Detailed description of each NCSS Dimension you are incorporating (Should have all four).

NCSS Core Themes	Description
Theme Number	Detailed description of each NCSS theme you are incorporating.

Handouts/Materials/Web Links

Handout/Materials:

Guiding Questions

What should students know or understand at the completion of the unit or lesson?

Primary Questions:

Additional Questions:

Important Vocabulary

List all of the important indicators of achievement (important people, places, and events) and vocabulary that students will need to know at the conclusion of the lesson.

Assessment Strategies

Lesson Plan Template • 373

| Describe the assessments that will be used during the unit. |

Teaching Strategies

Time		Time		Time			
				Time Remaining/ HMWK			
Time		Time					
		Times are highly flexible and should be adjusted according to number of sources used, length of introduction, period/block schedule, etc.					

Sparking Strategy/Warm-Up

Sparking Strategy (Lesson introduction)

Lesson Procedures

In a numerical list provide a step by step outline of what you plan to do in the lesson. Include questions you will ask the students and materials you will use.

Outline:

Differentiation

Think about your students' skill levels, intelligences, and learning styles. How are you going to make this lesson meet the needs of all of your students?

Scaffolds:

ESL Interventions:

Extensions:

Summarizing Strategies/Synthesizing Activity
What strategies are you going to use to allow students to summarize what they learned in the lesson?
Citations

APPENDIX B

HOLLYWOOD OR HISTORY LESSON PLAN/GRAPHIC ORGANIZER

Lesson Name:		
Part 1: Lincoln's Political Power Part 2: Lincoln's Reconstruction Plans		
Grade	**Subject**	**Topic**
7–8 (Can be Adapted for 5th Grade U.S. History Courses)	U.S. History	Civil War/Reconstruction
Era Under Study	**Estimated Time Needed for Lesson**	
Era 5: Civil War and Reconstruction (1850–1877)	55 minutes (Part 1) 55 minutes (Part 2)	

Teaching Middle Level Social Studies: A Practical Guide for 4th–8th Grade (3rd Edition),
pages 375–381.
Copyright © 2022 by Information Age Publishing
www.infoagepub.com
All rights of reproduction in any form reserved.

State and Common Core Standard Connection	
State	Detailed description of each standard you are discussing.
Georgia	**SS8H5 Analyze the impact of the Civil War on Georgia.** a. Explain the importance of key issues and events that led to the Civil War; include slavery, states' rights, nullification, Compromise of 1850 and the Georgia Platform, the Dred Scott case, Abraham Lincoln's election in 1860, and the debate over secession in Georgia. b. Explain Georgia's role in the Civil War; include the Union blockade of Georgia's coast, the Emancipation Proclamation, Chickamauga, Sherman's Atlanta Campaign, Sherman's March to the Sea, and Andersonville. **SS8H6 Analyze the impact of Reconstruction on Georgia.** a. Explain the roles of the 13th, 14th, and 15th Amendments in Reconstruction. b. Explain the key features of the Lincoln, the Johnson, and the Congressional Reconstruction plans.
Illinois	**SS.IS.4.6-8.MC:** Gather relevant information from credible sources and determine whether they support each other. **SS.H.3.6-8.MdC:** Detect possible limitations in the historical record based on evidence collected from different kinds of historical sources
Washington D.C.	**8th Grade U.S. History:** Describe Abraham Lincoln's presidency and his significant writings and speeches and their relationship to the Declaration of Independence (e.g., his House Divided speech in 1858, Gettysburg Address in 1863, Emancipation Proclamation in 1863, and inaugural addresses in 1861 and 1865). (P)
Washington (State)	**H3.6-8.4** Analyze and interpret historical materials from a variety of perspectives in United States history (1763–1877). **H3.6-8.5** Analyze multiple causal factors to create positions on major events in United States history (1763–1877).
Common Core	CCSS.ELA-LITERACY.RH.6-8.6 Identify aspects of a text that reveal an author's point of view or purpose (e.g., loaded language, inclusion or avoidance of particular facts).

NCSS C3 Framework

Description	Dimension	Detailed description of each NCSS Dimension you are incorporating (Should have all four).
D1.5.6-8.		Determine the kinds of sources that will be helpful in answering compelling and supporting questions, taking into consideration multiple points of views represented in the sources.
D2.His.6.6-8.		Analyze how people's perspectives influenced what information is available in the historical sources they created.
D3.3.6-8.		Identify evidence that draws information from multiple sources to support claims, noting evidentiary limitations.
D4.1.6-8.		Construct arguments using claims and evidence from multiple sources, while acknowledging the strengths and limitations of the arguments.

NCSS Core Themes Descriptions

Theme Number	Detailed description of each NCSS theme you are incorporating.
Power, Authority and Governance	Social studies programs should include experiences that provide for the study of how people create, interact with, and change structures of power, authority, and governance
Individuals, Groups and Institutions	Social studies programs should include experiences that provide for the study of interactions among individuals, groups, and institutions
Time, Continuity, and Change	Studying the past makes it possible for us to understand the human story across time. Historical analysis enables us to identify continuities over time in core institutions, values, ideals, and traditions, as well as processes that lead to change within societies and institutions, and that result in innovation and the development of new ideas, values and ways of life.

Handouts/Materials/Web Links

Handout/Materials: Hollywood or History? Graphic Organizer

Web Links:
a. Link to Film Clip(s):
- CNN (2012) (Warm-Up) "Lincoln filmmakers get it wrong" https://www.youtube.com/watch?v=50bxP9b0aso
- Lincoln (2012) (Part 1): "Buzzards guts, man" (Lincoln as a Tyrant) https://www.youtube.com/watch?v=1qjtugr2618
- Lincoln (2012) (Part 2): "Liberality all around" (Presidential Reconstruction under Lincoln) https://www.youtube.com/watch?v=BAunpxS8GXo

b. Primary Source(s):
- Letter (Part 1) Abraham Lincoln, Letter to Horace Greely. August 22, 1862. Avail: http://www.abrahamlincolnonline.org/lincoln/speeches/greeley.htm
- Abraham Lincoln's Second Inaugural Address (Part II); endorsed by Lincoln, April 10. Avail: https://www.loc.gov/rr/program/bib/ourdocs/lincoln2nd.html

c. Secondary Source(s):
- Article Excerpt (Part 1): Hutchinson, Dennis J. (2010). "Lincoln the Dictator." South Dakota Law Review 55: 284 298.
- Textbook (Part 2): Shi, D. E & Tindall, G. B. (2016). America: A Narrative History, Vol 1. 10th Edition. New York: W.W. London and Company, 582–583.

Guiding Questions
What should students know or understand at the completion of the unit or lesson? **Primary Questions:**<ul><li>Explain the impact that the Abraham Lincoln had on the United States during the Civil War and on the office of the President.</li><li>How has Abraham Lincoln become a fixture in the national memory of the United States?</li><li>What do you think the Stephen Spielberg depicted Abraham Lincoln in the way that he did in the film Lincoln?</li><li>According to the primary and secondary sources is the depiction of Davy Crockett's death at the Alamo 100% fact, 100% fiction, or somewhere in between? Which movie clip do you believe is more accurate?</li><li>How do historical films (or other historically-themed materials) work to shape our understanding of historical figures and events?</li></ul>**Additional Questions:**<ul><li>What is a primary/secondary source?</li><li>What are ways to gain a better understanding of an historical event or person?</li><li>Which type of source is the most accurate primary/secondary? Why?</li></ul>
Important Vocabulary
List all of the important indicators of achievement (important people, places, and events) and vocabulary that students will need to know at the conclusion of the lesson.<ul><li>**Congressional Reconstruction** (1866–1867): The period when the South was placed under the authority of Congress. As a result, southern states were required to pass the 14th amendment in order to be readmitted into the Union.</li><li>**Greely, Horace** (1811–1872): an American author and statesman who was the founder and editor of the New-York Tribune, among the great newspapers of its time. Long active in politics, he served briefly as a congressman from New York, and was the unsuccessful candidate of the new Liberal Republican party in the 1872 presidential election against incumbent President Ulysses S. Grant. (Wikipedia)</li><li>**Lincoln, Abraham** (1809–1865): an American lawyer and politician who served as the 16th president of the United States from 1861 until his assassination in April 1865. Lincoln led the nation through the American Civil War, its bloodiest war and its greatest moral, constitutional, and political crisis.[2][3] He preserved the Union, abolished slavery, strengthened the federal government, and modernized the U.S. economy. (Wikipedia)</li><li>**Presidential Reconstruction** (1865–1866) During this plan, President Johnson, a native of Tennessee who stayed loyal to the Union, was extremely lenient with the southern states. His plan, based on that of Abraham Lincoln who had been assassinated in April of 1865, allowed the South readmission in into the Union if 10% of the population swore an oath of allegiance to the United States. They also were required to ratify the 13th amendment, which officially ended slavery in the United States. (GA DOE 8th Grade Georgia Studies Teaching Notes).</li><li>**Thirteenth Amendment** abolished slavery and involuntary servitude, except as punishment for a crime. In Congress, it was passed by the Senate on April 8, 1864, and by the House on January 31, 1865. The amendment was ratified by the required number of states on December 6, 1865. On December 18, 1865, Secretary of State William H. Seward proclaimed its adoption. It was the first of the three Reconstruction Amendments adopted following the American Civil War. (Wikipedia)</li></ul>

Assessment Strategies

Describe the assessments that will be used during the unit.
    Formative Assessment—Round table discussion, History vs. Hollywood worksheets, Line of
        Contention.
    Summative Assessment- "What do you Think? History vs Hollywood" essays.

Teaching Strategies (Part 1 and 2)

10 min	Roundtable Group Discussion/ Lecture	15min	Primary Sources and Secondary Source Analysis Completion of Graphic Organizer/position statement	10min	Line of Contention
5min	View clips from: Lincoln (2012)	10min		Time Remaining/ HMWK	History vs. Hollywood?: Conclusion/Summary/ Extension
		\multicolumn{4}{l}{Times are highly flexible and should be adjusted according to number of sources used, length of introduction, period/block schedule, etc.}			

Sparking Strategy/Warm-Up

Sparking Strategy (Lesson introduction)
    Have students discuss some movies, video games, documentaries or books that focus on historical topics. Ask students how reliable they think these sources are in describing historical events. Show CNN News clip about the inaccuracies of the film Lincoln (2012).

Lesson Procedures

In a numerical list provide a step by step outline of what you plan to do in the lesson. Include questions you will ask the students and materials you will use.

Outline:

Part 1:

1a. Start with a roundtable group discussion – spark ideas about how social elements like movies, video games, documentaries, or books that focus on history shape our understanding of people and events. Provide a few examples; ask students to provide additional examples and explanations. Then ask to students to discuss which sources are "more accurate" than others and why. After this discussion have students watch the CNN News Clip about the inaccuracies of Lincoln (2012). Ask students why they think the film makers would include such inaccurate information about Connecticut's 13th Amendment vote.

1b. Alternatively, teachers might instead begin the lesson with a similar discussion about a more localized topic that is linked to the broader concept of the Civil War, Reconstruction, or Abraham Lincoln. Other questions could be about how famous people and events from this era have impacted the United States, socially, politically, etc.

2.	Deliver a mini-lecture on the Abraham Lincoln's role as president during the Civil War with special emphasis on the immigration from the Lincoln's political power, his role in passing the 13th amendment, and his Reconstruction plans (much of this should have been taught in a prior lesson). Reveal to students that they are going to learn about an aspect of these events and why it is important to understand the strengths and limitations of primary and secondary sources in our understanding of history.
3.	Explain to students that there have been several films depicting Abraham Lincoln. Explain to students that Lincoln has been the subject of several books, movies, T.V. shows, and plays. However, the films may or may not attempt to offer an accurate account of the events of Lincoln's life and Presidency. Introduce the Hollywood or History? graphic organizer handout and work with students to detail how they can use the outline to record information during the film clip and document analysis that they will take part in.
4.	Display the Part 1 clips of the Lincoln (links included above and on handouts). If teachers want to show the entire films, we recommend finding time to show the film in full but breaking it up into sections and have students use multiple sources to analyze each segment of the film.
5.	Have students analyze their primary source and secondary source. Multiple sources have been included to provide teachers with a variety of options. For more advanced students, teachers may elect to use more than one primary/secondary document, or, alternatively, to run through the initial phases of the exercise and introduce new documents after students form their initial perceptions.
6.	Students individually conclude whether the "Buzzards guts, Man" scene is History, Hollywood, or both by drafting a short statement/paragraph citing evidence from each source. Space is included on the graphic organizer handout.
7.	Use a "Line of Contention," or similar whole group debriefing approach, to allow students to share their thoughts. Draw a line on the board to demonstrate the continuum of thoughts. On one side of the line, write 100% history. Students who stand there are making the claim that the movie clip is 100% accurate and factual. On the other side of the line, write 100% Hollywood. If students stand next to this part of the line they are making the claim that there is nothing factual about the scene they watched. Allow studies to stand at any point of the line they wish (i.e., 25% history, 75% Hollywood, etc.). Most important are student explanations and efforts should be made to reference the document collections.

Part 2:

1.	Tell students they are going to analyze a second clip for them film with additional sources. Go through the same process as Part 1 but using the "Liberality All Around" clip and Part 2 documents.
2a.	If time is available include a roundtable discussion with groups to re-evaluate their knowledge and what they learned from the Hollywood or History? assignment including one or more of the guiding questions provided.
2b.	Teachers might also elect to introduce one of the other documents to the discussion. How does this new piece of evidence change or reinforce students' original positions?

Differentiation

Think about your students' skill levels, intelligences, and learning styles. How are you going to make this lesson meet the needs of all of your students?

Scaffolds: Work with students individually if needed to answer questions and further explain any material. Make sure that the student table groups have mixed students so that higher achieving students are working with/helping their classmates.

ESL Interventions: Provide vocabulary terms pertaining to the era of prohibition with useful synonyms and definitions/description in order to give students background knowledge and vocabulary helps as they move through the lesson itself. Consider selecting among the sources with images, or finding additional documents, from the source collections provided.

Extensions: Have students write a letter or make a video telling a younger student about the complexities the potential biases and inaccuracies found in Hollywood film and what they should do to be better informed about historical figures and events that are portrayed in movies.

Summarizing Strategies/Synthesizing Activity

What strategies are you going to use to allow students to summarize what they learned in the lesson?
- Strategies we will use:
- Hollywood or History?
- Student-generated position statements with reference to documents/evidence
- Line of Contention
- Roundtable Discussion

Citations

Teaching with Film:
- Marcus, A., & Stoddard, J. (2007). Tinsel Town as teacher: Hollywood film in the high school classroom. +(3), 303–330.
- Marcus, A. S., Metzger, S. A., Paxton, R. J., & Stoddard, J. D. (2018). *Teaching history with film: Strategies for secondary social studies*. Routledge.
- Matz, K., & Pingatore, L. (2005). Reel to reel: Teaching the Twentieth Century with classic Hollywood films. *Social Education, 69*(4), 189–192.
- Roberts, S. L. (2014). Effectively using social studies textbooks in historical inquiry. *Social Studies Research and Practice, 9*(1), 119–128.
- Roberts, S. L., & Elfer, C. J. (2018). *Hollywood or History? An inquiry-based strategy for using film to teach United States history*. Information Age Publishing.
- Roberts, S. L., & Elfer, C. J. (2021). *Hollywood or History? An inquiry-based strategy for using film to teach World history*. Information Age Publishing.
- Russell, W. B. (2007). *Using film in social studies*. University Press of America.
- Russell, W. B. (2012). The reel history of the world: Teaching world history with major motion pictures. *Social Education, 76*(1), 22–28.
- Russell, W. B., & Waters, S. (2017). *Cinematic social studies: A resource for teaching and learning social studies through film*. Information Age Publishing.
- Wineburg, S., Mosborg, S., & Porat, D. (2001). What can Forrest Gump tell us about students' historical understanding? *Social education, 65*(1), 55.

APPENDIX C

25 RESOURCES FOR TEACHING HISTORY

APPENDIX C BEGINS ON THE FOLLOWING PAGE.

Teaching Middle Level Social Studies: A Practical Guide for 4th–8th Grade (3rd Edition),
pages 383–387.
Copyright © 2022 by Information Age Publishing
www.infoagepub.com
All rights of reproduction in any form reserved.

	Author(s)/ Organization	Title	Location	Description
1.	Kenneth Anthony and Mary Katherine Morgan	Ulysses S. Grant Manumits William Jones: An example of America's entanglement with slavery	https://www.socialstudies.org/middle-level-learning/September-2015	Explores the lesser-known history of Ulysses S. Grant. Provides primary-source documents.
2.	Anti-Defamation League	N/A	https://www.adl.org/education-and-resources/resources-for-educators-parents-families/lessons	This website hosts a variety of lesson plans that inspire inclusive social studies that teaches knowledge of the past in order to understand current injustices.
3.	C3 Teachers	N/A	https://c3teachers.org/	The C3 Teachers Website offers over 100 free inquiry-based history lesson plans. Topics include Ancient, European, United States, World, and local/state history.
4.	Jeremiah Clabough and John H. Bickford III	Birmingham and the human costs of industrialization: Using the C3 framework to explore the "Magic City" in the Gilded Age	https://www.socialstudies.org/middle-level-learning/september-2018	A lesson that blends economics with social justice. Using Birmingham Alabama as a case study, it asks the question: "Were the benefits of Birmingham's industrialization worth the costs?"
5.	Sara B Demoiny and Jessica Ferreras-Stone	Critical Literacy in Elementary Social Studies: Juxtaposing Historical Master and Counter Narratives in Picture Books	https://www.tandfonline.com/doi/abs/10.1080/00377996.2018.1451981	The lesson plan in this article describes how critical literacy can be used to teach about the forced removal of Indigenous peoples in a way that honors multiple perspectives and invites students to consider how different individuals might retell the story.
6.	Facing History and Ourselves	N/A	https://www.facinghistory.org	This site provides resources addressing racism, antisemitism, and prejudice in history and current day events
7.	Jessica Ferreras-Stone	Women's Suffrage: Teaching Voting Rights Through Inclusive Social Studies	https://www.socialstudies.org/social-studies-and-young-learner/33/2	This lesson describes how to teach about women's suffrage while attending to intersectionality of oppression. The lesson details ways to teach about Indigenous, Chinese and Black suffragists.

25 Resources for Teaching History • 385

	Author(s)/Organization	Title	Location	Description
8.	Jessica Ferreras-Stone and Sara B Demoiny	Why are People Marching? Using Picture Books to Discuss Justice-Oriented Citizenship with Elementary Students	https://www.socialstudies.org/social-studies-and-young-learner/32/1	The lesson plan in this article outlines how integrating children's literature, which presents accurate content regarding political activism, can lay the groundwork for discussing and answering student's curiosity regarding marches as a form of activism.
9.	Eric Chandler Groce, Tina L. Heafner, and Margaret Norville Gregor	Jim Crow riding shotgun: Navigating racial discrimination in America	https://www.socialstudies.org/middle-level-learning/66	This lesson plan series explores interrelationships between Jim Crow laws, Black Codes, transportation discrimination and the Black experience in the South.
10.	Dan Krutka and Michael Milton	Visions of Education	https://visionsofed.com/podcast/	This weekly podcast between an education professor and high school educator focuses on pertinent issues in the field of social studies.
11.	Montclair State University	Black Civil Rights and Black Lives Matter	https://www.montclair.edu/holocaust-genocide-and-human-rights-education-project/wp-content/uploads/sites/176/2018/10/BlackLivesMatterIILessonPlan.pdf	This lesson specifically seeks to understand the origins of and current objectives of the Black Lives Matter Movement. In particular, the lesson seeks to identify and correct possible misconceptions.
12.	NCSS Notable Tradebooks for Young People	N/A	https://www.socialstudies.org/notable-social-studies-trade-books	An annual curated lists of texts for K–8 students on a wide range of social studies topics.
13.	Our Family Coalition and FAIR Education Act Implementation Coalition	Teaching LGTBQ History	http://www.lgbtqhistory.org/lesson-plans/	This website has 20 middle grade lesson plans that describe how to teach LGTBQ History. For example, a lesson entitled "Brother Outsider" describes the role Bayard Rustin played in the civil rights movement.

	Author(s)/ Organization	Title	Location	Description
14.	PBS	Latino Americans	http://www.pbs.org/latino-americans/en/education/lesson-plans/	This website has five lesson plans focusing on Latinx and U.S. History. For example, one lesson describes stereotypes and statistics and another lesson focuses on Latinos at the ballot box.
15.	Scott L. Roberts	Keep'em Guessing: Using Student Predictions to Inform Historical Understanding and Empathy	http://www.socstrpr.org/wp-content/uploads/2017/01/MS06545-Roberts.pdf	Authors frequently discuss and provide examples of doing history in the social studies classroom. Few focus, however, on allowing students to predict the outcome of historical events before learning what actually happened. In this article, I describe an activity allowing students to make their own predictions informing their understanding of the historical events related to Articles of Confederation. I developed this strategy based on my evolving understanding of how to bring historical thinking into the classroom. I discuss adding the concept of prediction to a previously published lesson plan and how, during my subsequent year in the classroom, I enriched the lesson to elicit student empathy. Finally, the article offers suggestions for teachers developing their own lessons incorporating student predictions.
16.	Scott L. Roberts and Meghan K. Block	Using "Open" and "Inquiry-Focused" Standards to Study Important Women in Iowa's History	https://iowasocialstudies.org/resources/Documents/IJSS%20Summer%202020%2028(2).pdf#page=108	This article provides middle level social studies teachers with a lesson idea for purposefully studying important women at the fifth-grade level. This article offers a step-by-step inquiry-based lesson that will help integrate elements of literacy, the Common Core, and the NCSS C3 Framework.
17.	Scott L. Roberts and Jeremiah Clabough	Using the C3 Framework to Evaluate the Legacy of Southern Segregationist Senators	https://www.tandfonline.com/doi/abs/10.1080/00377996.2021.1871580?src=&journalCode=vtss20	This article offers middle level state and U.S. history teachers an inquiry-based lesson plan describing how to use the Great/Not So Great Framework to analyze historic figures.
18.	Scott L. Roberts and Charles Elfer (Editors)	Hollywood or History?	https://www.infoagepub.com/series/Hollywood-or-History	The Hollywood or History? book series offers several inquiry-based lessons about effectively using Hollywood film and T.V. shows in the social studies classroom.

25 Resources for Teaching History • 387

	Author(s)/Organization	Title	Location	Description
19.	R. Zackary Seitz and Prentice T. Chandler	Celebrate freedom Week: Recalling the "Literacy Test" to vote	https://www.socialstudies.org/middle-level-learning/57	This lesson series explores the unconstitutional barriers presented by literacy tests.
20.	Southern Poverty Law Center	Learning for Justice	https://www.learningforjustice.org/classroom-resources/lessons	The Learning for Justice Website offers over 250 free social studies lessons for middle grade learners ranging in various topics. These lessons specifically attend to how social justice can be taught in social studies.
21.	The Stanford History Education Group	Reading Like a Historian	https://sheg.stanford.edu/history-lessons	The Stanford History Education Group offers over 150 free inquiry-based lesson plans about U.S. and World history.
22.	Washington Office of Superintendent of Public Instruction	Since Time Immemorial	https://www.k12.wa.us/student-success/resources-subject-area/time-immemorial-tribal-sovereignty-washington-state/middle-school-curriculum	The Since Time Immemorial is a mandated Indigenous curriculum in the state of Washington. It serves as an example of how Indigenous knowledge can be taught in middle grades.
23.	University of Minnesota	Teaching Immigration with the Immigrant Stories Project	https://www.ilctr.org/wp-content/uploads/2018/10/Teaching-Immigration-with-the-Immigrant-Stories-Project-FINAL_opt.pdf	This compilation of lesson plans helps students learn about various aspects of United States immigration both past and present through the personal experiences of immigrants and refugees.
24.	Jing A. Williams, Deborah Check Reeves, and Paige M. Wright	Civil War drummer boys: Integrating music into social studies	https://www.socialstudies.org/middle-level-learning/65	This lesson explores the lives and stories of drummer boys in the Civil War. It provides some common drumming patterns used in the Civil War.
25.	Zinn Education Project	N/A	https://www.zinnedproject.org	This project supports the teaching of history in middle/high school classrooms and provides lesson plans and units organized by time period, theme, and resource type.

APPENDIX D

25 RESOURCES FOR TEACHING GEOGRAPHY

APPENDIX D BEGINS ON THE FOLLOWING PAGE.

Author(s)/ Organization	Title	Location	Description
1. Carol Bliese & Lindsey Bailey	Hands-on Human Geography for a Rapidly Changing Planet	https://www.socialstudies.org/professional-learning/hands-human-geography-rapidly-changing-planet	In this webinar, participants will discover hands-on activities that build global awareness on population dynamics, land use patterns and environmental impacts (deforestation, climate change, and biodiversity loss) while cultivating critical thinking and problem-solving skills, communication and creativity. The presenters will explore the many applications to the four dimensions of the C3 Framework and how to lead inquiry-based lessons around timely events and trends.
2. Lisa Brown Buchanan, Christina M. Tschida, and Seth N. Brown	Integrating Mapping and ELA Skills Using Giant Traveling Maps	https://eric.ed.gov/?id=EJ1226190	In this article, "the authors describe the traveling map program and related materials, present a geography themed text set to use in conjunction with map rentals, and offer suggestions for using the giant maps in your school."
3. C3 Teachers	N/A	https://c3teachers.org/	The C3 Teachers Website offers over 15 free inquiry-based history lesson plans for teaching Geography.
4. Nazlı Gökçe	An implementation of tolerance training in a Geography lesson: Students' opinions	https://files.eric.ed.gov/fulltext/EJ1080311.pdf	Integrates tolerance education into a geography class, with focus on religion, culture, and race.
5. Thomas Hammond, Alec Bozdin, and Sarah E. Stanlick.	Redefining the Longitude/Latitude Experience with a Scaffolded Geocache	https://eric.ed.gov/?id=EJ1033017	In this article, the authors present a simplified, scaffolded version of a geocache designed to fit within a single class period: working in pairs, students will use a GPS (or other geolocating device, such as a smartphone) to navigate among several targets set up by the teacher. Students' conceptions and opportunities for extension and application are discussed.

25 Resources for Teaching Geography • 391

Author(s)/ Organization	Title	Location	Description
6. Li-Ching Ho and Tricia Seow	Teaching Geography through "Chinatowns": Global Connections and Local Spaces	https://eric.ed.gov/?q=Paris&pg=3&id=EJ1006892	Chinatowns are familiar emblems of "Chineseness" in many countries and are among the most visible and tangible spatial manifestations of Chinese migration. Large and well-established Chinatowns can be found in diverse locales, including New York, San Francisco, Vancouver, Paris, Sydney, and Singapore. Despite sharing numerous easily recognizable features, the different Chinatowns also possess many unique and distinct characteristics. In this article, the authors suggest comparing two or more Chinatowns in different countries or regions as a means for teachers to illustrate key geographical understandings and concepts such as stereotyping, migration, cultural diversity, and governance.
7. Matthew S. Hollstein and Alan Chu	Examining the climate crisis in the social studies classroom" Public polling and mock trials	https://www.socialstudies.org/middle-level-learning/january-february-2020	This lesson series encourages students to blend research and survey techniques with exploration of public opinion and policy regarding climate change. This article has strong multidisciplinary and interdisciplinary potential.
8. Steven Jennings	Questions to Facilitate the Use of Maps As Primary Sources in the Classroom	https://www.tandfonline.com/doi/full/10.1080/00377996.2012.720306	This article discusses the kinds of questions that teachers and students can ask about maps to have a deeper understanding of the maps. These questions can be selectively used and overlap to some extent so that teachers can choose as needed for their classroom situation.
9. Joshua L. Kenna, Joshua and Sarah Potter	Experiencing the World from inside the Classroom: Using Virtual Field Trips to Enhance Social Studies Instruction	https://eric.ed.gov/?id=EJ1205455	This article provides a list of quality platforms, which teachers can use to locate VFTs.
10. Joshua L. Kenna and William B. Russell	Keeping it Animated: Utilizing Animated Films to Teach Geography	https://www.socialstudies.org/	This article offers readers several lesson plans for using cartoons to teach middle level students about geographical concepts.

Author(s)/Organization	Title	Location	Description
11. Dan Krutka and Michael Milton	Visions of Education	https://visionsofed.com/podcast/	This weekly podcast between an education professor and high school educator focuses on pertinent issues in the field of social studies.
12. Timothy Lintner	Using Children's Literature to Promote Critical Geographic Awareness in Elementary Classrooms	https://eric.ed.gov/?id=EJ872092	The cornerstone of sound social studies pedagogy is the ability of teachers to use materials that spur students to think critically, reflect honestly, and to participate purposefully and passionately. This article illustrates how elementary teachers can use select children's literature that prompts students to think critically about their geographic surroundings and encourages student-centered reflection and action.
13. Ava L. McCall	Promoting Critical Thinking and Inquiry through Maps in Elementary Classrooms	https://eric.ed.gov/?id=EJ922448#:~:text=The%20article%20suggests%20teachers%20encourage,the%20value%20of%20different%20maps.	This article encourages elementary teachers to offer opportunities for their students to critically analyze maps as part of powerful geography instruction in order to help them become well-informed and civic-minded citizens. The article reviews challenges to powerful geography instruction, including traditional geography textbooks and pedagogy and the additional efforts needed to encourage students to examine maps critically and identify distortions and biases.
14. Kelly McPherson	The Fifty States Project: Learning about America, One Care Package at a Time	https://www.socialstudies.org/	In this article, a fifth-grade teacher offers lesson ideas to help students engage with inquiries. She provides lessons about the geography, culture, and history of the United States over the course of the school year through her fifty states project.
15. Ronald V. Morris	Service Learning and the Compass Trai	https://eric.ed.gov/?id=EJ1101387	This article describes how students used a compass trail to show how they could perform service to their school.
16. National Geographic	Great Pacific Garbage Patch	https://www.nationalgeographic.org/encyclopedia/great-pacific-garbage-patch/	Provides stark photographs and informational page regarding the Great Pacific Garbage patch.

25 Resources for Teaching Geography • 393

	Author(s)/ Organization	Title	Location	Description
17.	NCSS Notable Tradebooks for Young People	N/A	https://www.socialstudies.org/notable-social-studies-trade-books	An annual curated list of texts for K–8 students on a wide range of social studies topics.
18.	C. Steven Page	Racing Around the World A Geography Contest to Remember	https://www.socialstudies.org/search-results?search=&sort_by=search_api_relevance&sort_order=DESC&page=363	This article offers readers a lesson plan for using technology to take 7th grade geography students on a race around the world.
19.	David Sobel	Place Based Education: Connecting Classroom and Community	https://magazine.communityworksinstitute.org/place-based-education-connecting-classroom-and-community/	This article offers readers ideas for using elements of place-based education in their classes.
20.	Bryan Smith	Engaging Geography at Every Street Corner: Using Place-Names as Critical Heuristic in Social Studies	https://eric.ed.gov/?q=Cities&pg=4&id=EJ1179912	This article explores an often overlooked feature of everyday life that can serve as a powerful heuristic for students to engage history and geography critically: everyday place-names.
21.	Robert L. Stevens and Julia A Celebi	A Treasured island: Human and geographic interaction on Cumberland	https://www.socialstudies.org/middle-level-learning/3	This lesson explores human-environment interaction, using the feral horses of Cumberland Island as a case study.
22.	Karen A. Thomas-Brown	Teaching for Geographic Literacy: Our Afterschool Geography Club	https://eric.ed.gov/?id=EJ949416	This research describes how enrolling students in an afterschool Geography Club affects their perception of the discipline and their geographic literacy. The creation of the afterschool club at this particular school came out of the recognition of the need to increase students' exposure to geographical content.

Author(s)/Organization	Title	Location	Description
23. Misty Galloway Tucker	Whose responsibility is it to protect the Amazon Rainforest: Using the C3 framework to explore complex issues	https://www.socialstudies.org/middle-level-learning/64	A unit of study that walks students through the creation of essential questions, examination of resources, and taking informed action regarding the rainforest.
24. Stephanie Wasta	"Be My Neighbor": Exploring Sense of Place through Children's Literature	https://eric.ed.gov/?id=EJ895115	This article explores using six National Council for the Social Studies Notable Trade Books to assist primary students in their understanding of place. By using realistic fiction and nonfiction picture books that focus on children's lives in diverse locations, the suggested activities enable teachers to address the five themes of geography and promote cultural awareness to elementary students in meaningful ways.
25. Valerie Widall, Muteb Alqahtani and Thomas Kraly	The Measurement and Meaning of Landmarks Integrating Social Studies and Math in Fifth Grade Lessons	https://www.socialstudies.org/	In this article, "the authors describe their experience integrating social studies and mathematics in a fifth-grade classroom. The authors strove to provide elementary educators with a lesson integration model that uses historical investigation as a vehicle for learning other subjects such as mathematics."

APPENDIX E

25 RESOURCES FOR TEACHING ECONOMICS

APPENDIX E BEGINS ON THE FOLLOWING PAGE.

Teaching Middle Level Social Studies: A Practical Guide for 4th–8th Grade (3rd Edition),
pages 395–399.
Copyright © 2022 by Information Age Publishing
www.infoagepub.com
All rights of reproduction in any form reserved.

	Author(s)/ Organization	Title	Location	Description
1.	C3 Teachers	N/A	https://c3teachers.org/	The C3 Teachers Website offers over 22 free inquiry-based history lesson plans for teaching Economics.
2.	Council for Economic Education	N/A	www.councilforeconed.org	This organization offers economic based resources, materials and standards to K–12 social studies teachers. The website also includes information about their annual conference, on-line teacher training, a free online personal finance video game, and K–12 lesson plans and videos
3.	Econedlink	N/A	http://www.econedlink.org/	This is a website sponsored by the Council for Economic Education that offers tools to both students and teachers to use in economic education. All lessons and interactive games are "online" and focus on basic economics concepts, current events, and personal finance.
4.	Federal Reserve Bank of New York	Educational Comic Books	https://www.newyorkfed.org/outreach-and-education/comic-books	The Fed in New York presents comic books to introduce students to simple and more complex economic concepts.
5.	Mary Francis, James D. Laney, and Thomas A. Lucey	Grabbing a Tiger by the Tale: Using Stories to Teach Financial Literacy	https://eric.ed.gov/?id=EJ1222736	In this article the authors "present for classroom use a sample story about two sons and offer debriefing questions that invite conversation about money and social responsibility."
6.	Eric B. Freedman	Life in an auto factory: Simulating how labor and management interact	https://www.socialstudies.org/middle-level-learning/48	This exploration of worker rights blends history with economics. Students work through a simulation in which management and labor work to find balance with one another.
7.	Jennifer Lynn Gallagher and Eibhlin Kelly	Economic Thinking with Jon Klassen's Animal Hat Books	https://www.socialstudies.org/system/files/2020-06/yl_320216.pdf	In this article, the authors share an idea to purposefully integrate economic thinking into elementary curriculum by exploring the economic principles in a popular children's book series—books that many teachers are already using in classrooms.

25 Resources for Teaching Economics • 397

	Author(s)/ Organization	Title	Location	Description
8.	Suze S. Gilbert, Tracey R. Huddleston, and J. Jeremy Winters	Design, Build, and Test a Model House: Using the C3 Framework to Explore the Economics of Constructing a Dwelling	https://www.socialstudies.org	In this article, the authors provide a lesson plan for using the C3 framework to integrate economics and the STEAM disciplines.
9.	Heather N. Hagan and Carolyn A. Webber	The global challenge of equal access for girls to an education: An investigation using inquiry	https://www.socialstudies.org/middle-level-learning/january-february-2018	This lesson weaves human rights, social justice, and economic considerations when discussing girls' rights to education in Guatemala, India, Malawi, Liberia, and Ethiopia.
10.	Dan Krutka and Michael Milton	Visions of Education	https://visionsofed.com/podcast/	This weekly podcast between an education professor and high school educator focuses on pertinent issues in the field of social studies.
11.	Ava L McCall	Teaching Children about the Global Economy: Integrating Inquiry with Human Rights	https://eric.ed.gov/?id=EJ1152106	The article focuses on recommendations for teaching elementary students in grades three through five about the global economy utilizing the pedagogical recommendations from the National Council for the Social Studies and curricular and pedagogical suggestions from economic educators, human rights educators, and research.
12.	Bonnie T. Meszaros and Stella Evans	It's Never Too Early: Why Economics Education in the Elementary Classroom	https://eric.ed.gov/?id=EJ878503	In this article, the authors provide reasons why economics should be taught in the elementary classroom. They argue that economic instruction needs to start early to ensure that students are well prepared for their adult roles as consumers, producers, investors, U.S. citizens, and global citizens.
13.	Bonnie T. Meszaros and Andrew T. Hill	Work, Education, and Income: Economics and Financial Literacy in the Early Grades	https://www.socialstudies.org/social-studies-and-young-learner/28/1/work-education-and-income-economics-and-financial-literacy	This article describes a K–5 lesson plans to help students understand a variety of economic principals at the elementary level.

	Author(s)/ Organization	Title	Location	Description
14.	Peter William Moran, Kimberly Miller, and Genee Witte	Paper Bag City: Exploring Geography and Economics in the Primary Grades	https://www.socialstudies.org/system/files/publications/articles/yl_28011520.pdf	This article offers a lesson plan about a project that allows students make relatively simple distinctions between goods and services, but also begin to explore more sophisticated concepts such as entrepreneurship, economic specialization, pricing, high and low order goods and services, and the role of incentives in economic decision-making. This lesson can be adapted for 4th and 5th grade students.
15.	NCSS Notable Tradebooks for Young People	N/A	https://www.socialstudies.org/notable-social-studies-trade-books	An annual curated lists of texts for K–8 students on a wide range of social studies topics.
16.	New York Federal Reserve	Comic Books on Basic Economics (New York Fed)	https://www.newyorkfed.org/outreach-and-education/comic-books	The New York Fed's Educational Comic Book Series teaches students about basic economic principles and the Federal Reserve's role in the economic system. Created for educators and students at the middle school, high school, and introductory college levels, the series can help promote economic literacy.
17.	Lee Ann Potter	Encouraging Student Interest in the Economic Context of the Constitution with Continental Currency	https://eric.ed.gov/?id=EJ1045328	Introducing students to continental currency may well encourage their interest in the economic context of the Constitution and their understanding of a wide range of economic concepts. This brief article describes a lesson to familiarize students with continental currency and its relationship to Article I, Section 8, of the Constitution and the American economy during the revolutionary and early federal periods.
18.	Jen Reidel	Discovering Economic Concepts and Criticism in Progressive Era Cartoons	https://www.socialstudies.org/system/files/2020-06/se_8402089.pdf	This article describes how teachers can use progressive era cartoons from the Library of Congress to discover the role economics played in history.
19.	Tracy Schottanes	Becoming Ethical Consumers and Making Wise Economic Choices	https://www.socialstudies.org/system/files/publications/articles/se_7903139.pdf	This article describes a three-week unit designed for third graders and requires approximately 10 class sessions for implementation but would also be appropriate for students in grade 4 and 5.

25 Resources for Teaching Economics • 399

	Author(s)/ Organization	Title	Location	Description
20.	Emma S. Thacker, David Hicks, and Adam M. Friedman	It Might Not be a Matter of Life or Death, But Does Soccer Really Explain the World?	https://www.socialstudies.org/social-education/81/4/it-might-not-be-matter-life-or-death-does-soccer-really-explain-world	This article explain how teachers can use sports, in this case soccer, to help students learn history, economics, and geography concepts
21.	U.S. Mint	Lessons by Grade	https://www.usmint.gov/learn/educators/lessons-by-grade	A searchable database of lessons regarding money and financial literacy.
22.	Lynda D Vargha	Buyer Beware! Economics Activities for Middle School Students	https://eric.ed.gov/?id=EJ1702248	In this article, the author contributes to the bridge-building by presenting four activities that teach basic economic concepts and consumer decision making through active problem solving.
23.	Annie McMahon Whitlock	Economics through Inquiry: Creating Social Businesses in Fifth Grade	https://eric.ed.gov/?id=EJ1059310	This study describes how a class of fifth-grade students engaged in the inquiry arc in economics through the One Hen unit, a curriculum in which students create social businesses. Students learned concepts and skills in economics, math, and language arts while developing questions, evaluating evidence, and presenting results of their work helping homeless youth in their community.
24.	Annie McMahon Whitlock and Kristy A. Brugar	How Does a Cowboy Make Money? Using Student Curiosities to Further Elementary School Inquiries	https://eric.ed.gov/?id=EJ1145115	This article explores examples of student-initiated inquiries (in Grades 1 and 5) and the opportunities and challenges with engaging in them.
25.	Teresa G. Wojcik and William Knous	Promote Inquiry about Child Labor with Online Historical Primary Sources	https://www.socialstudies.org/middle-level-learning/May-June-2014	This lesson discusses the economics and lived experiences of child labor in the late 1800s. Primary sources and essential questions are provided.

APPENDIX F

25 RESOURCES FOR TEACHING CIVICS/GOVERNMENT

APPENDIX F BEGINS ON THE NEXT PAGE.

Teaching Middle Level Social Studies: A Practical Guide for 4th–8th Grade (3rd Edition),
pages 401–405.
Copyright © 2022 by Information Age Publishing
www.infoagepub.com
All rights of reproduction in any form reserved.

Author(s)/Organization	Title	Location	Description
1. Patricia G Avery, Sara A Levy, Simmons, M.M. Annette	Deliberating Controversial Public Issues as Part of Civic Education	https://eric.ed.gov/?id=EJ1012546	This article describes the results of an evaluation of one ten-nation project, "Deliberating in a Democracy," which suggest that teachers can learn to conduct deliberations in secondary classrooms.
2. Ben's Guide to U.S. Government for Kids	N/A	https://bensguide.gpo.gov/	This is a website for K–12 students that offers "student friendly" definitions for several elements of government including "branches of government," and "how laws are made," along with games and activities. Additional links to government themed websites for students are provided as well.
3. Brooke Blevins, Karon N. LeCompte, Tiffani Riggers-Piehl, Nate Scholten Icon and Kevin R. Magill	The Impact of an Action Civics Program on the Community & Political Engagement of Youth	https://www.tandfonline.com/doi/full/10.1080/00377996.2020.1854163	This study present findings related to students' community and political engagement and activism after participation in an action civics institute.
4. C3 Teachers	N/A	https://c3teachers.org/	The C3 Teachers Website offers over 30 free inquiry-based history lesson plans for teaching Civics/Government.
5. Center for Civic Education	N/A	https://www.civiced.org/more-lesson-plans	This website has approximately 50 lesson plans that help teachers engage in conversations about civic responsibility. Some notable topics include 9/11 and the constitution, Women's History Month, and Voting Rights.
6. Jeremy Hilburn and Lisa Brown Buchanan	Immigration Today: Three Strategies for Teaching with Film	https://www.socialstudies.org/middle-level-learning/57	Discusses how The Lost Boys of Sudan, The Namesake, and Which Way Home can be integrated into class exploration of current immigration policy.
7. iCivics	N/A	http://www.icivics.org/	This is a program founded by Justice Sandra Day O'Connor to help prepare "young Americans to become knowledgeable, engaged 21st century citizens" by creating "free and innovative educational materials." These include several educational video games about the U.S. government.

25 Resources for Teaching Civics/Government • 403

	Author(s)/Organization	Title	Location	Description
8.	Jennifer Ingold	Mission Impossible: Turning Essays on Enduring Issues into Respectful Ethical Debates	https://www.socialstudies.org/middle-level-learning/65	This lesson presents a framework for encouraging students to debate in informed, systematic, and respectful ways.
9.	Dan Krutka and Michael Milton	Visions of Education	https://visionsofed.com/podcast/	This weekly podcast between an education professor and high school educator focuses on pertinent issues in the field of social studies.
10.	Learning for Justice	N/A	https://www.learningforjustice.org/	Formerly known as Teaching Tolerance, this site hosts a variety of classroom resources such as lesson plans, texts, and professional development webinars focused on social justice and its interconnections to history, geography, economics and civics.
11.	James Massey	Dialectical Discussion: A method at the Heart of our Democratic Process	https://www.socialstudies.org/middle-level-learning/may-june-2017	This article discusses the dialectical discussion method that "...invites students to listen actively, think deeply, and develop articulate understandings grounded in inquiry." (p. 2)
12.	Margit E. McGuire, Karen Nicholson, Allan Rand	Live it to Learn it: Making Elections Personally Meaningful.	https://www.socialstudies.org	This article describes a lesson plan where students participate in the developing story of a presidential election.
13.	NCSS	Teaching with Primary Sources to Prepare for Civic Engagement	https://www.socialstudies.org/tps/teaching-primary-sources-prepare-civic-engagement	In this webinar illustrates how teachers can build students' historical knowledge, foster historical thinking skills that are vital for civic engagement, and nurture students' civic dispositions through document-based lessons. Using resources from the Library of Congress and following the National Council for the Social Studies C3 Framework, it presents model lesson ideas that add pizzazz to history courses and prepare young people to change the world.
14.	NCSS Notable Tradebooks for Young People	N/A	https://www.socialstudies.org/notable-social-studies-trade-books	An annual curated lists of texts for K–8 students on a wide range of social studies topics.

	Author(s)/Organization	Title	Location	Description
15.	John Pagnotti, William B. Russell, III	A Problem-Based Learning Approach to Civics Education: Exploring the Free Exercise Clause with Supreme Court Simulations	https://eric.ed.gov/?id=EJ1077579	The purpose of this article is to empower those interested in teaching students powerful and engaging social studies. Through the lens of Supreme Court simulations, this article provides educators with a viable, classroom-tested lesson plan to bring Problem-Based Learning into their classrooms.
16.	Rethinking Schools	N/A	https://rethinkingschools.org/	A nonprofit publisher and advocacy organization, Rethinking Schools provides resources to promote equity and social justice within the social studies classroom
17.	Scott L. Roberts and Charles Elfer	"All Politics is Local:" Enhancing Media Literacy through State and Local Elections	https://www.infoagepub.com/products/No-Reluctant-Citizens	This book chapter offers readers two classroom-ready civic lesson plans to help educators teach the importance of both media literacy and state/local elections.
18.	Paige Lilley Schulte and Travis Miller	Making Choices: An Exploration of Political Preferences	https://www.socialstudies.org/middle-level-learning/32	This lesson introduces the concept of political preference to middle school students. The lesson has students determine their preference for various food items and then re-evaluate their positions given new information.
19.	Sarah B. Shear, Leilani Sabzalian, and Lisa Brown Buchanan	Affirming Indigenous Sovereignty: A Civics Inquiry	https://eric.ed.gov/?q=disregard&ff1=audTeachers&id=EJ1224860	In this article, the authors outline a four-part unit that incorporates academic keywords, provides a foundation for understanding Indigenous sovereignty, and deliberates current events related to sovereignty.
20.	Since Time Immemorial: Tribal Sovereignty in Washington State	N/A	https://www.k12.wa.us/student-success/resources-subject-area/time-immemorial-tribal-sovereignty-washington-state	This site shares a curriculum in WA state endorsed by all 29 federally recognized tribes with ready-to-go lessons to adapt for grades preK through high school.

25 Resources for Teaching Civics/Government

	Author(s)/Organization	Title	Location	Description
21.	Social Justice Book: A Teaching for Change Project	N/A	https://socialjustice-books.org/	This site shares curated lists of multicultural and social justice books for young adults and children, including a guide for selecting anti-bias texts
22.	Street Law	N/A	http://www.streetlaw.org/en/home	It is a non-profit organization that "creates classroom and community programs that teach people about law, democracy, and human rights worldwide." The website offers teachers programs that "empower students and communities to become active, legally-savvy contributors to society" as well as a "full range of resources and activities to support the teaching of landmark Supreme Court cases, helping students explore the key issues of each case."
23.	Stephanie L. Strachan & Annie McMahon Whitlock	Five ways that read alouds can help K–8 teachers address the College, Career, and Civic Life (C3) Framework	https://drive.google.com/file/d/0B5N0kEdFQZ-sYVMzcEpmQWlOSVE/view	This article describes fives ways K–8 educators can use read-alouds to address the C3 Framework.
24.	USvsHate	N/A	https://usvshate.org	This page offers a space for students to write for authentic audiences on topics of diversity, inclusion, and justice.
25.	Benjamin R. Wellenreiter	Within These Halls: In Situ Primary Sources in Your Own School	https://www.socialstudies.org/middle-level-learning/january-february-2018	This article describes a lesson series encouraging students to explore their schools for examples of the relationship between government and the individual. Title IX, taxpayer spending, health and life safety codes, and a multitude of other opportunities await students as they find primary sources all around them.

ABOUT THE AUTHORS

SCOTT L. ROBERTS, Ph.D., currently serves as an associate professor of Social Studies Education at Central Michigan University. He teaches courses in elementary social studies education, current educational issues, research methods, and educational technology. A former middle school teacher, he received his doctorate from the University of Georgia in social studies education in 2009. He is the author of multiple publications concerning history education and is the co-editor of *Hollywood or History: An Inquiry-Based Strategy for Using Film to Teach United States History* (2018) and *Hollywood or History: An Inquiry-Based Strategy for Using Film to Teach World History* (2021). His research interests include state history, discussion-based strategies, history education, and educational technology.

BENJAMIN R. WELLENREITER, Ed.D., is an assistant professor of Middle Level Education in the School of Teaching and Learning at Illinois State University. He teaches courses in middle level social studies teaching methods, curriculum and lesson plan design, classroom management, and the application of learning theories in educational contexts. Before entering teacher education, Ben taught middle level U.S. History and World Geography for 19 years. Ben has publications in *Middle School Journal*, *The Clearing House: A Journal of Educational Strategies, Issues and Ideas*, *Middle Level Learning*, *The Counselor: A Journal of* *the Social Studies*, and *Teaching Social Studies*. Ben's research interests include adolescent socialization patterns, state social studies mandates and standards, and patriotism education.

JESSICA FERRERAS-STONE, Ph.D., is an associate professor of Elementary Education at Western Washington University. She teaches elementary social studies courses as well as multicultural education courses. A former teacher and school administrator she earned her doctorate degree from the University of Tennessee, Knoxville in 2016. Jessica has published in *Social Studies and the Young Learner, The Counselor: A Journal of the Social Studies, and The Social Studies*. Her research interests include teaching inclusive social studies that honors historically marginalized voices, using podcast as a teaching tool and integrating literacy and social studies instruction through critical literacy.

STEPHANIE L. STRACHAN, Ph.D., is an associate professor of Elementary Education at Western Washington University where she serves as the Director of the Language, Literacy, and Cultural Studies program and teaches preservice and M.Ed. courses in early literacy, assessment, research methods, and elementary social studies. Prior to her current position, she worked as a K–2 educator, literacy coach, and curriculum developer. Her research interests include early literacy instruction, project-based learning, disciplinary literacy, and mentoring of beginning teachers.

KARRIE L. PALMER, Ed.S., is the recipient of the 2019 Gilder Lehrman History Teacher of the Year award for the state of Georgia. She is currently teaching eighth grade Georgia Studies and seventh grade World Geography at Rising Starr Middle School in Fayette County, Georgia. For the past 20 years, Karrie has been a classroom teacher at both the elementary and middle school levels. She has also served as a Curriculum Teacher Leader for social studies to support other teachers with social studies instruction in their classrooms. Karrie's research interests include U.S. history education, the marginalization of social studies in public schools, inquiry-based strategies, and effective scheduling for student engagement.

CPSIA information can be obtained
at www.ICGtesting.com
Printed in the USA
BVHW042358090422
633834BV00004B/20